Treating Families
with
Special Needs

TREATING FAMILIES WITH SPECIAL NEEDS

David S. Freeman / Barry Trute

Editors

Alix Hirabayashi

Editorial Advisor

ALBERTA ASSOCIATION OF SOCIAL WORKERS
and
CANADIAN ASSOCIATION OF SOCIAL WORKERS

© 1981 Alberta Association of Social Workers
in cooperation with the
Canadian Association of Social Workers
Printed and bound in Canada
ISBN 0-9691085-0-8
ISSN 0710-4626

Published by
Alberta Association of Social Workers
in cooperation with
Canadian Association of Social Workers
Edited by David S. Freeman & Barry Trute
Editorial Advisor - Alix Hirabayashi
Cover - Alix Hirabayashi
Technical Advisor, Publication - Gweneth Gowanlock
Typesetting & Layout - Jean C. Somers

ALBERTA ASSOCIATION OF SOCIAL WORKERS
CANADIAN ASSOCIATION OF SOCIAL WORKERS
55 Parkdale Avenue, Fourth Floor
Ottawa, Ontario K1Y 1E5

ACKNOWLEDGEMENTS

Special thanks go to the Alberta Government, Department of Social Services and Community Health for its substantial financial contribution through the Alberta Association of Social Workers toward publication of this text.

We also would like to thank the Alberta Association of Social Workers for its financial contribution; the Canadian Association of Social Workers for its support, aid and financial contribution, in kind, in preparing the text; the five Western Canadian Schools of Social Work (School of Social Work, University of British Columbia; Faculty of Social Welfare, University of Calgary; School of Social Work, University of Manitoba; Faculty of Social Work, University of Regina; and the School of Social Work, University of Victoria) for their continual support in co-sponsoring the Western Canadian Conference on Family Practice, and to the Planning Committee for their endorsement; Gweneth Gowanlock at CASW for her administrative and technical publication advice throughout the publication process; Jean Somers, also at CASW, for her patience, efficiency and good humour during the final preparation of the text.

CONTENTS

CONTRIBUTORS

Lawrence M. Baldwin, PhD
Assistant Professor (Research)
Section of Psychiatry
and Human Behavior
Brown University
Providence, Rhode Island

Philip Barker, FRCP(C)
Professor
Psychiatry and Paediatrics
University of Calgary
Calgary, Alberta

Janice Bell, RN., MS
Assistant Professor
Faculty of Nursing
University of Calgary
Calgary, Alberta

Duane S. Bishop, MD
Clinical Director
Butler Hospital, and
Associate Professor, Psychiatry
Brown University
Providence, Rhode Island

Karin M. Buchanan, RSW
Social Worker, Neurosciences
University Hospital
Saskatoon, Saskatchewan

Walter Driedger, MSW
Assistant Professor
School of Social Work
University of Manitoba
Winnipeg, Manitoba

Grant Dunfield, MSW
Community Mental Health Worker
Department of Community Services
                    and Corrections
Portage la Prairie, Manitoba

Henry Enns, BSW
Chairman
Disabled Peoples' International
Winnipeg, Manitoba

Nathan B. Epstein, MD
Medical Director
Butler Hospital, and
Chairman, Section on Psychiatry
    and Human Behavior
Brown University
Providence, Rhode Island

Lillian M. Esses, PhD
Clinical Psychologist
Assistant Professor
Department of Psychology
University of Manitoba
Winnipeg, Manitoba

David S. Freeman, DSW
Assocate Professor
School of Social Work
University of British Columbia
Vancouver, British Columbia

James M. Gripton, DSW
Professor
Faculty of Social Welfare
University of Calgary
Calgary, Alberta

Howard Irving, DSW
Professor
Faculty of Social Work
University of Toronto
Toronto, Ontario

Derek Jehu, FBPsS
Professor
School of Social Work
University of Manitoba
Winnipeg, Manitoba

Joseph A. Kuypers, PhD
Associate Professor
School of Social Work
University of Manitoba
Winnipeg, Manitoba

Contributors

George MacDonald, MA
Community Mental Health Worker
Department of Community Services
and Corrections
Carman, Manitoba

Shelly Pearlman, DSW
Head, Sociobehavioral Treatment
Services, Clinical Institute,
Addiction Research Foundation
Assistant Professor
Faculty of Social Work
University of Toronto
Toronto, Ontario

Leah N. Quastel, MA
Assistant Professor
School of Rehabilitation Medicine
Faculty of Medicine
University of British Columbia
Vancouver, British Columbia

Ruth Rachlis, MSW
Assistant Professor
School of Social Work
University of Manitoba
Winnipeg, Manitoba

Ranjan Roy, MSW, AdvDipSW
Associate Professor
School of Social Work, and
Department of Psychiatry
Faculty of Medicine
University of Manitoba
Winnipeg, Manitoba

Ray Thomlison
Professor
Faculty of Social Work
University of Toronto
Toronto, Ontario

Karl Tomm, MD FRCP(C)
Director
Family Therapy Program
Division of Psychiatry
Faculty of Medicine
University of Calgary
Calgary, Alberta

Barry Trute, DSW
Professor
School of Social Work
University of Manitoba
Winnipeg, Manitoba

Mary Valentich, PhD
Associate Professor
Faculty of Social Welfare
University of Calgary
Calgary, Alberta

Lorraine M. Wright, RN, PhD
Associate Professor
Faculty of Nursing
University of Calgary
Calgary, Alberta

Allen Zweben, DSW
Head, Psychosocial Intervention
Research, Clinical Institute
Addiction Research Foundation,
and
Associate Professor
Faculty of Social Work
University of Toronto
Toronto, Ontario

PREFACE

Treating Families with Special Needs is the second in a series of publications on family theory, practice, research and policy being sponsored by the Western Canadian Conference on Family Practice. *(Perspectives on Family Therapy,* Freeman, 1981, was the first in the series.) It brings together a range of ideas concerning innovative approaches to helping families in which one or more members suffer a disability through physical, behavioral or developmental disorders.

While the emphasis in the past has been on treating the disabled in isolation from the family, this text emphasizes the importance of providing services, not only to the disabled member, but to the family as a whole. One of the messages developed consistently in these articles is that when a family is treated as a unit, it will be able to satisfy more of its individual members' needs as well as its needs as a whole.

The range of ideas, philosophies and innovative approaches developed in these articles should prove useful to the practitioner, teacher, researcher and policy analyst interested in better understanding the family and enhancing services to families.

The text is divided into four sections. The first focuses on models of practice with families. The second draws attention to the importance of contextual issues which frame family focused interventions. The third deals with the policy implication of providing services to the families of the disabled or ill persons. The fourth section focuses on the unique problems that the disabled experience in terms of their sexuality.

Future publications in this series will reflect the themes and issues identified by the Western Canadian Conference on Family Practice as being important for practitioners who serve the family.

INTERVENTIVE APPROACHES IN MEETING SPECIAL NEEDS

Over the past decade, there have been important contributions to the refinement of family-focused methods and the detailed articulation of interventive strategies. The opening section of this book contains six papers which deal with a number of important emerging models of family practice.

Duane Bishop, Nathan Epstein and Lawrence Baldwin, in their paper ("Disability: A Family Affair") provide an in-depth analysis of the McMaster Model of family therapy and illustrate its use in treating families with a disabled member. They discuss family functions that affect the emotional and physical well-being of family members and describe the range of family functions that appear necessary for the family to operate effectively in today's society. The authors also operationalize a number of principles that should prove helpful to practitioners wanting to experiment with this approach to family practice. In addition, they provide the reader with a literature review on families with a disabled member.

In his paper ("Behavioral Family Intervention with the Family of a Mentally Handicapped Child"), Ray Thomlison evaluates behavior modification as a tool for helping famlies who have mentally handicapped children and who are experiencing difficulties within the family and the community. After reviewing the literature on behavior modification and explaining its principles, Thomlison uses a case study to illustrate the practical use of behavior modification. His article will provide the reader with a thorough grasp of the utility of behavior modification as a treatment approach to families having difficulty with *any* member as well as those attempting to cope with handicapped children.

In their paper ("Worker Crisis in Crisis Work") Barry Trute and Joseph Kuypers address the issue of family crisis management. How a practitioner responds to a client's crisis can directly influence the client's view of that crisis and be a determining factor in the course of the crisis. The practitioner's response can increase the client's feelings of panic and urgency or reduce those feelings by giving the client a significantly different perspective. Trute and Kuypers also point out that, before practitioners can deal effectively with a crisis, they must first deal with their own feelings about the crisis. The authors provide a series of vignettes which identify common process hazards in crisis intervention which can disrupt effective practice and limit the worker's capacity to facilitate positive change.

In their paper ("Conjoint Treatment of Alcohol-Complicated Marriages: Conceptual and Methodological Uses") Pearlman and Zweben identify a number of conceptual, clinical and methodological issues concerning a systems-oriented conjoint therapy for alcoholics and their spouses. They discuss training of therapists, client engagement in treatment, assessment procedures and the timing of the intervention. They begin by reviewing the literature on different treatment modes for alcoholics, and then discuss in detail a program they established in Toronto using a systems-approach to treating the alcoholic problem. They take the readers through all the program phases, discuss the theoretical principles used in setting up the program and provide the reader with an understanding of the dynamics that can occur within the client system (and within the "professional family" system) that can defeat the success of the program. The paper presents a coherent model of practice that could be used in treating alcoholic marriages and/or families, and it could be used as a guideline to help agencies set up treatment programs for families with an alcoholic member.

Philip Barker, ("Paradoxical Techniques in Psychotherapy"), reviews the use of paradox as a technique in the family therapy field. He discusses what a paradox is, how it can be used in practice, and the indications and contra-indications for paradoxical intervention.

Karl Tomm's paper, ("The Milan Approach to Family Therapy: A Tentative Report"), addresses a recent theme in the field of family therapy. In the last several years, a group of Italian family therapists (Selvini, Voscolo, Cesshin, Prata) have been experimenting with a model of family practice now referred to as the Milan Approach to Practice. Tomm provides the reader with an overview of how the approach developed, the fundamental strategies employed, and what modifications have been made over the years. Most students of the systems approach to family therapy will find Tomm's paper instructive and informative.

Chapter 1

Disability: A Family Affair

Duane S. Bishop, Nathan B. Epstein and Lawrence M. Baldwin
Brown University, Providence, Rhode Island

Physical impairment and chronic disease often lead to significant disability in affected individuals. Disability has reverborating effects within the families of patients. The responses of involved families have significant effects on the course and outcome of the rehabilitation process.

In this paper, we will comment on the history of the interest in the psychosocial aspects of disability, review themes from the literature, and discuss a number of key conceptual issues. We will then describe our approach to the understanding of family functioning by means of a clinical illustration which demonstrates many important issues related to assessing and treating families with a disabled member.

Historically, the physical aspects of medicine were the initial and principal focus of people working with disabled patients. It was expected that technological advances such as special artificial limbs would ameliorate many of the problems and facilitate the adjustment of the disabled. While the new technological advances were frequently superb and wonderous, by the 1960's it became clear that the results achieved were often less than expected. (Shontz, 1959) Psychosocial issues then came to be recognized as crucial intervening factors. (Shontz, 1959)

The initial consideration of psychosocial issues centered on individual psychological processes. In the case of the disabled, this often focused on concepts such as denial of loss and rage, dependence-independence conflicts, and issues related to body image. In the case of the parents of the disabled, the concepts dealt with were denial of loss and underlying rage and a complex of guilt leading to detrimental reaction formation and over-protection.

While these concepts frequently are related to enlightened insights about behavior, a careful review of the literature reveals that little work has been done to bring them to a point where they can be optimally useful when dealing with disabled patients and their families. Most of these concepts originated in the study of the intrapsychic functioning of non-physically disabled patients and have then been applied to the field of disability and chronic illness without close empirical study. The concepts have not been operationally defined and are also often applied very loosely to a wide and confusing range of behavior. The real significance of behavior observed in chronic disabled patients and their families is then often missed entirely or distorted by the misdirected application of poorly defined concepts.

Some examples may help to clarify this. It is not clear whether and/or when denial is healthy or pathological, yet the 'concept' is frequently used by those working with the disabled and their families. Often this usage implies negative attributes or pathology that is unjustified on the basis of either the original definition and meaning of denial, or on a clear conceptualization of its real significance in disability.

The concept of dependency is a second example. The term can be used both in a psychodynamic definition and formulation as well as to indicate functional incapacity in disabled individuals. It is often not clear whether it is used in a specific way, both ways, or just loosely. Over time, common usage has added many nuances and additional implications. A psychodynamic concept of dependency never was easily operationalized and therefore seldom researched. Even less work has been done with regard to its application in disability.

Dependency is also an example of a concept with an original definition that may be narrow and reduce its possible utility in the disability field. Disability raises the importance of possessing a capacity to be appropriately dependent. However, few workers raise this issue because of a limited original concept and/or the bias of today's cultural values that imply health and importance to independence and pathology and negativism to dependency.

As a last example, parental guilt and overprotection have attained a central place in clinical lore relating to disability. This has occurred despite a minimum of reports which are in themselves limited by biased sample populations or reliance on anecdotal examples. However, many workers are still led to pre-judge parents and at times to confuse honest, assertive, enlightened, helpful and adaptive advocacy and intervention by parents or other family members with pathological guilt and overprotection.

Suffice it to say that key intrapsychic variables need further clarification with regard to their application to disability and chronic disease.

In the last decade attention has begun to focus on family issues. The shift has been fostered by rehabilitation professionals increasingly recognizing the importance of the family, by research and clinical work concerned with sexuality and disability, and by increased consumer advocacy on the part of the disabled and their families.

This change in focus goes beyond the family and highlights the need to take a much broader view of disability and to conceptualize and integrate behavior from a systems approach. Speigal (1971) has pointed out that such an approach incorporates the six levels of:

1. physical state of the universe;
2. individual-biological level;
3. individual-psychological level;
4. small group (including the family);
5. extended systems (extended family, work, school, etc.) and
6. societal values.

It is obvious that each level has direct application and importance when trying to understand behavior and disability.

We feel that the time is now right to shift to a systems approach. As part of this movement there is a definite need to focus on further developing and applying a family systems perspective to clearly aid our understanding and clinical work with disabled patients and their families. A shift from an individual to a family approach recognizes that individual concepts alone do not provide the required broad view obtained by looking at the total system.

LITERATURE REVIEW

There is an increasingly expanding literature that deals with family system functioning and its impact on disability. Summarizing, the articles suggest the following:

1. Family functioning affects the outcome of rehabilitation.

Litman reported on 100 orthopedically disabled patients undergoing rehabilitation at two centers (Litman, 1966). His results suggest that while there is no significant relationship between family solidarity and rehabilitation response, the family does play an important, supportive role in convalescence, and through this does positively affect outcome. Further, the likelihood of positive outcome is increased if treatment is directed toward the patient reentering the family.

Swanson and Murata compared the patient's view of pain problems with that of a primary family member and report that high agreement between patient and family member was associated with management problems and poor outcome (Swanson, 1980).

Waring states that marital and family dysfunction can play an important role in both the selection of chronic pain as a symptom and its perpetuation (Waring, 1977).

2. The family's involvement in treatment is important in primary, secondary,and tertiary prevention (Epstein et al,1976) and in compliance (Geertsen, 1970, Oakes, 1970).

3. Families require education in a number of areas (Bruhn, 1977, Dzau, 1978; Oddy et al, 1978; Thomson, I; 1974; Wright, 1960). Provided with this, they collaborate more effectively with rehabilitation teams (Dzau, 1978, Epstein, 1981) and their anxiety is reduced (Dzau, 1978).

4. Marriage and the quality of it (whether it occurs before or after the onset of disability) has effects which are unclear. The literature contains conflicting reports, but raises substantive issues (Crewe, 1979; El Ghatit, 1975; El Ghatit, 1976).

Renne, in a study of 4,400 families, suggests a relationship between dissatisfaction with marriage and the likelihood of reporting a physical disability or chronic illness (Renee, 1976).

5. Family role functioning is significantly altered by the disability of a family member (Bishop and Epstein, 1980; Bruhn, 1977; Carpenter, 1974; Cleveland, M, 1980; Crain et al, 1966; Crewe et al, 1979; Dzau, 1978; Friedman, 1970; Geertsen, 1970; Ludwig, 1969; Waring, 1977; Waring, (in print).

Cleveland reports that spinal cord injured sons challenge the father's role within one year after injury (Cleveland, 1980). She also indicates that the mothers correctly estimate the injured sons' ability but let them "off the hook" in terms of role task expectations and that the sons have trouble with male role and sexual identity. Lastly, she reports that parents feel they will never be relieved of their parental role.

Carpenter reports on a study of 93 families with a disabled husband. The major topics of concern were the need to change roles and disagreement over new roles (Carpenter, 1980). Friedman et al comment on the increased effects if the disabled individual previously filled the breadwinner role (Friedman, 1970).

Crewe and El Ghatit and Hanson (El Ghatit 1976) report that marriage after spinal injury is associated with the likelihood of being employed and fulfilling a financial resource role.

Waring speaks about the perpetuation of the chronic pain role in response to marital and family dysfunction (Waring, 1977; Waring, in print). Geersten and Gray also discuss factors influencing a mother's inclination to adopt the sick role (Geersten, 1970).

Croog et al report on the role of kin networks and helping patterns (Croog, 1972). This excellent study shows that individuals who use family members well in support roles also make better use of agencies and institutions. If these roles were used frequently prior to myocardial infarction, they provided more support after the event. No differences between rural and urban populations, social class or ethnic groups were associated with these findings.

Ludwig and Collette report on a study of two groups, one with and one without husbands dependent on their wives in activities of daily living (Ludwig, 1969). They report that dependency was associated with increased time spent together, but less time with friends and relatives. Dependent husbands were also less likely to be involved in decision making and couples were more likely to reflect conjugal role flexibility.

We have discussed a theory suggesting that the greater the incapacity the greater the role strain, and a study reporting the reverse (Bishop, 1980). We go on to present our own view which combines both. The reasoning is that minimal incapacity creates ambiguities about what can be expected of the disabled person while major incapacity clearly calls for significant role adjustments. Both therefore carry an increased risk of negatively affecting role functioning. With moderate but definite incapacity such strain is less likely.

6.   There is agreement that families with disabled members are faced with problems in the areas of health, pursuit of leisure activities, role changes, and difficulties related to specific disabilities (i.e. personality changes in multiple sclerosis) (Bishop & Epstein, 1980; Bruhn, 1977; Carpenter, 1974; Cleveland, 1980; Crewe, 1979; El Ghatit, 1976; Friedman, 1970; Geersten, 1970; Ludwig & Collette, 1969; Mohamed et al, 1978; Oakes et al, 1970; Waring, 1977; Waring, in print).

7.   The impact of having a disabled member in the family varies, depending on which member (husband, wife, child, breadwinner) is disabled (Friedman, 1970).

OTHER CONCEPTUAL ISSUES

There are a number of other concepts that are also important for clinicians, researchers, and teachers working with the disabled and their families.

First, there are a variety of individual and family *response and adaptation patterns* that follow the onset of disability. Some families are more successful in handling a member's disability while in other cases, the member's disability exacerbates already pre-existing problems. Faced with the onset of a family member's disability, most families experience at least a brief period of crisis with less than optimal functioning. As this phase subsides, many outcomes are possible. These can include a return to previous levels of functioning, a return to less than previously optimal levels of functioning, an improvement to a better than previous level or the development of a chronic maladaptive and repeating crisis pattern. It is not clear at this time which forces have the greatest impact nor which pattern can be expected. In clinical work it is important to differentiate the type of situation being dealt with; clinicians, therefore, face a challenge that demands careful assessment, sensitivity and sound judgment.

Second, it is important for clinicians to have a clear *guideline* that allows them to assess a *family's functioning* at any point in time. In order to do so, they require a conceptual model or framework as the basis for organizing their family data. To be effective such a framework should define those aspects of family functioning which are most likely to determine whether or not family members will present emotional or physical health problems. Because a family system is inherently complex, many dimensions must be assessed; oversimplification is not possible, and a general global rating does not provide enough information for clinical action.

For each area or dimension of family life, it is important to be able to describe a *range of functioning* from least to most effective. It is not sufficient to only ask "does this family communicate?". We must ask "how well or how poorly do they communicate?". It is particularly important to be able to designate most effective functioning. This is crucial in dealing with families with a disabled member, as they may have to compensate and function at above usual levels if optimal adaptation of the disabled member is to be achieved.

THE McMASTER MODEL OF FAMILY FUNCTIONING

We have developed and detailed the McMaster Model of Family Functioning which addresses the conceptual issues mentioned above in that it focuses on those dimensions of family functioning that impinge upon emotional and physical well being of family members; describes a range of family functioning from least to most effective; and is applicable to normal families (Epstein & Bishop, 1981; Epstein & Westley, 1981; Epstein et al, 1978).

The McMaster Model of Family Functioning is derived from empirical research and clinical work that led to the operational definition of six dimensions of family functioning. These are problem solving, communication, roles, affective responsiveness, affective involvement and behavior control. These dimensions identify clearly distinct aspects of family functioning but are interrelated in complex ways so that they are neither independent nor orthogonal in mathematical terms.

The model and dimensions have been clinically useful in a range of settings including family practice (Bishop et al, 1980; Comley, 1973; Epstein & Levin, 1973; Epstein et al, 1976; Epstein & McCauley, 1978; McCauley & Epstein, 1978; Weston, 1972; Gilbert, 1972), psychiatry (Levin et al, 1976; Woodward et al, 1978) and rehabilitation (Bishop & Epstein, 1980; Bishop et al, 1980). The model also formed the basis of treatment in an outcome study (Woodward et al, 1981) and in the selection of super functional families for a special therapeutic foster placement program (Levin et al, 1978).

Details regarding the model and its use in clinical assessment and treatment are found elsewhere (Bishop & Epstein, 1980; Bishop et al, 1980; Epstein & Bishop, 1981 a; Epstein & Bishop, 1981 b; Epstein & Westley, 1969; Epstein et al, 1978).

CLINICAL APPROACH

In this next section we will present a clinical case example and comment on the major concepts involved.

Case Example: Assessment

Mr. and Mrs. A were 50 and 48 years old respectively. Their 21 year old daugher lived with them and a 24 year old son was married and living a great distance away. They immigrated to Canada from Wales shortly after World War II and marriage.

Mrs. A was paraparetic from an episode of arachnoiditis five years previously. While partially mobile in braces she had problems because of spasticity which, when bad, prevented any walking and left her wheelchair bound.

Mrs. A, according to herself, had always been a "chronic worrier", which the husband and daughter associated with behaviors of fuzzy thinking, talkativeness, repeating the same thing over and over and a stance of demandingness, mixed with pessimism that nothing would work anyway!

Mr. A was a sensitive well-meaning laborer who wished to help in any way possible. He was a rugged individualist, a good provider for his family, and an executive of his union.

The daughter completed high school and technical training which led to a good job. She had been seriously dating a man for a long time but had been unable to seriously contemplate marriage.

A detailed assessment identified several important patterns. First, Mrs. A had always relied strongly on husband and had taken all problems to him. He was able to take a leadership role in resolving difficulties but included his wife in a way that maintained her self-esteem. The crisis produced by the onset of her medical condition and its disability had significantly increased her anxiety. She also worried that if she asked her husband for too much help he would be fed up with her and leave her.

The husband became hostile towards treatment services on two counts. To begin with, he felt that health professionals did not actively involve him in the treatment process. This was particularly difficult for him because of his previous high level of involvement with his family. He sensed that the behavior of health professionals undermined his leadership role. He withdrew and stated that "if the doctors can't help my wife, how can I be expected to". He had also felt put upon and accused during two previous attempts at family assessment. His feelings of being put upon centered around the fact that those meeting with the family made interpretations without first attempting to understand the family and its individual members, (i.e. interpreted without sufficient data). This reinforced his desire to withdraw.

In an attempt to assuage his feelings of frustration and isolation, the husband took a course in meditation and also began studying French at a local college. His wife's constant complaining continued to frustrate him. He withdrew further into his studies and went to the basement to do this - a place where she could not follow him. This heightened the wife's fears that she would lose him. She kept these fears to herself rather than discussing them with her husband. As her tension increased, so did her spasticity and she was almost constantly wheelchair bound. When she could contain the feelings no longer, there were episodes of yelling and screaming which would force him to come from the basement. When he arrived she would feel ambivalent about talking and the issue would not be clarified or resolved.

A second pattern identified was that the daughter now found it impossible to consider leaving home as she felt that both her parents needed her. She had assumed many of the role tasks previously looked after by her mother and also became concerned about her father's withdrawal. When she was on dates she felt guilty about not being at home to look after her mother.

A home visit revealed the third pattern. While the house was a moderate size, there were problems in one corridor in terms of the wheelchair and the ability to turn it. In particular, the bathroom door was hard to get through, although fortunately once this was accomplished, there was reasonable room for functional mobility and handrails had been installed. In the living room, dining room and kitchen, there were numerous bric-a-brac and small items of furniture that tended to get in the way of easy wheelchair passage.

Previous failure by the treatment team to engage this family as a collaborative component of the rehabilitation process significantly interfered with their functioning in many areas. When the *problem solving* dimension was examined in this family, the following findings emerged:

Problems were not being communicated to the appropriate resource people. Mrs. A was not talking to her husband about problems as she had in the past, and was turning to the clinical team members instead. The daughter had also stopped taking her difficulties to her mother and was unable to talk to her father as she felt he was preoccupied with his own stress. The effect was that everyone disengaged and the family systems problem solving mechanisms were disrupted.

In an earlier research study by Westley and Epstein (Epstein & Westley, 1969), it was found that most families seem to deal with a similar range of difficulties and problems. The effectively functioning families solve their problems, whereas ineffectively functioning families seem incapable of solving at least some of their problems.

To aid in assessing and understanding how a family solves problems, the McMaster Model of Family Functioning defines seven steps of problem solving.

These are:
1. Problem identification.
2. Communication of the problem to an appropriate resource.
3. Development of alternative action plans.
4. Deciding on a suitable action.
5. Acting to resolve the problem.
6. Monitoring that the action is carried out.
7. Evaluating the outcome of problem solving.

We postulate that the more steps completed, the more effective the problem solving. In the A family, their problem solving was disrupted at the second step - that of comr̃ ṇicating the problem to the most appropriate resource - and was thereby rendered ineffective.

This highlights a common problem. People working with the disabled often take on too many of the patients' responsibilities and foster the development of maladaptive dependency patterns. It is crucial to support and to make use of the family resources. There are of course situations where the family may quite reasonably turn to outside resources and effective families often do so. Helpers, however, should foster internal resources and take care to not short circuit them.

Role changes had also taken place. The husband's leadership and problem solving roles were undermined and the daughter assumed major responsibility in the home, leaving the identified patient with little to do. In response to this, the husband withdrew and the wife's self-esteem decreased. She became increasingly more anxious and this led to increasing spasticity. The daughter was not able to deal with her developmental task of leaving home and the family was not able to support her in this.

The McMaster Model of Family Functioning outlines a number of necessary role task functions that must be dealt with if the family is to be effective and highlights the issues of allocation and accountability and their importance in satisfying role functioning.

In the A family, the husband and daughter took over all the role functions without any open discussion of the reallocation process taking place. Mrs. A was then shut out of any opportunity to participate in and to contribute to the functioning of the family.

It is important to be clear about the actual functional capacity of the disabled individual. Families with a disabled member require education about what can and cannot be expected of the disabled one.

Many authors indicate that disability demands role changes and there is a strong suggestion that disabled members do poorly if clear family roles are not allocated to them. In particular, role task changes may be required around: income and finances, accommodations, household chores, power and decision-making processes, health-related issues, the sexual area, and social support. All these areas are listed as necessary functions within the McMaster Model of Family Functioning.

Family communication became masked by Mrs. A's mixed messages, by her tendency to avoid conflict by focusing on her braces and the fact that her mobility was restricted, and by reticence on the part of the husband and daughter to put things on the line: albeit, partially on compassionate grounds that Mrs. A had enough to deal with.

The McMaster Model discusses communication styles derived from looking at two independent factors labelled as clear versus masked and direct versus indirect. The A family developed a masked pattern exemplified by Mrs. A's fuzziness and her tendency to displace her anxiety onto her braces rather than talking about the family issues which bother her. It is not uncommon, when dealing with the disabled, for instrumental issues around braces, wheelchairs, etc., to become the focus when feelings such as personal inadequacy (I can't do it = braces are no good) or family difficulties are the real issue. The reluctance of both the husband and daughter to discuss the issues bothering them also contributed to the masked communication pattern which developed in the A family.

It is important for health professionals to appreciate the very real and substantial difficulties that restrictions of mobility, communication and activities of daily living present for the disabled. Studies have shown that health professionals fail to recognize the importance of such issues for patients and their families. Instead they tend to rate issues such as sexual functioning and grief as the highest priority items to be dealt with. This discrepancy of perception is obviously of great importance and must contribute to difficulty in collaboration between the professionals and the patients and families in the rehabilitation process.

Once the basic issues of mobility etc. are dealt with, then the other issues usually come to the fore. Helped with the basic issues, the disabled and their families are often capable of resolving these other issues on their own and fequently in a most effective fashion. Their seeming problems can often be the result of our failure to help with the basics. Financial assistance, advocacy and aid with home access can be powerful therapeutic intervention techniques!

Case Example: Treatment

Formulation of the case followed careful assessment of the A family. A treatment strategy and plan was then initiated that incorporated fostering the use of previously existing strengths in the dimensions of the family's problem solving, role functioning, and communication. We will now briefly summarize the treatment process.

The husband was engaged as an active and important part of the treatment team. A meeting was held with him, the physio-therapist and Mrs. A. It was agreed that physiotherapy for Mrs. A's physiological spasticity would be useful and greatly enhanced if she were relaxed when she attended treatments. As the husband was quite knowledgeable in the area of meditation and relaxation techniques, he was given the task of carrying out relaxation sessions with the wife on a regular basis, and also just prior to appointments with the physio-therapist. In return, the wife agreed to take a more active role at home. The couple worked out how she could carry out a significant amount of meal preparation and they rearranged furniture to facilitate this. Mrs. A's anxiety abated, her spasticity improved and the couple's time together improved.

The husband then openly broached his desire to have his wife get out of the house with him. She expressed her anxiety but agreed that if it was important to him she would do so. They planned weekly outings, and he insisted on following through despite her initial protestations. On the second outing, and without prompting by the therapist, he took her to dinner, thanked her for responding to his needs and presented her with a rose.

As the parents became more involved with each other and able to leave the home to socialize more, the daughter began discussing her desire to be independent and subsequently moved out. Husband and wife continued to meditate together regularly and he studied upstairs near her!

A number of important clinical intervention issues are raised by this case. Considerable time was spent in orienting the family to what the therapist was going to do and their active permission and collaboration was obtained at each step.

In addition to assessing the presenting problem in great detail, the family was assessed in each of the dimensions of problem solving, roles, communication, affective responsiveness, affective involvement and behavior control using the concepts of the McMaster Model of Family Functioning. In the course of the assessments not only was the current functioning of the family appraised but also their functioning prior to the onset of the disability. This helped clarify the family's strengths and facilitated their use and integration in the therapeutic process.

The A family had problems in the dimensions of problem solving, role functioning, and communication. The McMaster Model dimensions of affective responsiveness, affective involvement, and behavior control were handled with reasonable effectiveness. Each family varies, of course, and in a different family, the situation could be reversed. Assessing families on all six dimensions determines the specific pattern and enhances the clinicians' understanding of the presenting problem and key family transactional processes.

The assessment took three sessions, one of which was a home visit. While a home visit is not always possible, it certainly provides an excellent first-hand impression of the realistic difficulties that can occur in the family home. An office visit cannot achieve such perceptions.

Treatment moved rapidly and took place over four sessions that were spaced out over time. The treatment strategy in this case was to attempt to change the family structure and organization, particularly in the dimensions of problem solving and roles. In this case, changes in these areas led to spontaneous improvement in the communication dimension. Developing such strategies is impossible without an adequate and detailed assessment. It cannot be stressed enough that a detailed and adequate assessment is a prerequisite for treatment and often shortens time requirements for later therapy interventions. We have discussed treatment issues in more detail elsewhere (Epstein & Bishop, 1981 a; Epstein & Bishop, 1981 b).

FUTURE RESEARCH

More research is obviously needed in the area of interaction between disability and family functioning. We currently are finalizing developments of two instruments that allow quantification of family functioning on the six dimensions of the McMaster Model of Family Functioning. The Family Assessment Device is a paper and pencil questionnaire filled out by all individual family members over the age of thirteen.

The McMaster Clinical Rating Scale is a rating scale filled out by either the clinician doing a family assessment or an observer. Anchor descriptions of the most ineffective (rated 1), non-clinical (rated 5) and most effective (rated 7) levels of functioning support ratings on seven point Likert scales for each dimension.

We are beginning to develop studies using these devices with families who have either physically or psychiatrically disabled members.

Disability is a family affair. The responses of involved families have significant effects on the outcome of the rehabilitation process. A family systems approach to work with the disabled is therefore needed, and this requires careful clinical assessment and treatment planning. Both our family functioning and treatment approach are useful and hopefully our future research in this area will further their clinical utility.

BIBLIOGRAPHY

Anthony, E.J. **1970**. "The Impact of Mental and Physical Illness on Family Life". 127. *American Journal of Psychiatry*, 138-146.

Bishop, D.S. and **Epstein**, N.B. **1980**. "Family Problems and Disability". In Bishop, D.S. (Ed.). *Behavior Problems and the Disabled: Assessment & Management*. Baltimore: Williams & Wilkins.

Bishop, D.S., **Epstein**, N.B. and **Baldwin**, L.M. **1980**. "Structuring a Family Assessment Interview". 26. *Canadian Family Physician*, 1534-1537.

Bruhn, J.G. **1977**. "Effects of Chronic Illness on the Family". 4(b). *Journal of Family Practice*, 1057-1060.

Bruhn, J.G., **Hampton**, J.W. and **Charaler**, B.C. **1977**. "Clinical Marginality and Psychological Adjustment in Hemophilia". 15. *Journal of Psychosomatic Research*, 207-213.

Carpenter, J.C. **1974**. "Changing Roles and Disagreement in Families with Disabled Husbands". 55. *Archives of Physical Medical Rehabilitation*, 272-274.

Chen, E. and **Cobb**, S. **1960**. "Family Structure in Relation to Health and Disease - A Review of the Literature". 12. *Journal of Chronic Diseases*, 544-567.

Cleghorn, J. and **Levin**, S. **1977**. "Training Family Therapists by Setting Learning Objectives". 43. *American Journal of Orthopsychiatry*, 439-446.

Cleveland, M. **1980**. "Family Adaptation to Traumatic Spinal Cord Injury: Response to Crisis". 29. *Family Relations*, 558-565.

Comley, A. **1973**. "Family Therapy and the Family Physician". *Canadian Family Physician*, 78-81.

Crain, A.J., **Sussman**, M.B. and **Weil**, W.B. **1966**. "Effects of a Diabetic Child on Marital Integration and Related Measures of Family Functioning". 7. *Journal of Health and Human Behavior*, 122-127.

Crewe, N.M., **Athlestan**, G.T. and **Krumberger**, B.A. **1979**. "Spinal Cord Injury A Comparison of Pre-Injury and Post-Injury Marriages". 60. *Archives of Physical Medical Rehabilitation*, 252-256.

Croog, S.H., **Lipson**, A. and **Levine**, S. **1972**. "Help Patterns in Severe Illness: The Roles of Kin Network, Non-Family Resources and Institutions". 34. *Journal of Marriage and the Family*, 32-41.

Dzau, R.E. and **Boehme**, A.R. **1978**. "Stroke Rehabilitation: A Family-Team Education Program". 59. *Archives of Physical Medical Rehabilitation*, 236-239.

El Ghatit, A.Z. and **Hanson**, R.W. **1975**. "Outcome of Marraiges Existing at the Time of a Male's Spinal Cord Injury". 28. *Journal of Chronic Diseases*, 383-388.

El Ghatit, A.Z. and **Hanson**, R.W. **1976**. "Marriage and Divorce After Spinal Cord Injury". 57. *Archives of Physical Medical Rehabilitation*, 470-472.

Epstein, N.B. and **Bishop**, D.S. **1981(a)**. "Problem Centered Systems Therapy of the Family". *Handbook of Family Therapy*. Gurman A., Kniskern, D. (Eds). New York: Brunner/Mazel.

Epstein, N.B. and **Bishop**, D.S. **1981(b)**. Problem Centered Systems Therapy of the Family. Jan. 7 (1). *Journal of Marriage and Family Therapy*, 23-31.

Epstein, N.B. and **Levin**, S. **1973**. "Training for Family Therapy within a Faculty of Medicine". 18(3). *Canadian Psychiatric Association Journal*, 203-208.

Epstein, N.B., **Levin**, S. and **Bishop**, D.S. **1976**. "The Family as a Social Unit". 22. *Canadian Family Physician*, 1411-1413.

Epstein, N.B. and **McCauley**, R.G. **1978**. "A Family Systems Approach to Patients' Emotional Problems in Family Practice". *Family Medicine, Principles and Application*. Medalie, J.H. (Ed.), Baltimore: Williams & Wilkins.

Epstein, N.B. and **Westley**, W.A. **1969**. "The Silent Majority. San Francisco: Jossey-Bass.

Epstein, N.B., **Bishop**, D.S. and **Baldwin**, L.M. **1981**. "McMaster Model of Family Functioning: A View of the Normal Family". Froma Walsh (Ed.). *Normal Family Processes*. New York: Gilford Press.

Epstein, N.B., **Bishop**, D.S. and **Levin**, S. **1978**. "The McMaster Model of Family Functioning" Vol. 4. *Journal of Marriage and Family Counseling*, 19-31.

Friedman, E.A., **Goodwin**, N.H. and **Caudhry**, L. **1970**. "Psychosocial Adjustment of Family to Maintenance Hemodialysis II". Vol. 70 (March). *New York State Journal of Medicine*, 767-774.

Geertsen, H.R. and **Gray**, R.M. **1970**. "Familistic Orientation and Inclination Toward Adopting the Sick Role". 32. *Journal of Marriage and the Family*, 638-646.

Gilbert, J.R. **1971**. "The Primary Physician: A Unique Role". March 106. *Canadian Medical Association Journal*, 1007-1010.

Goldenson, R.M. (Ed.). **1978**. *Disability Rehabilitation Handbook*. Dunham, J.R. (Ass. Ed.). McGraw Hill, Chapters 1 and 3.

Levin, S., **Rubenstein**, J.S. and **Streiner**, D.L. **1976**. "The Parent-Therapist Program: An Innovative Approach to Treating Emotionally Disturbed Children". 27(6). *Hospital and Community Psychiatry*, 407-410.

Litman, T.J. **1966**. "The Family and Physical Rehabilitation". 19. *Journal of Chronic Disease*, 211-217.

Ludwig, E.G. and **Collette**, J. **1969**. "Disability, Dependency, and Conjugal Roles". 51. *Journal of Marriage and the Family*, 736-739.

McCauley, R.G. **1967**. "Family Practice: A proposed solution to the problem of meeting the medical needs of the community". 96. *Canadian Medical Association Journal*, 1036-1039.

McCauley, R.G. and **Epstein**, N.B. **1978**. "Application of Family Therapy Principles in Family Practice". *Family Medicine, Principles, and Applications*. Medalie, J.H. (Ed.). Baltimore: Williams and Wilkins.

Mohamed, S.N., **Weisz**, G.M. and **Waring**, E.M. **1978**. "The Relationship of Chronic Pain to Depression, Marital Adjustment, and Family Dynamics". 5. *Pain*, 285-292.

Oakes, T.W., **Ward**, J.R., **Gray**, R.M., **Klauber**, M.R. and **Moody**, P.M. **1970**. "Family Expectations and Arthritis. Patient Compliance to a hand resting splint regimen". 22. *Journal of Chronic Disease*, 757-764.

Oddy, M., **Humphrey**, M. and **Uttler**, D. **1978**. "Stresses upon the Relatives of Head-Injured Patients". 133. *British Journal of Psychiatry*, 507-513.

Renne, K.S. **1971**. "Health and Marital Experience in an Urban Population". 33. *Journal of Marriage and the Family*, 338-350.

Rohrer, K., **Adelman**, B., **Puckett**, J., **Toomey**, B., **Talbert**, D. and **Johnson**, E.W. **1980**. "Rehabilitation in Spinal Cord Injury: Use of a Patient-Family Group". 61. *Archives of Physical Medical Rehabilitation*, 225-229.

Shanfield, S.B., **Heiman**, E.M., **Cope**, D.N. and **Jones**, J.R. **1979**. "Pain and the Marital Relationship: Phychiatric Distress". 7. *Pain*, 343-351.

Shontz, F.C. **1978**. "Psychological Adjustment to Physical Disability: Trends in Theories". 59(11). *Archives in Physical Medical Rehabilitation*, 516-517.

Speigel, J. **1971**. *Transactions: Interplay between Individual, Family and Society*. (Ed.). New York: Science House.

Swanson, D.W. and **Maruta**, J. **1980**. "The Family's Viewpoint of Chronic Pain". 8. *Pain*, 163-166.

Thomsen, I. **1974**. "The Patient with Severe Head Injury and his Family". 6. *Scandinavian Journal of Rehabilitation*, 180-183.

Van der Spuy, M. (in preparation). "Clinical Rating Scale". McMaster University.

Waring, E.M. **1977**. "The Role of the Family in Symptom Solution and Perpetuation in Psychosomatic Illness". 28(1). *Psychotherapy, Psychosom*, 253-259.

Waring, E.M. (in print). "Conjoint Marital and Family Therapy". *Pain Patient - A Psychological Perspective*. Tunks, E. (Ed.), Williams and Wilkins.

Weston, W. **1972**. "Emotional problems - A Family Affair". June, 1972. *Canadian Family Physician*.

Wright, E.A. **1960**. *Physical Disability - a Psychological Approach*. New York: Harper and Row Publishers.

Woodward, C.A., **Santa-Barbara**, J., **Striener**, D.L., **Goodman**, J.T., **Levin**, S. and **Epstein**, N.B. **1981**. "Client, Treatment, and Therapist Variables Related to Outcome in Brief, Systems Oriented Family Therapy". 20(2). *Family Process*, 189-197.

Chapter 2

Behavioural Family Intervention With The Family Of A Mentally Handicapped Child

Ray J. Thomlison
University of Toronto, Toronto, Ontario

Within the past twenty years, the clinical approach of behaviour modification has become increasingly effective in its application to mentally handicapped children (see Yule and Carr, 1980). Originating in the late 1950's (Gardner, 1971), behaviour modification of these children has burgeoned into one of the more influential contemporary approaches.

Such an observation is supported by many of the reviews on research into this area of practice. It is further substantiated by Gardner's extensive inventory of studies from which he concluded that behaviour modification and programme instruction were "the largest of the content areas in learning research with the mentally retarded" (Gardner, 1970:633).

The significance of the behavioural approach to the mentally handicapped relates specifically to three areas: a) the training of children by professionals within institutional or residential centres; b) the training of individual parents within the institutional setting to carry out home-based programmes for their children; and c) the training of groups of parents within formal settings to design and implement behavioural programmes with their handicapped children.

Direct child training by professionals within residential settings may continue to be the mainstay of behavioural training for the mentally handicapped child. However, it appears that the demands placed on the parents and siblings of this child will increase in future times. Extra pressures have already been felt to some degree as a result of the many deinstitutionalization movements across the country.

In response to these movements, parent training programmes have become exceedingly helpful in assisting parents with learning new methods of dealing with their mentally handicapped child. However, the emphasis has been on *training* the parents (usually limited to the mother), with little time devoted to the concerns of the total family unit. If the family system is recognized as the foundation unit for individual affective and instrumental behaviours, then it seems to follow that professional child training and parent training are major adjuncts to a more important family systems modification.

This paper will develop a model of family interactional modifications (family intervention) for the family of a mentally handicapped child. In order to systematically construct this behavioural family intervention approach, it will first be necessary to review the existing behavioural work on training children in behavioural skills as well as on reducing maladaptive or undesirable behaviours. Parent training, both individual and group, will be examined for both its historical significance and its substantive contribution to behavioural family intervention.

BEHAVIOURAL MODIFICATION
OF THE MENTALLY HANDICAPPED

(a)   Programmes Within Institutionalized Settings

Behaviour modification within institutional and residential centres has traditionally focused on the development of techniques to enhance the behavioural skills of the child. The variety of reports related to a child's behavioural repertoire are too numerous to list since almost every conceivable facet of daily life has been examined. The following examples from the literature do give some indication of the range: brushing teeth (Abramson and Wunderlink, 1972); self-feeding (Albin, 1977); toilet training (Azrin and Foxx, 1971); dressing (Azrin et al., 1976); talking (Cook and Adams, 1966); and self-help skills (Westling and Murden, 1978).

Often, problematic behaviours emerge which are socially inappropriate and inhibit the handicapped child's developmental progress. Programmes administered within the institutional setting have again been carried out to reduce maladaptive behaviours and increase adaptive or desirable behaviours. Such programmes have dealt with aggressive behaviours (Boe, 1977); self-injurious behaviour (Corbett, 1975); stereotypic behaviour (Flavell, 1973); undesired meal time behaviour (Henriksen and Doughty, 1967); tongue protrusion (Kaufmann et al., 1977); throwing of temper tantrums (Sailor, et al., 1968); and a multiplicity of other behaviours (for further examples, refer to Thompson and Grabowski, 1972).

Two researchers were able to categorize the research of one half a decade on behaviour management with the mentally retarded into six groups of problem behaviours. They discovered that out of 56 studies published between 1971 and 1975, inappropriate social behaviour was the focus of 21% of the programmes. In decreasing order of frequency, the studies reported on classroom disruptions (20%), aggression (18%), self-injurious behaviours (16%), stereotypical behaviours (14%), and noncompliance (11%). Of further interest, 55% of these studies reported on programmes which took place in an institutional environment. An additional 29% of the programmes were based in a classroom setting, while only 7% of the reported programmes took place within a home situation (Bates and Wehman, 1977:10).

To some extent these data reflect the history of behaviour modification with the mentally handicapped child. In the beginning, the technology required environments wherein each procedure could be systematically applied with the resultant impact on the child's behaviour observed and recorded. It was through this observational approach within the more controlled environment of a hospital or residence that the effectiveness of behavioural techniques was demonstrated.

(b)   Parent Training Programmes

Accompanying the development of behavioural techniques within the institutional setting was another revelation. Since many children spend more time with their parents than with professional helpers, it seemed only appropriate to train the parents in the techniques of behaviour modification.

This was a pragmatic approach which could be utilized by non-professionals. Furthermore, traditional one-to-one approaches to treating the child were becoming increasingly suspect due to their relatively poor performance on outcome measures (Levitt, 1957, 1963). The new approach could prove cost effective, reducing the costs of treatment by transferring to the parents a greater responsibility for the training and management of their handicapped child. (The debate on this issue is acknowledged in Mira, 1970 and Rose, 1974.)

The behavioural parent training movement was quickly judged a success and became one of the most frequently reported behavioural interventions with the family during the seventies. It was examined in relation to a wide variety of skill training, including language (Seitz and Hoekenga, 1974), play (Mash and Tendel, 1973) and a range of self-help skills (Lance and Koch, 1973). Parents have also been trained to deal with the problematic behaviours of their mentally handicapped children (refer to examples of Callias and Carr, 1975; Doernberg, 1972; Freeman and Thompson, 1973; Rose, 1974; and Tavormina, 1975). Complete reviews of parent training may be found in Berkowitz and Graziano, 1972; Doernberg, 1972, Johnson and Katz, 1973; O'Dell, 1974; Tavormina, 1974; Yule, 1975; Gordon and Davidson, 1981.

Before commencing an intensive exploration of the behavioural approach to parent training and family intervention, a brief overview of the behavioural paradigm will be presented. The behavioural techniques of positive and negative consequences, extinction, shaping, chaining and modelling will also be discussed briefly as they play an important role in behavioural intervention with the mentally handicapped.

THE SOCIAL LEARNING THEORY OF BEHAVIOUR MODIFICATION

(1) The Behaviour Modification Paradigm

In order to achieve a basic understanding of the social learning approach to behaviour modification, three concepts must be understood. These concepts are outlined in the following behaviour modification paradigm:

FIGURE I

THE BEHAVOUR MODIFICATION PARADIGM

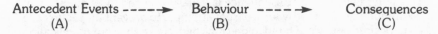

Antecedent Events ----→   Behaviour ---- →   Consequences
        (A)   (B)   (C)

In this theory of human behaviour, behaviour is viewed as being maintained by those environmental events which occur both before and after the identified behaviour. If behaviour is to be altered in terms of its frequency of occurrence and/or its intensity, then changes must be made both in the antecedents and the consequences of this behaviour.

(2) A Case Illustration

To illustrate this paradigm, imagine that a father complains because his child will generally not do as he is asked. Suppose, for the sake of illustrative simplicity, that the father's greatest concern centres on the child not coming to the dinner table when he is asked. Behavioural observations of this problem might produce the following sequence of exchanges:

Antecedent Event ---→	Behaviour -----→	Consequence
#1 John come to dinner-→	No response from John-→	Do you hear me?
#2 John get in here for dinner before I come-→ in there and get you	I'll be there in a minute ---→	I said now!!

After some elapsed time

#3 John, this is your last chance. Get in here. If-→ I have to come in there you are going to be in trouble!	John presents himself reluctantly at the table---→ and begins to eat	Father silent

What is depicted here is not an atypical parent-child exchange. From the social learning perspective, the non-compliant behaviour appears to be maintained by the father's commands and threats at the antecedent level combined with the threats and lack of acknowledgement at the consequence level. For example, when John finally arrived for dinner, his father ignored him.

This brief illustration serves to demonstrate one other major aspect of social learning theory. It is an interactional theory with emphasis on behavioural exchanges between people. While one person's behaviour may be briefly isolated for the purpose of analysis, the behaviour of those people involved in the interchange is considered to be an integral part of that analysis.

(3) Positive and Negative Consequences of Behaviour

Returning to the example of non-compliance provided by John and his father, some further explanation   of the behavioural model is needed for this dyad to be helped. It is known that consequences differ in terms of quality and purpose. Some consequences are of a positive or pleasing nature while others are of negative, aversive or displeasing variety.

This latter category of consequence is usually referred to as punishment and is frequently observed when a parent attempts to prevent the recurrence of an undesired behaviour by spanking the child. As a behaviour modification technique, the use of punishment as a consequence is acknowledged as a means of decreasing the frequency of a behaviour. In fact, the definition of punishment as a concept in the behavioural approach is rooted in its reduction effect on behaviour. However, punishment is viewed as an unacceptable manner through which to modify behaviour because in many instances it suppresses a behaviour without providing an alternative, more desirable behaviour.

The use of positive consequences to increase desirable behaviour is the strength of the social learning approach to behaviour modification. The results of more than a quarter of a century of research in the clinical area of behaviour modification have demonstrated that behaviour increases in frequency over time when it is followed by positive consequences.

(4) Coercion and Extinction in Behavioural Exchanges

Up to now, two techniques of behaviour modification have been identified as possible means of helping John and his father: use of aversive consequences (punishment) and/or use of positive consequences, with the former type reducing behaviour and the latter type increasing behaviour.

However, it was observed in the illustration that the father was employing two other tactics in his attempts to modify John's behaviour. First, the father attempted to get John to the dinner table with a verbal command. When this did not produce the desired results, he intensified the tone of the command by adding the threat of aversive consequences.

Trying to control another's behaviour by command and threat is familiar to most of us. In many instances, however, it has the effect demonstrated by John and his father. The commands and threats escalate until finally the child complies in order to terminate the yelling. By the time the child obeys the parent's command, the parent has become agitated enough to lose any motivation for acknowledging the child's compliance. This exchange is known as a "coercive exchange" (Patterson and Reid, 1970) or negative reinforcement. The main effect to remember for clinical assessment is that this exchange will result in an *increase* of the undesired behaviour (in this case, not coming to the table when requested).

A final concept in social learning theory must be identified as it labels a technique incorporated into almost all behaviour modification programmes. When the positive consequences for a behaviour are withheld over time, the behaviour will increase in frequency. This technique of withdrawing positive consequences or "ignoring" a behaviour is known as extinction. It should be pointed out that when John did sit down at the table, his father chose to ignore John's behaviour. In other words, in the absence of positive acknowledgement for the desired behaviour, the likelihood of increasing compliance is low because it is part of an extinction programme.

(5) Illustration of Intervention

In order to help John and his father alter their undesirable behavioural interaction, the therapist will need to devise a programme by which the father can give positive consequences for John's compliance with arriving at the dinner table on time. However, as the situation now stands, John and his father have trained one another in a manner which prevents John from arriving upon the first request and this in turn causes the father to be non-responsive when John does comply.

Intervention requires that a target behaviour for desired change be isolated. In this case, such a target might be labelled as "John coming to the dinner table when called". New antecedents must be identified and new consequences for the desired behaviour must be identified and agreed upon by John and his father.

An agreement to change might well be formalized in a contractual statement detailing the new behaviour, its antecedents and its consequences. An example could be the following:

CONTRACT

TARGET BEHAVIOUR: John comes to the dinner table when called

ANTECEDENTS: Father agrees to call John for dinner by saying "John it is time for dinner, please come to the table." (or some approximation to this verbal request) Father must call only once and he agrees not to repeat the request by yelling at John.

TARGET BEHAVIOUR: John agrees to come to the table when called by his father.

CONSEQUENCES: When John arrives at the dinner table as requested, his father agrees to verbally express his positive acknowledgement (praise) and to place a check mark on John's tally sheet.

If John chooses not to respond to father's request, father will begin eating alone, ignoring John's absence. John will forego the opportunity for his father's praise and tangible, positive acknowledgement for this dinner time.

While a programme of behaviour modification is usually more complex than this illustration, the points demonstrating the basic techniques of analysis and intervention are similar. It should be noted that the purpose of the check marks on John's tally sheet is two fold. First, it offers his father the opportunity to concretely acknowledge the compliance in a manner which, given a predetermined number of check marks, might be traded for a special event. Second, these tally sheets become important data collection devices for the therapist to monitor the change process.

(6)   Some Additional Techniques Applicable to Behaviour Modification

Additional techniques utilized in the behaviour modification approaches can be found in a number of introductory books (e.g. Bandura, 1969; Tharp and Wetzel, 1969; Patterson, 1971; Graziano, 1975; Kazdens, 1975; Craighead, Kazdin, Mahoney, 1976). In discussing family intervention with mentally handicapped children, three additional techniques must be briefly identified.

(a)   Shaping: When complex behaviours are to be taught to a child, it is essential to break the task down into its incremental behaviours. A complete list of these "successive approximations" to the desired complex behaviour is then compiled with the least complex behaviour being the first behaviour training objective.

Through the use of positive consequences, this behaviour is strengthened in the repertoire of the child. When this behaviour is established, the next behaviour in the heirarchy is targeted for learning. Positive consequences are now given only for the second behaviour. This procedure of positively reinforcing a behaviour until it is established and then withdrawing the positive reinforcers and holding them contingent upon the next behaviour is repeated until the complex behaviour is accomplished.

Most of us learn complex behaviours by some means of shaping behaviour. In the case of the handicapped child, behaviours such as eating, dressing and talking are examples of behaviours which may be trained through the use of a shaping technique.

(b) Chaining: This is a technique which resembles the shaping procedure in that its goal is to train complex behaviours by moving the child through the incremental parts of the complex task.

However, in the chaining procedure, the child is positively reinforced for the last incremental behaviour in the "chain" of behaviours which make up the complex task. For example, if a mentally handicapped child is to be taught to make his/her bed, the chaining procedure would begin by reinforcing the child for the last behavioural task in bed making - such as placing the bedspread over the blankets.

Once the child has demonstrated consistent ability to perform this task, the second to last bed making task would be introduced and reinforced in conjunction with the last task. This procedure would systematically retrace each task back to a completely unmade bed. In this manner, the child learns the sequence of required tasks by being positively reinforced for increasingly complex chains of incremental behaviours.

(c) Modelling: In its simplest form, modelling is a technique which utilizes a person's (child's) natural tendency to learn by imitation. Complex behaviours may be taught by demonstrating the desired behaviour to the child. When successful imitation is observed, the child is positively reinforced.

This technique is easily used but very often forgotten particularly in parent training programmes. For example, it is more effective to model certain behavioural procedures for parents, such as time out, than to describe the procedure in the hope that the parents understand the description well enough for it to be carried out.

BEHAVIOURAL FAMILY INTERVENTION

THE RATIONALE AND BASIS FOR BROAD BASED BEHAVIOURAL FAMILY INTERVENTION WITH THE MENTALLY HANDICAPPED

There is little doubt that behavioural parent training has had a positive effect on the behaviour of most parents and children that have participated in the programmes (Doernberg, 1972; Griffin, 1979; Callais, 1980). For the most part, behavioural parent training will remain a major thrust in the field of family intervention with the handicapped. This will be particularly true in teaching general behaviour modification skills to parents within the group context (Rose, 1974; Tavormina, 1975) because of its relative economic advantages in therapist time.

However, even in view of the acknowledged attractiveness of the parent training approach, a number of factors loom on this horizon which would argue that a broader family-based approach is needed. Such an approach would combine both the advantages of working with the family as a system and the advantages of a behavioural approach obtained from parent and child training programmes.

Those factors which appear to support a behavioural family systems approach have generated from the work of parent trainers themselves. First of all, there is the factor of recognition of the parents' need for more than simply training in behavioural management skills. As Tymchuk observes, "the parents come with an entire experimental history of failures, of dashed expectancies, of real or imagined social pressures, of incredibly complex personal feelings and even of family disintegration. Training parents to be trainers of their children when these same parents have come to reject their child may in effect curtail the chances of the success of such training" (Tymchuk, 1975:19). While most parent trainers would be sensitive to these needs, the reality of a parent training agenda places them in a secondary position to the behavioural procedures. Questions such as "Why did this happen to us?" or "Why do we have to work so hard at being parents?" cannot be adequately dealt with in a parent training group.

A second but related factor supporting the family behavioural systems approach has been the inability of the parent trainer to deal with individual problems which present themselves in discussions about the handicapped child. For example, problems related to other children in the family or marital distress or perhaps even maternal depression might possibly arise during parent training and be deferred in order to continue with the training session.

A third major impetus for a broad based family approach stems from the realisation that most parent training has been done with the mother (Gordon and Davidson, 1981:528) to the exclusion of other family members. Although data is lacking at this point which strongly supports inclusion of other members, it is apparent that changes in the behaviour of the handicapped child impact upon the behaviour of siblings. (Arnold, et. al. 1975; Lavigueur, 1976; Humphreys et. al. 1978). Conversely, it has been shown that siblings can be trained to function as behaviour modifiers for the identified child (Lavigueur, 1976; Colletti and Harris, 1977).

Unfortunately, studies are lacking on the role of the father in the family as a behaviour modifier. Notwithstanding this reality, it does seem to make clinical sense that individual behavioural change could be more effectively achieved if all members of the family were participants in the change process.

It could be further argued that the stability of change would be strenthened if all family members were more aware of the change process and the maintenance conditions for it. As the family is given more and more responsibility to care for its mentally handicapped child, a stronger support system will be needed to maintain behavioural successes and develop additional skills.

Two final points must be made in support of the family approach. It seems that an adequate assessment of a child's problems, his/her parents' strengths and resources, and the sibling relationshps can only be done by observing the child within his/her family context. For example, parental choices of target behaviours in parent training programmes may be at a level of expectation inappropriate for the family and child. Furthermore, parental perceptions of their handicapped child may well influence their reports on the behaviour of the identified child and siblings (Seitz and Hoekenga, 1974). In order to increase the accuracy of parental and child reports, all members should be seen in an interactional setting.

Finally, although the outcome data are reasonably positive for parent training, there is a group of parents that does not seem to be responsive to the approach (Berkowitz and Graziano, 1972). Also, the relatively high dropout rate among parents involved in group training does suggest that alternative approaches must be developed (Gordon and Davidson, 1981).

In light of the above factors, a model of behavioural family intervention is herein proposed as a means of broadening the assessment and treatment base for families with mentally handicapped children. Within this model the family becomes the locus of treatment, and the refined techniques of child training and parent training become adjunct approaches within the family approach.

A PROCEDURAL GUIDE FOR BEHAVIOURAL FAMILY INTERVENTION

A recent article identified three types of behavioural family intervention: parent training, parent-child contingency contracting, and family negotiation, systems, or problem-solving training (Blechman 1981:222). The interventive approach outlined in this section incorporates each of these approaches as elements to be integrated in the process of family behavioural change.

Behavioural family therapy is more than parent training, contingency contracting or problem solving. At the outset, it attempts to demonstrate to the family members that each person's behaviour does influence, and in turn is influenced by, others in the family. Individual behavioural problems have an impact in some way on all family members. Individual change and the maintenance of successful change becomes as much a responsibility of the family as it does of the individual.

As with the systems approach of family intervention, the behavioural family approach requires that the family be examined in the context of its community. This includes the work setting, school, health, social services and any other environment in which the family might interact. Such a perspective on the family is even more important for the family with a handicapped child because it is extremely difficult and even undesirable to attempt behavioural skill training without utilizing community services for the child and the family.

An attempt has been made to render the behavioural family intervention procedure as explicit as possible within the space requirements. The following Figure 2 provides the framework for this approach. The reader is advised to consult the references provided if elaboration is necessary.

ASSESSMENT PHASE

Involvement of the family with the mentally handicapped child in the assessment phase is not intended to suggest that all members have problems or that there is family pathology. Rather, the assessment phase is an information gathering period during which time the therapist identifies family perceptions of the handicapped child, the family's interactional and relationship patterns, as well as concerns, issues and problems which may emerge in the session. Assessment information must also be collected concerning problems or potential problems within other community systems. The major objective of this assessment is to identify the most effective strategy for intervention.

For those families with identified concerns and problems about their mentally handicapped child or other family members, the assessment procedure focuses on the problem behaviours which can be identified by those in the family. The ultimate goal is to identify existing family problems, to gain family acknowledgement of their existence, to secure a commitment to action for their alleviation and to identify the most appropriate means by which change may be accomplished.

PROCEDURES DURING ASSESSMENT PHASE

(1) Compilation of the problematic behavioural inventory

   (a) begin by asking for someone in the family group to identify their perception of the problem(s) that has resulted in the meeting

   (b) attempt to clarify individual definitions of these behaviours by asking for examples

   (c) as each person gives his/her perception of the problem, there is a high probability that discussion and disagreements will be stimulated. Sometimes it is difficult to know how to handle these exchanges. It is important to observe who disagrees with whom and over what behaviours and therefore you should allow these interchanges to occur. However, they can very soon become counterproductive to the objective of the assessment. At this point, you should intervene by requesting the family members to stop their debate, acknowledging that you would expect them to have different ideas about the problems but that arguing is not going to resolve the problems. Assure all members that you are interested in their perceptions of the problems and that *all* will have an opportunity to talk. *Make sure you follow through on this promise.*

(2) Classification of identified problems

   (a) if the family group identifies its priority problem behaviours as primarily the result of the limited behavioural skill repertoire of the mentally handicapped child, then a decision must be made regarding family intervention versus child and/or parent training intervention.

   (b) if the handicapped child is not already in formal behavioural training,

FIGURE 2

PROCEDURE FOR FAMILY INTERVENTION WITH THE FAMILY OF A MENTALLY HANDICAPPED CHILD

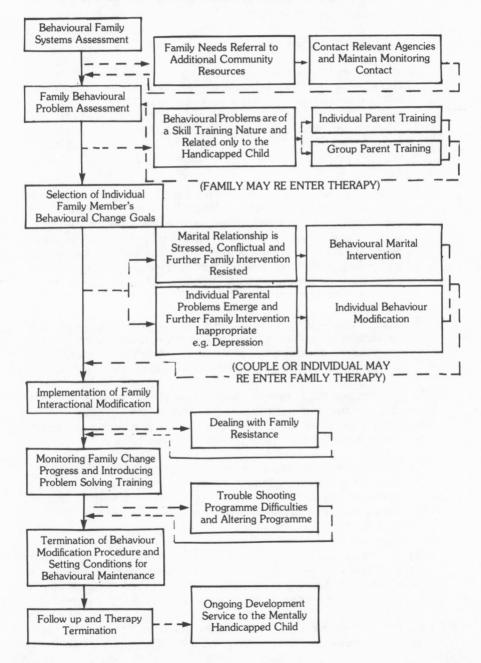

arrangements must be made with the appropriate community resource (see Yule and Carr, 1980, for examples of options).

(c) in order to enhance the skill training of the child, the parents must become involved in either individual or group training. For a discussion of individual training see Doernberg (1972); for group training see Rose (1974); and for the advantages and disadvantages of both, see Gordon and Davidson (1981) and Callais (1980).

(d) in those instances where parents may be uncertain or confused about parent training, it is helpful to assign readings to the family that will be discussed prior to embarking on parent training. There are a variety of such books and manuals available. For general and relatively easy reading refer to Patterson and Guillion, 1968; Becker, 1971; and Patterson, 1971. For examples of specific training manuals, see Baldwin et. al. 1973; Miller, 1975; Baker et. al. 1976; O'Dell et. al. 1977; and Carr, 1980.

(e) parent training may occur independently or concurrently with behavioural family intervention. When it occurs concurrently, the therapist must ensure that the programme objectives for both interventions are compatible and not at cross-purposes. One means of increasing the compatibility is to focus the parent training programme on behavioural skill development and focus the family therapy programme on the reduction of undesired behaviours and increase of desired behaviours.

(f) finally, if the family group identifies its priority problem behaviours as interactional in nature, for example when all family members state observations of displeasure about one another's attitudes, feelings, and behaviours, then family intervention should continue.

(3) Having obtained the decision to continue with behavioural family intervention, the therapist must return the focus to the identified priority behavioural problems. However, the objective is now to identify the controlling conditions for these problem behaviours.

(a) attempt to identify the antecedent events of at least those behaviours which arouse a higher level of intense feeling on the part of family members. Antecedent events are those conditions existent immediately prior to the occurrence of a target behaviour, e.g. what are others doing or not doing.

(b) identify the consequences of those problem behaviours which elicit the more intense family feelings. Consequences are those events which occur after the target behaviour, for example, what do others do after one of these problem behaviours occurs.

(4) Identify the contingencies existent for the provision of these consequences - what rules appear to govern the conditions under which these

consequences are provided. For example, when a child is spanked versus when he is not.

(5) Identify recurrent behavioural patterns in the family exchanges

   (a) observe and record behavioural exchanges, e.g. coercive exchanges, shouting, avoidance responses, excessive demands, etc.

(6) Secure a commitment from the family system in an attempt to ensure that:

   (a) they will work as a unit on these family problems and

   (b) they, as individuals, will work toward behavioural change.

   (c) at this point in the assessment phase, the therapist should be able to demonstrate to the family the interconnections of their individual behaviours in that when one individual behaves, all family members must respond in some manner. For example, when the handicapped child throws his food at the dinner table, the laughter of siblings serves to positively reinforce his behaviour. The probability that they will be scolded by the parents causes increased ill feelings at the table. These feelings may in turn be reflected back to their handicapped sibling in some form. With repeated occurrences, dinner time becomes an aversive or unpleasant time to be dreaded by all. The result is that all family members have a legitimate complaint about the dinner table "climate" and they may blame the handicapped child when in fact each family member is responsible.

(7) Begin to identify possible behaviour targets for change. These target behaviours should be "desirable" behaviours with the objective of increased frequency of occurrence.
   Two questions must be answered by each family member:
   a) How could you behave differently to make this a happier family?
   b) How would you like to see others behave differently to make this a happier family?
These questions may be given as a homework assignment with the instructions that each person provide as many answers as possible to each question. Also, remind them that you are essentially intersted in working with desirable behaviours. Point out that the challenge of the assignment is to identify behaviours which they would like to see occur more often rather than behaviours they would like to see stopped.
Note: these questions must be written down for each family member. Every effort must be made to assist the handicapped child with contributing his/her responses. Where the child is preverbal/nonverbal, the therapist will be required to make decisions for the child based on the assessment data.

(8) Select appropriate behaviour targets for modification - on the basis of the family's homework assignment

(a) select behaviours which are too accelerated in frequency in order to maximize the opportunities for positive consequences.

(b) select behaviours which appear to be most relevant to enhancing this family's definition of happiness.

(c) strive to select behaviours which are incompatible with the occurrence of undesirable (problematic) behaviours.

(d) select at least one behaviour for each child which is "low risk" for change. A low risk behavioural target is one that can be easily attained by the child and one which, if performed by the child without positive reinforcement (a violation of the change contract), will not jeopardise the growing trust of the child. An example of a child's low risk behavioural target might be combing his/her hair in the morning or taking the garbage out each evening.

(e) attempt to select behaviours which are commonly identified among family members, e.g., dinner time behaviour, family "get togethers", doing the dishes co-operatively, and playing with all siblings.

(f) remember that a behaviour must be observable to all and therefore it is necessary to explicate the indicators of some behaviours in order to minimize debates over whether the behaviour has occurred. e.g. the behaviour labelled "cleaning his room" may at first appear to be obvious but it is most important that specific behaviours be pinpointed, such as picking up clothes, making bed, etc.

(9) Allow time for all family members to present their concerns and their support for the target behaviours. Certain behaviour choices will elicit strong feelings from some family members. Negotation must take place before selected behavours are settled upon, and must always take place within the "spirit" of the agreement or commitment for change. If one or more members wish to re-evaluate this commitment in light of the selected targets for change, then this request must be honoured. Such re-evaluation may, however, have to take place within the context of the "consequences of no change". That is, all persons have a right not to be required to change. However, there are certain consequences for not changing. What are they for the individual and his family?

For the mentally handicapped child, the ability to cognitively appraise the consequences of no change may not be possible. If this becomes an issue, the consequences of no change can be demonstrated by way of comparison with the consequences of change in the target behaviour. For example, the family can be asked to demonstrate its withdrawal of attention in response to the child's temper outbursts. Alternatively, the family can demonstrate its approval and praise for the target behaviour of "appropriate talking".

(10) When behaviour targets have been agreed upon, set the conditions for a baseline measure (see Patterson, 1971).

(a) before instructing the family to change, request that the parents monitor the frequency of occurrence of the target behaviours. This will give a rough "before" measure that will help you assess ongoing performance.

(b) appoint the parent(s) as the monitors of the behaviour targets. Give the parent(s) a tally sheet and instructions to place a check mark in the box corresponding to the target behaviour each time the behaviour occurs. (see Becker, 1971, or Patterson, 1971).

(11) During the assessment phase, the therapist may identify problems with an individual or the marital couple which require specific attention. For that matter, some studies have indicated that further work focusing on the training of the child may not be appropriate. (Bernal et. al. 1972; Ferber et. al. 1974). Behavioural marital intervention is compatible with the assessment in progress. With the couple's agreement, family intervention may be temporarily suspended in light of the recognized need to concentrate on the dyad's problems. (See Jacobson and Martin, 1976). Similarly, there are a variety of behavioural approaches available to work with problems specific to the individual, (see for example, Gelder, 1979).

IMPLEMENTATION PHASE

The implementation phase of the programme is marked by the identification of new contingencies between identified behaviours and their consequences. To this point, the focus has been on the appropriate targeting of behaviours for change. At the time that a programme for change is to be operationalized, a contingency contract must be formulated in order to facilitate a systematic, co-operative effort of the family system toward change. The following objectives must be understood as part of the implementation phase:
1) Identification of *acceptable* positive reinforcers.
2) Securement of a contingency contract specifying the reciprocal behaviours of all family members.
3) Identification of acceptable sanctions to be employed in response to contract violations.
4) Tally recording for the purposes of monitoring individual change.

PROCEDURES FOR THE IMPLEMENTATION PHASE

1) Establish new cues or antecedent events for the target behaviours.
2) Establish new consequences to be mediated in relation to the occurrence or absence of a targeted behaviour.
3) Formulate a written contract specifying the following conditions:
   a) The target behaviours for change and their pinpointed elements.
   b) New antecedents (cues) to be given and by whom.
   c) New positive consequences which includes both tangible, e.g., check marks or tokens and social reinforcers, e.g., affection, praise.

    d) Specify sanctions to be mediated when an aspect of the contract is not met, what happens - maybe the person should be "costed". If swearing occurs, contrary to the contract - maybe it is to be ignored, e.g. put on extinction.

    e) Specify any bonus reinforcers to be given, e.g., "extra points for extra good behaviour".

    f) Specify who is to tally record (monitor) behaviour occurrences - usually one or both parents.

    g) Contracts may be written in a variety of ways, but they must all contain the conditions "Who does what to whom under what conditions!" Examples of contracts may be found in Patterson 1971; Stuart, 1971; Weathers and Liberman, 1975; and Blechman, 1977.

4) Instruct in the procedures of tally recording.

5) After implementing the programme, follow-up telephone calls must be made at least the first day and four days after the beginning of the programme. The purpose of these telephone calls is to answer any questions arising out of implementation of the contract and to ensure that implementation did in fact take place. These calls need not take long and should be limited only to the pragmatics of programme implementation.

6) The next series of family interviews will deal with monitoring the programme and the problems arising out of implementation.

7) Difficulties in implementing the programme are inevitable. These problems usually pertain to such things as problems in tally recording, differences in target behaviour definitions, and lack of "co-operation" on the part of certain family members. In order to deal with these problems, you must remember that the contract is your reference point. Once agreed to, all problems arising with the behavioural changes must relate to the original document. Changes in the contract must be negotiated by all members of the family.

Remember that all problems related to the implementation of and adherence to a contract for family interactional modification may eventually have to be related back to the original commitment for change agreed to by the family.

8) Each interview after implementation should begin with an examination of the tally recording and the systematic positive reinforcement by the therapist of behaviour changes on the part of all family members.

9) Next, discussion should focus on any problems arising between sessions related to the programme. Where problems are identified they must of course be dealt with.

10) Discussion may then flow to more general aspects of the family functioning with the therapist helping the family focus on the controlling conditions of other problematic behaviour.

11) Special techniques such as role playing, modelling and behavioural rehearsal may be introduced in an effort to deal with specific problems arising from the family's efforts to change.

12) Since much of the family's energy goes into problem solving activity and conflict resolution, the therapist must spend time on these areas of family life. For examples of these techniques see Vincent et. al. 1975; Thomas, 1977; and Jacobson and Margolin, 1979.

13) Where monitoring indicated that behavioural changes are not taking place, or where the programme is not being implemented to the satisfaction of therapist and/or family, it may be necessary to alter certain aspects of the programme. Depending on the area in which the programme is failing, it will be necessary to consider changes in:
   a) Target behaviours
   b) Consequences (positive and/or aversive)
      or to assess whether people are in fact following through on the requirements of the contract. For example, it might be that although a particular consequence is being held on contingency, you find another very potent positive consequence being provided at random.
14) When target behaviour(s) have achieved the desired level of frequency:
   a) Identify new behaviours for change.
   b) or move toward termination of your involvement.

TERMINATION PHASE

The purposes of the termination phase are:
1) To terminate therapeutic involvement.
2) To review progress in relation to reciprocal behavioural changes.
3) To set conditions for behavioural maintenance.
4) To arrange for follow-up interview.

PROCEDURES FOR TERMINATION

1) Together with the family system, evaluate the progress in relation to the objectives of the contract.
2) If the decision is to terminate, then set the conditions for behavioural maintenance.
3) Behavioural maintenance requires the therapist to review with the family the basic learning principles identified during the modification of the target behaviours; e.g., positive consequences vs punishment; reciprocity vs coercion.
4) Instruct the family to continue the tally recording over the next four weeks but without your regularly scheduled appointments.
5) Set an appointment for four weeks from this last interview, asking the family to bring the tally records with them.

FOLLOW-UP

The follow-up interview should be an assessment interview related to whether or not the behavioural changes have been maintained. If these changes have not been maintained at a level consistent with the expectations of the therapist and/or the family, it will be necessary to reinstitute the programme structure. If, on the other hand, all is well, then visits may be stopped with the understanding that the therapist could be called at any time that the family might wish consultation.

A CASE ILLUSTRATION: THE B FAMILY

Description of the Family

The B family is comprised of mother (age 38), father (age 43), Susan (age 14), Charles (age 11), Robbie (age 9). Father is employed as a pipe fitter and mother is not employed outside the home. The couple has been married for 16 years and appear to have a stable marriage.

Susan is mentally handicapped and functions at a mental age of 10 years. She has lived with the family since birth and has been attending a community based programme for mentally retarded children for the past six years. Her progress in this programme has been good although she has periodically presented the staff with disruptive behavioural problems such as temper tantrums, throwing objects and shouting. Within the school setting these problems have been of relatively short duration. Charles and Robbie are reportedly doing well in school and enjoy positive peer relationships. Generally, the family has coped well with Susan's difficulties and family relationships have been positive until recently.

Reason for Referral

Mrs. B has maintained on ongoing contact with a mother's group affiliated with Susan's school. Over the past six months she had been complaining about the children and in particular her inability to deal with Susan's behaviours. Mrs. B had also been feeling depressed primarily because she felt that her "job" as mother seemed to be an ever increasing burden. The thought that she was now losing her ability to parent her two younger children was causing Mrs. B to become increasingly self-critical. As the result of a number of her comments during group meetings it was suggested that she should see one of the agency's counsellors to help her with her feelings of depression.

Assessment Information

The total family was seen for assessment even though Mrs. B had contacted the counsellor requesting individual counselling. This interview produced a good deal of information concerning Mrs. B's problems in particular, and the family problems in general.

In essence, Mrs. B was very distressed over the very disruptive behaviour exhibited by Susan and the lack of assistance she received from her husband in dealing with the children. She felt that the boys were "out of control and wouldn't do a thing they were asked". Susan was particularly obnoxious at the dinner table and according to Mrs. B had succeeded in making supper almost unbearable for all. Her most disruptive and unpleasant behaviour was to scoop food from her dinner plate with her hand and throw it against the kitchen wall. From Mrs. B's observation this would occur at least 4 or 5 times during meal time. If Mrs. B reprimanded her for this Susan would overturn her chair and throw a temper tamtrum by screaming, throwing objects from the dinner table and physically striking out against the nearest family member.

Father presented a less verbal image than did his wife. He tended to agree that the children were presenting difficulties but felt that these would be overcome in time. Mr. B did admit that Susan's behaviour concerned him although he thought it was just another one of "those things" a retarded child would do. It was evident that Mr. B tended to leave the discipline of the children to his wife, however, it was apparent that he was an interested and involved parent.

Charles and Robbie remained rather quiet during the interview responding only to questions put to them directly. Susan on the other hand was verbal and often interrupted the conversation of others. Her interrupting was most prominent when the counsellor attempted to elicit information from her two brothers. She would attempt to answer for them and/or she would get out of her chair attempting to physically interact with the boys. Interestingly, neither parent intervened to inhibit Susan's interrupting behaviour until the boys' protests reached a volume requiring parental intervention. At this point Mr. B would instruct the boys to be quiet and for Susan to return to her chair. With repeated instructions from mother, Susan would eventually comply.

Although the two boys did not offer much additional information about family members' behaviour they did defend themselves against Mrs. B's complaints by saying that she yelled at them a great deal. Mrs. B, understandably, responded by arguing that if they did what they were supposed to do she wouldn't have to yell at them. During this type of exchange Susan and her father remained quiet while the boys and mother argued.

The assessment pertaining to the problem inventory is summarized below under the headings of the behavioural model. As with any assessment not all information is dealt with and therefore only the priority problem behaviours and their controlling conditions are present.

SYNOPSIS OF PROBLEM INVENTORY

Antecedent Events	Problem Behaviour	Consequences
Susan: - family sitting at dinner table, usually engaged in conversation - a warning from any family member to behave herself and eat her dinner	- disruptive dinner table behaviour, e.g. throwing food	- reactions from all family members (including father) reprimanding her - threats that she will have to leave the table - often laughter from Charles & Robbie - family dinner conversation interrupted
- after repeated food throwing one of parents (usually mother) removes Susan from table	- temper tantrums when removed from table	- continued disruption of dinner - family members attempt to calm Susan down - mother often leaves table to hold Susan
- wants something from family member - wants something done for her	- yelling at family members	- parents usually comply with her demands - brothers tend not to comply - brothers yell at Susan

Antecedent Events	Problem Behaviour	Consequences
-non-compliance by other family members to Susan's requests - attempts by other family members to correct Susan's behaviour	- hitting family members	- brothers return the hitting - yelling at Susan and brothers by mother - ignored by father
- mother tells Susan to tidy her room and/or pick up her clothes	- does not help with assigned household tasks, e.g. tidy room, hang up clothes	- mother scolds Susan - boys complaining Susan never has to do her jobs - mother does the jobs for Susan
- upon arising in the morning Susan dresses for school and goes to breakfast	- neglects personal hygiene, e.g., brushing teeth, and hair, washing	- mother reminds Susan to wash, etc. - Susan eats breakfast and and leaves for school - brothers tease Susan and call her names, e.g., pig

Charles:

Antecedent Events	Problem Behaviour	Consequences
- Charles is responsible for cleaning his room and taking out the garbage. With his brother he is to do the dishes each night - often mother reminds Charles to complete one of his assigned tasks	- will not complete assigned household tasks e.g. has to be reminded frequently to help with dishes, won't tidy his room, won't take out the garbage	- mother begins to scold Charles and the scolding escalates into a yelling exchange between mother and Charles. - mother cleans his room - father takes out garbage
- wants something from mother - engaged in argument with mother, usually concerning lack of task completion	- yells (sometimes swears) at his mother	- mother "grounds" Charles i.e. says he can't go outside after supper, must come home directly after school - mother has hit Charles - often both mother and Charles terminate this yelling exchange by one leaving the room - other family members remain quiet
- mother requires all children to let her know where they are after school - goes to play with friends	- does not report in after school	- mother expresses her anger - mother tells him that he is "grounded" for the week, but fails to follow through
- disputes over toys, comics and T.V. - disputes over certain task assignments, e.g., dishes	- fights with Robbie hitting and kicking him	- mother or father intervenes, sending both boys to their rooms with a spanking

Robbie:

Antecedent Events	Problem Behaviour	Consequences
- Robbie is responsible for cleaning his room, picking up his clothes and helping Charles with the dishes - mother reminds Robbie to complete his assigned tasks	- will not complete his household assignments, e.g. tidy his room, put clothes in hamper, and hang up his clothes	- mother scolds Robbie - mother cleans Robbie's room

Antecedent Events	Problem Behaviour	Consequences
- wants mother to do something for him - engaged in argument with mother	- yells at mother	- mother reciprocates the yelling - mother leaves the room
(same as for Charles)	- fights with Charles	- (same as with Charles)
- usually occurs during meal times - playing with sibs	- calls both his siblings names, e.g. pig, bum, ugly etc.	- sibs retaliate with name calling - mother becomes upset with the names that are directed at Susan and sends Robbie to his room - sibs begin to physically fight

This summary of the problem focused inventory demontrates how a number of reported problems may be distilled by the worker into a manageable number of problems to be worked on. Although the behavioural inventory focuses on the behaviour of the children it is extremely important to understand the interactional relationship of the parents. For example, mother is seen as a very active participant in the children's problem behaviours while father is significant by his apparent absence from most of the problem exchanges.

Since the behavioural family model employs the children as the most pragmatic and functional beginning agents of the family change, it is necessary to identify their problem behaviours as a focal point for the analyses of the parents' functional and dysfunctional behaviour. In this manner, the worker's assessment data may be organized within the behavioural approach to develop certain intervention hypotheses which will *require* the parents altering their own behaviours in order to affect changes in the behaviours of their children.

TARGET BEHAVIOURS FOR CHANGE

Upon completion of the problem inventory the approach to family interactional modification focuses on the identification of behaviours for desired change. This phase is followed by the identification and agreement among all family members of new antecedents and consequences for each of these target behaviours. Each of these therapeutic tasks is negotiated and eventually formalized in a written contract for change. The negotiation of this contract requires the agreement of all family members with regard to the identified change goals as well as who among the family is required to behave differently when the target behaviours occur. In order to illustrate this process the B family contract is presented below. Note that while the focus of the change contract is on the children, the parents are required to engage in a much higher level of positive reinforcement for desired behaviours.

FAMILY CHANGE CONTRACT

All family members agree to work toward the following changes. Susan, Charles, and Robbie agree to do the behaviours listed below, in return mother and father agree to give the required recognition for the children's behaviours. Further, mother and father agree to avoid yelling and spanking as methods of changing the children's behaviours.

Target Behaviour #1: Good dinner table behaviour
Target Person: Susan

AGREEMENT: Susan agrees to sit at the dinner table with the family and eat her dinner. She may talk at the table. In return for this mother and dad will mark the tally card for each 5 minutes of good dinner table behaviour. They will also tell Susan she is being good at the table with such phrases as, "good for you Susan", "well done", "you are doing well tonight", etc. Charles and Robbie agree to talk with Susan at the table.

AGREEMENT VIOLATION: If Susan becomes disruptive at the dinner table, mother and father are permitted to remind Susan that this is not good dinner table behaviour and she must stop the disruptive behaviour. If Susan chooses to continue the disruptive behaviour she will be asked to leave the table and sit in the living room. If Susan throws a temper tantrum she will be required to go to the time out spot at the entrance to the recreation room for a period not longer than 5 minutes after which time she will be allowed to return to the table.

If Charles or Robbie laugh or encourage Susan's undesirable dinner table behaviour they will be required to leave the dinner table and go to their respective rooms for a period of 5 minutes.

Points: Susan will be given 1 tally point for each 5 minutes interval of appropriate behaviour. Charles and Robbie will be given 2 tally points for each meal appropriately completed by Susan.

Target Behaviour #2: Cleaning Room
Target Persons: Susan, Charles, Robbie

AGREEMENT: All children agree to make their beds in the morning, to pick up their clothes, placing dirty clothes in the hamper and hanging up clothes. In return for this mother and dad will mark the tally sheet with 1 point for each of the completed tasks of making the bed, and picking up clothes. In addition, parents will acknowledge the completed tasks by praising each child for the task completed.

AGREEMENT VIOLATION: If any child fails to complete the target behaviour mother or father is entitled to remind the child once. If the child fails to comply, the task is left incomplete and no tally points granted. Parents are instructed not to engage in any yelling in attempting to get the job done.

Points: Susan, Charles, and Robbie will each receive 1 point for making their beds and 1 point each for picking up their clothes.

Target Behaviour #3: Doing Dinner Dishes
Target Persons: Susan, Charles, Robbie

AGREEMENT: All children agree to help with the dinner dishes. Mother and father will draw up a schedule whereby each evening's dishes will be the responsibility of two children with the third receiving the "night off". When the dishwashing has been completed mother and father agree to recognize the children's task completion with verbal praise and 5 tally points each. If the child who has the night off chooses to help he/she will be given 3 tally points.

Points: The two children responsible for doing the dishes will each receive 5 points upon completion of the task. The third child will receive 3 points if he/she chooses to help out.

AGREEMENT VIOLATION: If any child chooses not to carry out the assigned task of dishwashing no points will be given for that evening and parents will help complete the task. If a child chooses not to complete the task two evenings or more per week 3 points will be deducted from each incomplete session.

Target Behaviour #4: Family Activity Time
Target Persons: Mother, Father, Susan, Charles, Robbie

AGREEMENT: All family members agree to reserve at least 1 hour on each of 3 evenings during the week to engage in one item from the family activity menu. All family members agree to be together to engage in the family activity which include family talk sessions, games, family outings and family projects. The family agree that their first assignment will be to identify their family activity menu and suggest the means by which activity choices will be made. All family members will be given 8 points for their cooperation and completion of a family activity.

AGREEMENT VIOLATION: If any family member chooses not to engage in a family activity session he/she will loose the opportunity to earn 8 points. At no time should coercion be used to force a family member to participate in an activity, however, the family must discuss repeated refusals and present the results of their discussion at the next family counselling session.

Points: Mother and father will give 8 tally points to each child who partici- pates in a family activity session. Mother and father will also point to those parts of the activity they enjoyed and praise the children for their involvement.

Target Behaviour #5: Personal Hygiene
Target Person: Susan

AGREEMENT: Susan agrees to wash her face, brush her teeth and hair each morning before leaving for school. She will receive no reminder from mother. Susan will receive 1 tally point for each behaviour and praise from mother.

AGREEMENT VIOLATION: If Susan does not wash, brush her teeth or hair before leaving for school, she will not receive the tally points for the behaviours not completed. At no time is mother to yell at Susan for not doing these tasks.

Points: Susan is to be given 1 tally point for each of the behaviours of washing, brushing teeth and brushing hair to a total of 3 points each morning.

Bonus Points: At the end of each week on Friday evening mother and father will total the tally points. For each child who has earned over 80 points a bonus of 10 points will be given.

EXCHANGE OF POINTS:

Since the children are not presently receiving an allowance it was agreed that the tally points would be exchanged for money. It was therefore agreed that each tally point would be worth 2¢ and the children would now be required to pay their own way to movies and pay for their own treats. It was agreed that a maximum of $2.00/week could be earned on this exchange programme.

Signature of all family members   _____
agreeing to this contract:

_____

_____

_____

The negotiation and development of a change contract represents an integral part of the therapy process. It is the culmination of the input from all family members concerning their feelings about desired changes within the family. The therapist must move at the family's pace anticipating that most identified behavioural changes will precipitate disputes between family members and concerns about what will happen if "I change and she/he doesn't". Negotiation of the contract demonstrates the interrelationships between family members and that individual change requires family change. It also demonstrates to the family that family disputes can be resolved and compromise is possible.

The selection of behaviours will differ in terms of type and number depending upon the family and its predominant problems. In the illustration provided here, the behaviours were selected on the basis of their importance to reestablishing the parents' use of positive reinforcers together with the necessity of managing the children's behaviour. Susan's behaviour was most disruptive yet the parents' concern about Susan's handicap prevented them from successfully correcting her behaviour. It was necessary to develop a more appropriate dinner table behaviour for Susan. To accomplish this objective required the family members to understand their respective roles in maintaining Susan's undesirable behaviour. However, understanding is not sufficient to facilitate change. A structure for new behaviours for the parents and siblings had to be established with instructions as to how all members were to behave. While the emphasis on changing Susan's behaviour was placed on encouraging the parents to respond positively at a high frequency, some provision had to be made for the parents when Susan resorted to her disruptive behaviour. The therapist had suggested a time out procedure whereby Susan would be placed in her room. The parents viewed this procedure in an unfavorable light because they felt they must be able to watch Susan when she is throwing a temper tantrum. The therapist and parents were able to identify a location in the home where the parents could see Susan but she could not see them, i.e., the stairs to the recreation room.

A final point should be made about a change contract. It is not cast in stone. It will continue to be the focus of further treatment sessions and there may be additional information which will require the re-negotiation and change in the contract. For the most part these contracts do not require major changes and it is usual for the initial contract to provide the structure for successful family interactional modification.

Succeeding interviews focus on the progress of the family toward the change objectives. At a point when the behavioural data together with the family's reports indicate that successful behaviour modification has been achieved the formal programme is gradually withdrawn. Emphasis is placed on the need for all family members to continue the use of positive messages to one another. In the case of the B family the withdrawal of the programme would see the fading of the token economy with the requirement that the children be continued on an allowance. The family should now be aware of the impact of positive reinforcers, the need to acknowledge desired behaviour, and most importantly, to be able to re-establish a new behavioural programme if one is needed.

CONCLUSION

The major objective of this paper has been to develop and illustrate the application of a behavioural based model of family interactional modification with the family of a mentally handicapped child. The approach is more than parent training which has been the predominant behavioural approach with mentally handicapped children and their parents over the past two decades. The family approach requires a commitment for change on the part of all family members. It is a retraining process for the total family system not its dyadic subsystems. Most importantly, the behavioural approach requires each family member to focus on the major components of human interaction "who does what to whom, under what conditions and with what outcome?". Through the analysis of each family member's perception of the family problems the question of who affects whom demonstrates family exchanges. The conditions under which problem behaviours exist highlight the contextual variables of family behaviour resulting in a natural partializing of the family's problems and a reduction of the natural anxiety in confronting change. With the focus on specific targets for behavioural change all family members become aware, through the monitoring process, of the successful outcome of their individual and collective efforts at change.

Finally, family interactional modification is an educative or learning process which guides the family system through the stages of learning simple problem-solving techniques through to the more complex problem-solving strategies. With these objectives met, the family system has successfully developed a new behavioural repertoire for family living.

BIBLIOGRAPHY

Abramson, E. and **Wunderlich**, R. 1972. 'Dental Hygiene Training for Retardates: an application of behavioural techniques'. 10(3), *Mental Retardation*, 6-8.
Albin, J. 1977. 'Some variables influencing the maintenance of acquired self-feeding behavior in profoundly retarded children.' 15(5). *Mental Retardation*, 49-52.
Arnold, J.; **Levine**, A., and **Patterson**, G., 1975. 'Changes in sibling behaviour following family intervention'. 43(5). *Journal of Consulting and Clinical Psychology*, 683-688.
Azrin, N., and **Foxx**, R., 1971. 'A rapid method of toilet training the institutionalized retarded.' 4. *Journal Applied Behavioral Analysis*, 89-99.
Azrin, N., **Shaeffer**, R., & **Wesolowski**, M. 1976. 'A rapid method of teaching profoundly retarded persons to dress by a reinforcement - guidance method.' 14(6). *Mental Retardation*, 29-33.
Baker, B., **Brightman**, A., **Heifetz**, L., & **Murphy**, D., 1976. 'Steps to independence: a skills training series for children with special needs.' Illinois Research Press.
Baldwin, V., **Fredricks**, H., & **Brodsky**, G. 1973. 'Isn't it time he outgrew this? or, A training program for parents of retarded children', Illinois: Charles Thomas.
Bandura, A., 1969. Principles of Behavior Modification. Toronto: Holt, Rinehart & Winston.
Bates, P., and **Wehman**, P. 1977. 'Behavior management with the mentally retarded: an empirical analysis of the research.' 15(6). *Mental Retardation*. 9-12.
Becker, W., 1971. 'Parents are teachers: a child management program campaign.' Illinois Research Press.
Berkowitz, B. & **Graziano**, A. 1972. 'Training parents as behavior therapists: a review.' 10. *Behavior Research & Therapy*, 297-317.
Bernal, M., **Williams**, D., **Miller**, W. & **Reagor**, P., 1972. 'The use of videotape feedback and operant learning principles in training parents in management of deviant children' in Rubin, R. & Festerheim, H., Henderson, J. & Ullmann, L. eds. *Advances in Behavior Therapy*. New York: Academic Press.
Boe, R., 1977. 'Economical procedures for the reduction of aggression in a residential setting'. 15(5). *Mental Retardation*, 25-28.
Blechman, E. 1977. 'Objectives and procedures believed necessary for the success of a contractual approach to family intervention'. 8. *Behavior Therapy*, 275-277.
Blechman, E. 1981. 'Toward comprehensive behavioral family intervention.' 5(2). *Behavior Modification*, 221-236.
Callias, M. 1980. 'Teaching parents, teachers and nurses' in Yule, W., and Carr, J. eds. *Behavior Modification for the Mentally Handicapped*. London: Croom Helm, 175-200.
Callias, M. & **Carr**, J. 1975. 'Behavior modification programmes in a community setting.' in Kiernan, C. & Woodford, F. eds. *Behavior Modification with the Severely Retarded*. Holland: Associated Scientific Pub.
Carr, J. 1980. Helping Your Handicapped Child: a Step-by-Step Guide to Everyday Problems. Harmondsworth: Penguin Books.
Colletti, G., and **Harris**, S., 1977. 'Behavior modification in the home: siblings as behavior modifiers'. 5. *Journal of Abnormal Child Psychology*, 21-30.

Cook, C. & Adams, H. 1966. 'Modification of verbal behavior in speech deficient children.' 4. *Behavior Research and Therapy*, 265-271.
Corbett, J. 1975. 'Aversion for the treatment of self-injurious behavior'. 19. *Journal of Mental Deficiency Research*. 79-96.
Craighead, W., Kazdin, A. and Mahoney, M. eds. 1976. *Behavior Modificiation: Principles, Issues and Applications.* Boston: Houghton Mifflin.
Doernberg, N.L. 1972, 'Parents as teachers of their own retarded children.' in J. Wortis ed. 4. *Mental Retardation: An Annual Review.* New York: Grune & Stratton.
Ferber, H., Keeley, S., & Shemberg, K., 1974. "Training parents in behaviour modification: Outcome and problems encountered in a program after Patterson's work." 4. *Behavior Therapy*, 415-419.
Flavell, J. 1973. 'Reduction of stereotypes by reinforcement of toy play.' 11(4). *Mental Retardation*, 21-23.
Freeman, S. & Thompson, C. 1973. 'Parent-child training for the MR.' 11(4). *Mental Retardation*, 8-10.
Gardner, J. 1971. 'Behavior modification in mental retardation. A review of research of analysis of trends.' in R. Rubin, H. Fensterheim, A. Lazarus, and C. Franks, ed. *Advances in Behavior Therapy*. New York: Academic Press.
Gardner, J., Brust, D., Watson, L. 1970. 'A scale to measure skill in applying behavior modification techniques to the mentally retarded.' 74. *American Journal of Mental Deficiency*, 633-636.
Gelder, M. 1979. 'Behavior therapy for neurotic disorders.' 3(4). *Behavior Modification*, 469-495.
Gordon, S., and Davidson, N. 1981. 'Behavioral parent training' in Gurman, A., & Kniskern, D. eds. *Handbook of Family Therapy.* New York: Brunner/Mazel, 517-555.
Graziano, A. 1975. *Behavior Therapy With Children.* Chicago: Aldine.
Graziano, A. 1977. 'Parents as behavior therapists.' in Herzen, M. Eisler, R., Miller, P. eds. 4. *Progress in Behavior Modification.* 251-298.
Griffin, M. 1979. 'Training parents of retarded children as behavior therapists: a review.' 151. *Australian Journal of Mental Retardation*, 18-27.
Henriksen, K. and Doughty, R., 1976. 'Decelerating undesired mealtime behavior in a group of profoundly retarded boys'. 72. *American Journal of Mental Deficiency*, 40-44.
Humphreys, L., Forehand, R., McMahon, R., Roberts, M. 1978. 'Parent behavioral training to modify child noncompliance: effects on untreated siblings.' 9(3). *Journal of Behavior Therapy and Experimental Psychiatry*, 235-238.
Jacobson, N. and Martin, B. 1976. 'Behavioral marriage therapy: Current status.' 83. *Psychological Bulletin*, 540-556.
Jacobson, N. & Margolin, F., 1979. 'Marital Therapy: Strategies Based on Social Learning & Behavior Exchange Principles, New York: Brunner-Mazel.
Johnson, C. & Katz, R. 1973. 'Using parents as change agents for their children.' 14. *Journal of Child Psychology and Psychiatry*, 181-200.
Kaufmann, J., Hallahan, D. and Ianna, S., 1977. 'Suppression of a retardate's tongue protrusion by contingent imitation. A case study.' 15. *Behavior Research and Therapy*, 196-198.
Kazdin, A., 1975. *Behavior Modification in Applied Settings.* Illinois: Dorsey Press.
Lance, W., & Koch, A. 1973. 'Parents as teachers Help skills for young handicapped children.' 11(3). *Mental Retardation*, 3-4.
Laviguer, H. 1976. 'The use of siblings as an adjunct to the behavioral treatment of children in the home with parents as therapists.' 7(5). *Behavior Therapy*, 602-613.
Levitt, E., 1957. 'The results of psychotherapy with children: An evaluation'. 71. *Journal of Consulting Psychology*, 189-196.
Levitt, E. 1963. 'Psychotherapy with children: a further evaluation.' 1. *Behavior Research and Therapy*, 45-51.
Mash, E., & Terdal, L. 1973. 'Modification of mother-child interactions: playing with children.' 11(5). *Mental Retardation*, 44-49.
Miller, W. 1975. *Systematic Parent Training.* Champaign: Illinois Research Press.
Mira, M. 1970. 'Results of a behavior modification training program for parents and teachers.' 8. *Behavior Research & Therapy*, 509-511.
O'Dell, S. 1974. 'Training parents in behavioral modification: a review.' 81. **Psychological Bulletin**, 418-433.

O'Dell, S., **Blackwell**, L., **Larcen**, S., & **Hogan**, J. **1977**. 'Competency based training for severely behavioural handicapped children and their families.' 7. *Journal of Autism and Childhood Schizophrenia*, 231-242.

Patterson, G. **1971**. *Families: Applications of Social Learning to Family Life*. Champaign: Illinois Research Press.

Patterson, G. & **Guillion**, M. **1968**. *Living With Children: New Methods for Parents & Teachers*. Champaign: Illinois Research Press.

Patterson, G., & **Reid**, J. **1970**. 'Reciprocity & coercion: two facets of social systems.' in Neuringer, C. and Michael J. eds. Behavior Modification in Clinical Psychology. New York: Appleton-Century - Crofts.

Rose, S. **1974**. 'Training parents in groups as behavior modifiers of their mentally retarded children.' 5. *Journal of Behavior Therapy & Experimental Psychiatry*, 135-140.

Sailor, W., **Guess**, D., **Rutherford**, G. & **Baer**, D. **1968**. 'Control of tantrum behavior by operant techniques during experimental verbal training.' 1. *Journal of Applied Behavioral Analysis*, 237-243.

Seitz, S., & **Hoekenga**, R. **1974**. 'Modeling as a training tool for retarded children and their parents.' 12(2). *Mental Retardation*, 28-31.

Stuart, R. **1971**. 'Behavioral contracting with families of delinquents.' 2. *Journal of Behavior Therapy and Experimental Psychiatry*, 1-11.

Tavormina, J.B. **1974**. 'Basic models of parent counselling: a critical review.' 81. *Psychological Bulletin*, 827-835.

Tavormina, J. **1975**. 'Relative effectiveness of behavioral and reflective group counselling with parents of mentally retarded children.' 43(1). *Journal of Consulting & Clinical Psychology*, 22-31.

Tharp, R. & **Wetzel**, R. **1969**. Behavior Modification in the Natural Environment. New York: Academic Press.

Thomas, E. **1977**. Marital Communication and Decision - Making Analysis, Assessment and Change. New York: Free Press.

Thompson, T. and **Grabowski**, J. eds. **1972**. Behavior Modification of the Mentally Retarded. New York: Oxford University Press.

Tymchuk, A. **1975**. 'Training parent therapists.' 13(5). *Mental Retardation*, 19-22.

Vincent, J., **Weiss**, R., & **Bichler**, G. **1975**. 'A behavioral analysis of problem solving in distressed and non distressed married and stranger dyads.' 6. *Behavior Therapy*, 475-480.

Weathers, L. & **Liberman**, R. **1975**. 'Contingency contracting with families of delinquent adolescents.' 6. *Behavior Therapy*, 356-366.

Westling, D., & **Murden**, L. **1978**. 'Self help skills training: a review of operant studies. 12. *Journal of Special Education*, 253-283.

Yule, W. **1975**. 'Teaching psychological principles to non psychologists: training parents in child management'. 10(3). *J. Association of Educational Psychology*, 5-16.

Yule, W. **1975**, and **Carr**, J. eds. **1980**. *Behavior Modification for the Mentally Handicapped*. London: Croom Helm.

Chapter 3

Worker Crisis in Crisis Work

Barry Trute and Joseph A. Kuypers
School of Social Work, University of Manitoba

In observing health workers as they attempt to help people and families in crisis, we have come to appreciate how the form and substance of our training (and subsequent practice) as "helpers" is often a poor preparation for crisis work. Upon considerable reflection as to why this is the case, we have come to what appears to be a deceptively simple explanation. A first premise of our explanation is that the behaviors displayed by people "in crisis" are decidedly out of the ordinary. When experiencing the full impact of a crisis, a person may act in ways which, by our usual standards of decorum or politeness, are quite unusual, seemingly unpredictable, and often quite emotionally extreme. Furthermore, the tempo of interaction may be dramatically different and the subjective sense a person "in crisis" has of his experience may be quite different from that of a less involved observer. The crisis literature documents the extraordinary characteristics of individuals who are experiencing a crisis in their lives (Caplan 1964, Brockopp 1973).

By itself, this first premise would mean little, except to highlight that behavior in crisis is unique in certain describable ways. And so, our second premise becomes the crucial one in our argument. That is, that the worker is required to *interact with* the person who is experiencing a non-ordinary reality and who may be behaving in extraordinary ways. This interaction imposes specific requirements on the worker: to heal, comfort, stabilize, clarify and much more. While interacting with a client and their family, the worker must negotiate on many levels. The worker is not a disconnected observer (as an audience of a stage play might be) but becomes enmeshed in the crisis and required to influence the client in ways which lend "help". It is in this inter-personal involvement where problems for both the worker and client emerge; problems in interaction and communication which if unresolved, often render the worker useless as a crisis resource.

When face to face with the behavioral uncertainty and volitility of a person in crisis, we observed that workers are often thrown into chaos themselves and display many of the behavioral signs of being "in crisis". It appears as though the worker, while engaged in crisis work, is often drawn into defensive and repetitive positions which do not relate well to the needs of the client, and at these times, the worker often professes confusion as to what is happening. In effect, the polite and predictable give and take of usual social interaction is missing in much crisis work and this fact, by itself, deprives the worker of his confidence and clarity as to what to do.

The consequences for the worker of this second premise (that the worker must interact with an unpredictable client and that this prompts chaos for the worker) are elucidated, we think, by use of the concept "interaction ritual" as discussed by Erving Goffman in his book by the same title (1967). In this work, Goffman shows the degree to which our everyday behaviors are ritualized; sequences of actions and interactions which are so practiced and repetitive that we seldom take much notice of them. He explains, further, that momentary violations of those rituals, in everyday encounters, prompt immediate efforts to repair and correct the violation. In other words, in the "normal" world of practiced interaction, we act in ways which maintain a high degree of ritual. In so doing, we establish a sense of certainty, comfort and predictability. According to Goffman, a good deal of our behavior can be seen as complex ways to maintain and constantly recreate the ritual basis of everyday life. We think this theory helps explain how, in crisis work, a chaotic situation is created for the worker and indicates why he has difficulty when he attempts to deal with it. In Goffman's analysis, the behaviour of a person "in crisis" would constitute a ritual disruption for all parties involved. The natural effect would be for all parties to attempt to repair the ritual as disruptions occur. According to Goffman "at this point one or more participants find themselves in an established state of ritual disequilibrium or disgrace, and an attempt *must* (italic added) be made to re-establish a satisfactory ritual state for them. The imagery of disequilibrium is apt here because the length and intensity of the corrective effort is nicely adapted to the persistence and intensity of the threat" (Goffman, E., 1967, p. 19).

This is precisely what we have repeatedly seen when workers are presented with a crisis situation. Worker and client can be quickly thrown into a chaotic interaction. The worker is challenged to stabilize the interaction, making it more consistent with social ritual. On the client's part, the power of the escalating crisis experience may sometimes override the ability to repair violated social rituals and may serve to heighten feelings of embarrassment, guilt or powerlessness. For the worker, concerns may be prompted regarding his own competence and professional identity. Often the worker will attempt, usually without self-awareness, to get the client to "act right" or to act according to familiar social ritual as a precondition for further interaction. According to Goffman (1967), successful ritual repair efforts are essential for continuance of human interaction and fundamental personal concerns (of authority, of control, of identity) underlie the struggle to maintain social ritual. Hence, we see that, for the worker in particular, there is a high investment in his being able to influence the client to act in certain ritualized ways; for to fail in this task is to also threaten the worker's image of his own power and competence.

In family practice, the "communication theorists" (see: Okun and Rappaport, 1980) offer a frame of reference that is most appropriate to family focused crisis intervention. There are similarities between a family practice orientation and the crisis intervention model in that both are concerned essentially with human transactions within social networks (Goldenberg and Goldenberg 1980, Caplan 1974) and both appreciate a "homeostatsis model" of human functioning (Rappaport 1962, Jackson 1968). The family communication theorists have drawn attention to the rules governing communications and to the interactional consequences of these rules. In this context, the challenge to the crisis worker is to restore the family to a level of equilibrium in which they can proceed to employ "normal" rules of communication to resolve their family difficulties.

Perhaps the most interesting aspect of communication theory, in terms of the theme of this chapter, is the dictum that when one person communicates with another, there is an implicit maneuvering to define the interpersonal relationship (Haley 1963). This maneuvering to define social relationships is heavily ladened with social ritual. In times of crisis, many of the rules of social interaction and human communication are ignored or violated. The challenge to the crisis worker then becomes that of controlling the communication chaos with the intent of establishing a helping identity and securing the collaboration of the family unit to work towards crisis resolution.

When face to face with a family "in crisis", the temptation will exist for the worker to attempt to quickly normalize the interaction. This may require the client to act in certain ways in which they are not yet capable of acting. If and when the client, by virtue of being in crisis, cannot accommodate this expectation of the worker, an impasse occurs. At this moment, when the worker's efforts to ritualize are failing and the dynamics between worker and client systems are non-productive, we say that the worker may be caught in a "process trap". (Essentially, the worker is trapped when he is drawn automatically into ritual repair work.) When this happens, as we will show below, the worker has also dramatically reduced his clinical options and has most certainly lost the capacity for flexible responses to the crisis situation.

We now turn our attention to the major focus of this chapter: the study of commonly occurring process traps. While the danger of an unnoticed and repetitive trap may be quite powerful, inherent in the trap itself is often the germ for a creative and significantly "helpful" opportunity. Even though the "trapped" worker has temporarily lost the capacity to positively influence the crisis situation, the "trap" itself may also be the pivotal point through which actions which are most helpful and corrective can be initiated.

The notion of process traps emerged as a result of our experience in teaching crisis intervention techniques to hundreds of graduate students and health care professionals. An important aspect of our teaching method has been the use of crisis scenarios which are presented by professional actors. Students are required to intervene in a crisis situation and their actions are recorded on video- tape. The video-tapes are then carefully analyzed and through focused feedback attempts are made to identify some of the moment to moment choices and dilemmas facing the crisis worker. While observing many students in their response to the same scenario, frequent and persistent process traps have been observed. We now use the concept of the process trap as a focus and analytical tool for teaching and supervising crisis practice.

The examples of process traps we offer in this chapter are taken directly from the crisis scenarios we have used in teaching crisis intervention methods. Some of the examples given are not immediately drawn from intervention with family groups but we would argue are still directly relevant to family focused crisis work. The traps also have some relevance to non-crisis related therapy but they are particularly profound as process hazards in crisis practice. In essence, recognition of these traps does not lead to detailed intervention tactics that can be routinely applied in crisis practice. The traps do represent important themes of process disruption that, when recognized, may strengthen the worker's ability to respond more productively.

THE "AUTHORITY" TRAP

Situation:

It has become evident to the worker that the father of the adolescent girl is being unreasonable in his demands that she be in by 8:00 o'clock each night and that she assist in cooking all the meals and do the cleaning of dishes after every meal each day. The worker proceeds to explain in a rational manner that the father is wrong in his expectations. In seconds the father and the worker are locked in a battle as to what is right for the girl. It is a situation of competing authorities.

Crisis intervention is seen as being more focused and directive than is traditional psychotherapy. Because we are responding to human situations that are chaotic, emotionally charged, and filled with a threat of impending danger, the worker must respond quickly and at times take the initiative in crisis situations. However, danger lurks in the social roles we create by assuming authority and taking control. This invites a challenge from our clients. Certainly the will to exercise control in social situations can be seen to have positive as well as negative aspects. It tells us a great deal about our client's ego strength and social response patterns. The trap exists for workers who are unconsciously pulled into an open (or subtle) battle with their clients and find that they are out of control and do not have the capacity to disengage or soften the dispute without losing "social face" (Goffman 1967) and inevitably their clients. In effect, the client is given the power to define or destroy the worker's authority. Even if the worker does maintain authority and control by winning the argument, described in our scenario, there is a great likelihood that any future work with this family system will be scuttled. The worker will be identified as the protector and ally of the daughter and will have thereby eroded his intervention potential with the family system.

There are no simple and direct solutions to this process hazard. Some workers are proficient in avoiding control struggles in that they are skilled at defusing such situations before they can emerge. However, once it becomes evident that a control struggle is occurring (and workers can cue into their own escalating emotions as a warning signal) then several different responses may be appropriate depending on the unique circumstances within that specific crisis situation. The objective of the worker's response should be to help bring what is happening to a conscious and open level for all persons involved and to act as a mirror, rather than a target, of the action.

THE "EGO" TRAP

Situation:

The frustrated mother spins around and hisses at the child welfare worker, "Goddamn social workers...always sticking your noses in people's business...what can a smartass social worker like you do but make more problems...why don't you bugger off and leave us in peace?"

The "Ego" Trap may represent the most powerful of all process dangers for a crisis worker. It occurs whenever a situation is created in which the worker may personalize a client's expressed emotion. That is, workers feel as if they themselves are the target of the client's feelings, and take the client's emotion as being directed at them personally. This may occur either in situations that are perceived as being negative and represent a "hostile attack" or in situations that are perceived as being positive and represent an attempted "seduction".

What is perceived as a hostile attack may quickly escalate into actual physical danger if the worker responds in a manner which fuels the client's anger. The challenge to the worker is to deal with the reasons behind the anger (e.g. "there's been a lot of people dealing with your family lately"), to reframe the direction of the emotions ("your daughter has run away, let's try and figure out what to do, then I'll leave") or to join in with the client and share the anger ("if I were in your shoes I'd be angry too ... it's hard having outsiders poking around, especially with your daughter missing..."). Of course, there is no fixed response that will be the single right solution to these situations. The important factor is the worker's ability to consciously appreciate the nature of the client's anger and to resist personalizing the anger as an attack on his own ego or self identity.

Our intent here is to caution workers that the most dangerous maneuver is to "counter-attack". Workers frequently will respond to such situations by either trying to defend themselves and to explain their self-worth ("I'm just a nice person who's trying to help") or they try to lay down rules ("I'm here because I have to be and you will cooperate with me because you have no choice in the matter"). Such responses are invitations to disasters as they serve to heighten the client's anger and leave limited responses open to the client. It can serve as a prelude to violence.

A primary injunctive of the Japanese martial art of Akido is that one must never meet force with force. This principle can be most effectively applied in crisis intervention. When one is faced with a personal attack, the correct response is one which deflects, defuses or redirects the power that represents a threat.

Practitioners who are familiar with the phenomenon of "transference" may appreciate a profound variation of this particular process trap. In simple terms, transference occurs when a client directs emotional energy at a helper when in fact that emotional energy is actually targeted at a person with significant personal meaning to the client. We do not wish to reflect further here on transference in the context of crisis practice, other than to point out that in situations in which clients do transfer anger to the worker, care must be taken by the worker to exercise sensitivity and flexibility in response. To identify personally with the client's anger and to then defend one's position as a helper will often court disaster.

THE "DRAMA" TRAP

Situation:

The worker enters an interview room to find a woman sitting with her head bowed and a handkerchief in her hands. Her husband sits mutely beside her staring at the floor. When the worker introduces himself, nothing is said in response other than the non-verbal acknowledgment by the woman of brief eye contact. When the worker asks direct questions about the woman's circumstances, she answers in a quiet trembling voice. Soon the worker's voice drops to a quiet tone and the whole situation becomes framed by a quiet, depressed mood. The worker doesn't notice his altered style and is trapped in the mood and pace of the client system. This trap controls the range of his responses.

The setting of a mood or pace in communication represents one aspect of control that can be exercised in a social situation. In effect the mood or pace of communication can become the "stage prop" of a crisis situation. Such a prop can vary from the depressed scenario we have described to one which is fast moving and filled with highly charged, rapid communication. In this instance, the worker is swept along, joining the mood and pace of the crisis situation. At times the worker may be fascinated by what is happening in front of him, not appreciating the control that the client is maintaining over the manner of communication as well as over the avenues that may be taken in resolving the problem presented as a focus of crisis. The essential feature in this situation is the level of awareness the worker has about the client system's control over the mood and pace of communication. Once there is a cognizance that communication is being restricted, the worker has many options. He may allow the mood and pace to continue in his efforts to establish a closer rapport or to collect more information about the crisis. In this case, the worker becomes untrapped simply by becoming aware of the trap and by choosing to do nothing. The worker may also, while he acknowledges in his own mind that the client has control over the mood and pace, plan the next steps that might be taken to appropriately change the mood and tone of the communication which is occurring. He may "reframe" the entire situation so that an alternative atmosphere is created within which the interaction between helper and client can proceed. This may call for the use of humour, the raising of a subject that provides a more "neutral" emotional tone, or taking the client to an alternative physical location or environment. The important point here is that intervention potential may be severely limited when the worker is oblivious to the fact that he is caught in an emotional atmosphere set by the persons in crisis and is being pulled along by the established mood and pace of the crisis situation.

THE "I'VE GOT TO DO SOMETHING" TRAP

Situation:
The police officer arrived at the house, introduced himself to the victim's wife and explained that her husband had been accidentally killed in a highway mishap. The wife burst into tears and wept bitterly. The officer watched as her two teenage children comforted her and shared their common shock. The officer went to the window and stared out into the yard. After a time the room became quiet and the officer walked over to the family members, and once again expressed his sympathy. He asked if they had any questions and indicated that he would help them with some of the practical matters that needed immediate attention.

This type of situation, which involves people in great psychological pain, seems to be particularly troublesome for some novice crisis workers. There is a tremendous need on the worker's part to do something. It is often not apparent to the worker that they have the choice of non-intervention and that at some particular point in time it may be the most appropriate response.

Because of their own pressing need to do something, workers may push ahead into areas that their client (or client group) are not yet ready to contend with. In the example situation, the overly eager worker may wish to move forward and initiate what is conceived to be "necessary grief work". The worker's inappropriate sense of urgency and lack of appreciation of what would constitute the right timing for intervention may trigger a reaction from those he wants to help and create a serious process breakdown which will inhibit further work.

Another hazard, in trying to "do something", is the potential disruption that may occur in natural social support systems. Care must be taken by the worker that the normal support network available from the client's family, friends and associates can be mobilized to provide ongoing and comprehensive assistance. If the worker moves in too quickly, such natural networks may be inappropriately co-opted in that the worker may be usurping what should be the more extensive assistance of a natural social support system.

During times of crisis, the crisis intervention worker may need to provide time-limited support as a surrogate "significant other" and intervene as part of the client's network of relationships. Rappaport (1962) describes this as a function of crisis intervention which is sometimes required to assist individuals through periods of extreme crisis. Danger exists in the over-extension of the worker's involvement if the worker moves with inappropriate speed, builds unnecessary long-term dependency, or causes the under-utilization of more meaningful natural networks of social support. Rusk (1971) cautions the worker in this regard that "the golden rule...in crisis intervention is to do for others that which they cannot do for themselves, and no more!"

THE "QUESTION-FOIL" TRAP

The "I've Got to do Something Trap" is a hazard facing workers who are intent on moving fast and being active in their crisis resolution efforts. It is an impatience with the speed at which "change" is happening in crisis work. The "Question-Foil Trap" is a similar process hazard but one that is enmeshed in the impatience to provide greater resolution of "content" issues in crisis work. That is, with an impatience to find the right answer to a crisis problem.

The steps in this particular trap play out in the following manner:

Client: Tell me what to do?
Worker: O.K. Try this solution.
Client: But I have and it didn't work!

This pattern can continue in an endless cycle of failure. The worker is trapped into finding the "magic" answer thinking that if he can only find the right words, the right answer, then everything will be resolved. The client, in turn, is intent on undoing the worker's power and knows full well that there are no "magic solutions" to what is perceived by the client as an insolvable situation. Eventually exhaustion sets in. The client thinks the worker is a jerk and the worker thinks the client is manipulative. Those appreciative of transactional analysis will recognize this as Berne's (1967) "Why Don't You ... Yes But" game.

Helpers must often contend with the "layers of problems" clients carry with them. These layers are comprised of past "attempted solutions" that failed. Consequent secondary problems emerge as a result of a history of incomplete and ineffectual solutions. The helping process then becomes one of working through (or circumnavigating) the residue of solutions that failed until one can strike at the primary problem. This is a simple example of the profound analysis of Watzlawick, Weakland and Fisch (1974) that the problem is not the problem ... the problem is all the attempted solutions that failed.

THE "SELF-IMPOSED PRISON" TRAP

Situation:

> To his surprise, the crisis worker discovers that the adolescent daughter of a psychiatric patient has barricaded herself in her bedroom closet. When the worker enters her bedroom, he comes close to the closet door and begins to speak. The adolescent girl screams "get out of here ... leave me alone ... I've got a knife". The worker plants himself beside the closet and tries to coax the girl out. A routine develops between helper and girl in which the worker physically crowds the closet door and tries to reason the girl out. The girl blocks each sortie of reason with a barrage of verbal abuse and screams her demand that the worker "get out ... get away from me".

In situations such as the one described, we have found that many workers commit themselves to a physical posture (planting their feet in front of the closet and not moving) and a line of action (verbal reasoning) that clearly will not work. Instead of experimenting with alternative routes or tentatively pursuing a different line of action, the worker is caught in a "behavioral program" he created for himself. It is as if the worker had made a firm contract with himself as to how he would handle the situation and will not budge from the contract. Maintaining his "face" or image seems to require that he be consistent and follow through with his plan regardless of its utility. This process trap is often created in the first few minutes of an encounter. Although his approach is obviously failing, many a worker will push ahead, repeating the one solution for what is defined as "the problem" and will not (or cannot) budge from that inadequate solution. The worker knows (on some level) his attempted solution is a failure but feels compelled to keep trying to make it work. Paul Watzlawick has described a similar class of attempted solutions as the "more of the same impasse". (Watzlawick, Weakland and Fisch, 1974).

The frightened girl barricaded in a closet can be viewed as a metaphor for many people who are in need of crisis services. Part of our task as helpers is to provide a way for them to leave the protection of their personal "closet". We may then engage with them to find other ways of coping and to help resolve the factors that make them want to withdraw into the safety of their personal barricade.

The worker's capacity to respond to the momentary intricacies of the encounter is a key factor in such circumstances. Responding in this context implies a capability to acknowledge that a particular attempt at finding "the right way" is not working and that other approaches should be tried. Implicit is the capacity to judge when it is appropriate to abandon an attempted solution, and to move smoothly from one approach to another. Workers experience awkwardness and feelings of failure when they abandon what originally seemed like the correct approach to take. The task of leaving the "Self-Imposed Prison" is often quite difficult.

THE "I DIDN'T SEE YOU DO THAT" TRAP

Situation:

> The father pauses in his description of his home situation and leans toward his daughter who is slouched in her chair. The father quickly gives his daughter a slap on the leg, mutters "sit up like a normal person" and continues his description of what life has been like in the family home for the past few months, and how his daughter is now "totally out of control". The worker doesn't move but sits quietly and listens to the father's presentation of information about the family.

If the worker were questioned after the interview, he would likely acknowledge that he had noticed the father's action in slapping the daughter and would claim that he didn't feel right about doing something in response to that action. Everyone in the situation was aware that the action had occurred but, by colluding in silence and by not acting in any way, the worker has transmitted a message to the father and to the daughter. The father may feel a sense of control and feel less threatened by the worker while the daughter may see the worker as being someone who will not protect her. Most certainly, the worker has by his inattentive behavior given an implicit sanction to the father's violence and has set that behavior outside the limits of their work together.

The message here is not that one must respond to everything that occurs in an interview. What is important is that the worker develop a capacity to respond in a manner that transmits the message he wishes to communicate. Often workers see a limited range of alternatives available to them in such situations and feel that either one must ignore the father's action or one must attack it. Both these responses are possible. However, there exists a range of choices between these two extremes. For example, some workers "flag" the situation rather than choosing the deal with it at that moment. That is, they verbally acknowledge that the father struck the daughter and they further note that perhaps that can be "talked about" after the father had finished describing the home circumstances. This allows the process to continue but lets all the people in the situation know that significant actions will not be ignored, and that the worker claims the right to make comment on what transpires in the session.

THE "CONTENT" TRAP

Consider the last situation in which the father struck his daughter during the interview. This provides a suitable scenario for discussion of another important process hazard - "The Content Trap". A critical difference between this and the "I Didn't See You Do That Trap" may have to do with how conscious workers are about what is happening in front of them. In the prior scenario, some workers will be so engrossed in the content of what the father is saying that they will be oblivious to the fact that he even struck his daughter. The worker is so preoccupied with trying to integrate and analyse the father's verbal information that he will literally not see much of the behavioral complexity as it happens. (This, incidentally, argues for the teaching utility of video recording.) Sometimes, when questioned following the interview, the worker will not recall that such an event occurred at all.

It seems that workers who are concerned about doing a "full assessment", making a definitive "diagnosis", or in collecting details about the past to enhance their understanding and analysis of the "history" of the problem are most vulnerable to this trap. Professionals who are trained in methods where building a content based history is the *sine qua non* of good practice may become inhibited in the speed with which they can respond to fast moving crisis events.

Clients may, at times, lure the worker into this trap. Because individuals may be highly aroused during a crisis, they may look to the worker for clarity in the defining of the elements of the crisis. This may serve to push the worker to try to collect as much relevant "history" as is possible. However, the crisis worker must ensure that he is sensitive to the situational circumstances that are occurring in front of him during the process of crisis intervention. We do not mean to say that workers should ignore content and only attend to what is happening at the moment. Placing the current situation in historical context may play an important part in the eventual resolution of the crisis. But, if the worker feels that he must keep communication clear, focused and content oriented above all else, and if the client can't contribute to that process, the trap is set.

THE "I CAN SEE IT WHY CAN'T YOU" TRAP

Situation:

> The welfare mother has returned to seek help with her family situation. Her face is badly bruised. Her common-law husband returned home late one night last week and was angry and intoxicated. While he beat his wife, her two young children escaped to the streets. He took what little money was left in the house and stormed out the door. Now, a week later, he had telephoned to say that he wanted to move back in with the woman and that he would return that evening. This sequence of events had occurred several times before. The welfare mother wants the worker to "tell her what to do".

Crisis practitioners will invariably find themselves in situations in which "the problem" seems evident and its "solution" obvious. However, when they attempt to transmit this understanding to the individual in crisis, the response can be one of confusion and non-compliance. This is a "trap" when the crisis worker cannot believe that the crisis is not readily resolvable.

Fundamental to this process trap is the crisis worker's appreciation of the function of "resistance" as it occurs in any process of human change. Resistance can be considered to hold both negative and positive potential for the ultimate resolution of a crisis. It can reflect client strength as well as weakness. When one studies resistance as it occurs in the process of crisis intervention, two general themes emerge - "negative inertia" and "trust and hope".

"Negative inertia" may be the movement by the person in crisis to gain control over what seems to be an unmanageable circumstance or to slow down a process which threatens to make the crisis situation more personally confusing or damaging. Because clients are highly susceptible to efforts of a helper during the crisis period, they may signal through their resistance to a "solution" to their "problem" that they are temporarily overloading their personal resources by engaging in a process of crisis resolution. It may be that they wish to reduce the *speed* of change that is occurring during the process of crisis resolution and in so doing it appears that they are resisting "solutions" which seem quite logical to the worker. The notion we are suggesting here is that when individuals, families or systems are in crisis, they may offer resistance to crisis resolution if that solution causes rapid moving changes in interpersonal roles or places too much of a demand on what may be limited social resources. The failure of the person, family or social system to respond to the crisis worker may be a message that the worker is moving too fast and must slow down to move in harmony with the individuals in crisis. In this respect "resistance" is an indication of inappropriate intervention rather than a negative aspect of the client or client system.

"Negative inertia" may reflect a very important warning that the change process itself cannot be successfully concluded because of inadequate but necessary personal and social resources that will be crucial if a state of positive "equilibrium" is to be maintained. One indicator of client deprivation of social resources is the belief on the client's part that there is nothing to replace what will be lost through the process of crisis resolution. In our example situation, the woman who is physically abused by her husband may choose not to confront the husband legally or challenge her husband's behavior for fear of ultimately losing him. In her mind the isolation and loneliness she stands to suffer if she loses him holds greater pain for her than the physical punishment she may suffer by continuing in her situation. If she is alone without a social support network other than that which is provided through the companionship of her husband, she may stand to lose more than she gains (in her own mind) by challenging her husband's behavior. To the intervention agent, the resistance which emerges should serve as a significant indicator of insufficient social network resources to adequately facilitate change.

Some individuals may perceive the change process itself as being one of great psychological pain. Resistance in this instance is a reflection that the steps of change "hurt too much". Parents who experience a death of a child may consciously understand that they are containing their grief, fear and anger and that this suppression draws them into continuous rumination about the death of their child. However, the process of resolution of the death, of finally saying "goodbye" to the child may be a process which, at that particular point in time, is one that represents too much pain to the parent. Any attempts to initiate steps to work toward death resolution, catharsis, and intense grief-work will temporarily be blocked.

The second theme which underlies client resistance is that of "trust and hope". In highly charged crisis situations, workers may overlook the necessary development of a "relationship" between them and the people they are attempting to help. Perhaps the most evident example of this failure occurs when adults deal with children who are hostile or frightened. In completing what is seen as crisis intervention tasks, the worker may not take the time to ensure that adequate trust has developed in the client system so that communication will be honest and open.

At times, client resistance will clearly communicate to the helper that what the helper is doing "doesn't make sense". It is a simple message indicating the erosion of trust and hope. The client signals that greater care must be taken to move in concert with them, through the steps required in adequately resolving their crisis.

Lack of "investment" in crisis resolution by individuals who are integral to the maintenance of a crisis situation may underlie apparent resistance to change. Children or adolescents brought to a crisis counsellor may feel involved through no choice of their own. In this instance, the crisis worker must first establish a purpose and a rationale for the reluctant participant before proceeding with attempted solutions for crisis resolution. In this, as in all resistances which are reflective of an absence of trust and hope, the first task is to develop a communication bridge, which will help create a social context in which individuals can find purpose in cooperating with a change agent.

There are many other reasons for client resistance. However, we have found these two themes, the theme of "negative inertia" and of "trust and hope" to be frequent concomitants to the situation in which the worker gets caught in the "I Can See It Why Can't You" trap. This "trap" occurs when workers see their clients as being "manipulative" or "uncooperative", when in fact the process of constructive change is being blocked by their own inability to respond to the fundamental needs of those they are attempting to help.

THE "CLARITY" TRAP

Situation:
   The psychiatrist is called in to consult with the duty doctor in the emergency ward. The patient is an "agitated" adolescent boy who is severely depressed and anxious. When the psychiatrist asks the boy if he wants to sit down, the boy shakes his head and stands in the corner slowly rocking back and forth. The boy speaks openly about the only answer to his problem, which is suicide. However he will not tell the psychiatrist why he wants to kill himself. When invited a second time to sit down, he shakes his head and sobs quietly.

The situation we describe is not a simple one. In fact, the young boy had a vibrator lodged in his rectum and was in a panic state. He was terrified that his parents would find out about the vibrator and was convinced that this would destroy their relationship and cause them great shame. Death seemed to be the easiest way out of this predicament.

We have recreated this situation, which occurred at a local health facility, as a practice scenario for our students and have found that two errors frequently occur. Both have to do with a *mistaken sense of clarity* on the helper's part about what is wrong with the boy. In this trap, workers come to the conclusion, commit themselves to a definite line of intervention and are locked into their interpretation of what must be done to solve the problem (as they themselves have defined the problem).

The first process error is the over-reliance on messages that are transmitted indirectly through social ritual. Because the boy refuses to sit after being given several invitations to do so, workers interpret this to be a symbolic communication signalling a lack of social comfort on the boy's part and a resistance to communicate in a friendly and open manner. The workers then become uncomfortable themselves, feel that the boy's refusal to sit is a major issue and become more formal and cautious in their response to the boy. Frequently practitioners overlook the fact that there may be a physical reason for the boy's refusal to sit. Frequently practitioners assume that the boy really can't communicate at this point and consider the possibilities of involuntary commitment for what appears to be a high risk suicide situation.

A second process hazard which is common to this particular scenario is the practitioner's need to diagnose a syndrome and then apply the "proper" treatment. When the practitioner doesn't receive the responses he expects to his "simple" questions, a determination of this case as a "probably psychotic depression" may be made. In fact, it can be a very serious error on the practitioner's part. Before the boy can tell the helper his "secret" or offer any important information to facilitate a social assessment, trust must be established.

The challenge this trap represents to workers is one which urges crisis intervention agents to be more frank about their interpretation and more reliant on the client to give adequate and appropriate feedback (either verbally or non-verbally) which accepts or disputes the helper's conclusions. It is the maintenance of an attitude on the worker's part that the client and the worker should be moving in close concert with each other.

IMPLICATIONS FOR PRACTICE

The process traps we have described range quite widely in form and substance. Nonetheless, we would argue that these themes in crisis practice hold generic value in that they may be relevant to many workers across a number of practice situations. At the least, they offer the worker a series of potential process hazards which may often disrupt practice but which may be relieved through heightened worker awareness.

We believe that the first step in becoming untrapped lies in developing the capacity to see and understand the traps while they are happening. This capacity to see what is happening, in many cases, is sufficient to re-open the possibility of choice on the worker's part, dislodge the sense of a process impasse, and thereby release the trap. Coupled with this fundamental requirement of worker *awareness* is the necessity for workers to gain the capacity of *respondability*. That is, having the capability to respond to situations as they unfold and not to lock oneself into one approach or commit oneself to one solution in resolving a crisis state. We have suggested that crisis intervention does not neatly fit into a series of single skills that may be followed through simple stages, but calls for the capacity to respond to client need through a range of intervention alternatives. A number of training programs for crisis workers (particularly the police) tend to focus on crisis resolution through "diffusing techniques". That is, the primary concern of the crisis intervention agent is to reduce the threat that the crisis will escalate in intensity and build potential physical and emotional danger. In following this approach, crisis practitioners limit their range of interventions to one that is largely a calming influence directed at restoring "reason" to a social situation. We would challenge practitioners to extend their repertoire of process directions to include practice responses which may appropriately (i) escalate crisis (for example, join the family in their anger, help them release pent-up emotions, and open new parameters of expressing negative feelings), (ii) work towards a change in how the problem is perceived by the family so that it no longer subjectively holds a crisis inducing threat, (iii) work towards helping people act more adequately in coping with their crisis by providing them with more behavioral alternatives, (iv) assist clients to build the capacity to temporarily disengage from their crisis (without using tranquillizing drugs or alcohol) by consciousness raising techniques, relaxation exercises, and other approaches in psychological disengagement.

In many situations crisis intervention will call for minimal input with the individual but more profound effort with the family, personal network or social system. We believe there is truth to the adage that "families are either part of the problem or part of the solution in crisis situations" (Golan, 1978).

Our primary intent has been to establish that an important element of crisis practice involves the worker's capacity to understand and be aware of salient process hazards while intervening in a crisis situation. The ten common process traps we have discussed may offer guidelines which serve to assist practitioners in the analysis of their own intervention efforts. At the least, they point to aspects of crisis intervention which may call for heightened "informed caution" on the part of the practitioner when proceeding to assist others caught in crisis.

REFERENCES

Berne, E. **1964**. "Games People Play". New York: Grove Press.
Brockopp, G.W. **1973**. "Crisis Intervention: Theory, Process and Practice" in Lester D. and Brockopp, G.W. (Eds.) "Crisis Intervention and Counseling by Telephone". Illinois: Thomas, Chapter 6.
Caplan, G. **1964**. "Principles of Preventive Psychiatry". New York: Basic Books.
Caplan, G. **1974**. "Support Systems and Community Mental Health". New York: Behavioral Publications.
Goffman, E. **1967**. Interaction Ritual: Essays on Face to Face Behavior 1st Edition. New York: Anchor.
Haley, J. **1963**. "Strategies of Psychotherapy". New York: Grune and Stratton.
Jackson, D. (ed.) **1968**. "Communications, Family and Marriage" Vol. 1. California: Science & Behavioral Books.
Kuypers, J., and **Trute**, B. **1980**. "The Untrapped Worker: A Precondition for Effective Family Practice" in Freeman, D. (ed.) *Perspectives on Family Therapy*. Vancouver: Butterworth and Co.

Okun, B.F. and **Rappaport**, L.J. **1980**. "Working With Families: An Introduction to Family Therapy". California: Duxbury Press.

Rappaport, L. **1962**. "The State of Crisis: Some Theoretical Considerations". 36(2). *The Social Service Review*.

Rusk, T.N. **1971**. "Opportunity and Techniques in Crisis Psychiatry". 12, May. *Comprehensive Psychiatry*, 249-263.

Watzlawick, P., **Weakland**, J., and **Fisch**, R. **1974**. *Change: Principles of Problem Formation and Problem Resolution*. New York: Norton.

Chapter 4

Conjoint Treatment of Alcohol Complicated Marriages: Conceptual and Methodological Issues

Shelly Pearlman and Allen Zweben
Addiction Research Foundation and University of Toronto

Clearly, the beliefs one harbors about the etiology and persistence of a problematic set of behaviours determine in large measure the strategies to be utilized to alter those behaviours. This general observation is particularly relevant to the field of alcoholism, where many diverse hypotheses and viewpoints have evolved that continue to shape our understanding of and attempts to intervene with individuals abusing alcohol.

Initially, alcohol abuse was perceived from a predominantly moralistic perspective. The alcoholic was seen as incorrigibly self-indulgent, lacking in self-control, insensitive to the needs of others and generally "weak". "Treatment" typically consisted of exhortations on the part of religious or quasi-religious leaders to dramatically change the drinker's moral character or, when that failed, simply incarcerating the offender to protect the rest of society from exposure to his shortcomings.

This viewpoint gradually yielded to the medical model of alcoholism, a perspective that emphasized physiological dynamics in describing the etiology and consequences of alcohol abuse. Thus, treatment became the province of the physician who predictably focused on predisposing factors, the physiological symptomatology, the course of deterioration as excessive drinking continued and the notion of "loss of control" once the alcoholic started to drink (Jellinek, 1952).

Alcoholism has also been viewed as a manifestation of unresolved psychological problems. This psychodynamic perspective postulates that alcoholism is a behavioural manifestation or symptom of inner conflicts and that these intrapsychic "roots" must be the focal point of therapeutic intervention. Merely to attempt to redress the drinking, without appropriate attention to the underlying causes of the problem, is described as clinically inadequate within this perspective, since new symptoms may simply replace the drinking. Similarly, behavioural approaches, while eschewing the notion of symptom substitution and focusing more directly on drinking as a learned behaviour related to specific antecedents and/or consequences, continue in the tradition of conceptualizing alcoholism within the context of an individually oriented framework.

Beginning in the 1950's, an alternative approach to understanding alcoholism and other clinical difficulties began to emerge. This new approach focused on family dynamics in terms of understanding the etiology and persistence of symptomatology. Systems theory, communication theory, role theory and cybernetics all contributed to this interactional and interpersonal perspective on a wide range of disorders, including alcoholism.

With this change in perspective, the alcoholic came to be referred to as the "identified patient", "index patient" or "symptom carrier for the family". These various designations underscored the conceptual shift towards the family as the unit of treatment.

Thus, specific behaviours, such as alcohol abuse, previously thought to be determined primarily by individual genetic and intrapsychic factors were seen to be related to the demands of the interpersonal system within which the individual interacts. These behaviours began to be perceived as "syntonic" or complementary to the ongoing functioning of the system in that they are subtly or covertly elicited and/or maintained, assuming significance as systems maintaining or homeostatic mechanisms.

As Steinglass (1976) points out, it was only in the late 1960's and early 1970's that family and systems theory came to be applied extensively in the field of alcoholism. Davis   *et al.*, (1974) clinically documented several adaptive consequences of excessive drinking within the family. Berenson (1976) described the role that such drinking fulfilled in terms of serving a systems maintenance function for the family, by providing a release for the family's underlying strain and tension thereby effectively diverting attention away from more basic and threatening sources of conflict. Steinglass *et al.*, (1977) significantly contributed to the burgeoning development of a systems perspective in a controlled study of the reciprocal relationship between alcohol abuse and marital functioning. In this seminal work, couples in which one spouse was abusing alcohol were conjointly hospitalized. "Experimentally induced intoxication" was employed as a research strategy to provide an opportunity for direct behavioural observation of the couple's interaction during both sobriety and intoxication. Interaction during periods of intoxication was found to be less restricted in the areas of problem-solving, displays of affect and sharing of information. Alcohol use tended, for some couples, to signal stress when usual coping mechanisms were beginning to break down in the marital system.

Thus, alcoholism, in addition to its obvious destructive and debilitating effects on both individual and family functioning, gradually has been linked to adaptive or functional consequences for marital and family relationships as well. Both Orford (1975) and Meeks and Kelly (1970) suggest that in instances in which alcoholism is treated without an appropriate appreciation of and concern for the role it plays in systemic terms, other difficulties within the family or marital subsystem are likely to emerge in response to the threat to typical patterns of functioning.

The marital subsystem, in particular, has become a primary focal point in the integration of systems theory and treatment in the field of alcoholism. A number of studies have documented the importance of the marital system in attempting to intervene clinically with alcoholics (Edwards & Orford, 1977; Orford *et al.*, 1976; Paolino & McCrady, 1977). In fact, conjoint treatment of the alcoholic and spouse in a variety of contexts, including group and inpatient therapy, has been enthusiastically endorsed by practitioners and, to some extent, by preliminary research findings (Orford *et al.*, 1976; Gerard & Saenger, 1966). Although there are virtually no well controlled rigorous clinical studies of the efficacy of a marital systems approach to the treatment of alcohol abuse, the approach itself is growing in terms of its general acceptance among clinicians as a viable treatment modality. With the adoption of this interactional approach, the framework of treatment has been considerably broadened to include a concern with a variety of aspects of marital dynamics and functioning in addition to the alcohol related difficulties. Communication, decision-making, rules covering interaction, division of authority, sexual interaction, and problem-solving are several of the dimensions of interactional behaviour that are germane to a marital systems approach to the treatment of alcohol abuse. While the alcohol abuse remains the primary concern of the clinical intervention, the marital relationship provides the context or "gestalt" for understanding and ultimately effecting change. In fact, therapeutic goals typically are expressed not only in terms of actual alcohol related behaviours but in relationship to marital functioning and satisfaction as well (Steinglass, 1977).

With this increasing use of marital and family therapies in the alcohol treatment field, several concerns and problems have emerged. These relate to both conceptual and methodological issues as therapists continue their effort to apply systems concepts and techniques in working with marital relationships in which alcohol abuse is a primary presenting problem. The remainder of this paper will address these issues, offering specific suggestions regarding their resolution. Extensive references will be made to an ongoing research project, the Marital Systems Study, that the authors are currently engaged in at the Clinical Institute of the Addiction Research Foundation in Toronto, Canada. That project is examining the efficacy of short-term communication-interaction based conjoint therapy offered on an outpatient basis for couples where alcohol abuse has been identified as the primary problem.

1. *The Therapist Variable.*   Relatively few therapists during the course of their clinical training are thoroughly exposed to systems based treatment modalities. For most, marital and/or family approaches constitute an elective course or series of courses within the broader curriculum. Upon graduation, the practitioner either gravitates to a setting in which family treatment is well entrenched, thereby further consolidating skills in this area; participates extensively in post-graduate training, seminars or conferences in the family field to regenerate interest in and commitment to family approaches; or most typically, develops an "eclectic" treatment style in which intervention with couples or families is sporadically pursued.

As a consequence, even those clinicians who identify themselves as advocates of a family systems approach tend to evidence extremely wide variations in terms of their knowledge of and actual experience in conjoint treatment. It is unfortunately not unusual for therapists purporting to be utilizing a systems framework to conduct family interviews in such a way that the sessions are predominantly psychodynamic rather than interactive in orientation and thrust. In essence, these interviews are examples of individually oriented sessions in which the spouse and other family members serve as little more than witnesses or occasional sources of clinical leverage in the attempt to effect change in the individual symptom carrier.

This discrepancy between actual and alleged utilization of systems based treatment is compounded by the virtual lack of any comprehensive applications of the theoretical model to clinical practice in the family literature. It is only recently that such articles have begun to appear as guides to the practitioner and supervisor (Cleghorn & Levin, 1973; Tomm & Wright, 1978; Sluzki, 1978; Kniskern & Gurman, 1979). These general comments are particularly relevant to the field of alcohol treatment, where there are few detailed descriptions of ongoing programs or even clinical trials of conjoint therapy within the context of research studies. Only Meeks and Kelly (1970) offered a detailed outline of the treatment approach employed within their research study. Thus, as Steinglass (1976) points out, there is very little detailed "technical" information available for the therapist working with couples or families in which alcohol abuse is a predominant problem.

As a result, a concerted effort on the part of those responsible for the training and supervision of clinicians is needed to ensure that therapists are provided with a useful, relevant guide for conducting therapy on a conjoint basis. This process involves at least three distinct phases. The first stage consists of ensuring that the conceptual model of alcoholism from a systems perspective is well integrated by prospective practitioners. This requires didactic input to deal with the material at a cognitive level, as well as experiential learning e.g., role playing, reviewing audio or video tapes of marital and family sessions, to afford opportunities to apply the model clinically. Thus, specific interventive techniques such as stimulating interaction between the spouses, clarifying communication, and focusing on issues from an interactive perspective can be learned, practiced and integrated by the therapist in simulated clinical situations until he/she is comfortable with and confident in them. A comprehensive training program along these lines was made available to therapists in the Marital Systems Study over an extended period of time prior to the first actual clients being seen in the pilot phase of the Study.

The second stage of this training and supervisory process involves systematically reviewing and monitoring the therapist's actual interviews to ensure that a systems focus is maintained throughout the process of treatment, as opposed to the therapist slipping back into the more routine and traditional individually oriented framework. The critical question that is addressed by this monitoring procedure is: "Is the prescribed systems based approach actually being used?" Within the Marital Systems Study, a specific procedure has been developed to ensure fidelity to the treatment model among the therapists. All sessions are audio-taped and then are randomly subjected to a content analysis that focuses specifically on the therapist's statements. Each therapist statement is coded according to whether it relates directly to marital interaction and communication or not. For instance, therapist statements directed at initiating spouse-to-spouse communication are examples of marital systems based interventions. A ratio is then computed by dividing the frequency of marital communication statements by the frequency of all statements made by the therapist. This ratio, the Marital Communication Focus Ratio, MCFR, controls for differing degrees of verbal activity on the part of the therapists. A minimum value of the MCFR can then be defined as constituting evidence of fidelity to the treatment model. Within the Marital Systems Study, for instance, therapists are expected to maintain a minimum MCFR of .60*. Feedback is

---
* Sessions are monitored independently by two project staff who have consistently evidenced a high reliability coefficient.

systematically provided to the therapists to help them identify deviations from the model and difficulties in implementing the approach in a consistent fashion.

The third and final aspect of this comprehensive training and supervisory process involves another dimension of monitoring sessions. The focus of this monitoring procedure is related to ensuring that the quality of the intervention is of the highest order. In this context, the critical issue becomes: "Is the treatment being delivered competently?" To deal with this quality of service issue, two experts in the approach review randomly selected segments of the taped interviews. The reviewers work collaboratively in evaluating the therapist's skills in the use of the model by systematically rating the therapist by utilizing the Therapist Rating Scale developed for the Study. The Scale identifies eight specific dimensions of skills typically associated with the communication-interaction approach to conjoint counselling. The eight dimensions constituting the Scale are:

1) Stimulating interaction between the spouses
2) Clarifying faulty or problematic communication
3) Explaining the systems rationale for the treatment process
4) Setting and redefining the contract periodically
5) Making linkages between individual symptomatology (alcohol abuse) and marital interaction
6) Making confrontations in the context of support
7) Suggesting more effective ways of communicating/interacting/problem-solving
8) Stopping blaming and accusing

From these specific ratings on individual items, an overall rating can be readily derived. Ongoing feedback is provided to the therapists to identify both strengths and also areas in which improvement is necessary in terms of their use of the model.

These three phases of ongoing training and monitoring provide an effective, comprehensive and stimulating means of ensuring that the therapists are familiarized with systems based therapy and subsequently deliver such therapy in a consistent, high quality fashion.

2. *Client Engagement in the Treatment Process.* Client initiated premature termination of treatment has been a troublesome issue in psychotherapy generally and in the alcohol treatment field more specifically (Baekeland, Lundwall & Shanahan, 1973). Hollingshead and Redlich (1958) were instrumental in directing attention to discrepancies between clients and therapists as important factors related to discontinuance of treatment. This trend has been greatly accentuated by the work of others (Lennard and Bernstein, 1961; Levitt, 1966; Frank, 1973; Briar, 1966; Meltzoff and Kornreich, 1970; and Heine and Trosman, 1960), all of whom have emphasized the lack of consensus between therapist and client in their respective perceptions of what they are to do together in explaining premature defection from treatment.

Clinicians offering conjoint marital or family therapy have become well aware of the inherent difficulties that family members typically have in genuinely conceptualizing problems in interactional terms. For instance, even when couples voluntarily seek marital counselling, they tend to reflect an individualistic rather than interactional frame of reference (Group for the Advancement of Psychiatry, 1970; Maluccio and Marlow, 1974). Clearly, the therapist's initial task is to broaden the client's orientation to a systems based perspective. Many failures in marital and family therapy can be attributed to the therapist's inability to help the client system make this conceptual shift (Loehner, 1967).

There issues are further accentuated in the alcohol treatment field where the traditional understanding of the etiology and course of the problem, alcohol abuse, has been strongly couched in individualized, psychodynamic terms. Since few alcoholics or their spouses approach treatment expecting therapy to be offered on a conjoint basis, some form of "socializing" these clients into role and expectational sets that are congruent with those of the treatment regimen is essential.

In order to resolve these difficulties, the Marital Systems Study has incorporated provisions for extensive "role induction" (Frank, 1973) and formal contracting into its design. The objective of these two procedures is to enhance the degree of agreement between the couple and therapist around their expectations of the treatment process in order to reduce the risk of client initiated premature termination of therapy. Role induction is essentially a special pre-therapy session designed to provide specific information about the rationale and direction of the proposed therapy. The value of such systematic preparation of clients for treatment has been documented in a number of studies that have shown higher rates of continuance in treatment for clients participating in some form of role induction interview (Hoehn-Saric *et al.*, 1964; Perlman, 1968).

Within the Study, clients are asked to attend the initial intake session together with their spouses and, at that time, the reasons for involving the spouse are discussed openly and directly. These reasons revolve around our need to know how the drinking effects and is effected by the marital interaction and how the spouse's interest in and concern about the identified patient can best be used to facilitate the process of change. We acknowledge frankly and explicitly that this may seem somewhat surprising and at times even upsetting to them, since many people have a radically different set of expectations concerning treatment for alcohol related difficulties. They are encouraged to verbalize any concerns or questions they might have and are offered reassurance that the proposed course of treatment is consistent with their overriding concern with the problematic drinking. The predominant theme that is addressed throughout this process is that the spouse's active involvement in treatment is of critical importance in terms of effecting change, even though such involvement may not have been anticipated by the couple when they initially sought help. This process of orienting the couple to the Study's approach continues during the assessment stage, which again requires the presence of both spouses to provide the information required to formulate a comprehensive treatment plan. Finally, the couple meets with one of the Study's investigators who reiterates our conviction about the usefulness and desirability of proceeding in treatment on a conjoint basis. At each of these stages, the couple is encouraged to verbalize any concerns or misgivings they may have about the proposed course of treatment.

Similarly, the Study has emphasized the importance of "contracting" during the initial phase of the actual treatment process. The contract is seen as a formal, detailed agreement between the couple and therapist covering logistical concerns as well as clinical issues such as goals and perhaps even the techniques to be used (Seabury, 1976; Maluccio and Marlow, 1974). For instance, the therapist utilizes the initial treatment session to review the couple's experience within the treatment system up to that point, to summarize some of the key assessment findings, to continue the process of redefining the alcohol problem into interactional terms and finally to operationalize these efforts in the form of specific treatment goals and strategies. Therapists are encouraged to be sensitive to the need for recontracting on a regular basis and to "legitimize" the questions and concerns that the couple may have about the course or direction of treatment. Questions are invited, resistance or ambivalence on the part of one or both spouses is actively explored and dealt with, and the rationale of the approach is presented with confidence and assurance by the therapist.

Our experience during the recently completed pilot phase of our Study tends to confirm the utility of such procedures. We were able to engage and sustain a higher proportion of clients in conjoint treatment than in the typical individual therapy program offered within the Outpatient Department, in spite of the need to alter the conceptual framework of the couples involved in the conjoint treatment. These results, we feel, may reflect the impact of our concerted and systematic efforts in the areas of role induction and contracting.

3. *The Focus of Treatment - Marital Dynamics and Alcohol Problems.* One of the current areas of controversy among practitioners of conjoint treatment revolves around the appropriate balance to be maintained in therapy between the presenting problem, alcohol abuse in this case, and the underlying systemic dynamics, the marital relationship. Among family practitioners working with alcohol related problems, there are those who conceptualize the drinking solely as a behavioural symptom of family or marital stress and tension. These therapists proceed to virtually ignore the overt symptomatology, alcohol abuse, in favour of concentrating exclusively on the more fundamental systemic disturbances during the course of treatment. The assumption underlying this approach is that improvement in the presenting problem will flow almost automatically from improved marital or family functioning. Thus, problematic drinking is relegated to a secondary level of clinical concern, and at times virtually ignored, with primary attention being directed towards altering various aspects of the marital interaction felt to be directly related to the persistence of alcohol related difficulties (Steinglass, 1977).

There are, however, two major unresolved issues inherent in this approach. Can change in the presenting problem be assumed to be the natural and inevitable derivative of alterations in the marital relationship, without addressing the specific problem itself in a direct, meaningful way during the course of therapy? Secondly, to what extent does the benign neglect of the clients' initial concerns in favour of a more esoteric and complicated preoccupation with the marital relationship contribute to frustration, confusion and concern on the part of the clients, ultimately culminating in premature termination of treatment? Clearly, extensive research in this area is required to resolve these issues conclusively.

However, in some respects, this controversy itself misses the essential point. A marital systems approach should not imply a de-emphasis on the presenting problem in favour of a complex and abstract examination of the nuances of the marital relationship. Rather, the adoption of the conjoint approach implies a conceptual shift in terms of how the problem drinking is perceived, understood and ultimately dealt with in treatment. Rather than simply ignoring or denigrating the significance of the presenting problem, the therapist is required to help the couple deal with it from a collaborative, interactional perspective. Thus, the marital dynamics that are explored in treatment should be those that can be related directly or indirectly to the problematic drinking. It is the responsibility of the therapist to ensure that the connection between the thrust and direction of the treatment and the clients' initial concerns remains clear and meaningful.

In essence, the issue is not one of choosing between dealing with the alcoholism or dealing with the marital system. Rather, marital dynamics constitute an important and effective leverage point in the primary therapeutic task of effecting change in the abusive drinking. In this regard, a clear trend has emerged within the family therapy field in recent years towards focusing more directly and purposefully on the family's initial concerns or presenting problem, albeit from a systemic perspective, throughout the course of treatment (Haley, 1976; Weakland et al., 1974; Epstein and Bishop, 1981).

The orientation of the Marital Systems Study is very much in line with this reaffirmation of the presenting problem as the appropriate focus of clinical intervention. Within the Study, there is a concerted effort to ensure that problems related to alcohol abuse remain the primary source of concern throughout the treatment process. The involvement of the spouse and the concern with marital interaction are presented as means of achieving resolution of the drinking problem. Thus, each treatment session is expected to feature a careful review of the current status of the drinking problem in relation to drinking goals, a restatement of the rationale of the treatment approach as it relates specifically to alcohol abuse, and an ongoing attempt to relate those specific aspects of the couple's interactional repertoire that have been or will be dealt with in treatment to the drinking problem. The manner in which these issues are dealt with will naturally vary from case to case, depending for instance on the degree of continuing resistance or uncertainty that the couple evidence around the interactional approach.

Obviously, treatment will deal with other aspects of both interactional and individual behaviour that are not so directly or immediately linked to the clients' immediate concerns around drinking. These latter target areas of change, however, are generally accorded a lower priority. In some cases work in these areas is deferred until some initial evidence of progress towards the primary treatment goal appears. In other cases, the therapist may contract to deal with a specific interactional dynamic to achieve a necessary shift in the marital homeostasis to enable the couple to cope with abstinence or non-problematic drinking. In such instances, the sequential nature of the contract is emphasized in that the resolution of the immediate or intermediate issues being dealt with is presented as a precondition for dealing, at a later point, more directly with the issue of alcohol. For instance, it may be necessary to help a couple arrive at a mutually agreed upon decision concerning the stability of the marriage itself before working on the alcohol problem more directly. The essential point to be stressed is that there is a concerted effort on the part of the therapists to ensure that both the overall approach of the treatment and the specific themes pursued in individual sessions are consistently seen by the couple as being responsive to their initial concerns around alcoholism.

4. *Assessment.* A valid and comprehensive assessment strategy is a necessary component of a treatment program for purposes of decision-making with respect to (1) engaging the couple in therapy (2) identifying priority areas and strategies for intervention and (3) providing a baseline for subsequently determining whether changes (improvement and deterioration) have taken place as a result of therapy.

The nature of the treatments being offered will influence the methods utilized in assessment. For short-term therapies such as the systems based intervention carried out in the present study, an assessment strategy which includes both a uniform test battery, i.e., a series of measurements or scales routinely administered to clients, as well as a clinical evaluation by therapists, is particularly useful. It combines a sound psychometrically-oriented methodology with clinical diagnostic formulations in implementing, assessing, and evaluating treatment.

A test battery is an efficient mechanism for accurately measuring problem areas in a consistent and thorough manner. It is a valuable tool for detecting latent areas of difficulty, that is, problems or issues which may not be readily recognized in the beginning sessions of therapy, but which may be of critical significance to the presenting problems. This is especially important for short-term therapies, since the treatments offered are contingent upon early development of hypotheses concerning ongoing interaction between presenting problems and these underlying issues.

Conversely, the clinical interview may provide therapists with relevant information not readily accessible from the questionnaires, (Jayaratne and Levy, 1979). For example, problems with relatives not presently living in the home, such as grandparents, siblings and others, are usually not significantly covered on many of these paper and pencil tests. Also, direct observations of patterns of interaction occurring in the clinical interview can provide therapists with a broader understanding of the dynamics and issues and can be strategically important in formulating the treatment plan. Such observations can be compared with response scores on the various self-report measures to further validate the data. The therapist may subsequently revise or update the picture of the system in accordance with the evidence presented in the clinical interview.

The use of a dual assessment scheme, that is, eliciting data from both the client and spouse on a test battery as well as in clinical interviews is recommended as an efficient, comprehensive and highly productive procedure. One final point to be made in favour of this approach is that by actively involving the spouse in the collection and formulation of assessment data, the systemic focus of the therapeutic process is further underscored. Such active involvement on the part of the spouse could be an important element in forestalling early dropout from care, particularly in an alcoholic population (Gerard and Saenger, 1966).

In the present Study, the assessment battery has been an essential resource in helping to formulate tentative hypotheses regarding the inter-relationship between factors in the marital subsystem and alcohol abuse. By systematically and formally examining the pattern of events accompanying excessive alcohol use, we gain some preliminary understanding of the role alcohol may play in the marriage.

The specialized assessment battery is administered to both the identified patient and spouse at multiple vantage points - pre-treatment, during the course of therapy and at several intervals post-treatment, to assess the ongoing validity of the data and to detect changes which may be resulting from the intervention. Couples are informed of these procedures at intake and are asked to sign a consent form before completing the required forms.

The specific instruments used in the assessment process were selected in accordance with the conceptual framework of the Study. They are aimed at examining general domains and events reflecting marital dynamics and adjustment and those depicting the severity of the alcohol problem. Those measures associated with the marriage include the Revised Marital Adjustment Scale (RMAS), Revised Marital Relationship Scale (RMRS) and the Primary Communication Inventory (PCI). The RMAS is actually a combination of the Locke-Wallace Marital Adjustment Scale (LWMAS) (Locke & Wallace, 1959) and the Spanier Dyadic Adjustment Scale (DAS) (Spanier, 1976), the latter being for the most part an adaptation of the LWMAS with some additional items so that common-law relationships can be included in the sample.

The LWMAS and Spanier DAS investigate global and specific elements related to marital or dyadic adjustment. They have been employed to determine the overall quality of marital interaction in terms of separating out distressed from non-distressed couples (see e.g., Weiss and Margolin, 1977; Brichler et al., 1975). Item responses have been factor analyzed in order to identify major problem areas such as difficulties pertaining to decision-making and companionship (See e.g., Locke and Williamson, 1958).

The Revised Marital Happiness Scale was adapted from Azrin's Marital Happiness Scale (MHS) (1973). Differences stemming from the handling of financial affairs, leisure time, and household tasks are explored in this scale. Azrin (1973), in employing the MHS, discovered that greater improvement was observed in areas dealt with during the course of therapy than those events not addressed. Such findings underscore the importance of the measure for monitoring specific aspects of change in the marital relationship during the course of therapy and post-treatment.

The Primary Communication Inventory developed by Navran (1967) is included among the battery of tests dealing with marital adjustment because it focuses on changes in a couple's pattern of communication, a particularly valuable source of information in the current Study. It has been used to measure both non-verbal and verbal communication in couples. Couples having higher scores on the PCI are more likely to discuss pleasant matters, feel more readily understood, have discussions concerning shared interests, and are less likely to break off discussions when disagreements occur. A high correlation has been observed between the PCI and Locke-Wallace Marital Adjustment Scale (Navran, 1967) indicating that changes in communication patterns will likely be accompanied by changes in other areas of interaction within the marriage.

The severity of the alcohol problem is determined by several indices: the Time-Line Followback interview, the Drinking Consequences Score, Medical Information Form, Michigan Alcoholism Screening Test and Spouse Hardship Scale. The Time-Line Followback procedure provides a detailed and accurate picture of the extent and style of drinking (Sobell, *et al.*, 1979; Sobell et al., 1980; Maisto *et al.*, *Sobell et al.*, *1979*; Sobell and Sobell, 1980). The method entails giving clients a calendar and with assistance from the interviewer they are asked to recall the amount of alcohol consumed per diem, as well as related activities such as the number of days hospitalized, spent in jail, or in residential treatment because of alcohol abuse for a one year period of time. These data are then categorized into the number of light and heavy drinking days, abstinent days, days hospitalized, days jailed and days in residential care for the given period.

Different methods are employed to facilitate data gathering using the Time-Line Followback procedure. "Anchor points" such as holidays, birthdays, vacations, and crisis periods - marital separations, loss of employment and death of a loved one, are identified on the calendar and by using techniques such as "exaggeration" (asking clients whether they had 2 or 20 drinks for a given day) clients are assisted in recollecting their drinking behaviour on the days before and after the particular event.

Recent findings have revealed the Time-Line Followback interview to be a reliable and valid method of gathering drinking data across different help-seeking populations as long as drinking has not occurred at the time of testing (Sobell & Sobell, 1978). O'Farrell *et al.*, (1980) compared responses between male alcoholics and their wives on the Time-Line Followback interview and found good agreement on the total number of drinking days, abstinent days and other drinking related events such as number of incarcerated days. In short, the evidence presented affirms the usefulness of this measure in assessing, monitoring and evaluating alcohol consumption.

The Drinking Consequences Score partially drawn from the Drinking Consequences Scale presented in the Rand Report (Armor *et al.*, 1978) and further developed by the Follow-up Unit at the Clinical Institute, along with the Michigan Alcoholism Screening Test (Seltzer, 1971; Skinner, 1979) essentially provide important information on the symptoms and various social consequences of alcohol consumption. Questions pertaining to legal offences, sleep disturbances, emotional stability, financial problems and job difficulties are covered on these scales. Husbands/wives of alcoholics are asked about arguments, physical violence and other interpersonal difficulties in the home on the Spouse Hardship Scale (Orford et al., 1975; Orford et al., 1976). Scores on the above measures as well as on individual items can be compared with similar clinical groups in order to gain a clearer understanding of the consequences of alcohol consumption.

Such an extensive assessment approach is particularly beneficial in establishing a preliminary treatment contract with the couple. The specificity and concreteness of the process assist in problem identification and with the establishment of realistic goals with couples. Scores on different domains such as intimacy, cohesion, affectional expression or on more specific items can be utilized in the initial treatment session to develop a coherent treatment plan and to help the couple integrate the Study's principle orientation of relating the presenting problem to ongoing interactional dynamics in the marital system.

For instance, attention may be drawn to communication issues as identified in the assessment stage in the first treatment interview. Matters pertaining to problematic communication patterns can be raised in the context of reviewing the findings emerging from assessment. The net result of this experience is that the couple and therapist are assisted in developing some initial consensus around the problems to be dealt with during the course of therapy. This contributes to reducing the risk of early dropout from treatment.

Data emerging from alcohol related forms can be used in contracting with couples regarding their drinking goals. Attempts to gain agreement between the identified patient and spouse or between the therapist and couple can become a major source of tension in the beginning stage of therapy. Many clients enter the program with the notion of reducing or gaining control over their alcohol consumption rather than abstaining. Some may have frequent alcohol related hospitalizations, extensive patterns of use of other drugs such as tranquilizers, major alcohol withdrawal symptoms, serious family or interpersonal discord resulting from alcohol abuse and no demonstration of previous control over their drinking behaviour; individuals having such characteristics are considered to be a higher risk for the non-problem drinking goal (Maisto et al., 1980; Polich et al., 1981; Sobell, 1978; Skinner, 1981).

Consequently, material on the assessment battery can be utilized to enable couples to set realistic goals and perhaps reduce or prevent conflict between therapist and clients over such goals. The specificity of the information on the battery or the way in which it is offered can have considerable influence on clients struggling to formulate appropriate drinking goals. By assigning clients to a particular category related to the consequences of alcohol consumption based upon standardized scores on that dimension, or discussing risk factors associated with non-problem drinking, clients may be helped to abandon inappropriate goals with respect to their drinking.

Presenting feedback on the assessment can be difficult when there are significant discrepancies in the data derived from the identified patient and spouse. We are not talking about differences concerning descriptive or demographic data, discrepancies which can usually be clarified or remedied at assessment. The issue here pertains to attitudinal variables related to various aspects of the marital relationship. Also, disparities may be observed on items related to the severity of alcohol problems such as the number of drinks consumed, physical care, sleeping problems, aggressive behaviour and other consequences of alcohol use.

Under such circumstances, feedback offered can precipitate difficulties. These can erode a couple's initial positive expectations or commitment toward therapy and ultimately result in their abrupt termination from treatment, not an infrequent happening with this clinical population.

Consequently, in dealing with such a situation, care is taken to point out the existence and extent of such differences of opinion in a supportive rather than a confrontational context. By relabelling reported discrepancies as a reflection of differing conceptions of the quality of their relationship or of their assessment of the actual drinking pattern, the therapist uses the information constructively in terms of establishing a focus for the subsequent treatment. Such a process also helps to move the couple away from an individual perspective of the alcohol problem with accompanying notions of "guilt" and "blame" and more towards a systems perspective in which discrepancies in attitudes, values and expectations are emphasized.

5. *Timing of the Intervention.* A major dilemma confronting professionals in the field centers on the timing of the intervention. Should conjoint therapy be offered following individual therapy in which abstinence or non-problem drinking has been achieved as an initial goal? Or conversely, should conjoint therapy be provided as the initial and principal modality of care?

The argument for phasing in the conjoint intervention is that the underlying dynamics of the family or marriage cannot be attended to with clients whose drinking problem is not under control. The disruptions in the home associated with the problem drinker and the amount of attention demanded by him/her, undermine any attempt to deal with fundamental marital or family issues such as communication, sexual problems or other interpersonal difficulties. Consequently, it is recommended that the alcoholic first be offered the opportunity to participate in a traditional course of treatment that may include such activities as detoxification, individual and group psychotherapy, Alcoholics Anonymous, and perhaps antabuse. Once the alcoholic is in the "recovery phase" of his treatment, a referral to marital or family therapy is considered appropriate.

Such an approach was followed by Meeks and Kelly (1970) who instituted family therapy after clients completed seven weeks of intensive treatment involving individual and group therapy. During the course of treatment, spouses were seen individually to lay the "groundwork" for family therapy. Similarly, Esser (1971) did not involve alcoholics in family therapy until they were first exposed to AA, based upon the assumption that "progress" in family therapy could only be attained after a period of sobriety.

In the Marital Systems Study, an alternative strategy is being implemented. Upon completion of assessment, clients and spouses are immediately referred to conjoint counselling. Only those clients with extremely poor verbal skills as evidenced by a low score on the verbal ability test, having major medical problems such as extensive liver damage requiring in-patient care, and a long history of previous hospitalization for a psychiatric disorder, are excluded from the Study. Clients admitted to the program are typical of others seen in most outpatient settings dealing with an alcoholic population (See e.g., Orford & Edwards, 1978). Most are male, blue collar workers, having had a long history of heavy alcohol consumption amounting to four or more standard drinks per day and suffering from a moderate degree of impairment related to their drinking pattern, i.e., medical, legal, marital and employment complications.

The perspective maintained in the present Study is that the drinking problem can best be treated within the context of the marital relationship *providing relevant back-up services are accessible and available*. The service delivery system within the Clinical Institute of the Addiction Research Foundation has been designed to support and facilitate research in order to minimize the risks which may result from such an approach.

For instance, every client is assigned a case manager called a primary care worker who meets with all prospective clients prior to their involvement in the Study and also upon completion of the assessment. The primary care worker serves as a liaison between clients and other services maintained by the Clinical Institute, such as detoxification, in-patient care, the emergency unit and medical clinic. The primary care workers are readily available during the client's involvement with the Study to ensure that appropriate linkages are made with these other resources if deemed necessary.

Moreover, a follow-up worker routinely monitors the performance of clients during the course of therapy and at several intervals post-treatment. This entails administering a battery of tests and observing the condition of the clients. If a crisis occurs, he/she will notify relevant personnel in order to ensure that the appropriate service is made available. Clients who abruptly terminate from the Study are seen by the follow-up worker to evaluate their condition and to offer further help if necessary and desired.

In short, a structured support system is a component of the treatment being provided. Within this context, we see no reason for postponing the introduction of the conjoint treatment. Such a strategy, we believe, helps to move the couple away from the notion of "blaming the victim" and closer toward our own position that both are "victims" of a disturbed interactional system. Once the rationale for the intervention is explained to the couples, most are amenable to the approach. To date, neither couples nor therapists (including follow-up workers) have found it necessary to make extensive use of support services in the agency during the course of treatment or in the initial follow-up period.

In summary, this chapter has identified a number of conceptual, clinical and methodological issues concerning the implementation of systems oriented conjoint therapy with alcoholics and their spouses. Matters pertaining to training of therapists, client engagement in treatment, assessment procedures, and the timing of the intervention were dealt with in the paper. Emphasis was placed on maintaining a balance between systemic issues and those directly relating to the presenting problem - alcohol abuse, in carrying out the intervention strategy. It is hoped that the ideas presented will be of benefit to both those currently involved in and those in the process of planning similar treatment programs, thereby improving service for this clinical population.

BIBLIOGRAPHY

Armor, D.J., Polich, J.N., and Stambull, H.B., 1978. *Alcoholism and Treatment*. New York: John Wiley and Sons.

Azrin, N., Naster, B., and Jones, R., 1973. "Reciprocity Counselling: A Rapid Learning-Based Procedure for Marital Counselling". 11. *Behaviour Research & Therapy*, 365-382.

Baekeland, F., **Lundwall**, L., and **Shanahan**, T., **1973**. "Correlates of Patient Attrition in the Outpatient Treatment of Alcoholism". 157(2). *The Journal of Nervous and Mental Disease*, 99-107.
Bell, J.E., **1967**. "Contrasting Approaches in Marital Counselling". 6(1). *Family Process*, 16-26.
Berenson, D., **1976**. "Alcohol and the Family System" in Guerin, P. (ed.), *Family Therapy*. New York: Garden Press, 284-297.
Birchler, G.R., **Weiss**, R.L. and **Vincent**, J.P.A., **1975**. "A Multimethod Analysis of Social Reinforcement Exchange Between Maritally Distressed and Nondistressed Spouse and Stranger Dyads". 31. *Journal of Personality and Social Psychology*, 349-382.
Briar, S., **1966**. "Family Services" in Maas, H.S. (ed.) *Five Fields of Social Services: Reviews of Research*. New York: National Association of Social Workers, 9-50.
Cleghorn, J.M., and **Levin**, S., **1973**. "Training Family Therapists by Setting Learning Objectives". 43(1). *American Journal of Orthopsychiatry*, 439-446.
Davis, D.I., **Berenson**, D., **Steinglass**, P., and **Davis**, S., **1974**. "The Adaptive Consequences of Drinking". 37(3). *Psychiatry*, 209-215.
Edwards, G., and **Orford**, J., **1977**. "A Plain Treatment for Alcoholism". 7. *Proc. Roy. Soc. Med.*, 344-348.
Epstein, N.B., and **Bishop**, D.S., **1981**. "Problem Centered Systems Therapy of the Family". 7(1). *Journal of Marital and Family Therapy*, 23-31.
Esser, P., **1971**. "Evaluation of Family Therapy with Alcoholics". 66. *British Journal of Addictions*, 251-255.
Frank, J.D., **1973**. *Persuasion and Healing*. Baltimore: Johns Hopkins Press.
Gerard, D., and **Saenger**, G., **1966**. *Outpatient Treatment of Alcoholism*. Brookside Monographs.
Group for the Advancement of Psychiatry, **1970**. 7(78). *The Field of Family Therapy*. Report.
Haley, J., **1976**. *Problem Solving Therapy: New Strategies for Effective Family Therapy*. San Francisco: Jossey Bass. Inc.
Heine, R.W., and **Trosman**, H., **1960**. "Initial Expectations of the Doctor-Patient Interaction as a Factor in Continuance in Psychotherapy". 23(3). *Psychiatry*, 275-278.
Hoehn-Saric, R., **Frank**, J.D., **Imber**, J.D. **Nash**, E.H. **Hone**, A.R. and **Battle**, C.C., **1967**. "Systematic Preparation of Patients for Psychotherapy". 2. *Journal of Psychiatric Research*, 267-281.
Hollingshead, A.B., and **Redlich**, F.C., **1958**. *Social Class and Mental Illness: A Community Study*. New York: John Wiley and Sons.
Jayaratne, S., and **Levy**, R., **1979**. *Empirical Clinical Practice*. New York: Columbia University Press.
Jellinek, E., **1952**. "Phases of Alcohol Addiction". 13(4). *Quarterly Journal of Studies on Alcohol*, 673-684.
Kniskern, David, P., and **Gurman**, Alan S., **1979**. "Research on Training in Marriage and Family Therapy: Status, Issues and Directions". 5. *Journal of Marital and Family Therapy*, 83-94.
Lennard, H.L. and **Bernstein**, A., **1967**. "Role Learning in Psychotherapy". 4. *Psychotherapy: Theory, Research and Practice*, 1-6.
Levitt, E.E., **1966**. "Psychotherapy Research and the Expectation-Reality Discrepancy". 3(4). *Psychotherapy: Theory, Research and Practice*, 163-166.
Locke, H.J. and **Wallace**, K.M. **1959**. "Short Marital Adjustment Prediction Tests: Their Reliability and Validity". 21. *Marriage and Family Living*, 251-255.
Locke, H.J., and **Williamson**, R.C., **1958**. "Marital Adjustment: A Factor Analysis Study". 23. *American Sociological Review*, 562-569.
Loehner, C.A. **1967**. *The Sick Thinking Family and Its Treatment*. California: Phalarope.
Maisto, S.A., **Sobell**, L.C., and **Sobell**, M.B., **1979**. "Comparison of Alcoholics' Self-Reports of Drinking Behaviour with Reports of Collateral Informants". 47. *Journal of Consulting and Clinical Psychology*, 106-112.
Maisto, S., **Sobell**, M.B., and **Sobell**, L.C., **1980**. "Predictors of Treatment Oucome for Alcoholics Treated by Individualized Behaviour Therapy". 5. *Addictive Behaviours*, 259-264.
Maluccio, A.N. and **Marlow**, W.D. **1974**. "The Case for the Contract". 19(1). *Social Work*, 28-36.
Meeks, D.E., and **Kelly**, C., **1970**. "Family Therapy with the Families of Recovering Alcoholics". 31(2). *Quarterly Journal of Studies in Alcohol*, 399-413.

Meltzoff, J., and **Kornreich**, M., **1970**. *Research in Psychotherapy*. New York: Atherton Press.

Navran, L., **1967**. "Communication and Adjustment in Marriage". 6(2). *Family Process*, 173-184.

O'Farrell, T., **Cutler**, H.S.G., **Dentch**, G. and **Fortgang**, J. **1980**. "Comparison of Reports of Male Alcoholics and Their Wives of the Husbands' Drinking Behaviour for a One Year Pretreatment Baseline Period". Unpublished paper.

Orford, J., **1975**. "Alcoholism and Marriage: The Argument Against Specialism". 36(11). *Journal of Studies on Alcohol*, 1537-1564.

Orford, J., and **Edwards**, G., **1977**. *Alcoholism: A Comparison of Treatment and Advice with a Study of the Influence of Marriage*. Oxford: Oxford University Press.

Orford, J., **Guthrie**, S., **Nicholls**, P., **Oppenheimer**, E., **Egert**, S., and **Hensman**, C., **1975**. "Self-Reported Coping Behaviour of Wives of Alcoholics and Its Association with Drinking Outcome". 36(9). *Journal of Studies on Alcohol*, 1254-1267.

Orford, J., **Oppenheimer**, E., **Egert**, S., **Hensman**, C., and **Guthrie**, S., **1976**. "The Cohesiveness of Alcoholism Complicated Marriages and Its Influence in Treatment Outcome". 128. *British Journal of Psychiatry*, 318-339.

Paolino, T.J., and **McCrady**, B., **1977**. *The Alcoholic Marriage: Alternative Perspectives*. New York: Stratton.

Perlman, H.H., **1968**. *Persona: Social Role and Personality*. Chicago: Chicago University Press.

Polich, J.M., **Armor**, D., and **Braiker**, H., **1981**. *The Course of Alcoholism Four Years After Treatment*. New York: John Wiley and Sons.

Seabury, B.A., **1976**. "The Contract: Uses, Abuses and Limitations". 21(1). *Social Work*, 16-21.

Seltzer, M., **1971**. "The Michigan Alcoholism Screening Test: The Quest for a New Diagnostic Instrument". 127. *American Journal of Psychiatry*, 1653-1658.

Skinner, H.A. **1979**. "A Multivariate Evaluation of the Michigan Alcoholism Screening Test". 40. *Journal of Studies on Alcohol*, 831-844.

Skinner, H.A., **1981**. "Benefits of Sequential Assessment". 17(11). *Social Work Research and Abstracts*, 21-28.

Skinner, H.A., **1981**. "Primary Syndromes of Alcohol Abuse: Their Measurement and Correlates". 76. *British Journal of Addictions*, 63-76.

Sluzki, C.E., **1978**. "Marital Therapy from a Systems Theory Perspective" in Paolino, T.J., and McCrady, B.S., (eds.) *Marriage and Marital Therapy*. New York: Brunner/Mazel, 366-398.

Sobell, L., **Maisto**, S., **Sobell**, M., and **Cooper**, M.C., **1979**. "Reliability of Alcohol Abusers' Self-Reports of Drinking Behaviour". 17. *Behaviour Research and Therapy*, 157-160.

Sobell, L, and **Sobell**, M., **1979**. "Validity of Self-Reports in Three Populations of Alcoholics". 46(5). *Journal of Consulting and Clinical Psychology*, 901-907.

Sobell, L.C., and **Sobell**, M.B., **1980**. "Convergent Validity: An Approach to Increasing Confidence in Treatment Outcome Conclusions with Alcohol and Drug Abusers" in Sobell, L.C., Sobell, M., and Ward, E. (eds.) *Evaluating Alcohol and Drug Abuse Treatment Effectiveness: Recent Advances*, New York: Pergamon Press.

Sobell, M.B., **1978**. "Alternative to Abstinence: Evidence, Issues and Some Proposals" in Nathan, P.E., Marlatt, G.A., and Coberg, T., (eds.) *Alcoholism: New Directions in Behavioral Research and Treatment*. New York: Plenum Press.

Sobell, M., **Sobell**, L.C., and **VanderSpeck**, R., **1979**. "Relationship Among Clinical Judgement, Self-Report, and Breath-Analysis Measures of Intoxication in Alcoholics". 47(1). *Journal of Consulting and Clinical Psychology*, 204-206.

Sobell, M.B., **et al.**, **1980**. "Developing a Proto-type for Evaluating Alcohol Treatment Effectiveness" in Sobell, L.C., Sobell, M.B., and Ward, E., (eds.), *Evaluating Alcohol and Drug Abuse Treatment Effectiveness: Recent Advances*. New York: Pergamon Press.

Spanier, G., **1976**. "Measuring Dyadic Adjustment: New Scales for Assessing the Quality of Marriage and Similar Dyads". 38. *Journal of Marriage and the Family*, 15-28.

Steinglass, P., **1976**. "Experimenting with Family Treatment Approaches to Alcoholism 1950-1975 - A Review". 15(1). *Family Process*, 97-123.

Steinglass, P., **Davis**, D.I. and **Berenson**, D. **1977**. "Observations of Conjointly Hospitalized Alcoholic Couples During Sobriety and Intoxication". 16(1). Family Process, 1-16.

Steinglass, P., **1977**. "Family Therapy in Alcoholism", in Kissen, B., and Begleiter, H., *The Biology of Alcoholism: Treatment and Rehabilitation of the Chronic Alcoholic*. New York: Plenum Press.

Tomm, K.M., and **Wright**, L.M., **1979**. "Training in Family Therapy: Perceptual, Conceptual and Executive Skills". 18(3). *Family Process*, 227-250.

Weakland, J.H., **Fisch**, R., **Watzlawick**, P. and **Bodin**, A.M. **1974**. "Brief Therapy: Focused Problem Reduction". 13(2). *Family Process*, 141-168.

Weiss, R.L., and **Margolin**, G., **1977**. "Assessment of Marital Conflict and Accord. in Ciminero, A.R., *et al.*, (eds.), *Handbook of Behavioral Assessment.* New York: John Wiley and Sons, 555-602.

Chapter 5

Paradoxical Techniques in Psychotherapy

Philip Barker
Faculty of Medicine, University of Calgary

It seems that paradoxical methods are increasingly being used by psychotherapists nowadays (Haley, 1976; Palazoli, *et al.*, 1978; Cade, 1979; Fisher, *et al.*, 1981). A stage has probably now been reached at which therapists can no longer ignore the possibility of using paradox in their work with certain clients, families and perhaps other groups. The bourgeoning literature on the subject can be quite confusing; the purpose of this paper is to review the current situation and make some sense out of the considerable amount of information that is available. It will concentrate on practical issues but it will also be necessary to consider briefly some theoretical points. Further information can be found in the excellent review by Soper and L'Abate (1977), and other useful sources can be located by the use of the bibliography of paradoxical methods in the psychotherapy of family systems compiled by L'Abate and Weeks (1978). Some of the material in this paper is also to be found in the book Basic Family Therapy (Barker, 1981).

WHAT IS PARADOX

According to Collins' new Dictionary of the English Language, paradox can have three meaning:
1. "A seemingly absurd or self-contradictory statement that is or may be true".
2. "A self-contradictory proposition, such as 'I am always a liar!'."

3. "A person or thing exhibiting apparently contradictory characteristics".
Yet another definition is that of Watzlawick and his colleagues (1967). These authors define paradox as "a contradiction that follows correct deduction from consistent premises".
While these definitions can be confusing, even mystifying (which is perhaps the essence of paradox), basically a paradox is something which is contradictory or appears to be so. And in psychotherapy at least, it seems that the contradiction is often between meanings given at two different levels of abstraction.
Examples are probably easier to understand than straight definitions. It is clear that statements like "I am lying" or "I will visit you unexpectedly this evening" are paradoxical. The reason is that both these sentences contain statements about the statements and the two conflict. The statements about the statements may be called "metastatements" or "metacommunications". In other words, there are two messages conveyed at different levels of

abstraction. Such statements violate Whitehead and Russell's (1910) theory of logical types. This states, essentially, that whatever involves all of a collection must not be one of the collection.

Thus the statement "I am lying" belongs to that collection of statements which describes things that people do. Others would be "He is telling the truth", "She is doing the shopping", or "They are going to bed". These are straightforward statements but beside them there can be another collection of statements, at a higher level of abstraction. These would be statements qualifying or describing the kind of statements that I have just mentioned, for example statements saying whether or not the statements about what people are doing are true. Some of the statements might be true, others might not. But the statement "I am lying" attempts to do both things. It attempts to be one of the collection of statements which describes what people are doing, and also to be one of the higher level collection of statements which describe whether or not these statements are true. So in reality, it is meaningless - at least according to Russell and Whitehead.

Once it is explained this may seem fairly obvious, yet such paradoxical statements are very common in ordinary human conversation and in daily life. People are told that they must be spontaneous, that they must make up their own minds what they want to do and so on. Despite being, strictly speaking and according to Russell and Whitehead, meaningless, it is a fact that many such statements, used in everyday life, do work. People *do* make up their minds when told to do so, at least sometimes.

Many visual examples could be given. In the book *Pragmatics of Human Communication* (Watzlawick *et al.*, 1967) there are a couple of striking examples: one is of a bridge with a sign saying "Ignore This Sign", the other shows a "Stop" traffic sign with a notice on the same post saying "No Stopping Any Time". Figure 1 is from the parking garage of the Clarke Institute of Psychiatry in Toronto. Figures 2 and 3 were noticed along Memorial Drive in Calgary.

All of these signs convey messages at two levels of abstraction. In daily life, people are able to use them to obtain useful information even though, regarded logically, they are meaningless. The therapist using paradoxical methods must, however, understand clearly the two levels of abstraction - the two orders - involved in such messages. Only when this is done, can paradoxical and many other strategic methods be effectively planned.

In truth, there is nothing new about the use of paradox in the dealing of human beings with one another. Look in any school playground and you will see children telling others to chase and catch them by saying, "You can't catch me". Examples are to be found in the bible too. St. Paul, in the 7th Chapter of his letter to the Romans, writes of how the harder he tried to obey the law - by which he meant the old testament Jewish law - the less successful he was. His solution, set out in chapter 8, is not, as you might expect, to try harder still. Instead it is to stop trying and to reframe the problem.

Watzlawick, Weakland and Fisch (1974), in their important book *Change*, quote many examples. One is from the French film *Carnival in Flanders*. The invincible Spanish forces are advancing on a small but prosperous Flemish village. A spanish emissary arrived and ordered the burghers to surrender the village or have it destroyed. He then left without waiting for their reply. The burghers were terrified, but decided they would have to do their heroic best rather than simply allow their village to be destroyed, their women raped and their wealth looted. But the women suggested a different solution. The men were to flee the village, abandoning the women to their fate. Thus there would be no men to fight or surrender. All the invading army would find would be a village of helpless women in need of protection by brave soldiers - a situation likely to appeal to the proverbial gallantry of the Spanish.

Sure enough, when the "conquering forces" found themselves warmly welcomed by the women, their conduct even exceeded the hopes of the villagers. Not only did they show the women valiant protection and respect, even though combined with many gallant amorous adventures which apparently did not displease the ladies, but when they eventually had to leave the village to continue their advance, they bestowed many gifts on the villagers in gratitude for the delightful and civilized hospitality.

So paradoxical solutions to problems are not new; it is only that a preoccupation with other modes of therapy has led to their being overlooked and neglected. The reasons for this will be discussed later.

DIFFERENT TYPES OF PARADOXICAL INTERVENTION

It is necessary to look at the different types of paradoxical intervention which can be used in psychotherapy. All involve giving messages at different levels of abstraction.

A. First we have *Simple Paradox* or *Prescribing the Symptom*. Many of the cases reported by Victor Frankl (1960), the originator of the term "paradoxical intention", come into this category. Some of his cases are quite puzzling in their simplicity, for example this report by a patient:

> "Once I had forgotten to lock the door and when I returned home it was open. That frightened me very much. After that, whenever I left the house I couldn't get rid of the feeling that the door was still open. I would go back again and again to check. This went on for 20 years. I knew the obsession was silly, for every time I went back the door would be locked, but I couldn't seem to keep from obeying the impulse. Life became unbearable. Since my interview with Dr. Becker (one of Frankl's assistants), however, things have changed completely. Whenever I have the compulsion to check whether or not the door is locked, I say to myself: What if the door *is* open! Let them steal everything in the whole apartment! And from that moment I am able to ignore the impulse and go calmly on my way".

And all she had received in treatment was a single interview with simple instructions!

Jay Haley, in his book *Problem Solving Therapy* (1976), provides excellent instructions on how to give paradoxical directives. A similar set of instructions, derived from Haley, appears in *Basic Family Therapy* (Barker, 1981).

B. The next type of paradoxical intervention I want to mention is *prescribing the system, but in a different context*. An excellent example was prescribed by Hare-Mustin (1975) who reported a case of a four-year-old with frequent and unpredictable temper tantrums. The therapist therefore negotiated with the child and his family where the tantrums should occur, picking a safe place at home. If the boy started to have a tantrum he was to be taken to that place - the "tantrum place". By the next session a week later Tommy had had only one tantrum. The therapist expressed some surprise and disappointment about this and then said it was necessary to decide at what time the tantrum should take place. The period 5 to 7 p.m. was agreed upon. If Tommy started to have tantrums at other times he was to be told to wait until 5 p.m. By the third session, the tantrums had stopped and they did not recur.

The literature is full of many such cases. Clearly, it is hard to produce a symptom at will at prescribed times.

C. A paradoxical directive can be presented as one or two or more *alternative choices*. For example, a family came for treatment expressing concern about their nineteen-year-old unmarried daughter who also had a son aged 1½. Father, mother, a thirteen-year-old son and a seventeen-year-old daughter all complained that the nineteen-year-old who - characteristically - had refused to come to the interview, took no part in caring for her son, consistently failed to contribute from her wages the sum she had agreed to pay for her keep, was dirty, lazy, self-centered, a liar and prone to take things without asking. She seemed totally in control of the household and the other members felt impotent but furious. As an infant, this girl had had a kidney removed for cancer. Her parents expected that she would die and had apparently indulged her greatly when she was younger.

The situation was explored thoroughly. The parents said they had tried everything but without success. The daughter just seemed to use the family apartment as a sort of hotel with a built-in babysitting service. I pointed out to them that she would undoubtedly continue to do this if allowed and that the only possible alternative would be to make staying in the household conditional upon specific things, such as paying her "rent", doing her share of caring for her son and of household chores and so forth. If the conditions were not met she would have to be asked to leave and live elsewhere; changing the locks or seeking the help of the police to remove her might even be necessary.

Having spelt this out, I then told the parents I believed this course of action would be impossible for them. Their concern and love for their daughter was too great. It would be better, and less distressing, for them to choose the alternative course of action, namely to accept continuation of the present situation. So I advised them against the first plan but not until after spelling it out in detail. The parents, led by the father, immediately said no, they *would* take control of their daughter. The present situation had gone on long enough. I expressed grave doubts about this, but the parents left determined to carry through with the plan. They agreed to phone me a few days later to tell me what happened.

The father did indeed phone, and he told me they had confronted their daughter - whereupon I expressed surprise - and that she had chosen to leave the family. They retained her son, of whom they had previously assumed guardianship, and a plan had been agreed for the daughter to visit the son from time to time. At follow-up a month later this situation persisted.

In this case, the family was challenged. It would have been easy to present the plan as direct advice to the family, but they had been given advice repeatedly in the past with no effect and in any case knew what they had to do but had been unable to do it. The paradoxical approach challenged them to do what was necessary and they responded to the challenge.

D. Finally, we have *more complex paradoxical interventions.* The last example is of course a simple example of strategic therapy (Barker, 1981) but many more complex and sophisticated strategic procedures are possible. Mara Selvini Palazzoli and her colleagues in the Milan group have been noteworthy for their work in developing and refining such therapeutic interventions. Much of their work is elegant and fascinating. Tasks may be set and written instructions or letters to be read at home, when the family is together, may be used. Their work is well described in the book *Paradox and Counterparadox* (Palazzoli *et al.*, 1978). Their methods were developed for, and are indicated for use in, the more severely disturbed families. These will not be considered in this paper.

REFRAMING

Reframing is an important technique which is usually necessary when paradoxical methods are used. The case just mentioned affords an example. The family wanted to control their daughter and knew what they needed to do. It would not have helped them for the therapist to have thought up and prescribed new and better ways of doing this; this had been tried repeatedly in the past. Instead, the problem was reframed. It became not what they should do to get the daughter to toe the line, but whether or not the parents had the resolve to accept the consequences of taking a firm line - since these might be that they would have to throw their daughter out of the house. The discussion was no longer about how to handle the situation, but had moved up to another level of abstraction. This dealt with the extent of the parents' resolve when faced by open defiance on the part of their daughter. Having reframed the question in this way, a paradoxical directive of the "alternative choice" variety was applied which challenged the parents to do what they needed to do.

Closely related to reframing is *positive connotation*, a valuable change-promoting device espoused by, among others, the Milan group; thus reframing can be used to label as strengths, that is to positively connote, what have been regarded by clients as pathological behaviors. Some parents I was seeing complained that their son, aged 12, constantly took radios, electrical gadgets and clocks to pieces and was then unable to put them together again. He was labelled a thoroughly destructive and expensive child. When I heard about this I expressed considerable interest and even surprise. The parents had given me to understand that there was virtually nothing good about this boy but I said I was pleased to hear that he had curiosity and interest in how things worked. Bob immediately brightened up and started to look more interested in the therapy. Acknowledging that the parents did not wish their appliances and clocks dismantled, I turned the conversation to the question of how they might obtain old radios, clocks, watches and other gadgets which Bob could take apart. This led to a discussion of the why and how of obtaining items which Bob could take apart and try to put together again. Some were already available in the household and others were obtained. From that day on nothing was heard of the symptom.

EVIDENCE FOR THE EFFECTIVENESS OF
PARADOXICAL INJUNCTIONS

The next question to be considered is, what is the evidence that paradoxical interventions are effective? In order to answer this we must first decide what we consider to be satisfactory evidence. Undoubtedly, there is a vast amount of anecdotal evidence, both in the literature and in the experience of therapists who have tried these methods to any significant extent. The work of that highly gifted therapist, Milton Erickson, as reported by Haley (1973) in his book *Uncommon Therapy*, is replete with examples. Many are to be found in the books *Pragmatics of Human Communication* (Watzlawick *et al.*, 1968) and *Change* (Watzlawick *et al.*, 1974) The work of Victor Frankl and many reports of individual cases seem to confirm that this sort of intervention can be effective. I also, from my own experience, can bear witness that these methods work, particularly in cases which have proved stubbornly resistant to more conventional methods. The anecdotal evidence does seem sufficient to justify the use of paradoxical intervention in cases in which more conventional methods fail. Nevertheless, control groups are usually absent, clinical details of the subjects being treated are sometimes minimal and follow-up in some cases is short or even virtually non-existent. Interestingly, however, paradoxical intention has been claimed by behaviorally oriented therapists as well as by non-behavioral ones, and if we look into the behavioral literature we do find a little reasonable research

Particularly interesting is the work of Turner and Ascher (1979), from Temple University in Philadelphia. These authors reported a controlled comparison of progressive relaxation, stimulus control and paradoxical intention in the treatment of insomnia. All were found to be effective but no significant differences between them were discovered.

The authors claimed this study as the first controlled demonstration of the effectiveness of paradoxical intention. They then went on to do a sort of replication study (Ascher and Turner, 1979). Twenty-one subjects with sleep disturbances were randomly assigned to three groups.

The people in the "paradoxical intention" group were told to attempt to remain awake as long as possible rather than continuing their efforts to fall asleep. They were not to engage in any activity which was incompatible with sleep, such as having the lights on, reading or watching T.V., but were to lie in bed in a darkened room, keeping their eyes open as long as possible. They were fully informed of the rationale of the procedure.

Those in the "placebo control" group were given a task previously described by Steinmark and Borkovec (1974) which involved imagining a number of bedtime activities and pairing them with neutral scenes.

The no-treatment controls were provided with no treatment during the four weeks of the study, but contact was made with them by brief telephone conversations, once every one-and-a-half weeks.

Four outcome measures were employed. These were the latency period to sleep onset; the number of awakenings during the night with difficulty returning to sleep; a seven-point scale of "restedness", seven being maximum restedness; and a seven point scale of difficulty experienced in falling asleep, seven representing no difficulty.

TABLE I

	Latency		Awakenings		'Restedness'		'Difficulty in Falling Asleep'	
	Baseline	Post-test	Baseline	Post-test	Baseline	Post-test	Baseline	Post-test
	(Minutes)							
Paradoxical Intention	61	29	2	0.5	3.5	5.1	3.1	5.2
Placebo	63	50	1.4	1.2	3.5	4.0	3.3	3.2
No-Treatment Control	70	62	1.4	1.7	3.5	3.4	2.9	3.1

(Adapted from Ascher, L.M. and Turner, R.M. (1979). *Behaviour Research and Therapy, 17*, 408-411)

Table I shows the results somewhat simplified. These were examined by a multivariate analysis of variance. The differences between the paradoxical intention group and the two control groups are significant on each variable except the rating of restedness. The placebo and no treatment controls did not differ from each other on any variable. The study is not methodologically perfect; for one thing the subjects slept at home and their sleep patterns were not observed by researchers. Nevertheless this study, and the preceeding one, seem important, both because of their results, and also because they do show that this kind of issue is susceptible to scientific investigation.

INDICATIONS AND CONTRAINDICATIONS

For the purpose of this paper, it may be helpful to divide psychotherapies into three categories:
1. Interpretive.
2. Educational.
3. Strategic.
These are not mutually exclusive and there can be considerable overlap, but the distinctions may be useful in considering the place of paradoxical interventions.

Interpretive therapies, the classic example being psychoanalysis, aim to produce insight, among other things. The use of paradox does not seem to be appropriate here.

Educative therapies, such as much behavior therapy, aim to teach people specific skills which will be of help to them in overcoming their presenting problems. As will be mentioned later, paradoxical interventions do not seem to have a place in the behavior therapy process itself, though they may be useful in overcoming resistance to therapy and facilitating clients' cooperation.

Strategic therapy is harder to define. A good effort is that of Brian Cade (1980). Strategic therapists do not seek to promote insight. They are not primarily educators. Instead they use what Peggy Papp (1977) calls "interventions aimed at changing the cycle of family interaction". She refers to the "use of planned strategies based on systemic predictions of change". Cade described the strategic approach as "essentially pragmatic and related to the belief that problems are produced and maintained by repetitive behavioral sequences... Directive in style....the approach concentrates on what is observable in interaction rather than making inferences about internal states and about relationships between internal states, on events rather than the meaning of events".

Common strategic therapy concepts are:
1. Reframing
2. Sequences
3. First and second order change
4. Directives
5. Metaphor
6. Paradox

Cade (1980) discusses each of these in turn. The point is that paradox is a technique primarily to be used as part of a strategic approach. It is not a therapy in itself but one technique which can be used as a part of a particular approach to therapy.

When in the course of strategic therapy should paradoxical interventions be employed? There is not a great deal of literature about this, though there seems to be a general consensus that situations characterized by intense "double-bind" processes have to be countered by "therapeutic double-binds" or by paradoxical or "counterparadoxical" methods of one sort or another. Thus methods of this sort have to be used for "families in schizophrenic transaction", as described by Palazzoli and her colleagues (1978) in the book *Paradox and Counterparadox*. These are severely disturbed families which are usually resistant to straightforward methods and require more highly specialized treatment programs.

While it certainly seems that there are simpler problems in which paradoxical methods can be of value, nevertheless some therapists do not use them. For example, the McMaster model of therapy (Epstein and Bishop, 1981) is based upon the straightforward setting of tasks for the family to accomplish without any use of paradox; indeed these authors appear to place a premium on honest, open dealings with families. There is no evidence that the results of the McMaster group are different from those of other schools of therapy, so it probably makes sense to try direct injunctions first. Moreover, the various ways in which the effectiveness of such injunctions can be increased should probably be tried before paradox is considered.

These include:
1.   Making the instructions more precise. Instead of saying: "Don't be rude to so and so", the therapist should specify precisely what the person is not to say.
2.   Enlisting other family members to remind the subject of the injunction, but in a calm, non-critical and non-judgmental way.
3.   Using the force of the therapist's personality. Among the special methods which can be used are hypnosis, though in most cases this is not necessary.
4.   Setting up some form of reward or punishment - preferably reward.
5.   Telling people to do something different rather than to stop doing something. The different thing has clearly to be incompatible with the thing which is to be stopped. So do not just tell the person who is being rude what not to say, but give instructions about what *to* say.
6.   Telling subjects to do things in a different sequence. This was an area

where Milton Erickson was especially skilled. (See Haley, 1973).

It is probably good practice only to use paradoxical methods if the above measures have been tried and have failed. It is also important to stress that adequate assessment should precede treatment. While some gifted therapists seem able to launch into paradoxical and other strategic measures very quickly, success in such circumstances requires either great intuitive skill, vast experience or an enormous amount of luck - preferably all three.

An example of inadequate assessment is the case of a 13-year-old girl I was asked to see in consultation by an exasperated therapist and two exasperated teachers from a special education class. Everything, they said, had been tried, but the child remained aggressive, rebellious and constantly at war with her fellow students. Her educational level was also poor.

The girl was able to construct a long list of behaviors which, she said, she used to keep students at a distance. It seemed that only a paradoxical approach held any prospect of success. Everything direct had been tried. So I expressed surprise that the list was no longer and congratulated Rachel on avoiding closeness with her fellow students and neighbourhood children. I said it would be unwise for her to get any closer to the other children since I did not think she could cope with close relationships. I explained this also to father who alone had come with Rachel, and to the teachers.

The plan was probably basically sound, but alas it had only partial success. A big factor was the lack of involvement, particularly in the first meeting with me, by mother. She was an important figure in the family, and had failed to come to the first session because she had no expectations that therapy would change things and therefore designated her husband to carry out this rather unimportant task. Consequently, the intervention, which needed to involve both parents, was not effective at home, though at school, where the excellent teachers understood what they were to do and carried it through, there was improvement. The family dynamics and structure had just not been adequately evaluated.

Are there other more positive indications for paradoxical intervention than the failure of direct injunctions? According to Frankl (1960), paradoxical intention is indicated where there is a clear history that the subject's symptoms have worsened as he or she has tried to fight them. This is a crucial point. It applies not only to the symptoms of individual patients, but to processes occurring in family and other groups. A clear history that things have worsened as counter-measures have been tried suggests that increasing the intensity of the counter-measures is probably not going to help.

Lack of the motivation to do the work necessary during therapy is a common phenomenon. The clients want the changes they specify, but not enough to be prepared to do what therapy involves. Such people are similar to the person who wants his hernia repaired but does not want an operation! Preliminary work, which may often have to involve the use of paradox, may be needed in such instances.

Fisher and his colleagues (1981) address the issue of indications and contraindications for the use of paradox in family therapy. These authors define three strategies which may be used, namely "redefinition", "escalation and crisis induction" and "redirection". They attempt to define the circumstances in which each of these three techniques may be used. They also mention some contraindications to the use of paradoxical interventions. These include "chaotic families", "childlike families" and some "impulsive families", as well as families which accept responsibility for their behavior and take therapeutic interventions at their face value with minimal opposition or negative response. The last group consists of course of those who respond to direct injunctions, as mentioned above. The authors also emphasize that very careful assessment of the family is important before the decision is made to use paradoxical methods. On the other hand, they fail to stress the value of positive connotation which, in my experience, is very helpful in ensuring that paradoxical interventions are accepted.

At this point, it may be helpful to consider briefly why it has taken so long for paradoxical interventions to come to be at all widely used in psychotherapy. The answer is probably to be found, in large measure, in Freud's enormous influence upon psychiatry. He set psychiatry on a particular course. Psychic determinism became so generally accepted that people stopped looking for any approach other than psychotherapeutic ones aimed at exploring and dealing with the unconscious roots of pathological behavior. Anthony Jay, (1969) in his book *Management and Machiavelli* says, "The uncreative mind can spot wrong answers, but it takes a creative mind to spot wrong questions". This seems to me an important observation. For years, therapists were asking, "What is going on in the person's unconscious to cause this problem?". But by sticking to this question therapeutic choice was greatly restricted. The right question might have been, "What is the best approach to changing this person's behavior?". This is a question at a different level of abstraction - a second order question compared with the first - or what we might call a "metaquestion".

HOW PARADOX WORKS

I would now like to turn to the question of how paradox works. Various suggestions have been put forward. Frankl emphasized the role of anticipatory anxiety which brings about precisely what the patient fears. A similar concept is that of seeking pleasure, for example through sexual intercourse. But, Frankl said, "pleasure belongs to that category of events which cannot be brought about by direct intention, but is a side effect or bi-product". So the more you strive for pleasure the less you achieve it. Similarly, the more anxious you are not to be anxious, the worse you get. So Frankl encouraged his patients to attempt to bring on or increase the symptoms, but in a humorous context and in a way that enabled the patient to place himself at a distance from the symptom, to detach himself from his neurosis. The reader will note that Frankl is here describing a second order change, that is an operation at a different level of abstraction.

It has also been suggested that the novelty or the apparent craziness of a paradoxical directive "shakes up" the family or the client, so that change is more likely. This may also promote "second order" operations, by causing the subjects to view their behavior in a different way.

Another theory suggests that people normally tend to think in terms of linear, cause-and-effect mechanisms, and paradoxical directives tend to reorient people by providing alternative, circular explanations. In other words, like the previous explanations, this theory suggests that paradox makes people think about things differently.

The most widely held explanation seeks to explain the fact that some clients come for help but are resistant to the help offered. As Andolfi (1979) has pointed out, they provoke the therapist to try and fail. This is of course paradoxical behavior, so a paradoxical treatment or if you like a counter-paradoxical one, is necessary.

If all the examples of paradox which have been mentioned are looked at carefully, including simple prescription of the system, it is clear that messages are being given at two levels of abstraction. It is not just that the therapist tells people to do something which represents the opposite of the desired change; there are two messages and there is always a reframing of the problem. Thus when a task is prescribed there is also an unstated message that the client has control over the ability to carry out the task. Thus there is an unstated, higher level message given along with the directive as it stands at its face value.

These ideas have been carried a step further by Watzlawick (1978) in his book *The Language of Change*. In this book he seeks to explain the effectiveness of the various types of injunction, and why these sometimes have to be paradoxical or apparently illogical. He believes that the left and right cerebral hemispheres are each responsible for specific language functions. The left hemisphere, the dominant one, is concerned with grammar, syntax, semantics, thinking, reading, writing, accounting and computing - that is to say with digital communication. On the other hand, the right hemisphere's language is archaic and undeveloped. "It tends to draw illogical conclusions based on clang associations and confusions of literal and metaphorical meanings, to use condensations, compositive words, and ambiguities, puns and other word games". It deals with images, wordles thinking and music competency.

Whether or not Watzlawick's localization of these two language functions into the respective cerebral hemispheres is accepted, the two functions certainly seem to exist. Much pathological behavior is based, Watzlawick believes, on right hemisphere functions. To change such behaviors contact must be made with the right hemisphere - or at least with those functions believed to be carried out by the right hemisphere. To use the case mentioned earlier of the parents who wished to control their daughter, there was no way change in the family situation could come by means of logical, digital - that is left hemisphere - communication. The parents already knew what they had to do and explaining further was futile. So it was a "right hemisphere" problem. If Watzlawick's theory is correct then I was able, by my intervention, to alter right hemisphere function.

How is this done? In Watzlawick's book there is a whole chapter (seven) in which he describes methods of "blocking the left hemisphere", which he sees as being a kind of logical watchdog guarding the right hemisphere. Reframing is one way of doing this and it was indeed used in this example. Having reframed the problem however it was converted from a logical, digital one to an emotional challenge. When the parents were told that it would be unwise for them to take a firm line with their daughter, because their concern about what would happen to her if they threw her out would be too upsetting for them, father responded in a critical voice: "She'll be OK, she always looks after herself". Anger was evident. Emotion had become involved and the family were changing not because of "digital" logic but, at least if you believe in Watzlawick's localization, because of what was going on in the right hemisphere.

There are also some interesting views in the literature on behavioral marital therapy. In Jacobson and Margolin's excellent book *Marital Therapy* (1979), which is strongly behaviorally oriented, there is some discussion about the use of paradoxical instructions. On the face of it this might seem surprising and indeed Jacobson and Margolin do state that paradox as a general strategy of marital therapy is inconsistent with the behavioral perspective. On the other hand, these authors do believe that at times "paradoxical instructions can be viewed as consistent with and facilitative within a behavioral exchange framework". They describe the case of a young couple entering therapy in a state of crisis. They fought frequently between sessions and their fights were very destructive, including physical violence. The fights threatened to compel a separation before therapy could begin to reverse this process and a paradoxical intervention was used to suspend temporarily the altercations between the couple.

The therapist commented upon the fact that the couple had such vicious fights at home, whereas in the therapist's office they were so polite and subdued. The wife stressed that they did have very ugly fights but the therapist said that his having not seen one made it difficult for him to evaluate their case. He asked them to have a fight so that he could see how things got destructive and hear the two of them acting destructively. The husband laughingly asked the therapist to come to dinner, whereupon the therapist responded by asking the couple to have a fight then and there. He proposed to leave the room and watch through the one-way screen. However, the couple were unable to stage a fight.

The therapist now stated that he was in a dilemma. However, he had an idea. He gave the couple a portable casette recorder to take home, and a tape. He instructed them, whenever they started to fight, to go into the living room, turn on the tape and fight in the living room. They could then bring the tape back to the therapist's office and he could hear a fight. The wife said, "You're suggesting that we fight and tape it?". The therapist replied, "Yes, I can't think of any other way to get the information". He convinced the couple to comply with the plan but when they returned the following week they had not engaged in one single argument. The therapist appeared bewildered and responded punitively. He insisted that they fight at least once during the following week; otherwise progress would be retarded. Alas, however, fighting between this couple was over and therapy subsequently proceeded smoothly.

I quote this example, partly because it is both fascinating and creative, but mainly because of the explanation which the authors give. They say that by giving the couple a casette recorder, the therapist was capitalising on his value as a discriminative stimulus for polite, rational behavior. Giving them the casette was equivalent to visiting them for dinner, since then any time the couple fought, they would be doing so in front of the therapist.

CONCLUSION

There seems little doubt that paradoxical interventions can be effective. We do not have any firm evidence on whether, and particularly under what circumstances, they are more quickly or more often effective than simpler, nonparadoxical methods. Nor do we know whether their effects are more or less long-lived than those of other methods. There is certainly a need for more properly controlled trials and as the one example quoted shows, these are not too difficult to carry out.

So on the one hand there is a need for more research. On the other, there is an enormous amount of anecdotal evidence for the value of paradoxical approaches. It seems reasonable to suggest that we can no longer deny our patients a trial of this approach if other methods have failed, even in chronic entrenched cases in which every other possible therapy may not have been tried. After all, the treatment is relatively non-invasive and cannot really do worse than allow the present situation to continue - except where the paradoxical approach aims to escalate symptoms. Certain technical points should, however, be mastered by those using these techniques. Some have been mentioned, particularly the importance of a proper assessment of the family and knowing whether the family does respond to straightforward, non-paradoxical directives.

Some other points which are important are:

1.   It is necessary to spell out a tightly argued rationale for what is suggested. An example is what was said to the parents of the 19-year-old girl mentioned earlier. In treating this family, the rationale was spelt out at much greater length than in this paper. Moreover, what was said was basically true, namely that it *was* hard for the parents to take a firm line with their daughter and there was a case for their not subjecting themselves to that stress and allowing things to continue as they were.

2.   It is usually important to refuse to accept credit for any change that occurs in response to a paradoxical intervention - indeed to express scepticism that the improvement will continue or is more than a chance happening.

3.   It is most important to treat the patient, or client, or family with the utmost consideration and respect. The use of paradoxical interventions is not "one-upmanship". Our clients are usually people struggling with serious problems and they are often in states of considerable distress. While humour may be useful we should always be laughing with our clients, never at them.

4.   Working with a team, or at least a colleague, can be helpful. This recommendation does not refer to co-therapy, but to having someone either observing behind a one-way screen or reviewing interventions subsequently on videotape. It can be difficult to think out an effective strategic intervention as therapy proceeds and taking a break to discuss the intervention with watching colleagues, or even to think about it on one's own, can be extremely valuable. I have found that families are surprisingly receptive to my request to take a short break to think about how best to help them, and I quite frequently do this - though it is not as good as having colleagues assisting.

So what is the place of paradox in psychotherapy in 1981? It is a useful technique for resistant problems and for individuals and families chronically entrenched in dysfunctional patterns of behavior. There is evidence that it works and I believe that it is no longer a technique for adventurous, unconventional or specially talented therapists like Milton Erickson. It is rather something which, in its simpler forms, should be in the armamentarian of every therapist.

REFERENCES

Andolphi, M. 1979. *Family Therapy: An Interactive Approach.* New York: Plenum Press.

Ascher, L.M. and Turner, R.M. 1979. 'Paradoxical intention and insomnia; an experimental investigation'. 17. *Behaviour Research and Therapy,* 408-411.

Barker, P. 1981. *Basic Family Therapy.* Baltimore: University Park Press.

Cade, B. 1979. 'The Use of Paradox in Therapy'. *In Family and Marital Psychotherapy,* edited by S. Walroud-Skinner. London: Routledge and Kegan Paul.

Cade, B. 1980. 'Strategic Therapy'. 2. *Journal of Family Therapy,* 89-99.

Epstein, N.B. and Bishop, D.S. 1981. 'Problem centered systems therapy of the family'. 7. *Journal of Marital and Family Therapy,* 23-31.

Fisher, L., Anderson, A. and Jones, J.E. 1981. 'Types of paradoxical intervention and indications/contraindications for use in clinical practice'. 20. *Family Process,* 25-35.

Frankl, V.E. 1960. 'Paradoxical intention; a logotherapeutic technique'. 14. *American Journal of Psychotherapy,* 520-535.

Haley, J. 1976. *Problem-Solving Therapy.* San Francisco: Jossey-Bass.

Haley, J. 1973. *Uncommon Therapy: The Psychiatric Techniques of Milton J. Erickson.* New York: Norton.

Hare-Mustin, R. 1975. 'Treatment of temper tantrums by a paradoxical intervention'. 14. *Family Process,* 481-485.

Jacobson, N.S. and Margolin, F. 1979. *Marital Therapy: Strategies Based on Social Learning and Behaviour Exchange Principles.* New York: Brunner-Mazel.

Jay, A. 1969. *Management and Machiavelli.* New York: Bantam.

L'Abate, L. and Weeks, G. 1978. 'A bibliography of paradoxical methods in psychotherapy of family systems'. 17. *Family Process,* 95-98.

Papp, P. 1977. 'The family that had all the answers'. *In Family Therapy: Full Length Case Studies.* New York: Gardner Press.

Soper, P.H. and L'Abate, L. 1977. 'Paradox as a therapeutic technique: a review'. 5. *International Journal of Family Counselling,* 10-21.

Palazzoli, M.S., Cecchin, G., Prata, G., and Boscolo, L. 1978. *Paradox and Counterparadox.* New York: Jason Aaronson.

Steinmark, S.W. and Borkovec, T.D. 1974. 'Active and placebo treatment effects on moderate insomnia under counter demand and positive demand instructions'. 83. *Journal of Abnormal Psychology,* 157-163.

Turner, R.M. and Ascher, L.M. 1979. 'A controlled comparison of progressive relaxation, stimulus control and paradoxical intention therapies for insomnia'. 47. *Journal of Consulting and Clinical Psychology,* 500-508.

Watzlawick, P. 1978. *The Language of Change.* New York: Basic Books.

Watzlawick, P., Beavin, J.H. and Jackson, D.D. 1967. *Pragmatics of Human Communication.* New York: Norton.

Watzlawick, P., Weakland, J. and Fisch, R. 1974. *Change: Principles of Problem Formulation and Problem Resolution.* New York: Norton.

Whitehead, A.N. and Russell, B. 1910. *Principia Mathematica.* Cambridge University Press.

Chapter 6

The Milan Approach to Family Therapy: A Tentative Report

Karl Tomm
Department of Psychiatry, University of Calgary

I INTRODUCTION

The theoretical views and treatment methods of the "Milan Team" have been known in Europe for some time. In North America they were virtually unknown until two or three years ago. However, it now appears that their approach is having a substantial impact. It is becoming increasingly common to hear of family therapists in Canada and the U.S.A. forming "teams" around one way screens, taking extended breaks during the interview for intensive discussion, carefully preparing end-of-session interventions, positively connoting the homeostatic tendency, prescribing rituals, etc. These clinicians are modeling themselves after the Milan Team and hope to achieve the same dramatic results with "difficult" families that the Milan Team report.[1] Occasionally the approach works for them as well and a remarkable transformation does occur (e.g. an anorectic eats normally after two sessions, or an intensely conflicted couple relate to each other with mutual respect, humor and affection after three sessions). Far more often, however, there appears to be little or no effect at all. This is particularly true when first exploring the new treatment method. Nevertheless, the sudden, dramatic changes that do occur in some families, have been witnessed often enough to entice more and more clinicians to experiment with this new approach. To some of these "explorers", the Milan approach has been one of the most significant innovations in the field of family therapy during the past decade. Whether this is an overstatement, or an understatement, is difficult to say. Only time will tell how their contributions should be regarded.

This chapter offers an overview of some of the major concepts and techniques utilized in the Milan approach. The report must be regarded as tentative for two reasons. First, the author regards himself as still studying and exploring the approach. He became aware of the work of the Milan Team three years ago and has had two and a half years of experience applying their particular treatment methods. He is aware of the fact that his current understanding of the approach is limited and that his own biases have strongly influenced the content of this report.[2] Second, the approach itself appears to be continuing to develop and evolve. For instance, the Milan Team no longer use the sibling rescue intervention (Selvini et al 1978a, p. 99) because they found that it often intensifies sibling rivalry. Other more circular interventions which include the whole family have been found to be more useful. The background information used in preparing this report includes written works by the Milan Team (see references), a selection of videotapes of their interviews and periodic informal discussion with members of the team, especially Dr. Boscolo and Dr. Cecchin.

II. ORIGIN AND DEVELOPMENT

Between 1965 and 1967, Dr. Mara Selvini Palazzoli, who had already established herself as an expert in anorexia nervosa, became increasingly disillusioned with the inefficiency of the psychoanalytic method. After years of work in individual psychotherapy these patients made only modest gains. In exploring the professional literature she "wandered" into the family therapy field. She was intrigued by the results reported when interventions were directed towards the family unit. Breaking with psychoanalytic tradition, she started to become involved with whole families. In 1967, Dr. Luigi Boscolo began collaborating with her in her exploration of families as "systems" and in 1971, Dr. Gianfranco Cecchin and Dr. Juliana Prata joined to complete the Team at the "Centro Per Lo Studio Della Famiglia" in Milan, Italy. All were physicians and had had training in psychiatry and psychoanalysis. Dr. Selvini also had a prior background in internal medicine. The team of four collaborated very closely for almost ten years in developing their ideas and techniques. Some of the major early conceptual influences were "Strategies of Psychotherapy" by Jay Haley (1963) and "Pragmatics of Human Communication" by Paul Watzlawick et al (1967). In late 1971, Dr. Watzlawick was invited to make a series of visits and consult with them in Milan. Then, in 1972, they initiated a project of exploratory research on the families of young schizophrenics. The team had been launched and a process of creative innovation was underway.

Their initial and major task was to make the "conceptual leap" from a linear psychoanalytic orientation to a circular systemic one. Dr. Selvini describes this as "almost a painful process". She felt she was often "groping in the dark". The members of the team found that they learned best from their own mistakes. For an extended period, the group deliberately insulated themselves from direct contact with other well known and established family therapists. The reason for this was that they wanted to learn directly from clinical material and become more consistent in their own thinking and methods. Subsequently, they ran across and began reading Gregory Bateson's "Steps to an Ecology of Mind" (1972) which had a profound influence on their theoretical development. In 1975, they published their major book "Paradox and Counterparadox" which became available in English in 1978. Probably their single most important paper to date has been "Hypothesizing, Circularity and Neutrality: Three Guidelines for the Conductor of the Session" (1980a). This report draws most heavily from these latter two sources.

The members of the Milan group emphasize that the nature of their early collaboration as a team was instrumental in facilitating their creative productivity. Although the team as a whole was led by Dr. Selvini, each member cooperated voluntarily as an equal in the working group. Each was an independent clinical practitioner and was not financially dependent on the Research Centre. Thus, they were relatively free of political hierarchies and other constraints characteristic of large institutions. As a group they placed a premium on allowing the better *ideas* to predominate. Functioning as a team of "multiple minds", their comments in discussion provided feedback to one another to stimulate conceptualization at increasingly complex and more systemic levels. Thus one important effect of their work as a team was to enhance the ability of each member to think more systemically. The results have been readily apparent to those who have had the opportunity to observe them work together clinically in an "orgy of hypothesizing". The agility and elegance of their thinking is fascinating to watch.

III. BASIC ASSUMPTIONS AND THEORY

A. *Circular Epistemology*. The Milan Team themselves insist that their major contribution has to do with introducing a new epistemology, a new way of *thinking* about clinical problems, rather than introducing new treatment techniques. They draw heavily from Gregory Bateson's philosophy of mind (1972, 1979) and use the term epistemology as he does, to refer to the way in which we know or understand the world around us. The epistemological assumptions we make determine how we think, how we act and how we organize our existence. This new epistemology is based on systems theory, information theory and cybernetics. It emphasizes circular rather than linear causality.

When it comes to clinical work with families, a circular cybernetic epistemology is considered *more useful* than a linear cause and effect epistemology. Within a linear framework, we tend to assume that people and objects "have" (i.e. possess) certain qualities or characteristics in and of themselves. Within a circular framework, we assume that people and objects "have" (i.e. show) characteristics only in relation to the contrasting characteristics of other persons or objects. "I know that I am small only because you (and others) are tall." *Differences* between perceptions/objects/events/ideas/etc. are regarded as the basic source of all information and consequent knowledge. On closer examination, one can see that a difference is always a *relationship* (between whatever is being compared) and that such relationships are always reciprocal or *circular*. If she is shorter than he, then he is taller than she. If she is dominant, then he is submissive. If one member of the family is defined as being bad, then the others are being defined as being good. Even at a very simple level, a circular orientation allows implicit information to become more explicit and offers alternative points of view. A linear orientation on the other hand is narrow and restrictive and tends to mask important data.

The clinician who can understand behavioural events in circular (or more complex) terms has a more complete understanding of the behavioural or mental phenomena in question. When working with families and using a circular epistemology, such a clinician tends to think expansively in terms of context, of reciprocity, of the effects of behaviour, of the effects of beliefs, of connections between behaviours, of sequences, and of patterns that form self-perpetuating loops, rather than being constrained by the linear trappings of content, of intention, of causes and of origins of behaviour. The linear view tends to be specific and atomistic while the circular view tends to be broad and holistic. For understanding mental events, a circular perspective is assumed to be more complete and thus more useful.

As noted earlier, the Milan Team found that moving from a linear to a genuine circular epistemology was extremely difficult. A major problem is that the use of verbal language predisposes towards linear thought (see Selvini et al 1978a, chapters 3 and 6). This is because the basic underlying structure of language is organized around the subject-predicate sequences of sentences. The team call this "the tyranny of linguistic conditioning" and credit Shands (1971) as well as Bateson (1972) for clarifying the problem. The Milan Team found that by disciplining themselves to substitute the verb "to be" in their discussion and thought with the verb "to show", it was easier to maintain circular assumptions. For instance, to say or to think "mother is depressed" is to attribute a characteristic to the mother and implicitly to separate her from the context and thus to orient one's thoughts in search of internal causes. On the other hand, to say "mother shows depression" implies that the depressive behaviour may be related to the context and one is oriented towards evaluating her behaviour in relationship to those to whom she may be showing her depression. Is the "depression" a signal to the children to indicate that the mother wants/needs more attention and support? Is it a form of reassurance to the husband that he is still needed and has an important role to perform? Clues for answers to these questions may be inferred from the specific responses to the depressive behaviour, and from the response to the responses, etc. Given a circular rather than a linear epistemology, the focus of interest is transferred from the symptom to its connectedness with other events in its context and from which it derives its meaning. The Milan Team members are much more interested in the *message* conveyed by the symptom than in the symptom as an entity in itself.

B. *The Nature of Truth*.   The Milan Team assumptions about the nature of truth are also circular. Their view of truth is "pragmatic". The statement that is most "true" at any particular moment, is that which is most useful. In fact, they go so far as to say: (the higher level truth is that) "there is no truth, there is only punctuation".[3] That is, when it comes to assessing the meaning of behaviour there are only different punctuations or points of view, no certainties or absolutes. In order to emphasize this and avoid confusion they prefer to use the term hypothesis rather than truth. The following discussion, however, will revolve around the concept of truth.

It is generally accepted in the philosophy of science that "The Truth" can never be known. Scientific laws and theories can never be proven, they can only be disproven or replaced by more popular, more elegant or more useful theories. However, most people in our culture live and act as if they "know" the "truth" about most events in their lives. Thus in day to day living, we tend to accept the linear assumptions of the "classical" notion of truth. We assume there is a direct one-to-one correspondence between statements and the objects or events (or relations between them) that they describe. This cultural predisposition accounts for the discomfort frequently experienced by some clinicians (and families) when they first observe or hear some Milan interventions that are based on pragmatic truth. Immediate reaction to statements in the intervention often are "but that's not true", "they are being dishonest to say that". These reactions derive from a linear (or classical truth) interpretation of a circular or pragmatic intervention.

To clarify this issue further, it may be helpful to contrast these two views of truth.[4] Classical truth revolves around two major variables: statements and the "real" world of objects and events. Statements are assumed to be true when there is a direct and accurate correspondence between specific statements and the perceived events/objects/relationships in the world to which they refer. Pragmatic truth, on the other hand, revolves around three major viarables: statements, the real world and values. One of the most prevalent values in the mental health field is for clinicians to be *useful* in facilitating constructive change when working with patients and families. Hence, statements which make more useful connections between certain statements and certain events are assumed to be more true than other statements. The criterion of usefulness is evaluated on the basis of feedback, i.e. on the subsequent responses of the patient or family. The "truth" of the therapist's statement in the intervention depends on how useful it was in enabling the family to make constructive changes. For instance, it may be true (in the classical sense) that a wife is depressed and a burden on her husband. However, to make this statement in therapy may not be useful. On the contrary, it may in fact be harmful by inadvertently impeding change and aggravating the problem. It may have the effect of making the wife feel even more depressed and the husband feel more justified in blaming her, etc. If instead the therapist offered an opinion based on pragmatic truth by stating that by showing her husband her depression, the wife has found a way to reassure him that he is needed and that by blaming her for being inadequate from time to time, he helps her to feel depressed and to continue in her work of reassuring him, the possibilities for constructive change may be greater. Having repunctuated the wife's depression as a positive contribution to the husband, she is likely to be more relieved than more depressed. Having connected the husband's blaming to the depression yet at the same time connoting it positively (as helping her to help him) he is forced to reconsider the consequences of his own behaviour. Whether or not the opinion contained some (pragmatic) truth is determined by the immediate feedback from the couple as the intervention is given and by the remote feedback at the time of the next session. There are of course many situations where the most pragmatic truth is a classical one.

C *Systemic Process.* The Milan Team regard the family as "a self regulating system which controls itself according to rules formed over a period of time through a process of trial and error" (Selvini et al 1978a, p.4). They accept most of the basic postulates of General Systems Theory such as 1. the whole is greater than the sum of its parts, 2. the part is best understood in the context of the whole, 3. a change in one part will effect every other part, and, 4. the whole manifests a "totality" with tendencies towards homeostasis, equilibrium, transformation and equifinality. However, there are some novel aspects of their view of systems. For instance, they emphasize more than most family therapists the capacity of family systems to change on their own. While they may subscribe to notions such as morphostasis and morphogenesis in systems, they seem to think more in terms of continuous (homeostatic) fluctuation and discontinuous transformation. The former descriptors tend to imply stable structure and gradual change while the latter imply fluidity and sudden change. This difference in emphasis may be subtle but is more significant than one might suspect. The Milan position probably represents "the other side of a watershed" and appears to be based on different assumptions. A definition of the two contrasting positions may help clarify this issue. Systems theorists rooted in the Western philosophical tradition tend to regard the stable *organization* of a complex of elements in a system as the crux of the systemic view. The system exists by virtue of its *structured* complexity. The Milan Team appear to hold a position closer to the Eastern philosophical view that systems in essence represent an ongoing process of everchanging interconnectedness. The system exists by virtue of its *changing* complexity.

What are the clinical implications of this difference? The therapist who assumes that family systems essentially represent interpersonal structures looks for patterns of interaction that reveal the problematic "deep family structure" of coalitions, alliances, splits, etc. He or she then conceptualizes a more adaptive structure (implicitly or explicitly) and channels his therapeutic work to realign the system accordingly. For instance, when a cross-generational, cross-sexual malalignment is identified (mother aligned with son and father aligned with daughter), the therapist would direct his interventions towards defining a clear boundary between the generations and strengthening the marital and sibling sybsystems. Thus the therapist deliberately *acts on* the underlying family structure and sees himself changing it in a predetermined direction. The schools of structural family therapy and strategic family therapy represent this approach.[5]

The Milan systemic therapist assumes that family systems represent a continuous process of change. The family only *appears* to be stable and presents *as if* it were maintaining fixed repetitive patterns. The assumption is made that there are one or more "points" (P_s) in the system which are "stuck" but that the rest of the system is in fact changing around those points. The P_s is described as "the point of a system at which the maximum number of functions essential to its existence converge and which if modified effects the maximum change with a minimal expense of energy" (Selvini et al 1978a, p.4). From a communications perspective one might describe the P_s of the system as the point at which particular ideas/meanings/beliefs/values/ etc. are connected and locked into a paradoxical tangle or strange loop (Cronen et al in press). The therapist's task is to identify the points at which the system appears to be stuck. He then develops an intervention which aims to introduce new connections or a new time factor at these points so that the system may be freed up to continue to change spontaneously on its own. A sudden change or transformation is then possible "because only some of the personal characteristics of the elements are fully absorbed and utilized by the system, others remain available and can be put to use in constructing a working family system, for instance when the equilibrium of the old has been destroyed.... this interaction does not demand hard and protracted work on the part of the therapist but only the ability to seize the right moment at the right time" (Selvini 1978, p.199).

There are other features on which the Milan view of systems may be distinguished from others. While these will not be fully elaborated here, a few comments may provide a flavour for the imaginative reader. On the notion of time, their view is becoming more Einsteinian. Not only do systems exist within a framework of chronological time (Newtonian time), the phenomenon of time is incorporated within the systemic process itself. For instance, every system has its own internal time, T_s, of actions and reactions for incorporating the unexpected and unsettling communication that may be given in the intervention (Selvini et al 1978a, p.15). On the issue of the most useful units to consider for an analysis of family systems the Milan Team do not regard the "skin encapsulated" person as the basic unit. The focus is on units of meanings, on rules of logical connections and on contexts. Families are regarded more as information systems than as physical systems of mass and energy. Since the most relevant elements of an information system are not necessarily isomorphic with the elements of the physicochemical system on which they depend, it may be useful to free therapists of the habit of thinking primarily of individuals, of dyads and of triads. New conceptual tools are needed and Bateson (1979) has offered a provocative start. Another valuable resource may be "The Coordinated Management of Meaning" (CMM) which is a recent development in communication theory (Pearce and Cronen, 1980), that appears to be fairly compatible with the Milan view of the internal workings of a system. CMM Theory emphasizes *reflexivity* in hierarchial systems. For instance, a higher level logical type (e.g. the relationship) usually provides the context for attributing meaning at a lower level (e.g. the episode) but there are occasions when the levels may be reversed and an interactional episode (e.g. violence) serves to redefine the interpersonal relationship. Thus the hierarchical relationship between levels of meaning is reflexive, not unidirectional. Applying this notion concretely to a family there may be times when it is useful for the children to be at a higher level in the hierarchy than the parents. "The parentification of a child... may be functional... depending on the transactional context in which this occurs" (Selvini et al 1978a, p.163). This view stands in stark contrast to the position of some therapists who hold the view that the organizational hierarchy of healthy systems is fixed and stable, e.g. the parents should always be in charge of the children (Haley, 1980).

IV. THERAPEUTIC PRACTICE

A. *Overall Pattern of Contact With Families.* The Milan approach is described as "long brief therapy" (in contrast to the Palo Alto brief therapy model). It is long in the sense that therapy often extends over many months and sometimes years. It is brief in that the total number of interviews and amount of direct contact with families is usually small. This is a result of planning a long time interval between sessions. This time is required for the family to organize a transformation. Furthermore, the intensity of therapy is not in direct relation to the frequency or total number of sessions. During the schizophrenia project (Selvini et al 1978a) the team routinely contracted with the family for 10 sessions over one year. At the end of this series, it was possible to re-negotiate for an additional 10 sessions. Recently, however, the team has become much more flexible. They now tend to proceed on an ad hoc basis, arranging one session at a time. The average number of sessions also appears to be decreasing. It is as if they have become more skilled and effective as their own approach has evolved.

As implied above, the time between sessions is an important aspect of the Milan model. In a recent paper entitled "Why the Long Interval Between Sessions?" (1980), Dr. Selvini elaborates on this issue. Time is required for new information to reverberate through any system. In families, each member responds to the intervention with feedback (one cannot not communicate) and provides feedback to the feedback of other members, etc. The time taken for this whirlpool of feedbacks to "settle" is the T_s of the system. Thus, a considerable length of time must elapse before the real impact of an intervention can adequately be assessed. In practice, the most common time interval used is four weeks. This is variable, however, and depends on the family, its current state and on the nature of the intervention used. For instance, the more precise and "powerful" the intervention seems to be, the further away the next interview is scheduled. This allows the transformation to unfold. On the other hand, when there is considerable uncertainty among the team members concerning the validity of the hypothesis or the usefulness of the intervention, a shorter time interval of two weeks may be used. The responses to the first intervention are then utilized to refine the next one.

During the overall process of therapy, any contact with the family outside the session, direct or indirect, is regarded as having potential significance. Telephone calls from family members or letters from third parties (e.g. other professionals) are scrutinized for possible attempts to disqualify the intervention in order to resist change. In contrast to individual therapy where postponement of an interview is often regarded as evidence of resistance, a family request for an *earlier* session (e.g. because of a new crisis) is regarded as resistance. It usually reflects an effort to disqualify the intervention by getting the therapist into a discussion to alter his position and opinions. Requests for elaboration or advice in telephone calls may have the same intent or may reflect attempts to get the therapist to relinquish his neutrality. In order to avoid "falling into a trap" during a telephone call, the Milan Team follow a rule of only accepting information during the call and not offering any advice or making any commitments. The therapist taking the call indicates to the family member that before he can respond he must first confer with his colleagues in the team. Given more time to reflect on the significance of the message, the therapist is more likely to avoid being ensnared by the family's disqualification process. Discussion with the team makes it easier for the therapist to retain his systemic stance and thus when he does return the call he is more likely to have a response that could strengthen the intervention and therapeutic process rather than weakening it.

When families do not appear to be changing during the course of therapy, the therapist broadens his field of enquiry. The question "what is the most relevant system here?" is addressed. Does it include the school, workplace, extended family or peers? Consideration is given to bringing in significant others, especially from families of origin. The choice of who should attend is very carefully reviewed as well as who (the therapist, the family or a particular member) should make that decision. Another interpersonal area that is carefully examined is that of other ongoing professional contacts that the family may have. Sometimes these professional involvements are very significant factors in inadvertently maintaining the status quo (Selvini et al 1980b). Interventions must then take these relationships into consideration. A final area of continuing concern at all times is the relationshp between the family and the therapist himself. Has the therapist entered in a self-perpetuating homeostatic pattern with the family? A number of novel therapeutic interventions have been devised to enable the therapist-family system to change when it appears to be stuck (Selvini et al 1978a, Chapters 11, 16, 17 and 18).

B. *Structure of a Single Session.* One of the more obvious trademarks of the Milan method is the five part session (Selvini et al 1978a, Chapter 2). These parts are:
1. the presession - a discussion among team members (5-20 minutes)
2. the interview - the therapist interviews the family while the rest of the team observes (50-90 minutes)
3. the intersession - a discussion among all team members while the family waits (15-40 minutes)
4. the intervention - the conclusions of the team are delivered to the family while the team observes (5-15 minutes)
5. the postsession - a discussion among the team members (10-20 minutes)

The most striking characteristic of this structure is the amount of discussion time in the team. The purpose of this is to help the therapist be more systemic in his thinking and remain in the 'T' (therapeutic) position, rather than succumb to the natural "pull" to join the family belief system and assume an 'F' (family member) position. In the 'T' position, the therapist retains greater conceptual freedom to consider and use alternative "truths" (or hypotheses) to the "reality" presented by the family. In effect, by defining this structure, the Milan Team prescribed a ritual to themselves (and to other clinicians) designed to help them maintain their circular epistemology and resist the pressure to adopt the family's linear view of the problem.

During the *presession* discussion, the team reviews the last session and any interim events to develop hypotheses about the family and the therapy process which could serve to guide the therapist's questions during the interview. For the first interview a great deal of importance is given to information about the manner in which the case is presented. How was the family referred? Who in the family called? What was their tone on the phone? How did they construe their situation? What overt or covert expectations did they have? In generating their hypotheses, the team members also drew on their general knowledge and their specific experience with families in similar situations. A wide range of hypotheses may be entertained or a particular focus may emerge. It is also useful to discuss the types of questions that could be asked to elicit data that might validate or disqualify specific hypotheses. Thus before he or she actually meets the family, the therapist has some ideas about where to proceed.

The *interview* itself is devoted entirely to eliciting information by asking questions. No explicit attempt is made to alter family member behaviour within the session, e.g. to stop blaming, be more supportive. The Milan Team assume that real change, if it occurs, will do so outside the session in the daily life of the family. The interviewing begins with general open-ended questions thus giving the family an opportunity to reveal their most pressing concerns at this time. As the interview progresses, the therapist moves fairly quickly from member to member in asking questions, never allowing one individual to speak longer than three minutes. Spontaneous interaction between family members is carefully observed when it occurs but is not deliberately stimulated.

During the early years, the team always had a heterosexual pair of therapists in the room conducting the interview while the other two team members were observing. At the time they felt this arrangement was "more physiological" (Selvini et al 1978a, p.10). Later they came to realize that it is the quality of questioning and the underlying hypothesizing that is critical. They also found that two interviewers in the room at the same time could be problematic in that too many hypotheses may be generated at once. Now they use only one interviewer with one or more observers behind the screen. The observers are in a supervisory role and may call the therapist out at any time to comment on the process or make suggestions for further enquiries (or phone in specific questions if a telephone is available).

The *intersession* discussion is a major and significant break in the interview when the team meet to discuss the data elicited, refine their hypotheses and generate the intervention. Essentially this is a period of intense brain-storming. Team members are encouraged to offer their intuitive impressions, even to "discharge" their linear hypotheses (e.g. "He is a *very* angry man.") and then move on to elaborate a more circular and fully systemic understanding (Why is he showing us this angry behaviour? What effect is it having on whom? etc.). The mental work entailed in synthesizing the data available, hypothesizing the systemic process and creating an intervention is both taxing and exhilarating. The discussion is a time for expansive speculation regarding possible connections and for rigorous analysis of probable effects. The failure to reach a clear consensus regarding a useful intervention is taken to mean that the team is confused. Depending on the data available, the complexity of the situation, and the skill of the team, the intersession may take some time. To avoid keeping the family waiting for excessive periods, a decision may be made to simply end the session with a request for the family to return after a few days or with a promise that a letter with the team's opinion will follow.[6] In the meantime the team may meet again to continue their conceptual work. Most often, however, the family simply waits and does so with growing anticipation and suspense regarding the team's impending conclusion.

The therapist returns with the *intervention* for the fourth part of the session. This may be in the form of an opinion, a prescription for no change, a "declaration of impotence", a prescription of a ritual, etc. The delivery is usually succinct and brief allowing only minimal further interaction with the family. The intent is to introduce some new information, something that is quite different from what the family already "knows". The intervention usually has the quality of being unexpected and thus leaves the family with some degree of confusion and perplexity. The team's rationale for the specific intervention is usually not provided although an explanation that is considered useful (as part of the intervention itself) is offered. To try to get the family to "understand" the intervention in the session itself is regarded as a mistake. Attempting to do so can only result in a weak assimilation of the therapist's ideas into their preconceived views. It simply takes time to genuinely accommodate to something new. Thus the therapist is encouraged to introduce the new information in the preplanned manner and escape the field of interaction with the family. The family is expected to struggle to make sense of it after they leave the session.

The *postsession* discussion focusses on the immediate reaction of family members to the intervention. This feedback is used to evaluate the relative validity of the hypothesis and the probable usefulness of the intervention. Attempts may be made to predict the family's response if the intervention appeared to have been on target. Experience has shown, however, that these predictions are usually inaccurate. The family is inevitably more creative in finding their own solutions. If on the basis of the immediate feedback the intervention appears to have missed the mark, the reasons for this are explored. Discussion also includes ways in which the intervention or delivery could have been improved. Alternative interventions that could be considered in future sessions are entertained. Finally, a synopsis of the interview with details of the intervention is recorded.

It is important to emphasize that the essence of the Milan approach does *not* center on the five part session or on teamwork per se. It is the method of conceptualization and consequent activity of the therapist that is most important. Once an individual clinician has learned how to think systemically and how to develop creative interventions on his own, he can apply the approach without a team. However, the chances of recognizing if, when and how he has become trapped in the 'F' position is greatly reduced. It is advisable for independent clinicians to maintain some intermittent supervision or at least to arrange regular opportunities for colleagial discussion. On the other hand, working intensively as a team with the full five part ritual is probably the most effective way of developing the perceptual and conceptual skills entailed in this approach. If the team is too small and inexperienced, it may have difficulty coping with the "power" of the family's construction of reality and their covert rules for maintaining it. If the team is too large, it may have difficulty achieving adequate coorientation to generate systemic hypotheses and interventions. Variations in the process of teamwork in this model would make a fascinating study in itself.

C. *Method of Interviewing.* The Milan Team suggest that "if the method is correct, no charisma whatsoever is needed" (Selvini et al 1978a, p. 11). This is a very encouraging statement but the method has proven very difficult to learn. Fortunately the team has been able to identify three core principles which guide the behaviour of the interviewer. These are hypothesizing, circularity and neutrality. The reader is encouraged to read the excellent original paper (Selvini et al 1980a) for an indispensible elucidation. Only a cursory overview with a few comments and examples will be given here.

Hypothesizing refers to the conceptual activity of the therapist in generating and revising hypotheses about the family. Hypotheses have to do with the connections that are postulated between certain events, behaviours, attitudes, meanings, etc. In general, they address the following question: Why is this family presenting for therapy in this way at this time? The possible answers to this question guide the therapist in what he should ask about. Thus the process of hypothesizing funnels the enquiry of the therapist into those areas of family functioning, patterns of interaction or life events that may be most useful to explore. Once the therapist has "located" a relevant area, the hypothesis orients him further to explore specific connections. The therapist never asks about the hypothesis directly. There are two reasons for this: 1. The system "requires" that the members not be aware of the most relevant connections, and 2. the suggestion would be met with denials and the family would strengthen its resistance. A useful method of uncovering important connections without revealing the hypothesis is to track relevant behavioural sequences. What specific behaviour follows what other specific behaviour, e.g. "When your father does..., what does your mother do?", "and then what does he do?", etc. An enquiry about observable behaviours is more useful than focussing on feelings or thoughts since the latter are more inferential. When the therapist builds his own inferences from descriptions of perceived behaviours (rather than from family member inferences), he remains a little closer to what actually happened. Thus by asking questions related to hypotheses, the therapist gradually creates his own "reality" (albeit a tentative one) about what is going on in the family.

The principle of *circularity* provides guidance in how to formulate the type of questions that are more likely to yield real information rather than mere "noise". As noted in the theory section, a difference is always a relationship, which in turn is always circular. Thus by deliberately orienting questions around differences, one obtains information about circular process. Three basic types of difference questions may be asked: 1. differences between individual family members on a particular characteristic or issue, e.g. "Who in this family shows their sadness the most?"; 2. differences between relationships, e.g. "Is George closer to his mother or closer to his father?"; and 3. differences between individuals or between relationships over *time*, e.g. "Were father and George closer or more distant after Sally was born?" It is useful to keep in mind that one is looking for differences that "make a difference". Therapists learning this approach often pick up the technique of asking difference questions very quickly but because they are still weak in the area of hypothesizing, end up asking about differences in matters that are trivial or irrelevant. The result is a rather superficial interview with little useful information. On the other hand, when a difference question is well focussed with a good hypothesis, the question alone has a powerful effect on the family system.

Another important aspect of the principle of circularity is the value of triadic questioning. When there are enough family members present, it is extremely useful to ask a third person about the relationship between another two (or a fourth regarding another three, etc.). For instance, if one were enquiring about whether father and his son George are getting along better or worse than before, it is more useful to ask mother or daughter Sally than to ask father or George directly. There are at least two reasons for this. First, George and father have a greater personal investment in how their relationship is to be regarded by others. Hence their response would be biased to give the desired impression. A third or fourth party is less invested and thus less liable to "manage" their response and more likely to say it as it is. The second reason is that from a circular point of view, it is the effect that the relationship (or its changes) has on others (such as mother and Sally) that is important and not the intentions of the interactants (which are linear). Father and George are more likely to tell the interviewer about their intentions rather than the effects of their behaviour whereas mother and Sally are experiencing the effects of the relationship and hence can offer that information more readily.

Triadic interviewing is extremely effective in by-passing resistance and is very efficient in eliciting circular data. When exploring a covert alignment between father and daughter, the therapist might ask the son "When your mother and sister are fighting, what does your father do?", "Does he go more on mother's side or on Sally's?" To take full advantage of these questions one must attend carefully to the analogic (non verbal) communications as well as the digital (verbal) responses. Thus, a series of furtive glances accompanied by the failure to articulate a response to such distinctions provides useful information. As might be suspected, this pattern of interviewing includes the children in the discussion much more than other approaches to family therapy. The effect of triadic questioning is to stimulate "gossip in the presence of others". It is quite remarkable how family members will sit riveted to their chairs in anticipation of the response to a triadic question about them. One useful habit to develop when learning this technique is to identify the person or persons about whom information is desired and then reflexly turn one's head to look at a third person and ask him the question.[7]

Neutrality refers to the therapist's pragmatic effect of remaining in a metaposition vis-à-vis the family system. It entails the absence of any alignment or of any moral stance on the part of the therapist. Thus neutrality may be considered in relation to the family members and to the information disclosed. With regard to the first instance, the therapist carefully avoids taking sides overtly or covertly. He never agrees with one family member and disagrees with another. Since the mere fact that directing a question towards a particular family member gives that member special status, the interviewer must move on and ask for information from others in order to maintain a rough balance in talk time. In the second instance, the therapist avoids passing judgement on any behaviour or opinion that is revealed. Particular events in the life of the family are not judged bad or good; their report is taken as information. Everything that is said by the family is accepted on one level, yet at the same time everything is rejected (or confronted) on another. For example, if the parents pour out a barrage of accusations about how bad their son has been, the therapist listens attentively for a while and then enquires about which parent feels most (or least) strongly that what the son has been doing is bad. "Who in the family holds the position most strongly that pointing out his mistakes makes it less likely that he would act in that manner again? Who thinks pointing them out makes it more likely?" To retain his neutrality, the therapist should not take a position on one side of an issue or the other. He should try to articulate the question in such a way as to avoid implying any implicit moral stance. To do this, the therapist might have to elaborate the question rather carefully. For example, "Do you think that pointing out to your son that he has made mistakes is more useful in helping him avoid them in the future, or that waiting for him to discover his own mistakes is more useful?" The family could construe either side of the question (or both) as positive actions. Because they are not sure where the therapist stands on the issue, the respondents are more likely to give more accurate information about how they think, feel and act, rather than try to manage the responses to look good in the eyes of the therapist. Thus a neutral position makes it less likely that the information yielded is an artifact of the relationship between the therapist and the family, and more likely that it is a reflection of what is happening in the family system. The failure to remain neutral not only results in the generation of poor data, it also results in slippage from the 'T' position to the 'F' position.

In their paper on these principles, the Milan Team raise a tantalizing question. They speculate that if the interview were in fact conducted properly, a formal end-of-session intervention may not be required at all (Selvini et al 1980a, p.12). The information elicited from the family solely through the method of interviewing may be sufficient to trigger a transformation. In their practice to date, however, a carefully prepared intervention is used more often than not. Perhaps this is because new information is fragile and the new connections need to be "welded" by the intervention.

D. *Intervention Principles and Techniques.* It is important to recognize that the Milan Team do not assume that they know the solution to the family's problem, or that they are able to tell family members how they should change to become problem-free. On the contrary, they assume that the family system has the resources required to transform itself to become asymptomatic. This is not to say that Milan interventions provide no direction at all. The intervention usually contains some content that implicitly orients the family (at a higher meaning level) to consider a certain direction or heuristic issue. No particular solution (at a lower concrete level) is specified. Like the Buddha, the therapist points the way; he does not take the family there. Thus the goal of the intervention is to trigger the potential in the system to find its own alternative solutions (to the symptomatic one that has been adopted). This catalytic effect may be achieved in two major ways, 1. by introducing new connections at those points at which the family appears to be stuck, and, 2. by introducing "time" when incompatible injunctions are operating simultaneously. The new connections are provided in the form of an opinion, a paradoxical comment or a systemic prescription. Time is usually introduced by prescribing a carefully prepared ritual which may or may not be accompanied by an opinion. To obtain an accurate impression of the complexity and precision of a good systemic intervention, a description of the case as well as the actual intervention is required. This would require considerable space so the reader is referred to their original articles (Selvini et al 1977, 1978b) for excellent examples of rituals and to their book (Selvini et al 1978a) for rich case material for which both types of intervention are used. The comments in this section will remain general.

A useful digression at this point may be to unpack the title of their book, "Paradox and Counterparadox". The Milan Team see the family coming for therapy as presenting the therapist with a basic paradox.[8] The family says in effect "Here is the individual who has a problem... and needs to change... but our family is fine... and we expect to remain the same". One of the basic tenets of systems theory is that a change in one part requires some complementary change in the whole. The therapist's task is to *counter* or go against the family's paradox. The therapist's response need not necessarily be paradoxical but often is. For instance, a very common intervention used by the Milan Team is to offer a systemic opinion and then prescribe no change. This injunction *not to change* is paradoxical in that the content message (at a lower level) contradicts the context message (at a higher level) which dictates that the therapist's function in the community is to help individuals and families to *change*. Thus the family's paradox is countered by the therapist's paradox.

The pathogenic and therapeutic potential of paradoxes and double binds need much more theoretical clarification and explanation. Hoffman (1981) offers an interesting balance theory to explain why Milan interventions work. Cronen et al (1982) offer an intriguing notion of strange loops to clarify paradoxes and point out that one must always take the third level into consideration. Further theoretical developments in this area may be expected in the next few years as a result of the stimulus provided by the striking effects of Milan type interventions. Be that as it may, it is useful to point out a crucial difference between the Milan paradox and other paradoxical strategies. In fact, the Milan Team only use one type of paradox: the prescription of no change in the context of change. This is very different than other paradoxes (often associated with the early Palo Alto group) which prescribe an escalation of symptomatic behaviours or thought. The latter approach is symptom focussed and based on the cybernetic principle of positive feedback. Asking patients (paradoxically) to intensify the symptom introduces the cybernetic problem of runaway which then activates some other negative feedback mechanism which in turn serves to control or reduce the original symptom. The Milan paradox does not target symptomatic behaviour per se, but the homeostatic tendency of the system which includes the symptomatic behaviour. "Homeostasis" is of course a circular process and hence the new connections made in the intervention must be circular and systemic.

A very important technique used by the Milan Team is *positive connotation* (Selvini et al 1978a, Chapter 7). When the behaviours of all family members including the symptomatic behaviour of the identified patient are connected in a circular pattern and connoted positively as "good for the family", the intervention is more readily accepted. Thus one important function of positive connotation is to enable the new information to gain entry into the family system. Another major function is that positive connotation serves to justify the prescription of no change. If a particular pattern of behaviour is construed as being "a good thing" then it follows that it should continue. However, an additional phrase like "for the time being" is always appended to a no change prescription. This phrase is extremely important since it implies that future patterns of behaviour may be different and also introduces an element of time. Again it is important to emphasize that what is being positively connoted is the homeostatic tendency which families experience as essential to their continued existence as systems.

However, the connections which are made in the intervention implicitly direct attention to alternative solutions and possible avenues for change. As a result, the therapeutic paradox is not binding but is implicitly open.

Positive connotation is not an essential component of every intervention but it does add an "aesthetic" element to the therapeutic process. It helps therapists and families overcome the prevailing negative stigma regarding mental health problems. It helps the therapist become more systemic in his thinking. Most significantly, however, it reduces the probability of a successful disqualification of the pragmatic truth offered in the therapist's opinion. The "strength" of an intervention tends to increase as one moves from offering a systemic opinion alone, to offering an opinion with positive connotation, to offering an opinion with positive connotation and prescribing no change. Additional variations of the opinion type of intervention include single vs. multiple punctuations (or truths) offered at the end of one session and the number of family members whose behaviours are included in the circular connections.

Prescribing a *ritual* refers to the type of intervention in which the therapist gives the family explicit instructions to carry out a carefully delineated task. Considerable attention is paid to providing details about what is to be done, the time, the day, the place, who should do what and in what sequence. With this intervention, the therapist is making a direct request for family members to behave in a precisely specified manner. On first glance, prescribing a ritual may appear to be incompatible with the Milan assumption that the family will discover its own solution to how they should relate to each other. However, the Milan Team do not insist that the ritual be carried out. It is often not important whether the task is done or not. It is the reaction of family members to the instructions and to the implicit ideas contained in the ritual that is the active therapeutic agent. At one point in the development of the Milan approach it was felt that the impact of the ritual derived from the fact that it implicitly challenged a covert rule or a myth in the system. These rules or myths were seen to be the basis for maintaining problematic patterns of behaviour. More recently, they have come to the conclusion that rituals introduce time into a timeless paradoxical system.[9] For example, one ritual used by the Milan Team specified that Monday was to be "mother and daughter day" and father should not interfere in their relationship, Tuesday would be "mother and father day" when daughter should not interfere, and Wednesday would be "father and daughter day" when mother was not to interfere. For the rest of the week the family should "behave spontaneously". In the past the team might have conceptualized this ritual as challenging a covert rule about a hidden alignment between daughter and father which was a source of great discomfort to the mother. Now they might say that by introducing the notion of a distinct and separate time for each dyad, the relationships between family members are more clearly delineated and defined.

An important group of interventions used by the Milan Team are those which target the therapist-family system. When it appears that resistance has emerged in the responses of the family to the therapist, an intervention may be devised to target the homeostatic pattern which has emerged. Examples include:

1.   taking the problem upon themselves a) within the team
     b) between family and therapist.

2. redefining therapy as not being therapy but as being family meetings or follow up interviews.
3. assuming a complementary position by a) admitting they have no opinion despite the family's cooperation, b) letting the family decide a particular issue, or c) declaring therapeutic impotence.
4. taking the initiative to terminate because therapy may be "too risky".

The Milan Team do not hesitate to emphasize their limitations or to admit to families that they have made a mistake in prior interventions. However, when they do, great care is taken to do so in a manner that is therapeutic. For instance, if the family returns saying that they were unable to perform the ritual for various reasons, the team would accept responsibility for having prescribed it too soon, or for having misunderstood the family. Thus the admission of therapeutic error becomes a crucial part of the next intervention.

V. CONCLUDING COMMENTS

Needless to say the Milan approach is not a simple or straightforward method of treatment. It is extremely complex and requires very sophisticated skills. Difficulties in applying the model commonly arise when therapists try to model themselves after the Milan Team by using interventions they have heard about before they have developed sufficient understanding of the underlying theory and epistemology. Every family situation is unique. In effect, a new intervention must be created for each family and because the family is always changing, for each session. The scope for making errors is enormous. If the results of an error are taken into consideration the intervention becomes a trial with resultant learning by the therapist, and the next intervention will be improved (Selvini et al 1978a, Chapter 5). As for the family, if the therapist misses the mark the family usually simply ignores the intervention and remains unchanged. Provided the therapist maintains his neutrality and avoids any heavy negative connotation, the family will "forgive him". At worst, the family will simply drop out of treatment with the impression that the therapist's ideas were rather strange and bizarre. These impressions would of course be correct if the therapist had in fact made erroneous connections and missed the point. The worst mistake of all is the failure to learn from mistakes by failing to take note of the responses of the family. This is most liable to occur when the therapist comes to believe that his hypotheses and opinions really are "true" in the classical sense. Interventions must always be regarded as methods of testing hypotheses which are more or less useful.

It would be erroneous to assume that a drop-out is always due to a mistaken intervention. Sometimes the therapeutic impact is too great and the rate of change too fast. The family simply requires more time to assimilate the new input and thus drops out. These cases are included among the group of "therapeutic drop-outs" which may constitute the majority of families exposed to this approach. When the therapist needs to initiate termination, this may be done abruptly by redefining the residual issues as no longer "psychiatric problems" but as "physiologic ones" (of normal growth and development) which the family is able to manage on its own. This is an effective normalization procedure.

One rather interesting feature of the Milan approach is that when a major transformation does occur, the family rarely attributes this to the therapy. The change is seen to be a result of their own actions and choices (which it is) or some other event outside the family. Sometimes families even become very frustrated and angry with the therapist for failing to give the advice they expected so they "had to do it on their own". The therapist never questions or challenges these perceptions - he only expresses puzzlement and perhaps some concern regarding the durability of the improvement. The gratification for the therapist comes from the realization that he may have had a possible catalytic effect. Participation in the team is of course an extremely valuable source of support for the therapist in this type of work.

Where does this new treatment method fit in relation to other approaches to family therapy and in the mental health field generally? At the present time, it is impossible to say. The fact that sometimes Milan interventions do appear to trigger dramatic changes in families (which are often "resistant" to other approaches) suggests that the approach is somehow reaching an extremely important aspect of mental process. Thus it should be taken seriously. On the other hand, there is grave danger in assuming that it *is* the best approach in any given situation. Much more experience and understanding of the Milan method will be necessary to determine in what situations it is the most useful and in what other situations other approaches are indicated. In keeping with the Milan philosophy, it is probably best to remain skeptical and to accept the Milan model as only *one* hypothesis regarding what type of thinking and action is most useful when conducting therapy with families.

NOTES

[1] This is not to imply that all therapists who use the ideas and techniques described in this paper have been influenced to do so specifically by the Milan Team. It does appear, however, that the members of the Milan Team have emerged as leaders in a "new wave" of experimentation which at the present time is rippling through the family therapy field.

[2] The author originally felt uncomfortable in preparing this chapter, thinking it was premature for him to do so. However, encouragement by the editor and an awareness of rapidly growing interest in the approach prompted him to proceed in the hope that the reader would tolerate some residual ambiguity and inconsistency.

[3] Verbal statement by the Milan Team at Calgary Workshop, March 1980.

[4] I am indebted to Dr. Benjamin Freedman for elucidating this distinction (formerly assistant professor of Medical Ethics at University of Calgary and currently Associate for Bioethics at the Westminster Institute for Ethics and Human Values, London, Canada).

[5] The author disagrees with the categorization of the Milan approach by Duncan Stanton (1980) as strategic.

[6] The use of a letter may be chosen deliberately as a method of dealing with the absent family member maneuver (Selvini et al 1978a, Chapter 13).

[7] This useful little "reflex" was first pointed out to me by John Burnham of the Charles Burns Clinic, Birmingham, England.

[8] The term paradox is defined here as a contradiction between meanings at different levels of logical type.

[9] This change in theoretical view was described by Dr. Luigi Boscolo in a personal communication, August, 1981.

REFERENCES

Bateson, G. **1972**. Steps to an Ecology of Mind. San Francisco: Chandler.

Bateson, G. **1979**. Mind and Nature: A Necessary Unity. New York: Dutton.

Cronen, V., **Johnson**, K. and **Lannamann**, J. **1982**. Paradoxes, Double Binds and Reflexive Loops: An Alternative Perspective. 21(1). *Family Process.*

Haley, J. **1963**. Strategies of Psychotherapy. New York: Grune and Stratton.

Haley, J. **1980**. Leaving Home. New York: McGraw-Hill.

Hoffman, L. **1981**. Foundations of Family Therapy: A Conceptual Framework for Systems Change. New York: Basic Books.

Pearce, B. and **Cronen**, V. **1980**. Communication, Action and Meaning: The Creation of Social Realities. New York: Praeger.

Selvini Palazzoli, M. **1974**. Self Starvation - From the Intrapsychic to the Transpersonal Approach to Anorexia Nervosa, Chauncer, London. Revised and extended edition (1978). New York: Aronson.

Selvini Palazzoli, M. **1980**. Why a Long Interval Between Sessions? The Therapeutic Control of the Family-Therapist Supra System, in Andolfi, M. and Zwerling, I. (Eds.) Chapter 11 in *Dimension of Family Therapy.* New York: The Guildford Press.

Selvini Palazzoli, M., **Boscolo**, L. **Cecchin**, G. and **Prata**, G. **1974**. The Treatment of Children Through the Brief Therapy of their Parents. 13(4). *Family Process.*

Selvini Palazzoli, M., **Boscolo**, L., **Cecchin**, G. and **Prata**, G. **1977**. Family Rituals: A Powerful Tool in Family Therapy. Family Process, Vol. 16, No. 4.

Selvini Palazzoli, M., **Boscolo**, L., **Cecchin**, G. and **Prata**, G. **1978a**. Paradox and Counterparadox. New York: Jason Aronson, Inc.

Selvini Palazzoli, M., **Boscolo**, L., **Cecchin**, G. and **Prata**, G. **1978b**. A Ritualized Prescription in Family Therapy: Odd Days and Even Days, Journal of Marriage and Family Counselling, Vol. 4, No. 3.

Selvini Palazzoli, M., **Boscolo**, L., **Cecchin**, G. and **Prata**, G. **1980a**. Hypothesizing - Circularity - Neutrality: Three Guidelines for the Conductor of the Session. Family Process, Vol. 19, No. 1.

Selvini Palazzoli, M., **Boscolo**, L., **Cecchin**, G. and **Prata**, G. **1980b**. The Problem of the Referring Person. 6(1). *Journal of Marital and Family Therapy.*

Shands, H.C. **1971**. The War With Words, The Hague - Paris: Mouton.

Stanton, M.D. **1981**. Strategic Approaches to Family Therapy, Chapter 10 in Handbook of Family Therapy, edited by Gurman, A. and Kniskern, D. New York: Brunner/Mazel.

Watzlawick, P., **Beavin**, J.H. and **Jackson**, D.D. **1967**. Pragmatics of Human Communication. New York: Horton.

CONTEXTUAL ISSUES
IN FAMILY PRACTICE

Family focused practice is emerging as an important interventive alternative in human services. Concommitant with the expanding application of family practice methods has come a heightened awareness of underlying concepts relating to the nature of families and to the dynamics of bringing change to a family system. This has resulted in the reconsideration of traditional human service assessment parameters and the emergence of alternative treatment objectives and procedures. In essence, the context of intervention has shifted from an emphasis on the individual person to an appreciation of the family system. The focus of change has expanded beyond individual behaviour to include inter-personal transactions.

Family focused intervention is framed by practitioners' conceptions of what constitutes a "family" and what are parameters that define adequate family functioning. Inherent to this understanding is the appreciation of social, environmental, and cultural forces that impact on the family system and set a context for its functioning. This section of our book highlights important contextual themes in the provision of family focused human services.

Lillian Esses and Ruth Rachlis ("Single Parent and Remarried Families: Reasons for Reconsidering Traditional Conceptual Models of the Family") draw attention to the serious limitations of traditional conceptualizations as to what constitutes "normal" family functioning and to the poor applicability of these concepts to non-traditional family forms. The special circumstances of "single parent" and "remarried" families are considered as two family groupings that are becoming more prevalent and that challenge traditional norms in evaluating family functioning. It becomes evident that values held by family practitioners are fundamental to the whole process of family focused intervention. Esses and Rachlis suggest that as a pre-requisite family practitioners must recognize their own value biases and consider how these impact on their engagement with alternative types of family groupings.

Appreciating the contextual implications of unique family systems is a theme which is central to the chapter on farm families prepared by George McDonald and Grant Dunfield ("Farm Families and Family Therapy"). Important distinctions are offered in regard to the special social and environmental realities of families residing in farm settings. The family practitioner working in farming communities must attend to contextual factors such as social isolation, the close inter-dependency of family members and the family's close collaboration in occupational tasks. McDonald and Dunfield consider the structural family therapy approach within the context of the farm family and offer case examples which highlight important themes from the structural frame of reference.

As one attends to contextual issues in family practice and adopts an ecological view of the family unit, the importance of social support systems and human networks become apparent. In the chapter on networks ("Social Networks in Family Therapy") Walter Driedger reviews the importance of human support systems and considers the implications of employing such networks both as the target of change and alternatively as the vehicle of change itself.

Divorce proceedings usually indicate the demise of a family unit. Escalating divorce rates in North America and the subsequent splintering of family units is a social concern that warrants careful consideration. Howard Irving ("Family Mediation: A Method for Helping Families Resolve Legal Disputes") identifies family mediation as an approach in assisting families who are proceeding towards a divorce. Family mediation seeks to ease the emotional and social stress inherent in divorce proceedings and offset the notion of fault and retribution that are created by a decision-making process that is rooted in the court-room setting. Divorce mediation is described as a rational process of negotiations which seeks equitable resolution of family disputes in terms of what is best for the children. Irving outlines basic principles and guidelines established in divorce mediation and details this methodology of co-operative conflict resolution.

Chapter 7

Single Parent and Remarried Families: Reasons for Reconsidering Traditional Conceptual Models of the Family

Lillian M. Esses, and Ruth Rachlis
University of Manitoba, Winnipeg

Family therapy is a process in which therapists engage with families to understand their interaction and dynamics, mutually define their current concerns and distresses and work to move the family towards an altered level of functioning. Differences in the degree of emphasis given to these three parts of the process are reflected in diverging theoretical frameworks that have been used to assess family structure and function along with pleas that assessment, in its traditional diagnostic sense, be abolished entirely (eg. Haley, 1971). However, most family therapists would argue that conceptualization is a necessary prerequisite to intervention and that one's theoretical base determines the hypotheses made, the goals set and the interventions carried out.

The purpose of this paper is to examine the various frameworks that have been used to understand, assess and treat the traditional nuclear family and to ascertain their relevance in both conceptualizing and dealing clinically with the ever-growing numbers of single parent and remarried families. Major structural and functional distinctions between these three family forms will be delineated and the therapeutic implications of using traditional schemata for examination and intervention with the latter two alternate family types will be assessed. Currently, widely accepted frameworks, such as the McMaster model (Epstein, Bishop and Levin, 1978) which have been developed and found useful for assessment and treatment of the traditional nuclear family, have been applied without much scrutiny to a variety of family types for lack of an alternative. It is the contention of the present authors that structural and functional differences between the traditional, single parent and remarried family are sufficient to require modification of contemporary schemas if they are to be equally useful for work with non-traditional family forms.

THEORETICAL MODELS IN FAMILY THERAPY: OUR CURRENT STATE OF KNOWLEDGE

The sociological study of the family and intervention with whole families began independently in the 1950's, but by the early 1970's both fields had developed similar theoretical constructs in their work (Broderick, 1971). The theories which have proven most beneficial have been the developmental, interactional, structure/functional and systems, and both sociologists and family therapists have attempted to integrate parts of these seemingly diverse conceptual models into a unified framework (Haley, 1973; Hill, 1971; Broderick, 1971). This has been accomplished by adopting the concept of history over time from the developmentalists, the concept of position, norms, task functioning, role cluster, and role differentiation from both the interactionists and structure/functionalists; and systems theory has provided a view of the family as a boundary-maintaining and equilibrium seeking system within a larger social context (Broderick, 1971; Hill, 1971).

The developmental life cycle approach to family studies (Duvall, 1971; Hill, 1971; Rodgers, 1974) based on the Eriksonian individual life cycle was first recognized by Haley (1973) as being a useful framework for family therapists to understand the phases of a family's developmental tasks, while taking into consideration the developmental needs and tasks of each of its members. Family structure, its boundary, its roles and functions change to accommodate each new phase of the life cycle determined by the number, ages and developmental process of the members. Stress in the system is said to occur during structural alterations which necessitate shifts in the interrelatedness of individuals. Haley (1973) claims that there is a relationship between stress in the family and symptom development in one of its members "Symptoms appear when there is a dislocation or interruption in the unfolding life cycle of a family or other natural group. The symptom is a signal that a family has difficulty in getting past a stage in the life cylce" (p.42). The assumption is that family members are unable or unskilled either to complete the "tasks" required in the past phase or to begin the new "tasks" demanded in the current stage.

The family developmental stages as originally conceptualized by Duval (1971) began with marriage and ended with the aged family, encompassing within its phases the birth, socialization and launching of children. The assumption was that barring hazardous events, a family typically proceeds through these stages in an orderly progression. Transition points in which a member entered or left the family placed new demands on the system in structural and functional organization. These transitions were attributed to normal events such as birth, death or launching of a member at age appropriate times, or hazardous events such as untimely or unexpected happenings.

Carter and McGoldrick (1980) suggest, however, that the life cycle frameworks developed up to this time are more applicable to the "normal" nuclear middle class family and offer the view that family formulations such as the divorced, separated and remarried ought to have supplementary phases added with new and additional developmental tasks defined. Culon (1980) also suggests that the applicability of current developmental models requires adaptation in working with the multiproblem poor family. Glick and Kessler (1974) claim that family task accomplishment is made more complex when basic food, shelter and clothing needs are problematic because of the family's limited resources. Most certainly this is an issue in single parent families where economic problems are evident.

A more comprehensive approach which identifies family tasks common to all families at any point in time (eg. provision of basic physical needs, development of marital/coalition, enculturation of offspring, maintenance of parental coalition and generational boundaries, adherence to appropriate sex-linked roles ((Lidz and Fleck, 1967))has greater potential as a framework for analysis of alternate family forms despite its stereotypical role allocation. This functional approach within family therapy has best been represented by the McMaster school and will be discussed from that perspective.

The McMaster family category schema was built on Parsons and Bales' (1955) structure/functional study of the family and was heavily influenced by Epstein and Westley's research (1969) "The Silent Majority". In this study, families of "problem-free" university students were analyzed and the assumption made that since these families functioned well, their organization was "right" and ought to be a goal to achieve in therapy with other families. The schema was and is an important contribution to a field which was, as early as a decade ago being practiced and accepted by many without adequate theoretical constructs. It defines family problems as existing either in the instrumental (mechanical aspects of living) or affective (emotional aspects of family life) areas.

The dimensions of the schema were defined as: 1) problem solving (instrumental and affective); 2) affective relationships; 3) affective involvements; 4) communication; 5) role allocation; 6) behaviour control; 7) autonomy; and 8) areas of psychopathology (Epstein lecture, 1974). Epstein presents postulates as to the range and quality of interaction which makes for effective family functioning. These postulates are reflective of an implicit value base regarding what constitutes health and non-health. They appear to be most applicable to traditional nuclear families, though today not all would agree that this normative grid applies even to this family type. For example, empathic involvement is presented as the most suitable and lack of involvement as least effective within the affective involvement dimension. The schema does not take into account how this may apply to a non-custodial parent who has casual involvement with a child, or a stepparent and stepchild who are at an early stage in their relationship and ought to be maintaining some distance. Similarly, within the role dimension, the original schema allocated stereotypical behavior to each of the parents. Father was to assume responsibility for being a successful breadwinner, making primary decisions and taking the ultimate authority position in the family. Mother's role was to assume responsibility for affective areas and to perform efficiently and happily as a homemaker and mother. A subsequent modification of the schema (Epstein, et. al., 1978) influenced by the changing social situation for women, defined these roles less rigidly and stated that what was important was the performance of these functions, responsibility for their allocation and accountability. It is therefore essential that family practitioners be aware of the value assumptions which underlie their orientation and that they make appropriate modifications when dealing with alternate forms such as single parents and remarried families as well as with nuclear families who may choose to organize and live their lives non-traditionally. Not only therapists but families themselves, can experience considerable distress as a consequence of identifying with traditional norms that are inappropriate to their structure.

Family organization or structure closely linked with family functioning has been analyzed by Kanter and Lehr (1975) and therapeutically utilized by the structuralists (Minuchin, Montalvo, Guerney, Rosman, and Schumer, 1967; Minuchin, 1974; Aponte, 1974) as their practice framework. Minuchin began his work with families of lower socioeconomic status (Minuchin et. al., 1967). Working with families of delinquent boys, mainly single parent and black, he and his colleagues subsequently developed and applied his techniques to middle class families (Minuchin, 1974) and to families in which there was a psychosomatic problem (Minuchin, Rosman and Baker, 1978). He conceptualized structural family therapy as "...a body of theory and techniques that approaches the individual in his social context. Therapy based on this framework is directed toward changing the organization of the family." (Minuchin, 1974, p.2.). He sees the key components of theoretical work as establishing boundary clarity between the individuals of the family (disengaged, clear, enmeshed) and between the various subsystems (parental, parent-child, sibling) and makes the explicit value judgement that a well-defined hierarchical executive system and age-appropriate distribution of power are necessary prerequisites of a well-functioning family.

The well-defined executive parental system has its roots in Haley's (1967) theory that systems (family or administrative) become pathological (and here he states that pathology also includes divorced) when "perverse triangles" are formed. These are defined as coalitions across generations or administrative ranks which are not acutely acknowledged. Haley (1967) makes the analogy between business and family: "The administrative levels in the hierarchy must be kept separate for the proper functioning of an organization" (p.17). He recognizes that research to test this hypothesis has major methodological problems, not the least of which is a precise definition for coalition, however, this hypothesis has been a major assumption underlying the structuralist approach.

In summary, then, many of the theoretical concepts for working with families have been developed by assessing adequate functioning of middle class families, defining a structure (the nuclear traditional family) which is organized to fulfill that function (Parsons and Bales, 1955; Bell and Vogel, 1968), and labelling alternate forms as unviable or deviant. Winch (1977) notes that family forms different from the traditional two or more adults and dependent children, require "considerable institutional support" and an alternate position for women in the economic social structure.

Our position is that we ought not to define a normative grid which we then impose on families. We must take into consideration societal changes regarding sex-role allocation, family mobility and trends in separation, divorce and remarriage. Contemporary concerns of families are related to their adaptation to alternate forms and structures, non-static family values and re-definition of appropriate task allocation throughout the membership. As therapists we ought to engage with families, knowing our own value biases in order to achieve a more objective stance which enables us to recognize the family's uniqueness. Families, no matter what their form, have many similarities in their history, structure and function. Their differences are normal if they are viewed within a wider context of familistic pluralism (Winch, 1977). We will examine the single parent and remarried families within the broadest structure/functional framework in order to identify the special issues faced by each.

THE SINGLE PARENT FAMILY:
A DEMAND ON THE SYSTEM TO RESTRUCTURE

The previous section presented the major theoretical models utilized by family therapists in assessing and intervening with families. While the models do make a contribution to specific aspects of conceptualizing the family (ie. development over time, its functioning, organization and structure), cautious judgement ought to be utilized in their universal application to all families. This section will examine the structural and functional characteristics of the single parent family that ought to be considered in working with this family type. The analysis will be limited to those that develop through separation and divorce and not through death of a spouse or never married situation. Many of the same dynamics do apply, however.

The 1976 Canadian census data show (Statistics Canada, 1979) over half a million single parent families in Canada, an increase of over 80,000 between the 1971 & 1976 census. Eighty three percent of these were headed by females. These statistics indicate that four out of five single persons remarry and that one half of these remarriages also end in separation or divorce. The remarriage rate, particularly for women, has declined since 1972, however, this does not take into consideration the "living together" households which one U.S. study indicates has increased by 800% in the last decade (Giele, 1979).

It is important to note that while 80% of divorced parents do remarry, most custodial parents spend two to three years as a single parent family unit before doing so, and therefore the single parent status represents more than a transitory phase of development (Keshet, 1980). During this phase, major restructuring occurs in the relationship, roles, and functioning of all members in the old and new family system. Wallerstein and Kelly (1979) state this restabilization process takes 3½ years for women and 2½ years for men. McGoldrick and Carter (1980) suggest that separation and divorce which produces severe dislocation in the family life cycle and requires additional steps for the family to proceed developmentally, actually begins with the parent's decision to separate prior to dissolution of the family.

Major structural changes result as a consequence of moving from a two person to a one person executive parental system. The diminished resources resulting from this restructuring must nevertheless provide for a full range of instrumental and affective needs of all family members. Co-parenting or joint custody suggested as a solution by some (eg. Gatley and Koulack, 1979) has been shown to be practical and effective only under certain conditions (Abarbanel, 1979) and does not compensate for the fact that the two parents no longer share the same space or simultaneously perform functions related to caring for children (Keshet, 1980).

Brandwein, Brown, and Fox (1974) identified four major areas of family functioning which are affected by the changes in organization and resources resulting from separation: 1) economic functions; 2) authority; 3) domestic responsibility (child care and housework); and 4) social and psychological supports. They claim that the adaptation and role restructuring required for effective functioning are impeded by two interrelated societal attitudes. The first, is the stigmatization of lone-parent females who traditionally derive their status from their husbands (Winch, 1977) and consequently are seen as positionless or alternatively as the "gay divorcee". The second, which would apply equally to men and women, is the difficulty of role performance in areas traditionally assigned to one or another sex, for example, male adults taking responsibility for child care and household tasks and females assuming authority roles both within the family and between the family and community.

Empirical research demonstrates that economic functioning of most single parents is severely affected. This is born out by 1976 Canadian census data which places them at the lower-end of the income distribution scale (Statistics Canada, 1979). Poverty appears to be both cause and effect of divorce since divorce is more prevalent in poor families (Brandwein et. al., 1974) and poverty is predominant in the 300,000 lone-parent families with children 17 years of age and under (Statistics Canada, 1979). For the one out of five lone-parents on Social Assistance in Canada, income levels are well below the poverty levels (Adams, Cameron, Hill and Penz, 1971). In the U.S., one half of lone-parent females depend on welfare payments as their main source of income (Wattenberg and Reinhardt, 1979). Maintenance payments, in addition to being an uncertain source of income, are paid by only one third of ex-spouses after the first year (Brandwein, et. al., 1974).

This lowered income creates considerable stress as the family adapts to a drop in consumption, change in housing (usually to poorer accommodation and neighborhoods), and the often resulting feeling of isolation and anomie (Brandwein et. al., 1974). In Canada in 1976, 50% of all lone-parents moved from one house to another (Statistics Canada, 1978). Mobility, which is itself a stress, also affects the availability of support networks for both parents and children (Wattenberg and Reinhardt, 1979).

The degree of change in domestic responsibility will vary depending on whether the custodial parent assumes a work-for-pay in addition to an in-home role. This latter functioning places an extra instrumental and emotional burden on the custodial parent and availability of community resources such as day care, lunch and after school, and homemaker programs become crucial (Winch, 1977). Their availability is dependent on government policy and resources, and regulations have been discriminatory with certain programs more readily available to one sex than to the other (Brandwein et. al., 1974).

Assistance received from extended family in domestic tasks, particularly from grandparents varies widely. Some studies and anecdotal reports from professionals working with single parents, state fathers are more readily offered help with childcare and housekeeping than single mothers (Beal, 1980; Brandwein et. al., 1974). Typically, however, black and native single parent women may have a mother living in the home who assumes many of those functions. In fact, some of the original family therapy literature assumed that this structure was problematic and led to delinquency in children of black families because of unclear parental roles and boundaries (Minuchin et. al., 1967).

Single parent mothers are often faced with the double-bind of staying home, receiving public assistance and having inadequate income or going to work and being concerned about their children's care. Wallerstein and Kelly (1979) state, however, that children of working sole support parents do not present clinically with any more difficulties than children of stay-at-home parents, providing they are available to the child during their time away from work.

Little research is available to provide information as to what constitutes appropriate sharing of the household tasks by children themselves. Heatherington, Cox and Cox (1978) found that households in which divorce had occurred, had greatly increased household disorganization including reduced consistency of discipline and the holding of fewer expectations for mature behavior for children. However, Keshet (1980) claims that children of single parents participate more in decision making and are often required to take care of the house, themselves, and each other. This mutual dependence, she states, results in greater equality between parent and children. This more egalitarian action may create difficulties for female-headed single parent families, particularly with regard to the mother's authority position within the family. Brandwein et. al., (1974) attribute the single mother's difficulty with discipline and behavioral control to society's non-ascription of this role to women. Keschet (1980) points out that single parent households tend to develop relationships which are more intimate and of a companionship nature. The models discussed in the introduction postulate that a heirarchical structure with parents "in charge" is the most effective way for households to be managed. As already mentioned, this is a severe limitation in applying traditional frameworks to the single parent family.

Whether the presence of an authority figure and an organization along democratic lines within the family is problematic, has not been adequately studied. There is some evidence, however, that indicates that a "head of a household" with power and status is important for the family in its negotiation with external systems such as schools, credit granting agencies, neighbours, landlords, and social institutions (Brandwein et. al., 1974). Single mothers can develop skills which enhance their gatekeeping abilities and there are group programs that have been designed for women on welfare with this goal in mind. Attitudinal change in society towards viewing women as competent authority figures is also required.

Epstein et. al., (1978) postulate that a family which has difficulty with instrumental functions will automatically have difficulty in the affective area. Research to support this assumption is not available. The number of single parent families who do manage and do not present to agencies with difficulties despite the fact that the single parent is the focus around which both instrumental and affective tasks are accomplished (Beal, 1980), would appear to disconfirm that particular hypothesis. Wattenberg and Reinhardt (1979) call for further study on those that do manage and argue that greater understanding ought to be developed as to how and why single families endure and what national economic and social policies need to be put in place to improve functioning of single parent families rather than to focus on their deviance.

The emotional impact of divorce on children of middle-class, single parents whose financial resources to deal with instrumental tasks are more adequate, has been researched by Wallerstein and Kelly (Kelly and Wallerstein, 1976; Wallerstein and Kelly, 1974, 1979). Dealing with affective issues has been viewed as an additional developmental task within the family life cycle of single parent families by Carter and McGoldrick (1980). Of primary importance, is dealing with the loss of an absent spouse/parent, and for all members of the old system to learn new ways of relating to each other. According to their view, optimum functioning is achieved under conditions where the custodial parent is willing to maintain parental contact with ex-spouse and extended family through flexible visiting arrangements, and is motivated to rebuild a new social network. The necessity for ongoing contact of children with the non-custodial parent has been supported by Wallerstein and Kelly (1979) in their research with children. They contend that children are less troubled in those families in which relationships with non-custodial parents are preserved. Keshet (1980), agreed with this goal, but identifies the dilemma, particularly for the custodial parent, of becoming the central figure of a number of subsystems each with different goals. She/he is expected on the one hand, to break from the ex-spouse, establish new social and emotional support systems and to parent independently; and on the other hand, to continue the communication with the ex-spouse in a co-parenting relationship. Not surprisingly, divided loyalty and role-conflict (Boszormenyi-Nagy and Spark, 1973) are significant themes of separated families.

Reconstruction of emotional and social support systems for all members of the single parent family is a necessary component in establishing adequate effective functioning. Wallerstein and Kelly (1979) state that children generally do best when the boundary between the single parent household and others is clear. They earlier (1977) stated, however, that preschool children who are able to reach out and use the support of teachers and other adults in their environment faired better than those children who could not do so. The research does not clarify whether these children were at baseline, sufficiently trustworthy, and safe with adults to risk the reaching out process. In a later analysis of the same data (1979), they concluded that children's self-esteem which is positively correlated with degree of contact with the absent parent, is a component in how well they adapt to the traumatic separation process. Woody (1978), building on needs of children in divorce as identified by the research, suggests that mutual aid and support groups for children are useful for prevention of problems.

Groups for separated and divorced spouses have been found to be helpful in aiding them to deal with loss of self-esteem, feelings of failure, loss of old friends, increased responsibility for the custodial parent and loss of children by the non-custodial parent. Resolution of these issues with the help of adult support systems can prevent either projection of unresolved business onto children or inappropriate dependence on them. Walker and Messinger (1980), postulate that more open boundaries between the family and external systems is advisable.

In summary, many single parent families experience major changes in their environment, their functioning in both instrumental and affective areas and the resources and roles allocated to perform these functions. The relationships within all the subsystems of the family prior to and after separation undergo metamorphosis. The process is a stressful one for all concerned and societal and professional attitudes ought not further increase the pressure by clinging to traditional models which lead to deviant labeling. Practitioners need to understand the structure and demands on single parent families in order to effectively and appropriately assess and intervene with them. This family form is here to stay. We need to respond to the successful establishment of the single parent household and work with them as a viable family system in their own right.

REMARRIED FAMILIES: A NEW PHASE IN THE FAMILY LIFE CYCLE

It is not absurd to suggest that the remarried family may become the most prevalent living unit to be found in North American households of the future. While in the past, death of a spouse was the most frequent situation that led to formation of a stepfamily, nowadays remarriage is in most instances preceded by divorce (Jacobson, 1979). Currently we can estimate that approximately one-fifth of all marriages in Canada involve at least one divorced person (Statistics Canada, 1975). This figure has already been exceeded in the United States and when rates of remarriage following death of a spouse as well as second remarriages were included in calculations, 1975 data indicated that there were 25 million stepparents in the U.S. with a million being added yearly (Roosevelt and Lofas, 1976; Visher and Visher, 1978).

This complex, ever-growing and as yet poorly understood stepfamily system, sometimes referred to as "remarried", "combined", "blended", or "reconstituted", suffers from erroneously being viewed as a second attempt at nuclear family living for lack of an adequate new conceptual framework (Visher and Visher, 1978). As practitioners gain a better appreciation of the stepfamily, its structure and particular problems of adjustment, it becomes apparent that current models for understanding family functioning require modification. At present, some major factors which continue to impede the process of reconceptualization include: entrenchment in existing models, insufficient knowledge regarding stepfamily dynamics, negative distortions which have been evoked by folklore (Jacobson, 1979; Schulman, 1972; Visher and Visher, 1979) and failure to recognize the remarried family's elements as outcomes of a developmental history through more familiar family forms (McGoldrick and Carter, 1980). In this section, the unique features of remarried families will be examined and implications for intervening and assessing this family type using traditional frameworks will be critically examined.

A first consideration in examining the remarried family is recognition of the developmental history that has led to its formation. While contemporary family therapists differ dramatically in the degree of emphasis given to historical and developmental issues, it becomes of utmost importance to acknowledge these dimensions when dealing with stepfamilies. Every remarried spouse once struggled to build a viable nuclear family and while he or she may speak casually of the interim without a partner as "between my marriages", most ex-spouses with children have spent considerable time restructuring and solidifying into a single family unit prior to what is often a jolt into stepfamily life (Keshet, 1980). A number of recent investigations (e.g. Kleinman, Rosenberg and Whiteside, 1979; McGoldrick and Carter, 1980; Visher and Visher, 1979) strongly suggest that difficulties encountered during remarriage adjustment are triggered by unresolved issues preceding stepfamily formation.

The single parent subsystem is not easily integrated into the stepfamily because as is evident from the above discussion, it has developed into a self-sufficient unit with new organization and structure and a strong outer boundary. Regardless of whether the spouse entering a remarriage has children of his/her own and in addition these children join the new living unit, all members of the remarried family carry into these new relationships emotional baggage of unfinished business from important past relationships. According to McGoldrick and Carter (1980), "So complex is the process whereby the remarried family system stabilizes and regains its forward developmental thrust that we have come to think of this process as adding a whole additional phase to the family life cycle for those involved" (p.265).

These authors have attempted to delineate developmental tasks that must be resolved in order for the remarried family to become a mature, stable system capable of meeting the emotional needs of its members. It is speculated that failure to deal with these common transitional issues makes it impossible to effectively problem solve difficulties arising within the newly formed family unit and may be responsible for the development of symptoms in a family member (Kleinman, et. al., 1979).

As much as the issue may be denied by spouses entering remarriage, a major structural difference between intact, nuclear families and stepfamilies is that in the latter case, the previous spouse of one of the marital partners is often alive, well and living nearby. Mourning the loss of the previous family which may be emotionally reactivated at the point of remarriage, appears to be a necessary and primary prerequisite to successful remarriage adjustment (Kleinman, et. al., 1979). For the divorced parent, this often requires dealing with the loss of a previously intimate and nurturant spousal relationship and resolving antagonism sufficiently to enable cooperative parenting so that children need not be the vehicles of leftover hostility torn by loyalty conflicts. For the child, the process commonly involves a painful, gradual giving-up of the hope for parental reunion and resumed intimacy with the absent biological parent. This fantasy is difficult for children to let go of and they may easily view living as a single parent household as a temporary state until their parents can "patch things up". A parent's remarriage not only forces children to face the reality of divorce but may result in significant changes in the relationship between children and absent biological parent which cannot help but have implications for the new stepparent's role (Keshet, 1980).

Guilt can be an especially difficult issue for the spouse who has left children of a first marriage and may result in a futile attempt at forced intimacy with stepchildren which is either premature or inappropriate (McGoldrick and Carter, 1980). Remarried families are formed against a background of old scars and past failures which can result in the unrealistic expectation of "instant intimacy" (Visher and Visher, 1979) and denial of hostile feelings referred to by Goldstein (1974) as "pseudomutuality". According to McGoldrick and Carter (1980), failure to resolve intense relationship issues of the first family, the wish for premature closure to end ambiguity and pain and inability to give up the ideal of the intact nuclear family are good predictors of difficulty in making the transition to remarriage.

Thus family therapists need to be alert to these developmental issues, the remarried family's difficulty in acknowledging them and the necessity of dealing with them early in therapy if the stepfamily is to integrate into a stable growth-promoting system. As much as the stepfamily may press for assistance with child discipline, a common presenting problem (Fast and

Cain, 1966; Schulman, 1972), it may be necessary for the therapist to first help free the family emotionally from important "unfinished business' and unrealistic expectations. Consequently, assessment of this particular family type, demands that practitioners both depart and expand on traditional schemes of evaluation. When assessing stepfamilies, the following questions need to be foremost in the therapist's mind: To what extent has grief concerning separation from former spouses been acknowledged and worked through? Is this stepfamily trapped by myths of "instant love" and "the re-created nuclear family?" To what extent are family members able to acknowledge ambivalence, live with temporary ambiguity and accept compromise? Structural and functional characteristics of the remarried family system differ markedly from both the traditional and single parent family and need to be understood if effective intervention is to take place.

In the previous section, it was pointed out that the single parent family encounters economic, authority, domestic and socioemotional problems as a consequence of a deficit in structure and inadequate societal resources to relieve this deficit. In contrast, many of the difficulties experienced by remarried families may be conceptualized in terms of structural excess and confusion (Zimmerman, 1980). The remarried family is forced to become a more open system in order to accommodate new members. The consequent structural shifts and confusions that inevitably occur in defining boundaries and roles have a dramatic impact on family functioning.

Structural aspects concerning who belongs in the remarried family system and how members are related to one another may include issues of membership, boundaries, space, time, authority, and roles (Visher and Visher, 1979). As Sager, Walker, Brown, Crohn and Rodstein (1981) point out, in stepfamilies, even the most basic aspect of membership is open to interpretation. Stepfamily members themselves may not agree on who is "in" and "out" and the sheer increase in the number of newly acquired members increases the complexity of relationships with which the family must cope. Typically there is at least one biological parent outside of the stepfamily unit, children hold membership in two households and there is an extra set of grandparents (Visher and Visher, 1979). Thus, the remarried household may be involved with a host of significant others, former spouses, grandparents, stepgrandparents, aunts, uncles, all of whom may be referred to as the "metafamily" system (Sager et al., 1981). This vast array of extended family with whom ties are maintained can either provide support or reinforce a tendency toward splitting (Kleinman et al., 1979).

Inevitably boundaries of the remarried family are more ambiguous and permeable than is the case in traditional and single parent families. While in physical, geographical terms, family membership may be easily discernable, the degree of physical closeness and intimacy that stepfamily and metafamily members share with one another, that is, psychological boundaries, may be very obscure (Walker and Messinger, 1979). Remarriage is often an abrupt shift leaving both stepfamily and kin little time for preparation and accommodation. The decision is made by two single adults, not the family as a unit, which makes the process of negotiating new relationships very difficult. In addition, the locus of parental authority, economic subsistence and filial affection often involves two households. Even if the absent biological parent is dead, he or she may be very much alive psychologically.

According to McGoldrick and Carter (1980), boundary difficulties encountered by the remarried family can encompass issues of membership (Who are the "real" members of the family?), space (What space is mine? Where do I really belong?), authority (Who is really in charge of discipline? money? decisions?) and time (Who gets how much of my time and how much do I get of theirs?).

Upon entering the stepfamily, the single parent subsystem must give up some of its special intimacy and companionship (Walker and Messinger, 1979). The new two member executive system often results in a redistribution of power whereby the adult system becomes more powerful and the children, less so (Keshet, 1980). Jealousy between parent-children subsystems and among stepsiblings is a frequent source of stress in stepfamilies (Schulman, 1972). In addition, less well-defined generational and sexual boundaries may be more easily trespassed (Sager et al., 1981). A problem rarely dealt with explicitly is the lowered "incest taboo" (Goldstein, 1974) most pronounced in the stepfather - stepdaughter relationship. Felt sexual attraction need not be acted upon to create considerable tension and may become masked by pseudohostility.

Related to the absence of well-defined boundaries is the role confusion that characterizes most newly formed remarriages. Members are often caught in the confusing state of not knowing what to expect, do or feel. In the absence of societal guidelines and prescriptions, each remarried family must generate its own behaviour codes and norms (Sager et al., 1981). Walker and Messinger (1979) contend that remarriage family roles differ from nuclear family roles in two major respects: degree of clarity and the degree to which roles are "ascribed" as opposed to needing to be "achieved". The most acute problems of role uncertainty involve the relationship between stepparents and stepchildren which accounts for the proliferation of literature dealing with this issue. Goldstein (1974) talks of the "parental role freeze" as the most typical and predictable dilemma of remarried families. Fast and Cain (1966) argue that as much as a stepparent may achieve the role of nurturer, provider and authority figure within the stepfamily, that he or she is always also to some extent a "nonparent". Much has been written about the loyalty conflicts that result for children if the influence of the absent biological parent is denied.

Roles most appropriate to remarriage household members cannot be prescribed. Variations in the age, sex and number of children, whether children of both spouses live together, desires for intimacy on the part of both stepparents and stepchildren and how much the biological parent is willing to yield to involvement from the new spouse, are all factors which make every remarried household unique (Walker and Messinger, 1979). Aldous (1974) suggests that members need to engage in "role making", experimenting with different roles until the best fit evolves. This, however, requires time and the tolerance to withstand instability which can be very stressful.

As is evident, the complexities in structure that result from the merging of subsystems into the remarried unit can create considerable strain and emotional conflict. Keshet (1980) analyzes stepfamily and metafamily structure according to its various subsystems and points out that difficulties in remarried families often arise as a function of conflict between the goals of two subsystems. She stresses the importance of recognizing the pivotal role of the person who is torn as a consequence of simultaneously being a member of two subsystems which are in competition with each other. Other authors have likened stepfamily formation to the merging of two corporations (Visher and Visher, 1979) or gaining dual citizenship (Walker and Messinger, 1979) in an attempt to more fully appreciate its structural complexities.

Given the structural characteristics of the remarried family, to what extent is this system able to carry out basic family functions of providing material and emotional support for its members and socializing its children?

When a remarriage takes place, people with different needs, expectations and life-styles are thrown together. Unlike a first family situation, patterns are more solidified and ingrained. Often the ramifications of bringing together two major subsystems with different histories, rituals and rules of operating are not anticipated. Inevitably conflicts arise over various aspects of day-to-day functioning as a consequence of differences in previous learning and current needs. Stepfamily members may disagree on a number of issues including discipline, handling of finance, eating habits, division of labour, household rules and obligations, use of alcohol and drugs, rules around sexual behaviour and expression of affect (Johnson, 1980). Clashes in any of these areas may create considerable stress if left unresolved.

Thus far, there are few sound methodological studies that can offer us more than descriptive information on aspects of family function that prove most problematic for stepfamilies and factors that make for successful adaptation (Walker, et. al., 1977). Bowerman and Irish (1962) measured intrafamilial feelings and conflicts and found that stepfamilies experience more stress, ambivalence and less cohesiveness than intact families. Messinger's (1976) study of remarried couples suggests that the greatest source of emotional upheaval is children followed closely by financial problems.

Many clinicians (e.g. Fast and Cain, 1966; Schulman, 1972) report that when stepfamilies request clinical intervention, the primary patient is the child. Research attempts to assess the effects of remarriage on child adjustment are as yet inconclusive. There are two large scale studies, however, (Langner and Michael, 1963) which report the mental health consequences for children living in a remarried family to be worse than living in a family broken by bereavement or divorce without remarriage; and both situations to be worse than living in an unbroken family. It appears that acquiring a stepmother and that adjustment to a stepparent is generally better if the stepparent replaces a divorced rather than a dead parent (Bowerman and Irish, 1962).

Clinical studies suggest that stepmothers may experience conflict in the remarried family as a consequence of having to cope with the "wicked stepmother" myth, attempts to be overly nurturant with stepchildren and to take it upon themselves to try to make everybody happy, inability to express feelings of ambivalence, jealousy and anger and insufficient husband support (Visher and Visher, 1979). Difficulties for the stepfather tend to revolve around his rights and role in disciplining the children. It appears that a stepfather who attempts to take on parental behavioural control without first establishing a friendship bond with his stepchildren, is doomed to failure (Stern, 1978).

Visher and Visher (1979) identify major issues that children must deal with in adjusting to the remarried family. Dealing with feelings of loss and fantasies of natural parents reuniting have already been mentioned. Additional difficulties may involve divided loyalties, membership in two households, less available time and attention from the natural parent and having to deal with a new adult, not necessarily by choice. There is some suggestion that older children have a harder time adjusting to the remarriage arrangement (Langner and Michael, 1963). This may be due to greater resistance in learning new roles and accepting stepparent disciplining, the stress of sexual issues and/or conflict between the adolescent's striving for independence and the stepfamily's push for cohesiveness (McGoldrick and Carter, 1980). Thus each member of the stepfamily, parent and child, faces unique adjustment problems that affect the others and emotional support and understanding may not always be available or attainable.

It is generally agreed, that if the remarried family is to build firm, supportive relationships, the marital couple's relationship is critical (Kleinman, et. al. 1979; Sager et al., 1981; Visher and Visher, 1979). Couples often find it less stressful to focus on problems with or differences over the children than on other conflicts that need to be resolved between them. Disagreements concerning child management can mask fundamental questions of commitment and the unspoken threat of another possible rejection and loss. This can put a great deal of pressure on newly remarried spouses who may be experiencing inceased vulnerability as a consequence of previous marriage break-up and who now often lack sufficient time and privacy to fulfill their own needs.

Research studies have demonstrated that higher socioeconomic status is related to better stepfamily functioning (Bowerman and Irish, 1962; Langner and Michael, 1963). Simon (1964) suggests that this may be due to the fact that lower class individuals tend to remarry primarily to replace an absent parent which may prove disastrous. Regardless of social class, however, conflicts over money can create tension as it does in all families. The distinction is that in most remarried families, there is a financial crunch and the source and distribution of monies can take on strong emotional overtones (Visher and Visher, 1979). Child support payments may be used as a battle ground between ex-spouses. A stepfather who supports step-children may feel that he has a right to greater authority in decision-making and disciplining. A stepparent may find himself/herself under tremendous burden in attempting to support two sets of children. Divorce is an expensive proposition and inevitably the standard of living is subsequently lowered.

In summary, recognition of stepfamily formation as a part of a developmental process and attention to its unique structural complexities and consequent difficulties in functioning as a system are essential to effective intervention with remarried families in distress. Unfortunately, as Visher and Visher (1978) point out: "Much of the counseling of stepparents by professionals is unproductive because the therapist, unable to step outside the nuclear family model of interaction, considers that the original nuclear family exists or that the family needs to operate within the nuclear family model" (p. 254).

Therapists must begin to modify and expand current assessment models and their accompanying value base if they hope to be able to assist stepfamilies in their struggle toward achieving a viable alternative family form.

SUMMARY AND CONCLUSIONS

Family therapy, though still a field in its infancy, has made tremendous strides in the last three decades. An aspect, however, that has always impeded progress, is that practice has invariably preceeded the development of sound conceptual frameworks. Though no uniformly agreed upon model currently exists, the development, interactional, structure/functional and systems approach have each offered valuable theoretical constructs to provide a more comprehensive appreciation of family dynamics and therapeutic intervention. It is becoming apparent, however, as the numbers of single parent and remarried families continue to increase that these models, based on traditional middle class norms of the nuclear family, do not provide an adequate conceptual framework for work with alternate family forms and that failure to recognize this fact may result in negative therapeutic outcomes.

The single parent family often experiences marked structural deficits, financial decline and diminished resources. Boundaries within the system may become more diffuse while the family's outer boundary strengthens in an attempt to cope with emotional and instrumental tasks under these conditions. Increased difficulty in carrying out basic family functions such as economic support, domestic and childcare responsibilities, authority and provision of social and emotional support is inevitable. Stress is further enhanced by the need to work through painful transitional issues involving parent absence and consequent restructuring of relationships. Traditional norms regarding role allocation, affective involvement, autonomy and behavioural control may not only be impossible to maintain but attempts to do so may hinder successful adaptation.

Similarly, the remarried family presents with structural characteristics and problems of adjustment that warrant re-evaluation of current conceptual schemas by family practitioners. In this case, structural overload is manifested in confusion over family membership, space, authority, and roles and the family functions that seem to be affected most are economics and child management. Affective problems accompanying the restructuring process may themselves be considerable and are compounded by developmental issues surrounding mourning the loss of the previous family. Above all, the stepfamily must be able to handle a good deal of ambivalence and ambiguity and must be able to let go of the intact nuclear family as the ideal.

Not only lay people but therapists as well, must be able to give up deeply ingrained stereotypes of what constitutes an intact family and must themselves be able to tolerate a society wherein no guidelines exist for defining a "normal" family.

REFERENCES

Abarbanel, A. 1979. Shared parenting after separation and divorce. 19(2). American Journal of Orthopsychiatry, 320-329.

Adams, I., Cameron, W., Hill, B., and Penz, P. 1971. The Real Poverty Report. Edmonton: M.G. Hurtig Limited.

Aldous, J. 1974. The making of family roles and family change. 23. The Family Coordinator, 231-235.

Aponte, H. 1974. Organizing treatment around the family's problems and their structural base. 48(2). Psychiatric Quarterly, 209-222.

Beal, E.W. 1980. Separation, divorce and single-parent families. In E. Carter & M. McGoldrick (Eds.), The Family Life Cycle: A Framework for Family Therapy. New York: Gardner Press Inc.

Bell, N. and Vogel, E. (Eds.) 1968. A Modern Introduction to the Family. Glencoe, Illinois: The Free Press.

Boszormenyi-Nagy, I. and Spark, G.M. 1973. Invisible Loyalties: Reciprocity in Intergenerational Family Therapy. Hagerstown, Missouri: Harper and Row.

Bowerman, C.E. and Irish, D.P. 1962. Some relationships of stepchildren to their parents. 24. Marriage and Family Living, 113-131.

Brandwein, R.A., Brown, C.A., and Fox, E.M. 1974. Women and children last: the social situation of divorced mothers and their families. 36. Journal of Marriage and the Family, 498-514.

Broderick, C.B. 1971. Beyond the five conceptual frameworks: A decade of development in family theory. 33. Journal of Marriage and the Family, 139-159.

Canada, Statistics Canada. 1977. Vital Statistics, Volume II: Marriages and Divorces, 1975. Ottawa, Ministry of Industry, Trade and Commerce.

Canada, Statistics Canada. 1978. Supplementary Bulletin: Housing and Families, Lone Parent Families. 1976. Authority of the Ministry of Industry, Trade and Commerce.

Canada, Statistics Canada. 1979. Single Parent Families in Canada, 1977. Consumer Income and Expenditure Division.

Carter, E.A. and McGoldrick, M. 1980. The family life cycle and family therapy: an overview: In E.A. Carter and M. McGoldrick (Eds.), The Family Life Cycle: A Framework for Family Therapy. New York: Gardner Press Inc.

Colon, F. 1980. The family life cycle of the poor family. In E. Carter and M. McGoldrick (Eds.), The Family Life Cycle: A Framework for Family Therapy. New York: Gardner Press Inc.

Duvall, E.R. 1971. Family Therapy. Fourth Edition, Philadelphia: Lippincott.

Epstein, N. 1974. Family Therapy. Lecture at seminar on family therapy, Saskatoon, Saskatchewan, March 21, 22.

Epstein, N.B., Bishop, D.S. and Levin, S. 1978. The McMaster model of family functioning. Journal of Marriage and Family Counseling, 19-31.

Epstein, N. and Westley, W.A. 1960. The Silent Majority: Families of Emotionally Healthy College Students. San Francisco: Jossey Bass.

Fast, I. and Cain, A.C. 1966. The stepparent role: potential for disturbances in family functioning. 36. American Journal of Orthopsychiatry, 485-491.

Gatley, D. and Koulack, D. 1979. Single Father's Handbook: A Guide for Separated and Divorced Fathers. Garden City, N.Y.: Anchor Press.

Giele, J.Z. 1979. Social policy and the family. 5. Ann. Rev. Sociology, 275-302.

Glick, I.D. and Kessler, D.R. 1974. Marital and Family Therapy. New York: Grune and Stratton.

Goldstein, H.S. 1974. Reconstituted families: the second marriage and its children. 48. Psychiatric Quarterly, 433-440.

Haley, J. 1971. Approaches to family therapy. In J. Haley (Ed.), Changing Families: Family Therapy Reader. New York: Grune & Stratton, 227-236.

Haley, J. 1967. Toward a theory of pathological systems. In G.H. Zuk and I. Boszormenyi-Nagy (Eds.), Family Therapy and Disturbed Families. Palo Alto, Cal.: Science and Behavior Books, Inc., 11-27.

Haley, J. 1973. Uncommon Therapy: The Psychiatric Techniques of Milton Erickson, M.D. New York: W.W. Norton & Company Inc.

Hetherington, E.M., Cox, M. and Cox, R. 1978. The aftermath of divorce. In J.H. Stephens Jr. and M. Matthews (Eds.), Mother-Child/Father-Child Relationships. Washington, D.C., National Association for Education of Young Children.

Hill, R. 1971. Modern systems theory and the family: A confrontation. 10(5). *Social Science Information,* 7-26.

Jacobson, D.S. 1979. Stepfamilies: myths and realities. 24(3). *Social Work,* 202-207.

Johnson, H.C. 1980. Working with stepfamilies: principles of practice. 25(4). *Social Work,* 304-308.

Kanter, D. and Lehr, W. 1975. *Toward a Theory of Family Process.* New York: Harper and Row.

Kelly, J.B. and Wallerstein, J.S. 1976. The effects of parental divorce: Experience of the child in early latency. 46. *American Journal of Orthopsychiatry,* 20-32.

Keshet, J.K. 1980. From separation to stepfamily: a subsystem analysis. 1(4). *Journal of Family Issues,* 516-532.

Kleinman, J., Rosenberg, E. and Whiteside, M. 1979. Common developmental tasks in forming reconstituted families. 5(2). *Journal of Marital and Family Therapy,* 79-86.

Langner, T.S. and Michael, S.T. 1963. *Life Stress and Mental Health.* New York: Free Press.

Lidz, T., Fleck, S. 1967. Some explored and partially explored sources of psychopathology. In G.H. Zuk and I. Boszormenyi-Nagy (Eds.), *Family Therapy and Disturbed Families.* Palo Alto, California: Science and Behavior Books, Inc., 41-47.

McGoldrick, M. and Carter, E.A. 1980. Forming a remarried family. In E.A. Carter and M. McGoldrick (Eds.), *The Family Life Cycle: A Framework for Family Therapy.* New York: Gardner Press.

Messinger, L. 1976. Remarriage between divorced people with children from previous marriages: a proposal for preparation for remarriage. 2. *Journal of Marriage and Family Counseling,* 193-200.

Minuchin, S. 1974. *Families and Family Therapy.* Cambridge, Mass.: Harvard University Press.

Minuchin, S., Montalvo, B. Guerney, Jr. B.G., Rosman, B.L. and Schumer, F. 1967. *Families of the Slums.* New York: Basic Books.

Minuchin, S., Rosman, B.L. and Baker, L. 1978. *Psychosomatic Families: Anorexia Nervosa in Context.* Cambridge, Mass., Harvard University Press.

Parsons, T. and Bales, R.F. 1955. *Family Socialization and Interaction Process.* Glencoe, Ill.: Free Press.

Rodgers, R.H. 1973. *Family Interaction and Transaction: The Developmental Approach.* Englewood Cliffs, N.J.: Prentice-Hall.

Roosevelt, R. and Lofas, J. 1976. *Living In Step: A Remarriage Manual for Parents and Children.* New York: McGraw-Hill.

Sager, C.J., Walker, E., Brown, H.S., Crohn, H.M. and Rodstein, E. 1981. Improving functioning of the remarried family system. 7. *Journal of Marital and Family Therapy,* 3-13.

Schulman, G.L. 1972. Myths that intrude on the adaptation of the stepfamily. 53. *Social Casework,* 131-139.

Simon, A.W. 1964. *Stepchild in the Family: A View of Children in Remarriage.* New York: Odyssey Press.

Stern, P.N. 1978. Stepfather families: integration around child discipline. 1(2). *Issues in Mental Health Nursing,* 50-56.

Visher, E.B. and Visher, J.S. 1978. Common problems of stepparents and their spouses. 48(2). *American Journal of Orthopsychiatry,* 252-262.

Visher, E.B. and Visher, J.S. 1979. *Stepfamilies: A Guide to Working With Stepparents and Stepchildren.* New York: Brunner/Mazel.

Walker, K.N. and Messinger, L. 1979. Remarriage after divorce: dissolution and reconstruction of family boundaries. 18(2). *Family Process,* 185-192.

Walker, K.N., Rogers, J. and Messinger, L. 1977. Remarriage after divorce: a review. 58. *Social Casework,* 276-285.

Wallerstein, J.S. 1977. Responses of the preschool child to divorce: Those who cope. In M.F. McMillan and S. Henad, (Eds.), *Child Psychiatry: Treatment and Research.* New York: Brunner/Mazel.

Wallerstein, J.S. and Kelly, J.B. 1974. The effects of parental divorce: The adolescent experience. In J. Anthony and C. Koupernick (Eds.), *The Child in His Family - Children at Psychiatric Risk.* New York; Wiley, 479-505.

Wallerstein, J.S. and Kelly, J.B. 1979. Children and divorce: A review. 24(6). *Social Work,* 468-475.

Wattenberg, E. and Reinhardt, H. 1979. Female-headed families: trends and implications. 24(6). *Social Work,* 460-467.

Winch, R. **1977**. *Familial Organization: A Quest for Determinants*. New York: Free Press.

Woody, J.D. **1978**. Preventive intervention for children of divorce. 59(9). *Social Casework*, 537-547.

Zimmerman, S.L. **1980**. The family: Building block or anachronism. 61. *Social Casework*, 195-204.

Chapter 8

Farm Families and Family Therapy

George MacDonald and Grant Dunfield
Department of Community Services & Corrections, Manitoba

There has been a scarcity of written material available on mental health practice with farm families in North America. Rosenblatt et al (1978) describe a similar lack in material on the sociology of the farm family. They indicate that a systematic bias has been operating that inclines students towards studying the urban family while neglecting the farm family. As mental health professionals employed in farming communities, our efforts to unearth both practical and theoretical studies relevant to farm family treatment has met with little success. While the work of Rosenblatt provides a detailed description of the sociological context of farm families, very little work has been done tying this unique context to the theory and techniques of family therapy. This paper builds on important sociological analysis of the farm context provided by Rosenblatt and his colleagues and links the context with relevant concepts of structural family therapy.

The reasons the farm family has been neglected in the mental health field are probably many and varied. Several factors strike us as important and worth mentioning in this respect. Mental health problems have for a long time been viewed by the psychiatric establishment as similar to medical problems. The contextual development of a particular mental health problem was not really taken seriously as a relevant and causative influence within the strictly medical framework of psychiatric illnesses. "A depression is a depression is a depression", no matter what the context, was the rule of thumb. Other reasons why the farm family has been neglected are more general. There has been an unfortunate tendency to view farm and non-farm families as similar. While this may be true with respect to some aspects of lifestyles, education and commitment to national goals, there are from our observations, some salient differences that should not be ignored. Finally, a recent article by the Proskys (1981) suggests another reason why farm families are neglected. They indicate that in this technological era our society is moving away from the beliefs, norms and values that provide meaning in the farming context. Where once survival meant a joint effort at working the land, there is now a great deal more emphasis placed on individual production and mobility. The prevailing ethos of the technological era is taken for granted as valid for the farming community as well.

Our experiences with farming communities in Western Canada lead us to the conclusion that farm families in relation to the larger society are cast in a role "between the devil and the deep blue sea". They cannot avoid being influenced by new and ever changing values (i.e. with emphasis on individual production and mobility), yet they cannot ever completely abandon the means of survival that have always been important to farmers and farm families. The clash of these opposing value systems is more evident in the bumper stickers pasted to farm vehicles - ("I am proud to be a farmer", "If you complain about farmers, don't talk with your mouth full"). To the outsider, these "signs of the times" provide important information about how farmers feel and about how they have been made to feel in relation to the larger society. While working in a farm community or with a farm family it is important to realize that you are working with a system that must, of necessity, maintain a "foot" in two diametrically opposed value systems. In this respect, it is imperative that mental health researchers and practitioners recognize the farm family as a unique, natural, social system that has evolved its own ways of organizing and transacting that are economical and effective for that group. An awareness of this uniqueness has not only helped us to determine our strategies, but has enabled us, as urban trained professionals to navigate in what were initially unfamiliar waters.

In addition to regarding the farm family as a unique social unit in and of itself, we also subscribe to ideas in the field of mental health that are still considered outside the mainstream. First of all, we think that the great majority of observable manifestations of mental health problems can be viewed as complex patterns of relationship and interaction that exist within unique contexts. We are less inclined to support monadic theories of individual psychology that have traditionally viewed symptoms and problems as the private misery of a single individual. In this respect, Watzlawick (1967) emphasizes the point that "mental health problems remain unexplainable as long as the range of observation is not wide enough to include the context in which the behaviour occurs". A large number of theorists are moving away from intrapsychic definitions in psychiatry, and in doing therapy, are maximizing exploration and manipulation of the individual's present life context (Minuchin, 1974). These writers see the context of individual problems as the proper locus of intervention and utilize the prospective approach of family therapy. In our work with the people of our farming communities, we view family therapy as an important aspect of the treatment approach.

A SOCIAL SYSTEMS APPROACH TO MENTAL HEALTH INTERVENTION WITH THE FARM FAMILY

As mental health professionals and individuals who had essentially been brought up in urban settings, our immersion in the Western Canadian farming community proved to be a unique experience. We noticed for instance, that farm families appeared more involved with extended kin than did their urban counterparts. When a mental health problem came to our attention in the Community Mental Health Centre, often we would discover that the significant actors in its evolution had as much to do with extended kin as it did with one's immediate family. From our particular vantage points, we concluded that the farm family was quite different from other types of families and that these differences had important ramifications for how we went about our business of psychotherapy. With this in mind, we set out to determine what were the attributes of farm living that made the farm family appear different.

A number of attributes of farm families had already been described by Rosenblatt et al (1978). Our observations confirmed their notions and fitted our own understanding of what we knew to be true about the farm families of Western Canada. Attributes that separated farm families from other types of families revolved around issues related to the economics of farming, time management on the farm, and finally, to issues having to do with farm work and geographical space. These attributes, succinctly stated by Rosenblatt, are paraphrased in the following:

ATTRIBUTES RELATED TO THE ECONOMICS OF FARMING

(1) Because of the high cost of farming, it is often necessary for immediate and extended family to work together on the same economic enterprise.

(2) Income from farming is variable, unpredictable and strongly influenced by factors outside the control of family members.

ATTRIBUTES HAVING TO DO WITH THE MANAGEMENT

(1) Few or no days off from work for at least one family member (as with dairy farms or cattle ranching).

(2) Farm families exhibit wide seasonal variations in work requirements (especially for families with crop farms).

ATTRIBUTES HAVING TO DO WITH GEOGRAPHICAL SPACE

(1) Work life and home life occur in the same or adjacent spaces. In addition, extended kin are often living in the same geographical space (for families who live on or next to the land they work), known as multiple family households.

(2) Relative isolation from outside contacts and activities.

ATTRIBUTES RELATED TO GENEALOGY

(1) Often farm families exhibit a stronger sense of ancestral heritage because they work the same land as their ancestors. Because of this, family loyalties often run deeper than in other types of families.

From a psychiatric or mental health standpoint, these special attributes of farm families often seemed to underly the creation and development of individual problems that masqueraded as standard forms of "mental illness". Indeed, we began to realize that a mental health problem that manifested itself in our farm communities did not differ symptomatically from those problems existing in other settings. We knew, however, that the context of these problems was very different and it was "in context" that we pursued our understanding of a problem's genesis. As early as 1914, Ortega Y. Gassett said, "I am myself plus my circumstances, and, if I do not save it, I cannot save myself. This sector of circumstantial reality forms the other half of my person; only through it can I integrate myself and be fully myself." (Ortega Y. Gasset, 1961). As mental health professionals working with farm families, we took seriously the circumstantial "other half" of what it meant to be an individual living in a farm family. We discovered in so doing, that mental health problems became more socially intelligible and our sucess with various problems increased.

The attributes of farm living described on the previous pages are interdependent and tied together in such a way as to shape the special gestalt of farm family life. It is because of these attributes that the farm family has organized itself around issues and concerns that are very different from the urban family. While the farm family has evolved from these unique sets of circumstances, they share with all other families everywhere a "transactional existence" or "organic wholeness" that is rule-governed and transcends the life of its individual members. We have found that the language best suited to understanding the family as a unity of interacting persons is the language of systems theory and structural family therapy. In the remaining part of this section, we will provide the reader with a brief overview of a systems approach to family practice for families in general. This overview is not intended to be an exhaustive review of systems theory or family therapy modalities. Ideas and concepts will be defined and described that we have found to be helpful in our work with farm families. In the concluding part of this paper, we will connect the special attributes of farm life to the concepts of structural family therapy and demonstrate how mental health problems are created in this context. Finally, a number of case examples will be presented to illustrate how we went about resolving problems in this special context. It is our hope that this structural family approach to working with farm families will be of significant practical value to those persons concerned with the treatment of mental health problems in farm families.

SOCIAL SYSTEMS AND THE STRUCTURAL FAMILY APPROACH

A system can be regarded as a set of interacting interdependent parts operating in a particular context (Minuchin, 1978, p.20). Family systems theory has its roots in the general systems theory formulated by Ludwig von Bertalanffy (Bertalanffy, 1934). His work was based on the biological sciences and focused on the interactions within organisms and between organisms and their environments. Social scientists built on his work to incorporate general principles of interaction for all systems, both biological and human. Some basic terms used by social scientists when talking about human systems are wholeness, feedback, homeostasis, and circularity.

Wholeness refers to the idea that a living human system is more than the sum of its parts. In other words, a family system forms a unity in Minuchin's phrase, which has a life of its own; it is a "multibodied organism" (1981, p.12). Minuchin regards a member of any family as both a part of something larger than itself and as an individual whole. When one person changes within a family constellation, according to the system's viewpoint, every member will have to alter his or her relationship to every other member. The structure or organization of the system will change with an alteration in the behaviour of one of its members.

Homeostasis refers to the tendency in all living organisms in a family system toward both maintenance and evolution. This, simply put, means that family systems have the capacity for change and are in a constant process of development and adaptation. Also, families, as do all living systems, have a capacity for resisting deviation from the normal or customary methods of interacting. In fact, *feedback* is a term used to describe the mechanism that systems use to provide information, both within themselves and outside to the external world. In terms of applying this concept to family systems, feedback can be understood as ways families have of controlling the influence of change on the family. According to the systemic view, change is a function of family disequilibrium. That is, a fluctuation in the typical ways members respond to one another, such that they engage in a new way of organizing themselves. This is what is usually happening at a point where a family system is in crisis around an issue.

Closely related to the concepts of wholeness, homeostasis, and feedback is that of circularity. A basic principle of the systemic view is that an individual's behaviour is both caused and causative. Most therapeutic approaches prior to the '50s were modelled on linear thinking. Behavioural or emotional dificulties were thought to originate from some organic or intraphysic source. The advantage of the systems framework is that we are now able, using this model, to think not of an ultimate first cause for emotional dysfunction but can develop hypotheses based on an understanding of the interactions within the organization of the family unit. These interactions are assumed to be continuous in the sense that one person's behaviour affects another person's behaviour such that it is impossible to say who is more affected by whom in any given interaction. Every person is both having an impact and being influenced in the daily process of being involved in a system of relationships.

Flowing out of these systemic rules is a direction for intervening with problems. Change or growth within a family system occurs through trying new behaviour when interacting with intimates. Self-defeating, destructive or negative behaviour is perceived within a systemic framework as occurring and being maintained because all the significant actors conspire to encourage the behaviour. For example, sometimes one person (often a child) will become the "identified patient" and his difficulties will tend to blur the larger reality of a more complex problem, such as conflict within the spouse system. The child's troublesome behaviour can effectively function to preserve the family system.

Various family therapy approaches have evolved to produce positive change within family systems. The particular school of family therapy which we have employed in our work with farm families is the structural school most commonly associated with Salvador Minuchin of the Philadelphia Child Guidance Clinic. This school emphasizes the importance of helping families change basic structures in their organization to effect change in their dysfunctional patterns. It may be important to emphasize at this point, that there are some fundamental differences between systemic notions of intervention and those that are derived from other models, such as behavioral and intrapsychic. One of the differences is that a systemic worker may set out to promote change by actually escalating crises within a family system. He does so by first allying himself strongly with various parts of a given system to allow sufficient risk-taking among family members, so that people are freed up to try another way of resolving an issue with a partner or child. The therapeutic alliance established between the systems-oriented counselor and family members is one of the fundamental underpinnings of successful intervention.

Another key element in utilizing this approach is the need for the therapist to gain a clear sense of the repeating interactional patterns which tend to reinforce a problem, in order to develop goals for change. Family systems are understood to be both growth seeking and resistive to changes that force new levels of organization such as when marital partners find that they have to alter their customary form of interaction (e.g. the compliant one decides to take more leadership and the authoritative one accommodates by taking more of a back seat on some issues). In dysfunctional systems, where one person's negative behavior has operated to detour from another important concern (i.e. a conflicted marital relationship) the job of the therapist is to block the interaction that maintains the problem. The spouses can then deal with their differences in a more direct way. This will produce a different way of problem-solving and the negative behavior (of an acting out child, for example) will cease to be necessary. The family system, if the intervention has been successful, will move to a new and more satisfactory level of organization and will achieve a new level of homeostasis.

In addition to the definitions presented on the previous pages from the systems literature, another important aspect of our work stems from the recognition that all families progress through a number of developmental life stages.

A number of writers have formulated models for examining universal transitions in family growth. (Kimmel, 1974; Duval and Hill, 1948; Duvall, 1971). Minuchin (1981) has a more simplified scheme in which he suggests four main stages organized around the growth of children. Included in these are couple formation, families with young children, families with school aged or adolescent children and families with grown children. He argues that successful negotiation of each of these stages is critical for effective movement of the system to greater levels of complexity. Beginning with couples starting to form during courtship, there is a need for a person to accommodate to another human being who is in some ways complementary, while also preserving a personal identity within the relationship. New rules must be evolved through trial and error around respect for each individual spouse's own values and personality. There will of necessity develop what Minuchin refers to as boundaries around each person as well as around the couple as a unit in relation to other systems to which they relate (such as friends, families of origin, work place, etc.). As children are added to the mix, rules governing relationships must be incorporated. New subsystems come into play: mother-child, father-child, and parental. The parents must achieve controls which provide them with a degree of intimacy with their children as well as preservation of their own parental authority.

At the stage of school-age or adolescent children, families proceed to the important developmental milestone of competing with the peer group for influence over their children. Issues of autonomy and control are constantly being negotiated as the emerging young adult increases in competence. As the family moves into the stage of grown children, the young adults ideally should be accomplishing a degree of differentiation from their parents. The parents must solve the challenge of returning to a subsystem of two again while including new spouses of their grown children. All of these transitions have to be accommodated by families over the course of a lifetime, according to Minuchin, and it is at these developmental milestones that families often come into therapy. Therapy, from this perspective, becomes the job of "unsticking" a system's balance in order to permit it to move to a different level of complexity:

> "...Therapy is the process of taking a family who are stuck along the developmental spiral and creating a crisis that will push the family in the direction of their own evolution". (Minuchin, 1981, p. 27)

The notion of boundaries are, for Minuchin, critical for the successful understanding of family structure. Family structure is simple... "the relationship of the subsystems to each other and to the whole system..." (Okun and Rappaport, 1980, p.11). Boundaries of a subsystem are the "rules defining who participates and how" (Minuchin, 1974, p.53). Boundaries perform the function of protection of the differentiation of the system. In marriage, for example, clear boundaries ensure that husband and wife are clearly enough defined as a separate system to be protected from interference by other subsystems. Clear boundaries ensure that the lines of responsibility have been developed and that authority has been defined.

Minuchin has described three kinds of boundaries: enmeshed, where there is an excessive degree of involvement between people; disengaged, where relationships are rigid and too distant; and clear, where relationshps fall somewhere between the two extremes. These boundary types fall on a continuum. Problems are likely to occur at one of the extremes of disengagement or enmeshment.

The last principle which we would like to highlight involves the role of symptoms and their connection to dysfunctional interactions. Haley (1976, p.2) has defined a symptom as "...a crystallization of a sequence in a social organization." Both Haley and Minuchin emphasize that symptoms operate to maintain the homeostasis of the family system. For example, an agoraphobic may suffer from anxiety which prevents him from attending social gatherings with his wife. From the position that a symptom is a kind of contract between people, the therapist would look at how fear of social gatherings enables the spouses to remain disengaged. The fear of social gatherings may be a part of a disengaged pattern with this system. The goal for change may well be redefining the couple's view of the problem so that an irrational fear becomes seen as an inappropriate way of avoiding involvement or dealing directly with conflict. Thus, as Haley points out, when "symptoms" occur within a family, they must be viewed as contracts between those people and therefore adaptive to their relationships. With this in mind, the therapist begins to think of therapy in a different way and to intervene in a family system where he recognizes that symptoms and individual behaviour are interlocked in some very intricate ways.

In summarizing then, it is our belief that a "therapeutic problem" is hardly ever a "one person" phenomenon. If one thinks of problems as existing in context, all therapy, including individual therapy, becomes an intervention into some particular social organization. We have found that an understanding of social systems and the structural family approach has been most helpful to us in working with farm families. Out of these two frameworks, we have described generally some important systemic principles and have emphasized some important concepts and ideas. In the remaining part of the paper, we will illustrate how the significant attributes of farm living create a unique social context and are especially relevant to both understanding and intervening with the farm family.

HOW FARM FAMILY SYSTEMS ARE AFFECTED BY THEIR CONTEXTS

Having introduced the unique properties of the farm context and some key concepts of the social systems framework, we will now describe how the attributes described earlier interact with the systemic rules within farm families. We will attempt to explain how some typical problems can arise, given the nature of the context.

If families everywhere generally encounter difficulties with achieving differentiation of their young adult members, then farm family systems have a context that potentially makes this an even more challenging task. It will be recalled from the section on characteristics of farm context that farming is frequently a shared enterprise encompassing several generations. Establishing clear boundaries when several subsystems of a family occupy a farm property can be a major task. A frequently occurring structure among farm families is the situation in which a son and his wife and children live on the same property as the son's parents and the son and his father share the operation. There are many variations on this theme such as two brothers and their families living on or near the same jointly farmed operation. Often three generations - grandparents, parents and grandchildren - can all be involved in sharing the responsibilities of farming. Living in proximity requires careful negotiation of responsibilities including drawing up agreements spelling out the division of income. Frequently, attempting to maintain a sense of personal identity can become a frustration when the rules governing the arrangement require re-investing profits for the sake of expansion or maintenance of the farm.

Loyalty to the farm and pride in being the member of the family (frequently the son) who is keeping the family farm alive can become a boundary problem if being "married" to the operation exceeds in priority the commitment placed on one's marital relationship. The way in which loyalty can become an intrusion into one's personal or marital boundary is that the strong value placed on maintaining the family connection to the land may prevent a couple from considering options other than farming at a critical stage where they are trying to negotiate greater distance from parents and siblings. Also the emphasis that is placed in some farm families on helping out one's immediate kin can be used as an obstacle to the husband and wife attending to their own needs within their marital relationship. Frequently wives play "second fiddle" to their husband's family loyalties.

Combined with the issue of loyalty is the expanding crisis within farm families around greatly increased costs for equpment and land. One method that in the past helped farm families get adult children involved in the business in a separate way was to sell parts of an original holding or expand an operation, allowing the sons to buy in. Also, people were at one time able to finance their own farm when land and interest rates were not so prohibitive. This often effectively contributed to the differentiation of young couples from their parents. These solutions are less available to young farmers today and the net effect is sometimes a prolonged waiting period for a couple at the important phase of young couplehood when issues of personal identity and identity within a relationship are being confronted.

The effect of living close together can produce several possible outcomes. The most common one encountered in our clinical work is one in which the boundary between marital partners is disengaged. The husband may be tremendously invested in the operation to the exclusion of his wife. The wife, in turn, can be so caught up in the day-to-day jobs that fall within her area of responsibility that she is as distant from her husband as her husband is from her. Because of the nature of farming, the investment of time required of everyone is potentially limitless. There are plenty of opportunities within a farm context for avoidance of conflict resolution, given the total involvement that is often necessary from family members.

A frequently encountered structure for us as systems therapists is an enmeshment between one or both spouse and his/her/their own parents and a disengagement between the spouses themselves. The factors of economics, loyalty to family tradition, living in spatial proximity, and the heavy commitment of time can all exacerbate these boundary problems. Financial dependency on parents can limit a couple's flexibility in moving to another location. Being physically adjacent in living arrangement can mean couples are more vulnerable to interference in decision-making by parents, siblings, or extended kin.

Loyalty to the family enterprise may intensify pressure on a husband to side with his parents against his wife on major issues (or vice versa). The amount of time consumed by one partner in farm work may leave a spouse feeling isolated. He/she may choose to obtain the nurturance of a child as a way of filling the void left by the unavailability of the partner. This in turn may restrict the child's age-appropriate development because the child may have to devote his/her energies to the involvement with the parent. This sort of pattern can produce psychiatric symptoms in youngsters, especially at the stage of adolescence when the young person is challenged by his peers and by his own needs to develop an individual identity. The purpose of symptoms, within a human system is to protect or stabilize a relationship structure from change. Symptoms such as depression, anxiety, or even psychotic behavior in teenagers can function to prevent growth from occurring. In the case of the farm family just described where the parents are disengaged and one parent is over-involved with a teenage child, the teenager's symptoms can very easily develop to protect against the necessity of facing his/her own need for more autonomy and against the parent's need to challenge his/her partner about their lack of closeness. It will be seen that, as has been stated earlier about the rules of systemic operations, each person's behavior has a profound effect on every other.

Before closing this section it should be pointed out that we are not suggesting that all farm families have dysfunctional structures that necessarily contribute to the creation of symptoms in their members. In fact, from both the literature reviewed and from our personal experience, we have the impression that many farm families in Western Canada achieve mastery of the key developmental stages and succeed admirably in the maintenance of effective boundaries within and between major subsystems.

The cases that follow will illustrate the evolution of systemic problems within farm families. Interventions using a structural approach will be described.

Case #1 - Mike M.

The patient, Mike M., was a twenty-one year old male, living with his family on their farm in a small rural community. He was the youngest child of a family of five, containing three girls and two boys. Only the boys were living at home at the time of referral. The farm itself was somewhat larger than average and was worked by the patient's father and uncle, with the help of the two sons. Mike's parents and family had a large house adjacent to his grandmother's where both she and his uncle lived. There was daily contact between these two families.

Mike was referred to the Community Mental Health Clinic by a Public Health Nurse for what she described as "depression". The nurse reported that this young man had recently refused to continue working towards a degree at University and was at home refusing to come out of his room. When certain members of his family attempted to communicate with him, he pulled his bedcovers over his head and ignored the communicator. He would communicate with his mother, but only through written messages which were pushed back and forth underneath his bedroom door.

Previous to the referral, Mike had been hospitalized in a large urban psychiatric ward for a two week period. Upon discharge, the hospital arranged a schedule of appointments for him to see a psychiatrist on an outpatient basis, appointments which he subsequently kept over a three week period. During this period, Mike began gradually to withdraw and became even more uncommunicative than he had been prior to his admission. Although the psychiatrist had prescribed two different medications for Mike, these did not seem to help. His parents felt that he was beginning to relapse and in some ways was getting worse than prior to his admission. It was at this point that the public health nurse made the referral to the Community Mental Health Service.

Both the drugs and Mike's hospital admission told us a great deal about the psychiatrist's medical orientation toward mental health problems, but we learned very little about the young man experiencing the problems. A number of telephone calls were made to Mike's psychiatrist but none were returned. The medical interventions attempted by the psychiatrist (i.e. hospitalization and use of medications) were viewed by ourselves as unhelpful.

When Mike was referred to the Community Mental Health Centre our organization was less in tune with the systemic notions that we now find so valuable. Without knowing it, we had to some extent accepted the idea that because Mike was referred, he was the problem.

Both parents expressed their concern and anxiety about their son's refusal to attend his university classes and his refusal to get out of bed and leave his room. Because we were more intrapsychically oriented at the time, we decided to see this young man on an individual basis for a period of time, primarily to enable him to adopt more socially adequate behaviors. The first month of counselling then was spent with one clinician visiting Mike weekly. During this time the parents, nurse, and family doctor were beginning to consider a rehospitalization. This pressure for hospitalization by the systemic forces outside the counselling dyad was successfully resisted by the worker involved and after a month Mike began to engage more freely in a dialogue with the counsellor. This movement on his part toward a more adequate social interaction was built on by demanding that if he wanted to continue further discussions with the worker, he must make appointments and come to his sessions at the clinic instead of the counsellor making home visits. He agreed to this reluctantly.

After Mike began coming regularly to counselling sessions, the approach utilized was to adopt a number of individually oriented techniques to further the goals of more adequate social interaction, growth and differentiation. Remember, Mike had changed from a young man who had attended university to a person who insisted he would never be able to handle that kind of social interaction again. He was shy, withdrawn and completely unable to take risks. We needed to help him achieve what we knew were still possibilities for him. The individual techniques used were cognitive restructuring, rational emotive therapy, goal-oriented counselling and relaxation training. He attended these sessions biweekly for almost a year and seemed to enjoy them. He did not, however, reach out to other people beyond his immediate family and the therapist. Even in this respect he claimed that the therapist was really the only person he ever talked to because most of his family was "too competitive". He also claimed that he did not feel a need to begin socializing with anyone else.

The worker involved with Mike began to have mixed feelings about the individually oriented approach to Mike's problem after this first year. The positives that were gained from these sessions stemmed from the huge amounts of family information gathered from him as he talked about his personal world. In addition, for a therapist who was not at that time completely convinced of the structural family approach, it provided us with enough contact time with the client to insist with a greater measure of certaintly that this young man was not biologically or psychiatrically disordered as his hospitalization and medication implied. At the same time, however, we had no real success in enabling Mike to begin more satisfying relationships in the larger world. He continued to behave and act as though he were a "hermit crab". At that point in time, we made a decision to begin involving more family members to see if they could somehow help Mike reach out more to the outside.

During the individual counselling sessions we were already beginning to formulate systemic hypothesis about the nature of Mike's family life that made it impossible for him to change. For example, in individual counselling we learned:
(a) that husband and wife disagreed over the value of a university education. The wife was a teacher, the husband a farmer.
(b) that ten years previously, the husband had threatened suicide and had been hospitalized in a psychiatric ward, ostensibly because of marital disharmony.
(c) that Mike himself felt that his parents used him and demanded too much of him. The father needed him to help out on the farm, the mother wanted him to complete his university education.
(d) that although the client was angry at both parents, he supported both of them in a way that made it impossible for him to act at an important stage of his life - the critical point of vocational choice and leaving home. Mike did not have to experience any anxiety about leaving home - which he was afraid of - because his parents made it impossible for him to do so.

(e) finally, we were made aware of a conflict that existed between Mike's father and Mike's grandmother who lived adjacent to the M. family. Mike indicated that there were disagreements about his father's ownership of the family farm and that his dad, at the stage of vocational choice himself, was only given it with "many strings attached". We also knew that the grandmother involved herself in Mike's family affairs in a way that made it difficult for Mike's father to achieve a sense of autonomy from his own family of origin. It appeared that in this farm family, receipt of the family farm upon retirement of the older farm couple was a bequest fraught with much familial strife for the inheritor.

Mike's current psychiatric problem seemed to be a repeated pattern of behavior handed down through the generations, especially at the critical point of vocational choice. Mike appeared trapped by his father's desire to have a son who would take over the farm as he had once done, while his mother disagreed with her husband and pushed her son towards more autonomy, which her husband had never been really able to achieve. The pressure the mother applied to the son in many ways was an indirect attack on her husband for not having liberated himself from the tyranny of his family of origin. The young man seemed hopelessly entangled between his parents in a marital dispute that was longstanding. He did the only thing possible for him. He became seriously depressed and got himself labelled a mental health case, and effectively "stopped the world and got off". In so doing, he paradoxically achieved a greater sense of control over his world and it allowed him to excuse himself from the frightening responsibilities of finally leaving home and becoming a fully functioning young adult.

We decided, as we developed systemic notions about Mike's problems that his behavior served many different and valuable functions in the context of this farm family. We also began to realize that helping Mike meant essentially creating a crisis for somebody else in his family.

At about the same time we decided to include more family members in Mike's counselling sessions, we received a frantic telephone call from his mother informing us that he had started behaving in much the same way as he had the year before. He had locked himself in his room and was refusing to come out. The mother viewed the problem as even more serious than the year before, because this time her son seemed to be eating less. (During these crises they would take his meals to his room and leave them on a tray outside his door. He would pull the tray into his room, eat and push it back outside when he was finished. The tray was picked up later and the sequence repeated at each mealtime - at no time was there any contact of a verbal nature). Metaphorically speaking, Mike, by his own inclination and with his family's unspoken agreement, had installed himself as a kind of "prisoner" in residence with his family.

We were unable to determine what precipitated this particular crisis, although we were able to speculate about some possible causes. First of all, it manifested itself around the same time as it had the previous year - harvest time. We knew that it was at this high pressure time for this father that he began to make more demands of his son. Their farm was relatively large and they did not have a hired hand. His crops needed to be harvested and he clearly needed some help in doing it. Also, harvest time came at about the same time that a student would be enrolling in university if he were going to be attending at all. Mike's problems then seemed to be related to these two things in some important ways. His depression made it impossible for him either to involve himself in the harvest or to attend university.

Instead of visiting Mike where he was "holed-up" in his bedroom, as the worker had the previous year, we decided to ask for more involvement from other family members and that everybody should come to our clinic. In this way, we were taking a firmer stand on organizing the family instead of having them organize us. We suspected that Mike would refuse to come to these family sessions, but we knew it was very important to begin our work with the other components of the family system. As it turned out, only the mother and father came to the clinic.

Both were worried about their son and were also experiencing some trepidation about their own responsibility for his problems. Again, because the clinician had been able to build a strong relationship of trust with the young man, we were able to say to the parents with confidence that his problems were not as serious as they felt and that what he needed was a strong sense of direction from *both* his parents. We emphasized the word *both*. The mother shared her fears that her son might commit suicide - we reassured her that he was not at all suicidal and reiterated to the parents the need to show their son that they were in agreement about wanting him to do something and that together, they would no longer allow him to stay in his room and remain depressed. They were to tell their son their decision by going to his room together and informing him of their new sense of direction. The father, in this situation, had many reservations about this idea and we were afraid that he would be unable to carry through with his wife. For this reason, before they left the first family session, we extracted from both partners a firm commitment that they would together confront their son and demand that within the very next day he had to be doing something different. We also told the parents that it would be a safe bet that Mike would become very angry by this confrontation and he may do something to frighten them and thereby weaken their resolve. We told them that this is normal and happens often when parents demonstrate executive leadership of their family together. They were told not to be frightened, but to keep insisting on new behaviors from their son.

One week later, the mother informed the worker that both she and her husband went home immediately and told their son they would not allow him to continue his life the way he had been. They insisted that if he intended to stay at home they would require him to pay room and board. In addition, his meals would no longer be brought to his room, but if he wanted to eat he should do it at the kitchen table where everybody else ate. They also expected him to make a decision within the day about university or helping out on the farm. He had twenty-four hours to think it over. Four hours after this conversation, Mike left his room, came downstairs, got into his car and drove wildly in circles around the farm house. The mother said at that point both she and her husband began to get frightened and wondered whether they had done the right thing. One hour later he came back into the house and informed his parents he would enroll at university the next day. The parents agreed it was a good idea and told him they definitely expected something from him.

Mike went back to University and recently received his degree after the two year absence. Although he switched faculties, he acquired a degree. Two years later Mike has not presented us with any other problems and is currently employed. His mother, however, did contact us to report that her husband was experiencing problems and wanted to come in for marital counselling. The husband subsequently refused although the wife came alone. She was seen individually twice by the worker and was able to acknowledge that in her family, mental health problems seem to move from person to person. Recognition by this woman that their individual problems were interlocked with other family members seemed to provide her with the impetus to begin a discussion with her husband about the nature of their family life together. On follow-up, the marriage is still intact and Mike has recently left home to get an apartment in the city.

SYNOPSIS

This particular case illustrates very well the contextual field of a dysfunctional farm family. It underlines for us the importance of focusing not just on the development of problems within the individual but on the farm family as a collection of interlocking individuals. As we worked with the client over the one year period since his referral, we realized that Mike did not "fall ill" in isolation, but that his "illness" was a farm family event. The attributes that we described in an earlier part of this paper - the working with extended kin, living in the same yard with grandparents, the necessity of starting to farm with the help of older farm couple, all helped to shape the organizational dysfunctioning of the family.

Because the father was unable to take the crop off himself, he pressured his son for aid in such a way that Mike felt overwhelmed. Indeed, in the language of structural family therapy, he was so pressured that he felt there was really no psychological boundary around himself that delineated his identity as separate. His mother contributed to his problem by suggesting other directions for his life. The young man, seeing the parental disagreement over his life, must have felt overwhelmed by the burden placed on him to go against the loyalty to one or the other of his parents. His choice to separate himself in his bedroom, with pillows and covers pulled over his head was in a symbolic way an attempt to create a clearer boundary around himself. In some ways it was a much more effective maneuver than what his father had done with his own life. Indeed, at the age of fifty-eight, his father was still having trouble with autonomy issues with his own mother, who at the age of eighty-two continued to live across the yard from the M. family. Not only were geographical boundaries very diffuse, but psychological boundaries were constantly being infringed on. Like Mike being caught between his parents, his father was caught between his mother and his wife - it was no surprise that in requesting support from his son, he too, infringed on a personal boundary.

A number of other aspects of this case make a great deal more sense when looked at from a structural family perspective. The concept of circularity, that an individual's behavior is both caused and causative, was clearly evident. Mike's problems existed because of an untenable triangulation between him and his parents. Simultaneously, his parents did not have to do anything about their marital situation because they had a son in their family who was a greater individual problem than they were together. Not only did his problem short-circuit change in the parental subsystem, it made their relationship appear at first glance to be a very harmonious one in that the parents were very "together" in their mutual concern for their offspring. At another level, Mike's "psychiatric" behavior was a challenge to the familial system itself, about the necessity of changing the status quo. Unfortunately, as Jay Haley (1973) points out, hospitalizations and psychiatric medications serve generally to promote stability in a dysfunctional system rather than create the necessary changes. We learned from this case that individual counselling served much the same purpose in preserving stability in a farm family that desperately needed change. As we mentioned earlier, after one year of individual counselling we witnessed similar development of symptomatology that had existed a year earlier. This repeated pattern of behavior was an important message to the clinicians. We know now that the real success with Mike occurred when the worker intervened with the parental subsystem and indicated that they needed to exert more executive control over his behavior together and that they needed to draw some clearer boundaries around themselves and the rest of their family, especially Mike. When Mike was able to see that his parents could function together in a proper heirarchial fashion in relation to himself, he was set free, with parental support, to become a young man with many things to accomplish in the world.

Case #2 - Donna T.

Donna T. was a twenty-six year old farm wife who contacted the Community Mental Health Service on the basis of a friend's advice. She reported by telephone to the worker that she had left her husband John the previous weekend because of an argument they had had over his parents. She also had indicated that she was depressed for the past half year and she wondered whether she was "going crazy". Because Donna's initial contact with our clinic was made by telephone over a party line, she was encouraged to come to the clinic to discuss her situation.

Upon arriving for her appointment, Donna described in detail the events that had led up to the current crisis in her marriage. She presented as distraught, depressed and confused and while speaking, frequently wept. She reported that she and her husband and their two year old son Dennis were currently living in a trailer beside John's parents, where both John and his father worked a section of land as a family farm. John's father had been a farmer all his life and had integrated John into the operation when John and Donna had been married.

Donna complained that her recent argument with her husband was related to his "inability to grow up". When he told her she was placing too many demands on him, she left their home with their son and moved in with a sister in another farming community some distance from their home. When she first arrived at the Community Mental Health Clinic she had already hired a lawyer and begun separation proceedings. Although she had gone to a lawyer, she claimed that she did not really want to separate, but wanted to impress on her husband the need for change in their marital relationship.

A number of things had precipitated the current crisis according to Donna:

(1) She was angry at John for eating breakfast and lunch at his parents' home instead of having it with herself and Dennis in the trailer.

(2) Donna was furious that John's parents persisted in buying clothes for their family, while Donna was not given any money by her husband to purchase them herself.

(3) For the past half year, neither of Donna's parental in-laws would speak civilly to her, yet they encouraged Dennis, the youngster, to spend time with them. On numerous occasions they counselled the little boy to ignore his mother when she attempted to discipline him.

(4) The parental in-laws suggested to their son, John, that his wife needed a psychiatrist and that "there was no shame" in needing that kind of help. They based their conclusion on the fact that Donna seemed so adamant about her need to buy her own clothes and those of her husband and son.

(5) Finally, Donna and John were about to move into a new bungalow they had just built beside their trailer and John's mother implied to him that perhaps they should take the old homesteading house and let the parents move into the bungalow.

Based on Donna's self-reports about this particular two-family system, we developed the systemic notion that many of her problems were being created by the enmeshed and intrusive nature of her in-laws' interaction with their son, her husband. Accepting Donna's remarks at face value meant that her husband John was probably experiencing serious problems with autonomy because of parental controls. At the same time we assumed he was experiencing much personal turmoil because he was figuratively being torn between his parents and the woman he married. On the basis of Donna's desire to restore their marriage, we requested that she contact her husband and ask him if he would be willing to come to the clinic to discuss their marriage problems. A subsequent call was made to John by the counsellor involved to allay any anxiety he might have had concerning the counselling sessions. Both husband and wife agreed to come to the clinic at a mutually agreed upon time.

By the time both husband and wife saw one another for their first appointment at the Community Mental Health Clinic, they had been apart for two weeks. The purpose of the counselling sessions was explained as an effort to restore their marriage, since that was what both people agreed they wanted to do. The counsellor asked John whether he was aware that his wife had gone to a lawyer and would it make a difference to him in terms of counselling. He indicated that he was aware but he also believed that his wife did want to save their marriage.

The first session began with Donna asking John for more support in relation to his parents. She explained to him that she felt hurt that her in-laws continued to buy their clothes and she resented it. John immediately countered that he didn't see anything wrong with it, because his parents also bought clothes for his older sister and her two children and she never complained. (This older sister had been recently divorced in the city and moved back to within six miles of her parents). When Donna again explained that she was not like her sister-in-law but that she wanted the freedom to look after her own family, John accused her of attacking him by attacking his parents - he insisted that his parents wanted only to "help her look good" by buying her the finest of clothing.

A good part of this first session consisted of a sequential pattern of the wife requesting support for herself in relation to her in-laws and the husband denying it and accusing the wife of needlessly attacking his parents "who had been so kind to them". The counsellor's initial hypothesis that the older parental subsystem was intruding on Donna's and John's marriage in an unhelpful way seemed confirmed.

Seeing that the husband in this context was being pulled in many different directions simultaneously, the therapist decided to join him and support him around the difficulty of being responsible for so many people. By joining him and supporting him, the therapist hoped to give him some strength in confronting the unreasonable demands placed on him by his parents and thereby block them from contaminating his marriage. The therapist told John a number of stories relating to how difficult it often was for parents to accept their children as adults and even when they got married parents often persisted in treating the newlyweds as though they were children. The therapist expressed the belief that because this kind of problem occurs so often in families, many wedding ceremonies incorporate in the ritual the necessity that "a man must leave his father and mother and be united with his wife" (Ephesians 5:31-32). The worker indicated that this process was made even more difficult by virtue of the fact that many young farmers also had to continue working with their fathers collaboratively in the farming enterprise.

At this point in the intervention, John began to cry in such a way as to convey the feeling of being in intense pain. His demonstration certainly underlined the power his parents wielded in relation to their son. At the same time, the worker increased the pressure on John to make a choice within a week, even though it would be a painful choice. Both Donna and John agreed to an appointment one week later where they were to decide on what important changes would be made to begin restoring their marriage.

Between this first session with this couple and the next appointment, John's mother made contact with the worker involved, by phone. Although there had never been contact between John's parents and the counsellor before, she demanded to know what was the purpose of marital counselling for her son when her daughter-in-law had already initiated separation proceedings. The worker gently suggested that perhaps she and her husband could come to their next appointment to help out in the process. She refused immediately, indicating that Donna was an unreasonable woman and would be very difficult for any man to please. The following day the therapist received a call from John saying that he would not be keeping his next appointment and that he had decided to "divorce the person who had caused him the most pain" - his wife. He informed her by letter that he was hiring a lawyer and beginning separation proceedings.

At this point in time, John is continuing to live at home on the family farm with his parents. Donna has custody of their son and is attempting to create an independent life of her own by finding an apartment, getting a job and placing her son in a day care centre during the day. Although we were unable to help this couple restore their marriage to a higher level of functioning, we view our intervention as a successful one in that it unbalanced their family system in such a way as to enable the couple to make clearer decisions about their life. In addition, through counselling, John was required to make a personal decision about his life. Up to that point he had been avoiding making decisions by allowing his parents and his wife to take over. Donna was able to separate from the relationship feeling that she was not entirely responsible for the break-up of their marriage.

SYNOPSIS

The T. family demonstrate in a classic sense, the problems and risks of too much togetherness in a joint farm family enterprise. They also illustrate in a very graphic way, the problems that occur at significant life stages for some farm families. Because important transitional life stages were limited within this multi-family group, neither the older or younger couple were able to move on to the next important stage of family development. We can say that both families were stuck homeostatically and it was only at the point of Donna's marital crisis and threatened separation, that they became "unstuck" briefly and the possibility for change existed.

It is important to emphasize at this point that within particular contexts we would be wrong to assume that any of the actors are either "bad, mad or malicious". When we look at the problems of the T. family as transitional life stage problems, we are "hard put" to determine who, if anyone was most responsible for the structural problems.

Like many young men who begin working the family farm jointly with the help of a father or father-in-law, John had serious difficulty with parental controls. John's father could be viewed as deliberately attempting to delay more responsible behaviour in his son so that he and his wife would not have to face their own issues of releasing their children and dealing with themselves again as a couple in their declining years. To the extent that John did not challenge his parents and demand more autonomy and responsibility around the farm, he reinforced the parental view that both he and Donna would always need looking after, even to the point of actually buying their clothes. Donna attempted to help her husband emancipate himself from what she knew intuitively to be destructive interaction that would eventually ruin her married life. At some level, she also realized that this interaction was somehow blocking both her and her husband from moving on to the next important stage of their life together, in their case, organized around the care of their own young child. Because John was unable to challenge his parents, he was in fact unable to help negotiate the marital relationship.

Another way of looking at this particular problem is that John's inability to confront his parents stemmed from a realization that to do so would create suffering for them and he felt a strong need to protect them. We speculated that John felt such a deep sense of concern for his parents that rather than upset their equilibrium and cause heartbreak "because they had done so much for him", he chose instead to believe his parent's reality and sacrificed his wife. This, of course, was highly inappropriate from a family structural point of view, but neither his partner nor the therapist were able to draw him out of an enmeshed family system that turned out to be much more powerful than either. Upon rethinking this case, we realized with hindsight that a more productive intervention might have been to insist that the extended family come with John and Donna to their first marital session. In so doing, the therapist would have had a much better chance of drawing clear boundaries around the older parental subsystem and freeing John to begin looking after his wife and child rather than protecting his parents from the reality of growing older.

We knew from Donna's self-report that she and John were experiencing problems because of the enmeshed nature of John's interaction with his parents. Although she had married him six years earlier, she had always felt like a "stranger in a strange land" when it came to feeling a part of her husband's family. Again, as with the previous case, we were presented with a group of people who lived in very close proximity to one another, and with whom psychological boundaries were extremely diffuse. Because Donna was the outsider and not caught up in the enmeshement like her husband, she was freer to "flag" the problem and to set the stage for systemic change.

To prognosticate a little bit about the individuals within this family context, we feel that Donna's future seems brighter. She made a decision with her husband's help to leave a contextual field that was debilitating to her as an individual and as a wife and parent. Although there will be some hard times for her, she has a much better change of learning new skills in a different context than the one she found herself in through marriage. We are less optimistic about John and his parents. John, for his part, chose the path of least resistance and decided to remain in his family of origin where "time stands still" and children are always children and parents never grow older. By keeping their son around them and dependent, the older couple misses the opportunity of being together again in a different way in their old age.

SUMMARY

This paper has been an attempt to expand the knowledge about, and intervention with, farm families. Drawing on the work of Rosenblatt (1978), important features of the farm family situation were described including close spatial relations, variable income, large investment of time in the enterprise, prohibitive economic cost, and a strong sense of ancestral heritage and loyalty. Salient elements of a social systems framework were considered in the context of farm families.

The structural model of family systems intervention was considered as a useful tool in working with farm families. Boundaries, the circular nature of family interactions, the homeostatic principle, the mastery of important life stages and the evolution of symptoms within farm systems can be identified as concepts vital to the understanding of family functioning.

Two case examples were offered to illustrate the application of these concepts and their utility in mental health practice with farm families.

REFERENCES

Bertalanlfy, Ludwig Von, **1934**. *Modern Theories of Development: An Introduction to Theoretical Biology*. London: Oxford Press.

Duval, Evelyn M. **1971**. *Family Development*. Philadelphia: J.B. Lippincott.

Duval, Evelyn M. and **Hill**, Reuben. **1948**. Report of the Committee for the Dynamics of Family Interaction - prepared at the request of the National Conference on Family Life, mimeographed.

Haley, Jay. **1973**. *Uncommon Therapy: The Psychiatric Techniques of Milton Erickson*, M.D. New York: W.W. Norton.

Haley, Jay. **1978**. *Problem-Solving Therapy*. San Francisco: Jossey-Bass.

Holy Bible, *Ephesians* 5:31-32.

Jahoda, Marie, **Lazarsfeld**, Hans zeisel. *Marienthal: The Sociography of an Unemployed Community*. Chicago: Aldine-Atherton. Originally published in 1933 as *Die Arbeitslosen Von Marienthal*.

Kimmel, Douglas C. **1974**. *Adulthood and Aging*. New York: Wiley.

Kohl, Seena B. **1976**. *Working Together: Women and Family in Southwestern Saskatchewan*. Holt, Rinehart and Winston.

Minuchin, Salvador and **Fishman**, Charles H. **1981**. *Family Therapy Techniques*. Cambridge: Harvard University Press.

Minuchin, Salvador, **Rosman**, Bernice L. and **Baker**, Lester. **1978**. *Psychosomatic Families*. Cambridge: Harvard University Press.

Minuchin, Salvador. **1974**. *Families and Family Therapy*. Cambridge: Harvard University Press.

Okun, Barbara F. and **Rappaport**, Louis J. **1980**. *Working With Families: An Introduction to Family Therapy*. Massachusetts: Dunbury Press.

Ortega Y Gasset, Jose. **1961**. *Meditation on Don Quixote*. New York: W.W. Norton.

Prosky, P. and **Prosky**, P. **1980**. Thoughts on Family Life. 48. *The Social Worker*, 15-18.

Rosenblatt, P.C., **Nevaldine**, A. and **Titus**, S.T. **1978**. Farm Families: "Relation of Significant Attributes of Farming to Family Interaction. 8. *International Journal of Sociology of the Family*, 89-99.

Watzlawick, P., **Beavin**, J.H. and **Jackson**, P.D. **1967**. *Pragmatics of Human Communication*. New York: W.W. Norton.

Chapter 9

Social Networks in Family Practice

Walter Driedger
School of Social Work, University of Manitoba

On the one hand Social Network is analogous to terms like "significant others" (Richmond, 1917; Cabot, 1915), "person-in-situation" Pearlman, 1952), "social circles" (Kadushin, 1969), "informal and formal resource systems", (Pincus and Minahan, 1972), and other terms which have been found in the social work literature over the past seventy to eighty years. On the other hand the concept holds high promise for becoming a major unifying framework and a guiding reference in clinical practice and research (Erickson, 1975; Turkat, 1979) which will enrich the provisions of family practice. Social network is not a concept which will replace "social systems" and "ecological systems" but will offer concrete interventive options in order to form a robust framework for practice.

Present day usage of the term social network originated with J.A. Barnes, a British social anthropologist who was examining the linkages between kinfolk in a Norwegian Island community of Bremnes. He recognized that kinship connections were too limiting. Friends, neighbours, workmates and fellow members in clubs and religious organizations could be as or more important to a person than kinfolk. Barnes (1954) defines social network in the following manner:

> "Each person is, as it were, in touch with a number of other people, some of whom are directly in touch with each other and some of whom are not ... I find it convenient to talk of a social field of this kind as a network. The image I have is of a net of points some of which are joined by lines. The points of the image are people, or sometimes groups, and the lines indicate which people interact with each other."

This definition indicates that connections or linkages between people can be represented in a multidimensional structure or on a map. Raymond Bradley (1975) prepared a model in which networks were set up in a manner analogous to a model of molecular structure in chemistry. He used styrofoam balls representing individuals or organizations and straws or stiff wire representing the ties between individuals or organizations to portray multiplex relations and social integration of urban communes. Morris and Cicero-Hilbert (1981) made use of a dart board with map tacks and string to represent rural natural helping networks. Carolyn Attneave (1975) uses four concentric circles, drawn on any flat surface to map out a person's and/or family's network. These structures or maps enable the practitioner and researcher to gain a better perspective of quantifiable factors such as: size (range of personal contacts), density (degree to which members interact with each other), multiplexity (are relationships based on multiple or single ties), direction (are the relationships reciprocal and symmetrical) and frequently of contact.

The empirical factor which is most easy to ascertain is size of social network. This factor has been studied numerous times. Pattison et al (1975) administered the *Pattison Psychosocial Kinship Inventory* to 200 subjects. This inventory asked the respondent to list the subjectively important people in his/her life under the categories of family, relatives, friends, co-workers, and social organizations. They found that the healthy person has 20 to 30 people in his/her intimate social network, the neurotic person has 10 to 12 others. Psychotic persons have 4 to 5 others. Erickson (1976) designed a study which included caregivers as well as network members in the sample. He interviewed 40 psychiatric patients, their respective caregivers and immediate others in Northern England. His findings indicated that the increasing severity and chronicity of the psychiatric condition correlated with a decreasing size of personal networks. In a study at Stoney Mountain Penitentiary, Manitoba, 60 inmates were sampled. Fifty percent (50%) had no friends on 'the outside' and stated that the friends they now had inside the institution would not be included in their lives once they were released. Another 50% also reported having no relatives (Saulnier, 1980). Justice and Justice (1979) and Weinberger (1976) in two separate studies found that the person who commits incest is introverted and relies on nuclear family members to meet all emotional and social needs. The lack of contact with others mitigates against leakage of information about such behaviour. Others have noticed significant positive correlation between size of network and general state of well being (Froland, 1979; Walker et al, 1977; Boissevain, 1974; McCallister and Fischer, 1978; Wellman, 1978).

Density, which refers to interaction and acquaintance, is another empirical factor which has been studied (Boissevain, 1974; Craven & Wellman, 1973; Wellman, 1973; Lauman, 1973). Llamas, Pattison and Hurd (1981) in a report pertaining to size and density state that personal support networks of urban, suburban and rural persons seem to indicate that a normal individual's set of "important" or "significant" others consists of 20-40 persons. Most individuals have three to six 'intimates'. These come from the kinship and friendship sectors. Nuclear family, relatives, friends, work associates and neighbours compose separate dense clusters. There is generally not much interaction from one cluster to another.

Wellman et al (1973) found that there is a relationship between density and support during times of crisis. Craven and Wellman (1973) found that relatively dense networks are generally small, and linkages among the members are quite strong. Those networks that are loosely knit tend to be quite large and their members are less deeply involved with one another. Granovetter (1973) found that loose-knit networks are more effective in the communication of new information and in providing help to attain tangible resources, job information and new social contacts. Litwak (1969) strengthens the above observation with the proposition that people who maintain a diversity of range of network members will generally be more likely to resolve troublesome situations.

In summary, a sizeable network composed of a variety of dense clusters has potential for emotional support, new information and stimulation from many sources. There is evidence that tightly knit ingroups which have highly defended boundaries do provide the greatest amount of emotional support. The closed boundaries however cut off the influx of new information. This phonemenon is observed in some primitive tribes and ethnic or religious ghettos. In the tightly knit ingroup with highly defended boundaries human maturation and general wellbeing can be stifled, retarded and even endangered. Differences become most suspect and preservation of ingroup norms takes on greatest priority. The most dramatic progression of such a situation would be exemplified by Jonesville of Guyana. Density, range and diversity have potential to provide the balance needed for wellbeing.

Studies indicate that multiplexity, (which refers to relationships which exist for several and more reasons), frequency of contact and reciprocity are other factors of importance to the well being of persons (Mitchell, 1969; Boissevain, 1974; Erickson, 1975; and Hirsch, 1979).

Walker et al (1977 p.35) sum up the importance of a social support network in the following manner: "The social network consists of a set of personal contacts through which the individual maintains his social identity and receives emotional supports, material aid and services, information and new social contacts." The needs of the nuclear family are not different in kind from the needs of the individual. Therefore, it seems to follow that assessment and intervention should not be limited to the boundaries of the nuclear or even extended family.

Assessment of social functioning of an individual or family must include understanding of the quantitative and qualitative aspects of the social network. Disregard for the vast implications of the social network factors will limit the interventive potentials. Social network focused assessment and intervention is a way of mobilizing the self help potential within the family, relatives, friends, neighbours, work mates, religious organization or club members and also caregivers. Attneave (1969) emphasized that the social network members can be mobilized into a social force which counteracts the depersonalizing trend in contemporary industrialized life patterns. Members of the social network can help articulate needed instrumental and affective resources and can collaborate in making these resources available to nuclear families and/or individuals (Garrison and Werfel, 1977). Furthermore, the social network intervention on the part of professional family practitioners is an exercise which can give the network members guided opportunity to learn to solve similar problems in the future (Reid and Epstein, 1972). If family practitioners incorporate the theory and first hand experience of social network practice in their family therapy, group work, parent and community education, a new wave of primary prevention can be initiated.

In the second part of this chapter I want to consider some clinical practice themes which have emerged in the literature and in my own practice. In a seminal paper Erickson (1975) has categorized four kinds of personal network. These four categories are 1) network as a curative grouping 2) network as a resource grouping 3) network as interpreter of help-seeking behaviour 4) network as mitigator of effects of multi-organizational involvements. Additionally I will include 5) network building and rebuilding (Collins and Pancoast, 1976; Turkat, 1980; Froland, 1979).

I *Network as a Curative Grouping.* Social network members hold keys to doors which professional caregivers cannot unlock. A team of professionals can unite their efforts with significant others taken from one or more of the network clusters connected to a family. This group can perform psychosocial treatment. Curative network intervention is well represented in the literature (Speck and Attneave, 1973; Rueveni, 1976; Garrison and Werfel, 1977). This form of intervention is used when traditional counselling and/or family therapy methods are not appropriate. It could involve a small number of people or a mass grouping of up to 100 people. This kind of professional activity calls for collaboration of two to five professionals depending on the size of the total number of people gathering at one time.

Network intervention usually is a short term method; one to six sessions should be adequate. Criteria for use of this method are proposed by Garrison and Werfel (1977, p.109):

a. Are there resources in the client's social environment that could be beneficial?
b. Are any other caregivers involved in the case open to a network approach?
c. Will the client consent to convening the important people in his/her life?
d. Can the clinician responsible for the case think of any reason not to use a network approach?

The following case illustration will help to portray network as a curative grouping.

Mrs. D. came to the Psychological Service Centre at the University of Manitoba during February. The presenting problem was that her son would not attend school. In the intake process it was revealed that John had refused to go to school in September. A major interdisciplinary agency had been asked by the school authorities to provide help. All attempts by this agency failed and so John was next referred and admitted to a psychiatric facility. He was presenting himself in such a way that the examining psychiatrist considered John to be in need of inpatient therapy. While in the hospital John became quite obstreperous on several occasions and was heavily medicated. He was truly living up to his label. A psychiatric resident, however, developed a good relationship with John, and by mid-October, John began attending school and was discharged from hospital. As soon as the resident was transferred to another service in early November he terminated contact with John, and immediately thereafter John quit school.

When we saw Mrs. D. she was quite afraid that Child Welfare authorities might be called in and John might be taken into care for truancy. A graduate student[1] in practicum was assigned to Mrs. D's case. She tried some additional intervention techniques — no change occurred. We set up an interventive team. The student informed Mrs. D. and a daughter about network intervention procedure. Mrs. D. made a list of people that were linked to her and invited them to a meeting regarding the problems of John's truancy from school. About twenty people came to the D. residence for the first meeting. Included were two or three daughters, one brother-in-law, several close neighbours, a teacher, several friends and some other members of the extended family. Four caregivers including a social worker from the Psychiatric Facility composed the interventive team. The procedures outlined by Speck and Attneave (1973) were used as a guideline.

At the first meeting most people were able to give their own viewpoint of the problem either to the whole group led by the graduate student or to smaller sub-groups led by one of the other team members. No specific solutions were attempted at the first meeting. At the end of the meeting people left with the challenge that they would bring back their own recommendations for a solution of the problem.

Some network members did not appear at the second meeting. John, who did not participate in the meetings, made a practice of sitting at the head of the stairs where he could hear what was going on. The relative and friendship sectors were quite irritable and resistant during the second meeting. These members did not bring complete plans but brought a few isolated opinions. They were angry with the caregivers and stated that professionals were needed. The team of caregivers had decided on the strategy which would be used if the meeting could not heuristically produce a workable plan. Mrs. D. and John were "too closely tied" to each other. For example, we had learned that when John was taken on a vacation with his sister and brother-in-law the previous summer, he returned by bus after being away one day. Another brother-in-law complained that John would not come fishing without his mother present. This person particularly disliked his mother-in-law. John, however, did have active friends in the neighbourhood.

After considerable time was spent in brainstorming with the whole group the team members proffered the following plan. We recommended that John be given the choice to go to school or to stay in his room. The consequence for choosing to stay at home would mean no T.V., no visits with friends and no meals with his mother. Mrs. D. was going to be supported by sequential visits from network members in order to help her enforce the plans if John chose to stay at home. John still did not choose to go to school. The mother failed in applying the agreed upon consequences. On the third meeting some people who had not been present earlier attended. Among them were John's single sister and a brother-in-law (Mr. A). Former plans and arrangements were reviewed. At a point of tension in the meeting the single sister dramatically pointed at mother and suggested that mother must be separated from her son. The eldest sister agreed and stated her mother should be removed from her son. Consensus was reached. John should be given the choice of staying in his bedroom or going to school. The group agreed that Mrs. D. would live with her eldest daughter. As long as John failed to go to school one of the network members would live in to take care of him.

The husband of the eldest sister volunteered to stay with John. He thought he would get caught up on his bookwork and do business by phone. Mother would be allowed to return on the evening of the first day of John's school attendance, and the above plan would be reenacted if John failed to attend the morning after. This latter contingency was not needed. The following morning John "chose" to go back to school. He continued to attend school without any problem until the end of term. We made several follow-up phone calls. Four months later we made a follow-up visit and were able to talk with members of the nuclear family and key in-laws. John had finished the school term and revealed no signs of abnormality. Also, the extended family had ironed out some significant interpersonal impasses.

The network meetings did not only solve the problem of John's truancy, they also reunited relatives who had been estranged from each other. Speck and Attneave (1973) observed this phenomenon and referred to it as "retribalization". In another situation, in which I was involved in network intervention, some of the relatives decided to hold monthly clan meetings following our termination, which would maintain a meaningful support network.

The above situation illustrated that relatives and friends can team up with caregivers to solve psychosocial and interpersonal problems. Family practitioners planning such intervention will find that full cooperation of the principal members involved must be obtained (Speck and Attneave, 1973;

Speck and Rueveni, 1967; Garrison, 1974). The key members must become comfortable with the fact that details of their problems will be revealed and network members will come in to "mind the business" of their friends and/or relatives. Those network members who are known to be nurturant and constructive can be entrusted with troubles other than their own.

II   *Network as Resource Grouping.* The foundations of a human support system lie in the fact that people have concern for others in general and a special concern for others with common heritage and culture. In this section I will describe and illustrate both of these assertions. Litwak (1960) and others have emphasized that even though the family in technological society is highly mobile, kinship ties are activated during crisis. Howard (1978) recently pointed out that people are devising non blood-linked 'clans' in which long lasting relationships are established. These groups function like committed relatives during good and bad times. As indicated earlier in this paper, these relationships are viable because of social exchange (reciprocity) potentials. We are all familiar with accounts of rural communities in which when a barn burned down a building bee was organized and a new structure soon appeared where the smouldering embers had just recently expired. Scores of neighbours responded and did weeks of work in one day. In today's urbanized society caregivers often need to initiate such process because a community member (natural helper) may not emerge at the appropriate time.

Benevolent cultural or religious societies have existed throughout the length of human existence. People acknowledge responsibility for others especially when these others share a common heritage and culture. Canadian Indians are no exception; they too care about their own people and want to share in being a resource network to their own people.[2] Without going into historical analysis of how Canadian Indians helped themselves over the ages I want to illustrate how Canadian Indians in one part of Manitoba and in British Columbia recently demanded involvement in child welfare dispositions. This will exemplify network as a resource grouping.

In the late 1950's Canadian Indian chiefs and elders in Western and Central Manitoba became despondent over the family problems which were apparent on the reservations. They determined that Federal Indian Welfare Services were not providing adequate services. They were unable to develop policy agreements with Children's Aid Societies of Western and Central Manitoba (hereinafter C.A.S.). By the early 1970's the relationships between CAS of Central Manitoba and one of the reservations were very strained. CAS workers were meeting open resisstance and often verbal invective. One of the agency supervisors[2] stated that he was greatly influenced by the implications of social network theory and therefore realized that their agency would need to team up with the resources apparent on the reservation. They developed new plans of service delivery which included a period in which much time would be spent with chiefs, band council members and natural helpers. The message which was clearly given by the people was that CAS workers were not allowing the people to share in decisions and care pertaining to their own lives. They were most incensed that their children were often removed from them and if they were returned they came back as strangers in their own homes. In brief, the CAS help was no better than that which Indian Affairs Department had previously provided. Family, kinship and friendship networks were being destroyed, and the greatest insult was that parents and elders could not use their own resources to alleviate their own problems. The agency study revealed that the reservation still wanted to make use of the expertise and fiscal resources which the CAS could offer, but they wanted to be involved in decisions and they also wanted a chance to provide care suitable to their own resources.

New administrative structures were established. A Native Child Care Committee was established and a native liaison officer was hired by CAS. The new arrangement provided means whereby full collaboration between agency and Reserve could flourish. The work of CAS no longer continued in clandestine manner. The resources represented in natural helpers were used and many more family problems could be handled by those people most closely affected.

Farquharson (1979) reports how Canadian Indians on a reservation in British Columbia were invited by student social workers to air their concern regarding child and family problems. The students spent much time listening to natural helpers who came up with many complaints about the fragmentation of family kinship and friendship circles due to interventions made by white agency representatives. These fact finding meetings between natural helpers and students resulted in a locally administered child care organization. The positive results which stemmed from tapping community resources are best illustrated in a 50% drop in numbers of children taken into care and the successful return and re-involvement in reserve life of the children previously removed.

Utilization of resources of client systems is a concept that dates back to social work which was described in the 1890's. The above illustrations, however, verify that professionals sometimes compromise their practice principles. Social network theory in this kind of situation is not introducing new ways of providing intervention but is strengthening old standards with the use of recently developed theoretical constructs.

III *Network as Interpreter of Help Seeking Behaviour.* In this sphere of network intervention caregivers work with network members in such a way that resistance, on the part of the target system needing change, is broken down by new information (or counselling or bargaining or persuasion) so that the target system will take on the client role. The persuasion and advice of network members is more powerful than that of strangers, even if the strangers are professionals.

The importance of the network in terms of convincing people they need help from social agencies is further supported in studies by Freedson (1972), Cantor (1975), and McKinley (1973). Freedson (1972) reported that the whole process of seeking help involves a network of potential consultants, from the intimate and informal confines of the nuclear family through successively more select, distant and authoritative laymen, until the professional is reached. Cantor (1975) speaks of the process of help attaining behaviour on the part of old persons. She found that these people generally exhausted informal supports before they approached formal services. Network members can be gathered together to develop a coercive thrust which is needed to bring some people into care.

The following illustrates how a personal network was instrumental in bringing an alcoholic into treatment.

The focal person was failing as a husband, father and executive, but he did not acknowledge this. He happened to be working for the kind of corporation that tried to help their employees through such problems, rather than dismissing them. The immediate supervisor called a meeting including the vice president, the wife and the only child. The focal person was confronted by each of these people with hard evidence of his over-indulgence in alcohol. He continued to resist. The vice president stated that he must go for treatment or be fired. The wife stated that he must go for treatment or she will leave him. The daughter supported the mother. The focal person denied his problem but quickly promised that he would stop drinking forthwith. The network members all agreed that they would give him one more chance. If he showed up intoxicated at work or at home he would go for treatment. A contract was finalized. Treatment was begun (Johnson, 1975).

In such illustrations the interactions in the nuclear family (as well as at work) are at the point of crisis. The behaviour of the person will not be tolerated any longer. Prior to the time when the person became dependent on alcohol he was highly valued by key network members and his efforts at work were prized. The network members and employers want the dependency on alcohol to be removed and are willing to give him another chance. Those who care about him coerce involvement in treatment. The treatment facility is aware of the concern that others have for the alcoholic person. They include key network members in the treatment and they count on strong network support after inpatient care has ended.

IV   *Network as Mitigator of Effects of Multi Organizational Involvement.* Throughout North America we find that there are clients with a multiplicity of problems and it often follows that many social service agencies are involved in service delivery to one client system (sometimes to one client). Most often these agencies all work independently. The client is pushed and pulled in many directions and is not able to discern self direction. Auerswald (1971) and Erickson et al (1974) discuss the need to stage meetings in which all the agencies providing services are brought to a conference *together with the "multiproblem family"*. My own experience with these conferences convinces me that this should become the treatment of choice for such situations as soon as a client indicates lack of progress and appears frustrated at demands for work made by various caregivers. The first line of action is to clarify the differences by telephone. When this seems not to work the conference should be called.

Negotiating conferences may be a very difficult task with some agencies. It is self evident that wherever more than one agency is providing helping services there is hazard of fragmentation and divergent planning. At these meetings, time is *not* spent on recitation of deviance and pathology among the family members, but on immediate problem solving and honest attempt to collaborate and to give responsibilities to the most appropriate persons. Contracts are ratified and witnessed and therefore commitments have much greater strength and potential to help appropriately and efficiently.

V   *Network Building and Rebuilding.* There are many clients of social agencies whose social network is shrivelled to the point of being non existent (Pattison et al, 1979). In order for individuals to have a more meaningful existence, and to attain any amount of independence from constant professional service, their friendship network may need to be enlarged. There are those clients whose networks are deleterious for the client's own well being. These clients need help to get involved in more constructive ingroups in which they can find meaningful friendship and support.

Turkat (1979) points out that in many cases severely disturbed individuals have rejected and have been rejected by their natural social networks. In many cases the lines of communication have been disrupted, mutual trust has been dissipated, and hence the relationship has become so stressful and unrewarding that focal persons do not even seek the support of network members during a crisis. In functioning networks there exists reciprocity of emotional and tangible exchanges. The severely handicapped have gone through periods when they were unable to give. They will need to relearn how to give of themselves so a network with reciprocal features can be built up around them. In an efficiency conscious society few people have enough patience to allow adults the remediation necessary in relearning how to give. Caregivers in mental health services must become more innovative in providing a gradation of after care services wherein the proportion of professional input is phased out as others, including self help groups, friends and relatives, take over increasing responsibility. I am thinking of a patterned continuum with many programs flowing from one to another, where the beginning of the flow is the initiation of professional services and the end of the flow is independent living. Caregivers will need to engage in community organization, group work training sessions, organization of recreational and vocational activities. No one profession is adequate for such a task. Interdisciplinary teams will have to work together. Included in these teams must be: high level of skill, mutual respect, trust, goodwill, and united purpose.

David Cutler (1978) points out that historically, natural community networks - churches and a wide variety of community-based organizations have always been utilized as refuges for persons who are rejected by society for deviant behaviours and appearances. The state hospitals took over this function for about 100 years and during that time the community forgot how to provide care for deviants. Those patterns that worked before the presence of large mental hospitals could again be called into service.

There are many ways whereby networks can be built and rebuilt. Following is one illustration of how a social worker attended to the needs of two alienated and lonely old folks in a small village:

An elderly woman had hit an elderly man on the head with a hammer. The woman was subsequently hospitalized in a psychiatric hospital and the man had to go for observation to the general hospital. These elderly people had both lived alone in a small village. Members of the village were very disturbed when they heard that Mrs. A., 'that old eccentric woman who had become crazy' was going to be returned to her home from the psychiatric hospital. According to the information they received via the grapevine and according to their stigmatized view of psychiatric treatment, they had reason to be frightened. Several natural leaders appointed themselves as spokespersons who would prohibit the return of Mrs. A. to the village. The social worker realized that the village people needed to be informed about what had really happened and they needed also to do something in order to help both Mrs. A. and Mr. L.

The social worker called several townhall meetings. He informed the people that Mrs. A. had hit Mr. L. on the head because he had persisted in making unwelcome sexual advances. This was her way of protecting herself. The social worker reported that Mrs. A. had been doing very well in hospital and listed reasons why it would be inappropriate to hold her in the psychiatric hospital. Several people came to Mrs. A.'s support and acknowledged that this 'strange woman' was probably not dangerous. She had, however, been alienated from the villagers for a long time. The villagers resolved that they could do something to help both these old people. They would provide for social interaction and human support. They would include them in more social activities of the village. The meeting ended on a positive, caring note. Village people, with some help from the social worker, became willing to provide a more nurturant and constructive environment for two lonely people.[3]

In the above example the caregiver was in touch with community spokespersons in regard to a controversial issue. He was willing to engage in community concerns on behalf of his client and the community. He organized a 'town hall' meeting. After two such meetings the villagers were willing to welcome two elderly alienated persons into their network.

Network building and rebuilding will take much energy and imagination. The strategies will include everything from serendipitous connections to match making. People with commonality are brought to one place at one time with the hope that friendship will develop.

Another large category of activity in the context of network building pertains firstly to the realm of self help group formation and secondly to collaboration with existing self help groups. Earlier it was stated that professional services must be organized in such a way that professional input is diminished in conjunction with increased self help. The interface between professional care and self help must become a focus of professional attention. This process should not be left to chance. The professional care-givers can give needed direction and support. Baker (1977) points out that lay people have often devised self help groups when problems were unattended to by professionals. There is nothing intrinsically wrong with this except that the process is often very slow and therefore costly in terms of human well being. Professional attention to these needs could speed up the development of appropriate care. Development of self help networks is a complex process. Professionals, as it were, sow seeds which will come to fruition in self help groups. In the early stages traditional group work methods (Schwartz, 1961) can be used to get people with common interests and concerns together. The caregivers must be clear that they will not take direct leadership past the beginning phase. They must take care to establish acceptance for governance by the membership. The role of the caregivers is clearly announced as providing help to get things going. Once the group is stabilized the caregivers provide help only as needed.

Relationships between established self help groups and professionals are often unsatisfactory (Baker, 1977; Katz, 1980). There is accusation on the part of the self help members that: the professionals do not really understand; they are too theoretical and that they make things worse. The professionals often accuse the self help group members of meddling, of undoing valuable progress. From what I have experienced in this regard the accusations cease when open and frank dialogue begins. Self help group members would like to use the expertise professionals have to offer.

Professionals appreciate what natural helpers can do to aid in ongoing care. There is growing literature which establishes the value of self help groups. (Katz and Bender, 1976; Gartner and Riessman, 1977). Interaction between self help groups and professional caregivers will greatly enhance early detection of problems, direction for focus of prevention programs and better after care for consumers of family and social services.

Network building and rebuilding are difficult tasks which need concerted efforts on the part of policy makers and social service agencies and individual caregivers. Collins and Pancoast (1976) as well as Froland (1978), Cutler (1978) and Turkat (1980) provide some useful models for network building.

CONCLUSION

Social network theory and social network intervention provide family practitioners with more tools to perform their work. These tools are being rapidly shaped and honed by many researchers and caregivers in North America and Britain. Social and family networks are the source for emotional (affective) and practical (instrumental) resources which the individual and family require not only for general well being but also for survival. The study of social networks will better help us to understand community life and the kinds of interventive programs needed.

Some rethinking and reorientation will be called for in family practice if a social network orientation is going to be taken seriously. The boundaries around the nuclear family become too limiting for comprehensive practice. An increased emphasis is placed on understanding the social systems in which individuals and families are embedded (Mitchell and Trickett, 1980). New practice models which encompass the collaborative efforts of professional and lay persons will need to be established. This collaboration with natural helpers is a logical outgrowth of social network intervention. It presents a challenge to professionals in the human services, maximizes natural human support resources, inherent in a person's environment, as a vital component of the helping process.

NOTES

[1] Dr. Mary Warmbrod, Asst. Prof., Psychological Service Centre, University of Manitoba is acknowledged as the leader of the interventive team. She was a graduate student in practicum at that time.

[2] John Chudzik formerly a senior supervisor at Children's Aid Society of Central Manitoba was directly involved in initiating and implementing the new model of interaction between the agency and Long Plains Indian Reservation. He invited the author to several meetings with natural helpers and Band Council members.

[3] Noel Thomas, Plantagenet, Ontario, a rural mental health social worker, provided this example in a workshop co-sponsored by the author.

162   *Treating Families With Special Needs*

REFERENCES

Attneave, Carolyn L. **1969**. "Therapy in Tribal Settings and Urban Network Intervention." 8. *Family Process*, 192-210.
Attneave, Carolyn L. **1975**. *Family Network Map*. Copyright, 1975. 5206 Ivanhoe Place, N.E., Seattle, Washington, 98015.
Attneave, Carolyn L. **1976**. "Social Networks as a Unit of Intervention" in *Family Therapy: Theory and Practice*. P. Guerin ed. New York: Gardner Press.
Attneave, Carolyn L. **1980**. "Social Networks and Clinical Practice: A Logical Extension of Family Therapy" in David S. Freeman, ed. *Perspectives in Family Therapy*, Vancouver, B.C.: Butterworth and Co.
Auerswald, E.H. **1968**. "Interdisciplinary Versus Ecological Approach." 7. *Family Process*, 202-215.
Baker, Frank. **1977**. "The Interface Between Professional and Natural Support Systems". 5(2). *Clinical Social Work Journal*, 139-148.
Barnes, John A. **1954**. "Class and Committees in a Norwegian Island Parish." 7. *Human Relations*, (Feb.).
Bott, Elizabeth. **1957**. *Family and Social Network*. London: Tavistock.
Boissevain, Jeremy. **1974**. *Friends of Friends*. Oxford: Basil Blackwell.
Bradley, Raymond T. **1975**. "Multiplex Relations and the Social Integration of Urban Communes". Working Paper #5, Urban Communes Project, Centre for Policy Research, and Columbia University: New York.
Cabot, Richard. **1915**. *Social Service and the Art of Healing*. New York: Dodd.
Cantor, Marjorie. **1975**. "Life Space and the Social Support System of the Inner City Elderly of New York". (Feb.). *The Gerontologist*.
Collins, Alice H. and **Pancoast**, Diane L. **1976**. *Natural Helping Networks: A Strategy for Prevention*. Washington, NASW.
Craven, Paul and **Wellman**, Barry. **1973**. "The Network City" 43:3 and 4. *Sociological Inquiry*, 57-88.
Cutler, David L. and **Madore**, Elizabeth. **1980**. "Community - Family Network Therapy in a Rural Setting" 16,2 (Summer). *Community Mental Health Journal*, 144-154.
Cutler, David L. **1978**. "Building Folk Networks for Chronic Patients", in Charles Froland and Diane Pancoast, *Networks for Helping: Illustrations from Research and Practice*. Portland, Oregon 97207. Regional Research Institute. Portland State University.
Driedger, Walter A. **1980**. "Prevention in Family Practice" in David S. Freeman, ed. *Perspectives in Family Therapy*. Vancouver, B.C.: Butterworth and Co.
Erickson, Gerald D., **Rachlis**, Ruth and **Tobin**, Margaret. **1974**. "Combined Family and Service Network Intervention". Vol. 41. *The Social Worker*, Ottawa, Canada, 276-283.
Erickson, Gerald D. **1975**. "The Concept of Personal Network in Clinical Practice". 14(4). *Family Process*, 487-498.
Erickson, Gerald D. **1976**. *Personal Networks, Mental Illness, and Social Work Practice: Framework for a Single Subject Approach*. Unpublished D. Phil. Dissertation, University of York, U.K. Dept. of Social Administration and Social Work.
Evans, Glen. **1979**. *The Family Circle Guide to Self Help*. New York: Ballantine Books.
Farquharson, Andrew. **1979**. "Self Help in the Provision of Child Welfare: The Stoney Creek Indian Band." Mimeographed, Victoria, B.C.: University of Victoria.
Freedson, Eliot. **1972**. "Client Control and Medical Practice" in *Patients, Physicians and Illness*. 2nd ed. E. Gartley Jaco, ed.
Froland, Charles and **Pancoast**, Diane L. **1978**. *Networks for Helping: Illustrations from Research and Practice*. Portland, Oregon, 97207. Regional Research Institute, Portland State University.
Garrison, John. **1974**. "Networks Techniques: Case Studies in the Screening-Linking-Planning Conference Method" 13. *Family Process*, 337-351.
Garrison, John and **Werfel**, Sandra. **1977**. "A Network Approach to Clinical Social Work" 5(2). *Clinical Social Work Journal*, 108-116.
Gartner, A. and **Reissman**, F. **1977**. *Self Help in the Human Services*. San Francisco: Jossey-Bass.
Gottlieb, B.H. and **Schroter**, Candice. **1978**. "Collaboration and Resource Exchange Between Professionals and Natural Support Systems". (Nov.). *Professional Psychology*, 614-620.

Gronovetter, Mark. 1973. "The Strength of Weak Ties." 78 (May). *American Journal of Sociology*, 1360-80.
Hirsch, B.J. 1979. "Psychological Dimensions of Social Networks: A Multi-method Analysis." 7. *American Journal of Community Psychology*, 263-277.
Howard, Jane. 1978. "All Happy Clans are Alike: In the Search of the Good Family". (May). *The Atlantic Monthly*.
Johnson, Vernon. 1975. "I'll Quit Tomorrow" *16 mm Film*, Minneapolis, Minn. 55441: The Johnson Institute, 10700 Olson Memorial Highway.
Justice, Blair and Justice, Rita. 1979. *The Broken Taboo: Sex in the Family*. New York: Human Sciences.
Kadushin, C. 1969. *Why People Go to Psychiatrists*. New York: Atherton.
Katz, Alfred, H. and Bender, E.I. 1976. *The Strength in Us: Self Help Groups in the Modern World*. New York: New Viewpoints.
Katz, Alfred H. 1980. "Commentary" Helping Networks and the Welfare State: A Symposium. Toronto: University of Toronto, School of Social Work.
Laumann, Edward, O. 1973. *Bonds of Pluralism*. New York: Wiley.
Litwak, E. 1960. "Geographic Mobility and Extended Family Cohesion" 25. *American Sociological Review*, 385-394.
Litwak, E. and Szelenyi, I. 1969. "Primary Group Structures and Their Functions: Kin, Neighbours and Friends." 34. *American Sociological Review*, 465-481.
Llamas, Robert, Pattison, E., Mansell, and Hurd, Gary. 1981. "Social Networks: A Link Between Psychiatric Epidemiology and Community Mental Health". 3(3). *International Journal of Family Therapy*, 180-192.
Lynch, James J. 1977. *The Broken Heart: The Medical Consequences of Loneliness*. New York: Basic Books, Inc.
McCallister, L. and Fischer, C.S. 1978. "A Procedure for Surveying Personal Networks". 7. *Sociological Methods and Research*, B1-148.
McKinlay, J.B. 1973. "Social Networks, Lay Consultation, and Help-Seeking Behaviour". 51. *Social Forces*, 275-92.
McLanahan, Sara S., Wedemeyer, Nancy V. and Adelberg, Tina. 1981. "Network Structure, Social Support, and Psychological Well-Being in the Single Parent Family". (August). *Journal of Marriage and the Family*, 601-612.
Mitchell, J.C. 1969. *Social Networks in Urban Situations*. Manchester: University of Manchester Press.
Mitchell, Roger E. and Trickett, Edison J. 1980. "Task Force Report: Social Networks as Mediators of Social Support: An Analysis of the Effects and Determinants of Social Networks." 16(1). *Community Mental Health Journal*, 27-44.
Morris, J.H. Jr. and Cicero-Hilbert, Judy. 1981. "Training Social Workers, Clients, and Students in the Use of Rural Natural Helping Networks and Rural Linkages" *Sixth National Institute on Social Work in Rural Areas*, Mimeographed. Columbia, S.C.: University of South Carolina.
Pattison, E. Mansell, and Defrancesco, Donald, et al. 1975. "A Psychosocial Kinship Model for Family Therapy". 132(12). *American Journal of Psychiatry*, 1246-1250.
Pearlman, Helen H. 1952. *Social Casework*. Chicago: University of Chicago Press.
Pincus, Allen and Minahan, Anne. 1973. *Social Work Practice: Model and Method*. Ithaca, Ill. F.E. Peacock Pub., Inc.
Reid, William J. and Epstein, Laura. 1972. *Task Centered Casework*. New York: Columbia University Press.
Richmond, Mary. 1917. *Social Diagnosis*. New York: Russell Sage Foundation.
Rueveni, Uri. 1976. "Family Networks: Healing Families in Crisis", (May-June). *Intellect*.
Saulnier, Kathryn. 1980. *A Study of Inmate Attributions*. Unpublished Masters Thesis. Winnipeg: Dept. of Psychology, University of Manitoba.
Schwartz, William. 1961. "The Social Worker in the Group." *The Social Welfare Forum*. New York: Columbia University Press.
Speck, Ross V. and Attneave, Carolyn L. 1973. *Family Networks*. New York: Pantheon Books.
Speck, Ross V. and Reuveni, Uri. 1967. Network Therapy: A Developing Concept." 8. *Family Process*, 182-191.
Turkat, David. 1979. "Devised Social Networks", *Current Psychology*, 19-20.

Walker, Kenneth, **MacBride**, A. and **Vachon**, M. **1977**. "Social Support Networks and Crisis of Bereavements", *Social Science and Medicine*, 35-41.
Weinberg, S.K. *1976*. *Incest Behavior* (Rev. Ed.) Secacus, N.J.: Citadel Press.
Wellman, B. **1979**. "The Community Question: The Intimate Networks of East Yorkers." 84 (March). *American Journal of Sociology*, 1201-31.

Chapter 10

Family Mediation: A Method for Helping Families Resolve Legal Disputes

Howard Irving
Faculty of Social Work, University of Toronto

This year alone in the United States and Canada over 1,000,000 couples will divorce. If one includes the children, in-laws, close friends, and business colleagues of each divorcing couple, the total number of people affected by the pain, frustration, and destructive emotional trauma of each legally contested divorce is staggering. The average cost of a contested divorce - $10,000 per spouse - is just as staggering. Members of the legal profession are fully aware that current legal attitudes toward divorce, based as they are on the venerable notion of fault, are socially irrelevant and psychologically dangerous. When a marriage is over, it is not the time for retribution and revenge, but rather the occasion to strike out for a new life while providing for and protecting the children.

Court contested divorce protects the legal rights of the individual but is totally unresponsive to emotional complications which often have the harshest effect on the children of the divorcing couple. Mediation is directed at people whose marriage is near breakdown or has already broken down, and has as a central goal, helping the family become rational and responsible enough to co-operate on making voluntary settlements that are least detrimental to everyone.

In many cases the emotional entanglement during separation, and later, may lead to a great deal of resentment on the part of one individual in the family. Before proper mediation can be effective, this individual may need to take advantage of more intensive psychological therapy outside the mediation process. This type of therapy is called crisis intervention and is also short-term. It may be simultaneous with the divorce mediation process.

It is important to understand that the mediator will be taking a "systems" approach to the family. That is, if one member is affected, the entire family "system" is also affected. It is therefore crucial that the mediator be able to see all family members who may be involved. The best way to describe the role of the mediator would be to define him or her as a "facilitator". The mediator's main objective is the resolution of family disputes in the context of what is best for the children.

The divorce mediation system is at least in part a combination of traditional labour relations techniques and the ability to understand the nuances of inter-personal relationships. The problem remains, of course, of how to implement this combined knowledge when dealing with divorce, a problem that seems on the surface to be unlike either a labour dispute or an administrative tribunal.

The actual method in divorce mediation derives from a process of negotiations in conflict resolution. The techniques utilized are always done in an atmosphere of support and trust. Communications theory is drawn upon quite heavily as is systems theory, learning theory, and role theory. Some of the general principles have become a worn truism. 1) One cannot not communicate. 2) Communication is multi level. 3) Interaction is a cyclical reverberating process. 4) The whole is greater than the sum of its parts. These principles provide the mediator with the understanding that he cannot operate in a vacuum by seeing the clients only on an individual basis. As a matter of fact, the same principles that apply to family therapy generally, also apply to divorce mediation. The mediator must be able to understand the patterns of communication which define the family rules. He must then be able to stimulate communication and help the family establish a therapeutic contract.

I find it very important that the rules of mediation be spelled out to all the parties. I even give them a typed copy of the rules. For example, each party must agree to put aside their anger and resentment and deal with a sense of fair play. Each agrees to be committed to reaching a resolution through mediation. Each agrees to share all information pertinent to the issues. Each agrees not to include other family members and especially children as confidants in matters discussed during the mediation. Finally, each member to the mediation is given an opportunity to state his own rules for the mediation. The structure is necessary to help people resolve issues and not necessarily change their personality. It is highly focused and as mentioned earlier, all of the interaction is conducted in an atmosphere of co-operation.

I would like to share with you my method of family mediation as well as some of our preliminary findings with approximately 300 families through a mediation project at the Family Court in Toronto.[1]

Initially, the mediator spells out to the family members and lawyers the general principles and guidelines for mediation and arbitration. It is paramount that the lawyers for both parties be involved as soon as possible and that the guidelines be spelled out and agreed upon by the clients and their lawyers. An example of these guidelines has been developed by myself and a legal colleague which takes the following form:[2]

It is understood that you consent to act as mediator and this letter will set out the terms upon which the mediation is to proceed. They are:

1) As mediator, you will attempt to bring about an agreement between the father and the mother as to the determination of the following questions: a) How much time should the child spend with each parent during school summer vacation? b) Should custody of the child be changed from the mother to the father?

2) In considering these questions, the parents and the mediator shall give primary importance to the needs of the child and how these needs, in the circumstances, can best be met.

3) In working out the custody and access arrangement which best meets the needs of the child, the parents may agree that: a) One or other of them shall have temporary custody of the child for a trial period; or b) Both of them shall have custody of the child as joint custodians, or first one parent then the other, during periods that are specified and set out in the agreement; or c) Neither of the parents shall have custody of the child but the periods of time which each child is to be with each parent are to be specified and set out in the agreement. These alternatives are

mentioned for the purpose of emphasizing that the parties are to make whatever arrangement is in the best interest of the child. Their choice may be one of these alternatives, or any better alternative that might emerge from the mediation meeting.

4)   The separation agreement entered into under date of the____ day of____ , 19____ , shall not be binding on the parties so far as the questions of custody and access are concerned.

5)   The question of the child's maintenance or financial support is excluded from mediation and, if it arises, shall be referred back to Counsel for determination.

6)   In attempting to bring about an agreement, the mediator may meet with and speak to the father, the mother, and the child separately, or jointly, and may consult such other persons and inspect such reports, records, or documents as he deems necessary.

7)   Any agreement reached shall constitute a settlement of the subjects under mediation and be produced for the information of the court in the legal proceedings pending between the father and the mother in the Supreme Court of____or in any other relevant proceedings.

8)   In the event that no agreement is reached within the period established for mediation, both parties shall have the right to pursue their legal remedies in the action pending between them in the Supreme Court of____or in such other action or proceedings as they or either of them may be advised to take.

9)   The period of time allowed for the mediation shall be established by the mediator in consultation with both Counsel after the mediator has interviewed both parents, but in no event shall be for more than six weeks from the date of this letter.

10)   Evidence of anything said or of any admission or communication made in the course of mediation is not admissible in the pending or any other legal proceeding.

11)   The mediator will not be called as a witness or on behalf of either parent in the pending or any other legal proceeding, and the mediator shall not be required or permitted in the pending or any other legal proceeding to give any opinion or to disclose any admission or communication made to him in the course of mediation.

12)   Except to inform Counsel that: a) no agreement has been reached; or b) what the terms of the agreement are, there shall be no report made by the mediator of the mediation process.

13)   Your fee for mediation shall be borne by the parents in equal shares and payable on such terms as are determined by you.

Mediation is agreed to by both parents in the confident expectation that, with your assistance, they can determine the questions above, in a way that will be more satisfactory than any settlement imposed by a court or other process.

Once the basic ground rules are set, divorce mediation is further defined to the couple. Any agreement reached would constitute a settlement of the subjects under dispute. Only this agreement, unlike an arbitrator's report, would be given to the court in the legal proceedings pending between them. If no agreement is reached in mediation the parents are free to pursue their dispute through the adversarial system. The period of time allowed for dispute resolution using divorce mediation would be established once the family had been interviewed and after consultation with their lawyers, but for no reason should it extend beyond a six-week time limit.

Point 10 of the referral letter is reiterated to assure the couple that none of the information gathered would be admissible in any legal proceeding. The mediator would only inform counsel either that no agreement had been obtained or, if an agreement was reached, what its terms were.

For couples who are unable to settle a dispute by mediation, it is often necessary to refer them for binding arbitration. This is a very different approach because all information is made available to the Court, and in effect, one is conducting an evaluation and writing a recommendation for dispute resolution. It should be understood that the mediator cannot function as an arbitrator if the mediation breaks down. All proceedings commence *de novo* (anew). In binding arbitration, the spouses agree in advance that the decision of the arbitrator will be binding on them with the same force as a Court order. This is only used as a last resort. All the information in the arbitrator's report can be cross-examined and challenged if the parties are unable to accept the arbitrator's recommendations.

PROCEDURES OF THE METHOD

The Initial Phase: Understanding Through Exploration

The first discussions are usually carried out with each individual family member. It is critical for the mediator to thoroughly explain the mediation process at this time. This is a period of individual introspection and the mediator simply tries to understand where each individual stands as well as what each wants to accomplish. The mediator will listen to what is said, but will also observe what is done.

The mediator's ability to empathize is critical to this phase. He or she must be able to accept, understand and support the family members so that real expression can take place. The focus is not only on how the individual feels about a specific problem at hand, but also on self-perception. This process creates an atmosphere of trust between client and mediator. The major intent is to identify and clarify problems, while offering constant emotional support. Each relevant family member is approached in the same way: given an opportunity to ventilate the anger and hurt according to each person's unique situation while being able to explore and focus on his or her unique problems.

Second Phase: Problem Solving

This is the critical negotiation phase which eventually leads to the resolution of disputes. During this period it is extremely important that family members interact with each other. The focus during this phase shifts from the mediator to the family, when joint interviews are held with the couple, or with the entire family if the situation demands collective consultation. Each person explains his or her goals and expresses what is really wanted.

The individual positions which were discovered in phase one are discussed among the parties involved. These views are discussed in two ways: 1) as stated by the individual and 2) as they are understood by other family members. When there is an impasse, the mediator attempts to reframe the conflict by broadening perspectives and offering options not previously realized. For example, in a situation where the parents are in disagreement as to the amount of time children should spend with each of them, they may be so concerned with their own objectives that they have not considered what would be best for their children. The mediator can help the parents see how they must set aside their own personal interests when those interests conflict with the best interests of the children. This is usually brought about during discussion with the children and parents together.

Final Phase: Resolution

This phase of divorce mediation usually takes a highly structured form. It is nearly contractual in nature and details what each party will do. Each step is monitored so that everyone concerned knows what action is being taken on any agreements made. If anyone does not act as agreed there will be almost immediate feedback. This reduced the "revolving door syndrome" of going back to the courts.

It is neither desirable nor necessary for individual lawyers to be taking any legal action during the divorce mediation process. The absence of lawyers at this point, quite apart from the expense involved, helps prevent the old spectres of the adversary system (fault finding and blame) from getting in the way of the issues at hand. In order to protect both spouses and the mediator, all meetings, information presented, or offers made are considered confidential and are not available for any subsequent court proceedings. In this way, the mediator will not degenerate into yet another "expert" witness. To make sure, the mediator will require as a precondition that he or she will not be called later to testify or produce documents in a courtroom. This is important to the spouses because it helps them feel at ease. They know they can discuss their feelings with a degree of openness and candour that will make it easier to arrive at a resolution.

Some lawyers also become uneasy when confronted with the divorce mediation process. They instruct their clients not to reveal certain information for fear that it will be held against them in a subsequent court case.

Due to the undeniable legal implication of divorce, the mediator should meet privately with individual lawyers, accountants, or any other relevant persons where such meetings might be appropriate. Each spouse is encouraged to fully disclose all information (financial statements, tax returns, and the like) that are requested either by the mediator or the other spouse when such information has an important bearing on the discussion. This type of discussion falls into the "fact finding" phase of the divorce mediation process.

Divorce mediation is not intended to be extended family therapy. There are agencies as well as private practitioners that provide family and marriage counseling, and such groups and individuals do provide long term therapy. The length of divorce mediation meetings as well as their number and frequency can be determined once it is clear that the entire process will be beneficial to the whole family. In any event, the number of meetings is not extended to the point where they might unduly delay legal divorce proceedings or increase costs. As a hedge against the mediation meetings becoming protracted, the couple may jointly specify an outward limit - six to ten meetings, for example. Fluidity is of prime importance, so all such limits may be waived at any time with the consent of all concerned.

Though maximum limits may be fluid, minimum limits should be firmly set. If mediation is entered into voluntarily, then a minimum limit of perhaps two meetings should be required. If, however, mediation or conciliation are ordered by the court, there is usually a limit of two meetings with a maximum of six. The Los Angeles Conciliation Court, for instance, requires one session of approximately one and one-half hours. During this meeting, the spouses are usually seen together first for a brief period to enable the conciliator to establish the ground rules, satisfy them of his or her impartiality, and to assure them that the welfare of the children is of primary importance. The parents are then seen separately and the entire session ends with a tripartite conference. If it appears that the process will be beneficial, a second meeting might be scheduled. From that point other meetings can be arranged if progress is made and if the process is improving the situation.

Once the couple is satisfied that mediation really is a rational and helpful alternative to the courts, that the mediator is impartial, and that the interests of the children come first, then attempts at a divorce settlement can begin. If agreement is reached, the details are written down, signed by the spouses and shown to the respective lawyers. This agreement is then submitted to the court as the basis of the divorce decree. The agreement comes solely from the mediation process and has nothing to do with fault or the adversary system. It is a result of mutual co-operative problem solving.

To sum up, the mediator must: 1) provide emotional support, 2) help identify the problem or problems, 3) elicit sufficient factual information to find a solution to the problem, 4) develop and identify all possible alternative solutions, 5) assist the couple to mutually select one of the alternatives and 6) develop an agreement as to the steps which must be taken in order for the selected alternative to be successful, and 7) follow up or monitor the success of such an agreement.

Divorce mediation is a method of co-operative conflict resolution that relies on compromising and confronting techniques where good will is the *modus operandi*. The mediator utilizes family self-determination and communication skills in enabling the family to reach an agreement that is in the best interests of the family.

When an agreement is signed by the parties, it is often helpful to put in a clause that allows for and encourages a return to mediation if the parties themselves are unable to resolve further conflicts. It is important to realize that practically all of the empirical studies have found that approximately 70% of the clients who go to mediation end up with an agreement rather than proceeding to litigation. Furthermore, these agreements are durable and although they change from time to time, they do not resort to the court as in a contested dispute. In effect, the families have developed a system of on-going mediation that they themselves conduct. Although much needs to be learned about mediation, the results of successful mediation are extremely promising.

Marriage is not, after all, a corporate merger. It is a willing participation in a social and emotional contract. The advantage of divorce mediation is that divorce is not viewed as any one individual's fault, but rather as a common responsibility. It is not for the courts to solve all interpersonal problems nor can we abdicate our own responsibilities for the conduct of our lives and those of our children.

BIBLIOGRAPHY

Irving, Howard. **1980**. "Divorce Mediation: The Rational Alternative". Toronto: Personal Library Publishers.
Irving, et al. **1981**. "A Study of Conciliation Counselling in the Family Court of Toronto". Toronto: Ministry of the Attorney General.

PERSPECTIVES ON DISABILITY
AND THE HELPING PROCESS

In this, the United Nation's Year of Disabled Persons, attention has been drawn to the circumstances and needs of the physically and mentally handicapped. A keynote address at the 1981 Banff Conference ("The Historical Development of Attitudes Toward the Handicapped: A Framework for Change") focused directly on the concerns of the disabled. This address is offered as a preliminary statement in this section of our book. In his presentation, Henry Enns considers attitudes in regard to the disabled and describes how distorted perceptions lead to inappropriate actions on the part of the general public and the helping professions. The intent of the chapter is to make professionals more cognizant of the role they have played in creating the societal image of the disabled as helpless and dependent. An alternative strategy, "the independent living paradigm" is offered for devising programs and service structures available to disabled persons. Inherent to this paradigm is the acknowledgement that in many circumstances the disabled can achieve the greatest benefit from self help activities in which they take an active role as the advocates, planners, and providers of their own services.

The choice of family intervention as a treatment alternative is often not adequately appreciated in human services. David Freeman ("Family Systems Thinking and the Helping Process: Misconceptions and Basic Assumptions") discusses common misconceptions about family therapy and clarifies the basic assumptions in this approach to human change. A "systems orientation" is identified as a fundamental conceptual framework which may guide practitioners employing this perspective in the helping process.

Physical disability and family dynamics are closely inter-related. The response of family members can profoundly influence the impact of disability on an individual. Concurrently, disability in a family member can directly affect ongoing family dynamics. Family practitioners can engage with the disabled and their families to promote inter-relationships that are conducive to improved health status in the disabled person. They may assist families to establish appropriate expectations and effective coping skills in dealing with crises associated with physical disability.

The response of the health care system in situations of illness and disability has traditionally been focused on the individual, rather than the family unit, as "the patient". Lorraine Wright and Janice Bell ("Nurses, Families & Illness: A New Combination") consider the implications of family focused intervention in nursing care and offer an alternative paradigm for service delivery. Within hospital settings, nurses may provide valuable information and psychological support in engaging with families to ameliorate the confusion and stress associated with serious illness.

Karin Buchanan ("The Impact of Critical Illness on the Family: Stresses and Responses") considers the impact of serious illness on the family. She outlines the practical problems and emotional stresses families may face in critical illness situations. As a framework for assessment, Buchanan identifies social factors and personality characteristics that will influence a family's response to life threatening circumstances.

The last chapter in this section on disability and the helping process ("Chronic Pain and Family Dynamics") by Ranjan Roy considers the treatment of chronic pain from the perspective of the family system. Family dynamics are viewed as they relate to the etiology and perpetuation of chronic pain. Case examples are offered to highlight the role of family members as these inter-relate with the person suffering chronic pain and to exemplify individual and family characteristics of the pain prone patient. Alternative approaches are identified which apply a family frame of reference in the assessment and treatment of chronic pain.

Chapter 11

The Historical Development of Attitudes Toward the Handicapped: A Framework for Change

Henry Enns
Disabled Peoples' International, Winnipeg

INTRODUCTION

Historically, handicapped people have been badges of shame and objects of pity and embarrassment to families and communities. They were often hidden from public view. Examples of these are numerous in popular literature such as "The Hunchback of Notre Dame" and Dickens' "Christmas Carol". In biblical writings, they were seen as beggars, sitting beside the road asking for alms. Later, they became candidates for poor houses and mental institutions.

Today, we like to think that this deplorable condition has largely vanished. But is this really true? In *Handicapping America*, Frank Bowe (1978), states that:

> The city of Chicago recently repealed an ugly law, similar versions of which remain in force in Columbus (Ohio) and Omaha (Nebraska). The Chicago statute read: 'No person who is diseased, maimed, mutilated, or in any way deformed, so as to be an unsightly, or a disgusting object, or improper person, is to be allowed in or on the public ways, or other public places in this city, nor shall therein, or thereon expose himself to public view .'

Society has created an image of disabled people that may be the greatest barrier towards full participation and equality during 1981, the International Year of Disabled Persons. We see the disability, the white cane, crutches, hearing aid and wheelchair, but not the person. Commonly held myths are that handicapped people are psychologically maladjusted, that they are "sick", feeble minded, in need of sheltering and protection and are asexual.

Attitudes towards handicapped people seem to be a mixture of fear, ignorance, optimism and discrimination. Attitudinal barriers influence and underlie actions. Teachers will not exert effort on, or expect performance from students they do not think can achieve. Employers will not hire applicants they do not believe will fit in or be able to do the job. In Canadian society handicapped people have been defined by their disabilities, not their abilities.

Proof of our attitudes can be seen by the way the communications media publish and broadcast "gee whiz" stories about physically disabled people who succeed in any endeavor. What a non-handicapped person does as a matter of course - what he is generally expected to do - often becomes noteworthy or extraordinary when done by a disabled person. Why should it be so noteworthy when a physically handicapped person graduates from a university, or attains some success in a business or professional career? Is it not because so little is expected of the physically handicapped?

This paper makes no attempt to review research studies on attitudes towards disabled people in societies past, nor is there any attempt to analyze literature on social service practices, or social policy in Canada. The aims are clear: to make professionals more critical of the role they have played in contributing towards the images of helplessness and dependency society has of disabled people in Canada, and to suggest a framework in which attitudinal change can take place. This framework is presented in an historical perspective and suggests a new role for rehabilitation services. If "full participation and equality" is ever to become a reality, disabled people must be seen as citizens with rights first and clients of social services second. It will be demonstrated throughout the paper that attitudes and treatment of disabled people are closely linked.

At least three phases can be identified in society's attitude towards disabled people. The first was before the arrival of special treatments and services which we recognize today. The second was the development of hospitals, special services and legislation to provide specialized programs. The third phase, initiated recently, was marked by the development of the consumer movement of handicapped people.

DEFINITIONS

According to the Report of the Special Parliamentary Committee on the Handicapped, there are two million Canadians who have a disability and seven hundred thousand who are severely disabled. (Obstacles, 1980). The World Health Organization study calculates that one in ten adults has a disability (World Health Organization, 1980). An understanding of the concept of disability is central to attitudinal change.

Disability has too long been viewed as a problem of the individual and not the relationship between an individual and his/her environment. It is, therefore, necessary to distinguish between *impairment*, any loss or abnormality of psychological or anatomical structure or function; *disability*, any restriction or lack (resulting from an impairment) of ability to perform an activity in the manner or within the range considered normal for a human being; and *handicap*, a disability or impairment that results in a disadvantage for a given individual in that it limits or prevents the fulfillment of a role that is normal for that individual (World Health Organization, 1980). These definitions point to the socio-economic and structural obstacles that hinder participation.

The distinction between *impairment, disability,* and *handicap* are more important than clarifying definitions. The prevailing notions that disability is *in the person* is an assumption in need of critical analysis. The closest to the real is impairment, because this refers to functional loss due to injury or disease. But when we get to disability, the capacity to perform cannot be assessed in terms of the person alone, but depends on the assistive devices and qualities of the social environment available to the impaired person.

Thus, disability is a relationship of a person's physical capacities to the enabling potential of the physical and social environment. By this definition, even the all-American football player is totally disabled when flying at a high altitude without oxygen and a liveable air pressure. *Handicap* is another kind of relation to the environment involved when an impaired person competes at a disadvantage with others in various activities.

This definition of disability is of fundamental important and its implications for re-deploying rehabilitation energies and resources are far reaching. It forces us to critically examine the expenditures on clinical vocational rehabilitation services, and a questioning by disabled persons as to whether they could be used better in the development of independent living centres, the organization of advocacy groups, or lobbying for more adaptive housing.

It is useful to define or analyze the status of the handicap population as an oppressed minority group. It is noted that members of oppressed social groups have often little in common apart from being the victims of systematic oppression. This fact has been illustrated with reference to European Jews in the 1920's and 1930's; also, more recently to women and the elderly (Gliedman, 1979).

Handicapped people have begun in this decade to see themselves as a minority group, united by a common set of pressures and barriers to human rights, discrimination, largely concentrated in the economic marketplace, constituting the "sociological fate" of the handicapped. This discrimination imposes a minority group identity on handicapped people, who have in most other respects as much in common with the general population as with each other.

PRE INDUSTRIAL PHASE

Historical evidence cited concerning the treatment of the handicapped appears to be somewhat conflicting. For example, Newcomer and Bard (1976) note that archeological evidence dating back 50,000 years indicates that an individual who was disabled by virtue of the lack of one arm and partial blindness was being provisioned and cared for by the members of his social group during ice age conditions. This evidence appears to imply stable social relations and gives a basis for the assumption that this individual was of value to his group. His value did not seem to depend upon his economic contribution, but was then, as now, a social matter (Newcomer and Bard, 1976).

Bowe (1978) notes that the concept that handicaps result from inter-ractions between disabilities and environments, is well illustrated in primitive culture. Survival there depends upon strength, agility and sensory acuity, so physical disabilities become handicapping. Intellectual superiority and the ability to read, calculate and artistically create are of little value in primitive cultures. Consequently, brilliant physically disabled children and adults may have been left to die while the moderately retarded were allowed to survive because their disabilities were less handicapping.

Medical treatment of disabilities has also changed over the years. It was not until the fifth century B.C. with Hippocrates' influence that medicine began to separate from superstition and attempts were made to diagnose and treat physical and mental disease. In spite of this, the Greeks were so enamoured of physical perfection that the Athenians cast defective children from a precipice and Spartans abandoned them on a mountainside. The only anticipation of modern methods was the Greek-Roman baths, which combined hydrotherapy with exercises and social interchange. The slow advance toward "enlightenment" came to a halt during the middle ages, when the primitive belief in spirits and demons again prevailed. It was not until centuries later that the ground work for a medical attack on disabilities was laid (Enns et al., 1979).

Until the end of the middle ages in Europe, handicapped persons were provided for in informal customary traditional ways without institutional arrangements. Production was primarily agricultural and the producer was tied to land and landowner. Society was rural and consisted of small communities. Relative to the present day there was little division of labor. Peasants could not shop around for the most favourable labor situation, nor could they be displaced; therefore, they were never separated from their means of production, In such a system, the handicapped were not separated from the rest of the people but absorbed into each household economy doing whatever tasks he or she could handle. The relevant societies were small, lending themselves to comprehensive knowledge of the capabilities of individual members (Newcomer and Bard, 1976).

In the few industrial cities, production was organized under the guild system, which included crafts, begging and theft. Handicapped people in the cities were reduced to begging. By 1531, the disabled were separated from the able bodied poor and given license to beg and accept charity; although the handicapped did not incur direct physical punishment as did the able bodied. Workhouses were characterized by work confinement and discipline intended to:

> deter the indolent and vicious, nothing but extreme necessity will induce any to accept the comfort which must be obtained by the surrender of their free agency, and the sacrifices of their accustomed habits and gratifications (de Schweinitz, 1943: 123).

The innocent were to be punished along with the guilty, for their existence and treatment functioned as a deterrent to indolence. From 1531 to the beginning of the 20th century workhouse type arrangements were the main forms of service provision for the handicapped. Phase one saw handicapped people as images of misfits, beggars, candidates for poor houses, mental institutions, objects of religious pity, sympathy and charity; but, part of the community.

PHASE TWO - SEGREGATION

Phase two marked the growth of hospital based medicine and the creation of large asylums. Institutions provided the physical means for segregating disabled people from their communities. The characteristic attitude was to view disabled people as suffering personal tragedies, being unable to care for themselves and consequently, in need of protection. This was markedly different from phase one where disabled people were socially active and responsible for their actions.

The twentieth century marked the beginning of new industries and professions developing the means of "rehabilitation". This development has been characterized by "specialization" into kinds of handicaps and various "specialized needs", all requiring special services. Thus, needs of the handicapped have become the basis of many forms of employment, largely for a professional class in our society as we know it today. Professionalism is based on the perception that a given field is so complex and intricate that only the practitioners can accredit themselves. The development of successful medical practitioners in hospitals ensured greater numbers of people with physical impairments surviving, and must have strengthened the connection between disabled people and institutions as well as facilitated the medical dominance in the field. The growth of professionals, particularly in the past two decades, has been phenomenal.

The development of the "medical model" by professionals at the beginning of the twentieth century has been instrumental in shaping society's attitudes towards the disabled. Thus, professionals must share the blame for the disability attitudes.

The acceptance of the medical model in our society provides a rationale for the exclusion of the handicapped from full participation. Under this model, the handicapped are segregated by specialized services, specialized schools, sheltered workshops, architectural and transportation barriers. Thus, interaction between the handicapped and non-handicapped is severely curtailed. This lessens the potential for attitudinal change.

Products designed for the disabled are marketed through the medical social services system; thus, disabled people are barred from behaving as independent producers, consumers and citizens. In order not to react cruelly due to fear and anxiety, we opt for the "enlightened" and "humane" approach of the medical model. Rather than blame the handicapped person, we blame the disease. This fosters an image in a social sense of the handicapped as chronic patients (Gliedman, 1980).

The difficulty this presents is that it allows the disabled person no scope for leading an adult social life, and places him in a functional category similar to that of children. In our society, a particularly destructive "sick role" is thrust upon the handicapped. Not merely powerless because of illness, the handicapped are also defined as incapable because they cannot even master the job of getting well. This situation deprives the handicapped of social power and political identity.

Professionals who work with handicapped people and who have vested interest are often painted as being among the worst offenders. Ivan Illich (1978) states that the development of professions has created disparities. He indicates that for generations professionals in education, welfare and medicine have been perceived as selflessly devoted to the good of the weaker members of society, thus enabling those who lack the capacity to fend for themselves to lead fuller, safer, and healthier lives. However, the question must now be asked whether the professions in fact provide their services so altruistically, and whether we are really enriched and not just subordinated by their activities. The professions have become stronger while the clients have become passive, dependent, and economically deprived.

The fact is that social workers and recipients view identical events very differently. Enns et al., (1979) point out that while recipients saw their primary non-financial problem as bad housing, unemployment or illness, social workers saw their recipients' problems as personal or emotional difficulties (even though one-fourth stated that their recipients did not have enough money to get through the month). There was little relationship between the recipients' problem and the type of service given (i.e. counselling was the only service given for bad housing, unemployment or illness).

The rehabilitation paradigm, which is evident in both medical and vocational rehabilitation, is the most prominent in disability policy today. In this paradigm, problems are generally defined in terms of inadequate performance or in terms of inadequate preparation for gainful employment. In either case, the problem is assumed to reside in the individual. It is the individual who needs to be changed. This approach is characteristic of the "blaming the victim" philosophy. To overcome his or her problem, the disabled individual is expected to yield to the advice and instruction of a physician, vocational rehabilitation counsellor or some other professional. The disabled individual is expected to assume the role of "patient" or "client". While the goal of the rehabilitation process is maximum physical functioning or gainful employment, success in rehabilitation is to a large degree determined by whether the patient or client complied with the prescribed therapy program (De Jong, 1980).

It is apparent that public policy reflects public attitudes. The Vocational Rehabilitation for Disabled Persons Act passed in 1961 defines disability as follows:

> Disabled person means a person who, because of physical or mental impairment, is incapable of pursuing regularly any substantially gainful occupation and vocational rehabilitation means any process of restoration, training and employment placement, including services related thereto, the object of which is to enable a person to become capable of occupation.

The Act's definition of a "disabled person" begs the question of cause and effect. It seems to imply that when handicapped people are unemployed, it is because of their personal disabilities. In contrast, a structural economic analysis suggests that deficiencies in our economy breed unemployed and poor employment; and that handicapped people are affected to a greater degree by the process. Although the Act's concept of "disabled" puts the onus of economic hardship on the individual without consideration to the economic structure, its definition of "vocational rehabilitation" is limited to persons regarded as potential candidates for some form of competitive employment. It strips the handicapped of individual and social dignity by stating that sources should be made available in order "to restore them to usefulness".

Vocational rehabilitation centres physically segregate disabled people from regular vocational programs with able bodied students. This creates an artificial environment and the skills developed are often not transferable to a regular job. Sheltered workshops have their origins in the workhouses first developed in the 16th century in England. They reflect a philosophy that handicapped people are not competitive in the labour market and therefore can appropriately be paid less than minimum wage.

PHASE THREE - EQUALIZATION OF OPPORTUNITY

The move towards increasing independence in the community marks the beginning of phase three. One of the most important areas of change has come with advanced electronic technology. This technology enables the most severely disabled person to control his environment sufficiently to enable him to live relatively independently in the community.

The third phase can be viewed as just a beginning in setting the context for a generation of new attitudes. The focus is the nature of society which handicaps disabled persons. Disabled people must be defined by the things they have in common with other people while taking into account their differences. Disabled people themselves are having a major impact on changing attitudes and directing their involvement in society. They want to be seen as citizens with rights; not clients of social services.

In Canada, the struggle for independence can be traced through a long line of attitudinal developments. It started with specialized services for the Blind in the late 1900's, and services to take care of crippled children in the 1920's and 30's. All the product of the volunteer charity ethic. The 1940's and 50's saw the formulation of parent organizations concerned with improving medical services, the growth of special recreation facilities, camps for disabled people, sheltered workshops and segregated housing institutions (all the trade marks of "phase two" attitudes of dependency and helplessness).

With the technological advancements after World War II, handicapped people started to become more involved in the community. The Wheelchair Sports Associations in the 1960's demonstrated the ability of disabled people in athletics. But it wasn't until the 1970's that handicapped people began to accept the responsibility to speak out on their own behalf. They no longer wanted to be seen as passive recipients, but as active partners in decision-making on matters affecting their lives. This led to the development, in the handicapped, of the "consumer ethic" and its impact on public attitudes has been profound.

Handicapped people themselves are their own best spokespersons, and the focus should be on the ability of people, not their disability. The two different approaches have been contrasted by Beatrice Wright as the succumbing and coping frameworks (Wright, 1975). The succumbing framework concentrates on the difficulties and heartbreak of being disabled. Emphasis is on what the person can't do; what is denied the person. The disability is seen as central. The person as an individual with a highly differentiated and unique personality is lost. The coping framework on the other hand, represents the constructive view of life with a disability. It orients the perceiver to appreciate the individual as having abilities that have intrinsic value. People with disabilities are regarded as active participants in their own life and the life of the community.

The growth of the consumer movement in Canada in the 1970's is unique and warrants special consideration. Out of it developed a new appreciation of handicapped people as persons with ability and a new philosophy of the role of service providers and consumers. During the 1960's, the consumerism, self-help and civil rights movements in the United States set the example for handicapped people in Canada to speak out for their own solutions. The movement in the United States resulted in organizational models, networking and advocacy models, recognition of rights and citizen participation. In Canada, the movement was initiated with the formation of provincial organizations in Alberta and Saskatchewan in the early 1970's and the Canadian Rehabilitation Council for the Disabled Conference in 1973 in Toronto. Subsequently, an organization was formed in Manitoba in 1974 and the formation of a national organization, The Coalition of Provincial Organizations of the Handicapped, in 1976.

The goals and objectives of these organizations were all very similar. They saw themselves as vehicles for public education, lobbying for changes to environmental barriers, evaluating and monitoring services, and membership development. Thus they incorporated a mixture of consumerism and self-help approaches. The initial thrust of these organizations was focused on human rights legislation, revision of the building code, establishment of public transportation services for the disabled, and efforts to improve employment opportunities through job creation and policy change.

Philosophically, their position was quite simple and direct though not always that well defined. They wanted to have the opportunity for full participation in society. To make that possible, attitudinal and architectural barriers would have to be eliminated. They talked as citizens about rights, not as clients of social services.

Not only should services be improved, but who delivered services was equally important. Regular community delivery systems should be utilized. Services available to the community as a whole should also be modified or supplemented to provide services for disabled people, i.e. Canada Employment Centres should provide employment placement, not Rehabilitation Agencies. Specialized rehabilitation services should be established only after every effort to utilize other services has failed.

Consequently, the acceptance of a limited definition of rehabilitation services emerged:

> whereas rehabilitation is a process aimed at enabling a person to reach an optimum physical mental and/or social functioning level in order to provide that person with the tools to direct his/her own life, independent living and community services are not and should not be part of that process. (Disabled People's International Charter, 1980)

Theoretically, the consumer movement in Canada has much in common with the Independent Living Movement in the United States. The Independent Living model is a reaction against the traditional rehabilitation delivery system. It is a reaction against the "sick" role of the medical model, the child-like moppet of the charity ethic, and the helpless, passive client in the professional ethic.

The Independent Living Paradigm has emerged in part, as a response to the anomaly of the severely physically disabled person. According to the Independent Living Paradigm, the problem does not reside in the individual, but often in the solution offered by the rehabilitation services. That is, the dependency inducing features of the physician-patient, or professional-client relationship. Rehabilitation is seen as part of the problem, not the solution. The focus of the problem is not only in the environment, but the social control mechanism in society at large. To cope with these barriers, the disabled person must shed the patient or client role for the consumer role. Advocacy, peer counselling, self-help, control by disabled people, and barrier removal are the trademarks of the Independent Living model (DeJong, 1980).

The theory of causation implicit in the Indepenent Living Paradigm asserts that environmental barriers are as critical, if not more so, than personal characteristics in determining disability outcomes. Disability research must give more consideration to the effect of environmental variables. Environmental barriers include the following: hospital milieu, stigma value of disability, social milieu, access to educational, recreational and avocational pursuits, socio-economic status, architectural barriers and availability of transportation, family and interpersonal support, legislation, cultural and ethnic influences (De Jong, 1980). Since there is a growing public debate about the extent to which society should subsidize the removal of environmental barriers like inaccessible public transportation, architectural barriers and unmet personal care needs, this research could be very meaningful. If it can be empirically demonstrated that these barriers are predicative of disability outcome, it may hasten reform. Environmental variables unlike individual characteristics can be changed through legislation and administrative actions.

What is unique about the movement of disabled people in Canadian society is their role in the process of social and policy changes. While in most industrial countries, consumers have also become providers of service; in Canada there has been a strong rejection of that. Their role in Canada is mainly focused on advocacy. Services should be provided by regular community services or rehabilitation services, but it is the responsibility of the consumer movement to evaluate and monitor services, make recommendations for change, and advocate for modification or creation of new services.

It is significant to note the impact the consumer movement has had on the Report of the Special Parliamentary Committee (Obstacles 1981). It calls for the amendment of the Human Rights Act, to provide comprehensive protection for disabled Canadians and not only in employment. It promotes architectural and communications system design modifications as being usable by all people, rather than as being necessary for accessibility for disabled people alone. It recommends changes to make public transportation systems, airline travel more usable for disabled people. It takes into account that design features for public housing must consider the needs of all Canadians, including the mobility, visually, and hearing handicapped. It recommends preferential hiring policies and job creation programs for disabled Canadians as being necessary to create equal employment opportunities. Recognition is given to total communication for the sensory handicapped as being essential for integration.

The consumer movement is more than a grass-roots effort on the part of the disabled to acquire new rights and entitlements; it is also reshaping the thinking of disability professionals and researchers, has initiated new service delivery models and has encouraged new research direction. As a paradigm, "independent living" is redefining the problem of disability and encouraging new interventions that are in marked contrast to the definitions and interventions provided by the rehabilitation paradigm.

CONCLUSION

The approaches of service providers have had a major impact on society's attitudes towards disabled people. It has been clearly shown that by increasing the role and power of the professional, the responsibility and dignity of the individual is eroded. It is therefore important for the professional to understand these dynamics and to see disabled persons not as clients, but as consumers, as ultimate decision makers in goal setting and case planning. Professionals should not respond defensively but should see a consumer's sense of independence as a good omen. It must also be understood that the dynamics of a disabled person's behavior may be functional for adaptation and not pathological.

Considering the brief history of the consumer movement in Canada, its accomplishments in legislation, services and raising of consciousness have been truly remarkable. But the movement has only begun and professionals should encourage its development and support its role, for only through some degree of consumer separateness will persons with disabilities be recognized as a significant power block to be reckoned with. Separate consumer based systems do not deny integration, mainstreaming and normalization. They affirm these goals. Integration as second class citizens is not "full participation and equality".

Paradigms have latent social functions. They prepare students, scholars and practitioners for membership in a particular discipline. They define the boundaries of professional practice. They confer legitimacy upon professional groups. The emphasis on environmental issues are expanding the focus of disability services from a narrow one-to-one clinical interaction to include lawyers, architects, economists and public health professionals.

The struggle of any minority group always involves the issues of who decides what for whom. Persons with disabilities must set the terms for their participation in society. Those terms should not be based on professional assumptions. The consumer movement has given disabled persons a voice in their own future and has fostered a new sense of dignity and pride that for too long has been denied them. This will continue to be its most important contribution in the years to come.

REFERENCES

Ball, Barbara. **1975**. *Poverty Causes and Social Policy*. Unpublished.
Bowe, Frank. **1978**. *Handicapping America*. New York: Harper and Rowe Inc.
DeJong, Gerben. **1980**. *Independent Living: From Social Movement to Analytic Paradigm*. Vol. 80 (Dec). Archives of Physical Medical Rehabilitation.
Derksen, Jim. **1980**. *The Disabled Consumer Movement Policy Implications for Rehabilitation Services Provision*.

Enns, H., **Ball**, B. **1979**. "An analysis of Social and Economic Inequality of the Handicapped." Unpublished.

Finkelstein, Vic. **1980**. "Attitudes and Disabled People: Issues for Discussion" presentation paper, Milton Keyness Open University, Great Britain, MK7 6AA.

Gliedman, John. **1979**. "The Wheelchair Rebellion." (August). *Psychology Today*.

Horne, Kathie, **Enns**, Henry. **1980**. *Consumer's Involvement: Administrator's Challenge.* Unpublished.

Illich, Ivan **et al**. **1978**. *Disabling Professions*. 19 Brewer Street, London Ontario: N. Boyars Publishers Ltd.

Linquist, Bengt. **1980**. *Full Participation and Equality*. Speech presented at World Congress of Rehabilitation International. Unpublished.

Newcomer, P., and **Bard**, L.E. **1976**. *An Investigation Into Rehabilitation and Employment of Disabled in Manitoba*.

Obstacles. 1981. "Report of Special Parliamentary Committee on Disabled and Handicapped.

Rothney, Russ, **Donner**, Lissa, **Stewart**, Brian. **1977**. *Labor Market Implications for Handicapped Manitobans*.

Wright, Beatrice. **1980**. "Developing Constructive Views of Life with Disability." Paper presented at a meeting of the Social Commission on Rehabilitation International, 14th World Congress, Winnipeg, Canada.

Charter Disabled People's International. **1980**.

World Health Organization. **1980**. *International Classification of Impairments, Disabilities and Handicaps*. Geneva.

Chapter 12

Family Systems Thinking and the Helping Process: Misconceptions and Basic Assumptions[1]

David S. Freeman
School of Social Work, University of British Columbia

A therapist who works with families with a disabled member should carefully consider his/her own attitudes, values and beliefs. When utilizing a family systems approach for dealing with a serious dysfunction within the family the theoretical framework we bring to bear and the assumptions we hold about how to proceed are significant factors. The therapist must recognize the impact of the disability on family functioning, while at the same time recognize how the family can serve as a resource to itself for dealing with its needs and difficulties. This point needs to be emphasized because families with a disabled member often have other professionals involved in providing support services that the family, i.e., nuclear and extended, quite possibly could provide for itself. If this point is not recognized by professionals their involvement in the family's life can become a bigger problem to the family than are the disabled person's problems.

The following discussion highlights some of the major misconceptions therapists have about working with families and applies to families with or without disabled members. It pinpoints major misconceptions and their significance to practice.

MISCONCEPTION ONE: The Family Therapist is the Expert in Resolving Family Problems

This misconception is popular because the traditional role of the therapist has been that of the expert who gathers information, diagnoses the problem, and provides the solutions. In this traditional model the therapist is viewed as the knowledgeable one who will figure things out based on the information the client or patient provides him. Many family members enter family sessions with this expectation, especially if they have had prior therapy.

I have discovered in my teaching and consulting with mental health professionals that many therapists and students also place these high expectations on themselves. It would appear that much of the anxiety that professionals have about their work lies in their accepting responsibility for solving problems that probably are insoluble as they are presented.

In a family systems approach, the experts are the family members. The goal of the therapist is to help the family develop its own way of discovering how it wants to move from point A to point B. One of the therapist's jobs is to encourage the family to assume the expert role. The expectation of the family early in therapy that the therapist will have the answers presents one of the first challenges to the therapist. Consequently, there may be an initial struggle between the therapist and the family to decide who is going to do what. If the therapist takes responsiblity for the solution of problems, then he must take responsibility also for the outcome. If the therapeutic endeavor works, it is because he is a bright therapist, if it fails, it is because he is inadequate. In either case, the family does not assume responsibility for resolving their problems.

One of the more powerful experiences a family has in therapy is the discovery that they have their own very effective ways and ideas about resolving their dilemmas. The therapist's initial task then, is to encourage the family to find their own solution. Typically, when families enter therapy it is because they have been ineffective in trying to resolve their problems. Often the definition of who has the problems is exacerbating the situation and preventing them from finding better solutions. Therefore, one of the first tasks in family therapy is to redefine the problems. To accomplish this task, the therapist must help the family understand how their problems are affecting the entire family. This process helps the family members gain a broader, more sophisticated definition of themselves as system. As this occurs a new set of ideas will emerge with the family about how they want to resolve their dilemmas. As the therapist focuses on the family's ideas the members begin to see themselves as experts in dealing with their problems.

MISCONCEPTION TWO: Significant Change Occurs in the Therapy Hour

The usual frequency of family therapy sessions is once a week. The idea that significant change occurs during this hour is unrealistic, as lasting change will occur only if the family is motivated to experiment with new ways of relating. The therapeutic hour can provide this impetus. The therapist, through his own inquisitiveness about how certain patterns develop within the family, helps them experience something new during the session. However, the emphasis must be on encouraging the family to continue the process outside therapy. In each session, the therapist might well ask the family what new matters they have been working on. Gradually, the family recognizes that the major work is accomplished through their own efforts outside the session.

Since the family systems therapist takes the position that change occurs in the environing social systems, that is, within families, schools and communities, he acts as a consultant during the therapeutic hour. His role is to help the family discover their internal resources and ways in which they can position themselves differently, with both the family and the community.

By the time a family enlists the aid of a therapist, their problems are usually long-standing and firmly entrenched. Often family members will fantasize that the therapist will agree with them that it is a particular family member who has the problem. Frequently, family therapy begins with the family telling the therapist that a certain member has to change. One of the family therapist's initial tasks is to help the family understand that change has to occur within the family, not simply within a particular member. For the family to experience and act upon this new perception, they have to begin to behave differently, not only within the session but, more importantly, outside it.

In order for significant change to occur, the therapist must concentrate on helping the family recognize whatever new methods for interacting the family has been experimenting with, and deemphasize the family's need to "understand" any one family member whom they have seen as the cause of the problem.

MISCONCEPTION THREE: A Major Goal of Family Therapy is Helping Family Members Develop Insight Into Their Problems

This misconception is related to the preceding one. The therapist who takes the position that understanding the problem will bring about a solution will emphasize the gaining of insight. In contrast, the systems therapist focuses on how family members relate to each other and what they expect in the relationship. He believes that the solution comes about as basic behavioural patterns change, whether or not this is accompanied by insight. Not until people begin to behave differently will they begin to experience anything new about each other. There are in fact times when understanding problems contributes to a lack of motivation to experiment with doing something differently.

MISCONCEPTION FOUR: Family Therapy Begins With the First Session

It is commonly thought that therapy begins at the time of the first interview. However, family systems therapy actually starts with the referral or initial request for service. One of the most important preparatory maneuvers of the family therapist is to ensure that the first session will bring people together in a way that will help the family perceive the situation in a new light. If the therapist begins by focusing on the identified problems or by accepting the family's ideas about who should be present, this may preclude his ever being able to offer the family a new perspective.

One of the most important decisions the family therapist makes is who to invite to the first session. This selection in itself helps the family begin to experience its difficulties differently. By inviting several family members to the first session, the therapist sets up a situation in which he can help them learn how to turn to each other for help and understanding in dealing with their problem, instead of turning to the therapist as the only expert.

MISCONCEPTION FIVE: The Major Role of the Family Therapist is to Help Family Members Express all Their Concerns

Central to this misconception is the idea that each family member should talk about everything that bothers him or her. In fact, one of the concerns that many family members have when they come into family therapy is that the therapist will in some way force them to talk about subjects which make them uncomfortable. It is critical for family members in family therapy to be able to hear things about and from each other that they have not been able to hear before. This is not accomplished by the therapist's encouraging one's most private thoughts out into the open, rather it is achieved by the therapist's maintaining an atmosphere that allows family members to hear each other differently. Often there are so many distractions in the family home that it is difficult for family members to listen to each other. The therapist, by controlling the atmosphere of the session, can create a neutral zone in which family members can begin to hear new things about each other. What they hear are not necessarily secrets, but rather ideas, goals, hopes, and expectations that have not been expressed before. Or, if they have been expressed, they have been misunderstood because of the charged atmosphere of the home.

Another aspect of this misconception is that it is most important to be able to communicate about the here and now. For many family members, however, the past is a much safer subject than the present. A family therapist should be skilled in being able to move back and forth through all three time dimensions: past, present and future. I have found that many family members can express their feelings more freely about the present by discussing what they wish they had done differently in the past. The skilled practitioner is able to make good use of the past and recognizes that people's hopes and ambitions for the future affect the way they deal with each other in the present.

MISCONCEPTION SIX: All Members of the Family Have to Change Equally if Family Improvement is to Occur

The ideal in family therapy is a change in each member and a group effort to solve the family problem, thereby effecting a significant improvement in the entire system. Of course, such an occurrence is rare. However, it is not necessary for all members of a system to change at once. If one or more family members begin to respond differently, while maintaining communication and contact with the rest of the family, a very powerful dynamic for change throughout the family is catalyzed. Hence one major task of family therapy is to identify the more powerful members within the family and to assist those members to respond differently. The others will respond in kind as change occurs at the top of the power structure.

These major misconceptions were discussed to illustrate that there are several areas of confusion about family systems work. For non-family therapists, the family is often seen as a backdrop to the problem. When the family is invited to a session by the therapist, it is mainly for the purpose of gathering information about the problem. The family therapist takes the opposite approach; he engages the entire family in a systems change. The family is not only the provider of information but the very mechanism through which change can occur.

THE ROLE OF THEORY IN FAMILY SYSTEMS PRACTICE

The practice of therapy should be guided by clear conceptual thinking. The clinician must have a theoretical framework to guide and orient his practice. This theoretical foundation does not diminish the intuitive or artistic aspects of practice, but rather brings perspective to the behavior families exhibit. Many therapists shy away from seeing families because they become confused and anxious about how families behave in front of them. A strong theoretical base helps dispel this confusion.

When working with families, practitioners need to have a well-developed set of concepts that help explain systems behavior. This set of concepts serves as a cognitive map of group behavior helping therapists to understand it. With this cognitive map, practitioners are less likely to see chaos in multidimensional family behavior, and more likely to develop hunches or diagnostic impressions about what is going on. In turn, these diagnostic impressions serve as guides for structuring therapeutic strategies. We must have a broad conceptual map which helps us perceive the widest range of behaviors. Systems concepts provide a broad understanding about behaviors and help us categorize behaviors in meaningful ways. Other concepts can be limiting, serving as blinders which pigeonhole our perceptions.

In family work, theoretical grounding is necessary for at least three system levels. It is necessary to have an appreciation of how individuals function and how they influence family behavior. Theoretically, we have to account for how the family influences the individual as well as how the individual influences the family. Our theoretical orientation should be sufficiently sophisticated to account for both types of influence. In addition to understanding the impact of the individual on the family, and vice versa, we also require a set of theoretical concepts to explain the family as a system. The third level of theoretical knowledge concerns the community. One may conceptualize the family as standing between individual needs on the one hand and environmental and community expectations on the other. The family can be seen and used as a resource in helping its members achieve their individual needs while at the same time satisfying and responding effectively to the expectations of the community.

(see Figure I page 192)

Figure 1 illustrates the three systems levels of therapist knowledge. The first and the smallest unit represents intrapsychic knowledge about the individual. The second represents family theory and the third represents community organization theory.

If the therapist has a good knowledge of these three theoretical areas, he can move between and within any one of these systems levels to produce change. There are times when the individual needs direct work, especially when the family is not available to him. There are also times when it is appropriate for the therapist to work with the family as a unit to produce intrafamilial change. And finally, there are times when the intervention or consultation should take place in the community.

At each of these levels it is important for the therapist to employ a set of theoretical assumptions to guide his interventions. The most important assumptions which guide family practice are as follows:

ASSUMPTION ONE: The Family as a Whole is Greater Than the Sum of Its Parts

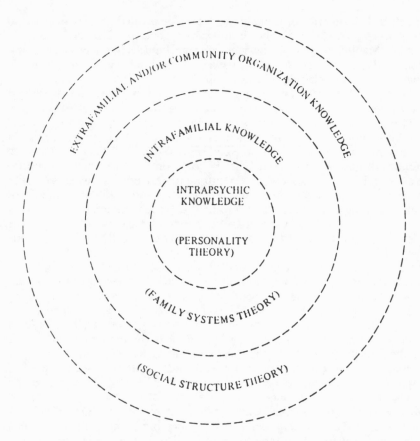

Figure I: Three Theoretical Levels of the Family Therapist's Knowledge

This assumption suggests that what a family produces as a group cannot be understood by knowing family members separately. Many practitioners have found that when a member is seen outside of the family context, he appears quite different. Behavior depends upon environment. When all family members are seen together, their behaviors are influenced by the emotional processes going on at the time in the group. However, when one member is taken out of the group, even the most bizarrely functioning member, his behavior and performance become significantly different.

During a recent consultation, a practitioner presented a family in which the husband was said to be causing the difficulty. The practitioner accepted the wife's description of his behavior as bizarre and unpredictable. The thought of having the husband involved in therapy frightened the wife. Both the wife and the children described the husband/father's behavior as psychotic and unanimously agreed that he would not be amenable to family therapy. When the therapist finished her presentation, another participant at the consultation said she knew this man and was totally surprised to hear this report about his behavior. She had always regarded him as being functional and appropriate. The practitioner who presented this case had relied on secondhand information about the absent member and was not able to determine its accuracy. On the other hand, the member of the group who had seen the husband/father outside the family context held a totally different perception of this individual. Who was accurate? In this context, both were. Bringing the family together would provide firsthand information on how the members behave as a unit. Although this assumption is widely recognized and accepted, many practitioners continue to be certain that the description they have received of a family member is accurate in spite of their not having seen him or her.

It is important for the family therapist to meet the family. Old myths and stereotyped ideas about individual functioning can be thrown into question when the whole family gets together. When one or more family members are absent it becomes more difficult to question ideas family members have about those who are not present.

ASSUMPTION TWO: If You Change One Part of the Family System You Change the Whole Family

This assumption stresses that change in one part of a system affects the rest of the system. For instance, if one member of the family refuses to play old games, that is maintain old patterns of behavior, but remains in contact with the family, the family has to adjust to this change. Unfortunately that person often distances from the family and has little or no interaction with them. Hence a void is created. This void has to be filled, but the chances are that it will be filled by someone else playing the distanced member's role, especially is that role is important to the family. The scapegoat process illustrates this point: if one member of the family is scapegoated to maintain emotional calm or distance among family members, it is likely that another member of the family will become the scapegoat when the first person refuses to maintain that position.

Practitioners who have worked in psychiatric hospitals are familiar with the scapegoat process. When a member of the family is hospitalized it is usually because his behavior becomes too disruptive to the family. Within a short time most hospitalized individuals appear much less disturbed. Emotional distance from one's family or community can change disturbed behavior quickly. However, soon after the person is returned to his family and community, the old behavior returns. The revolving door syndrome existing in many of our psychiatric hospitals is in part a result of this process. Unless the family changes with the individual, they will tend to put pressure on him to resume his old behavior to maintain the old balance. However, if the family can be involved and learn how the new behavior is in the best interests of the whole family, they will learn how to accommodate this behavior and appreciate the benefits of doing so.

Case Example: The N family requested family work because of concern over the behavior of the second eldest daughter, Judy. The family, and various members, had been in and out of treatment for over ten years, primarily because of problems with their eldest son, Sam. The two younger children, ages fifteen and twelve, were seen as asymptomatic. At one level the family recognized that theirs were family problems, but they presented the problems as being primarily in Judy. Shortly before the family sought help, Judy had been hospitalized for one month because of her uncommunicative behavior and refusal to take care of her basic needs. Soon after the hospitalization her behavior improved and she became more spontaneous, alive, and concerned about herself. When she was discharged and returned home, the old behaviors recurred. At this point, the family asked for help as a unit. Rather that focusing on Judy's behavior, I asked members of the family to define what they wanted to work on for themselves, and how the family as a unit could accommodate these areas. When the focus of attention was taken off Judy and placed on the rest of the family, Judy's behavior changed rapidly. As she improved, unresolved problems between the parents became a central issue. After several sessions the family recognized the attention had been focused on Judy so that the parents could avoid looking at the marital relationship.

This case vignette illustrates how change in one part of the family, ie, parent system, resulted in change occuring throughout the family. As the N family went through the process of family therapy and began experiencing more satisfaction and less anxiety, they had more energy available to work on other areas.

ASSUMPTION THREE: Family Systems Become More Complex and Organized Over Time

This assumption stresses that families are complicated systems which grow and develop over time. With the increase of information, resources and additional members, the family has to adjust, grow and adapt. The family must be perceived as an open system experiencing dynamic tension which constantly helps it to expand both its functions and its structure. General systems theory has emphasized that a universal characteristic of living systems is a tendency toward complexity. "Biological wholes achieve higher stages of organization in contrast to physical wholes, in which organization appears to result from the union of pre-existing elements" (Gray, Duhl, and Rizzo 1969).

If one were to apply this assumption to practice, it would be wise to take the position that one never really knows for sure how a particular family functions and what its structure will be at all times. Each family changes from moment to moment. Each day brings new information, energy and dilemmas to the family. How the family deals with these variables will have a direct effect on its overall functioning. The family as a whole continually has to negotiate between its internal needs, wants and resources and demands. The active negotiation between the internal and external components of a family will determine its course of action. Each time the whole gets together, a slightly different course of action is triggered. Because of this, it becomes very difficult to predict from one moment to the next how a particular family will react to a given stimulus. Therefore, a preferred therapeutic method is to question and requestion a family regarding its decisions to take one course of action over another.

As the family learns more about itself, its options, and how it has changed over time, so does the practitioner. One can view therapy as an ongoing learning process between the family and the practitioner. The better the questions the practitioner asks the family, the more opportunity the family will have to learn about itself. By contrast, the more statements the practitioner makes to explain the family's functioning to them, the greater the likelihood that the family will learn less about itself and rely more on the practitioner for explanations. The goal is to help the family realize that it is changing all the time and that change itself is natural. However, particular family changes and their consequences compose the information the family can provide for the therapist. The therapeutic position is to become a researcher for the family to help it learn more about itself.

ASSUMPTION FOUR: The Family is Open, Changing, Goal Directive and Adaptive

This assumption implies that the family has resources within itself to deal with both internal needs and external stresses. One of the goals for work with a family is to identify the resources within the family so that the family can actively help itself. This goal directly relates to the third assumption. Instead of seeing the family as a reactive system that fends off change, it is viewed as a proactive system which has the potential for coming up with its own answers and strategies to meet its needs. The bulk of family literature tends to depict families as closed systems with few resources of their own to deal with the problems at hand. This view has some accuracy for those families who are experiencing extreme stress and anxiety. However, most families are not in this category and with appropriate intervention they can discover internal resources for responding to their difficulties. This type of intervention highlights the family's positive growth potential, and identifies the resources it has used in the past to survive. It can safely be assumed that a family who has experienced life together for a period of time has learned something about how to manage its affairs. This assumption changes the therapist's role in relation to the family. Rather than getting the family to talk about problems, things that haven't worked, and disappointments in life, the therapist might ask questions about what has worked, what things have gone well, and what they see as their strengths and resources.

Case example: The D family sought help for Mrs D, who had been committed to a psychiatric hospital because of violent behavior directed toward her husband. This was her first hospitalization but the family felt that the problem had been growing over time and that her behavior was now uncontrollable. At the time of hospitalization, Mrs D was 45, Mr D was 47, and the two children Deborah and Sally were 19 and 18 respectively. The first family session involved the nuclear family and Mrs D's mother and younger brother. Mrs D described how unreasonable and inaccessible her husband was to her and the rest of the family. She explained her violent behavior as stemming from her feelings of desperation about trying to get her husband more involved with the family. Mr D denied that he had not been involved and accessible to the family. Rather, he felt that his wife was driving him away. The children tried to stay uninvolved, but as the session continued, they started to show distress about what was happening to the family. One began crying and the other asked to be excused. As treatment progressed, it became clear that members of the extended family, particularly Mrs D's mother were very much involved in the operation of the nuclear family. During one session, Mrs D's mother was asked to explain how she managed her family when her daughter was growing up. She said she had experienced difficulties with her husband who had a serious drinking problem and who was seldom available to the family. When Mrs D's mother was asked how she perceived what was happening to her daughter's family, she said that she didn't want to meddle because she was only the grandmother. At that point I said that grandmothers are very important people since they are the only ones (other than grandfathers) who have so much knowledge about all that has happened in the past. She responded by smiling broadly and began to share many of her ideas about how she managed her family and the role she was herself playing in her daughter's family. This action opened up communication between the mother and daughter, reduced the tensions between Mr and Mrs D, and provided a valuable resource person to diffuse the emotional intensity within the family. Rather than searching for the problems involved in family units, an attempt was made to highlight the strengths and to discover what did work for the family.

Families try to get the job of living done in the best way they know how. Some things have worked well and some things have worked badly. If one supposes that families are adaptive and goal directed, then one can also begin to ask questions about how it has managed so far and what other resources can be called into action from the family gestalt. This position is similar to social network therapy, in which the therapist involves many members of a family gestalt as a way of revitalizing a family system (Speck and Attneave 1973).

ASSUMPTION FIVE: Individual Dysfunction is a Reflection of an Active Emotional System

When an individual member within the family experiences difficulty, either physical or psychological, the family system has to respond to it in some way. This response will set up certain family behavioral patterns which could influence behavior after the original problem is gone. A family member who is seen as a family problem is being compared to those who are seen as healthy. Dysfunctional behavior can be seen to serve a certain role within a family. In order for that behavior to be carried out, reciprocal processes must occur. One family told me that the mother was the mediator in the family. All family members agreed that unless she mediated, there would be nothing but fighting. The mother stated that she didn't want to continue playing this role since it caused her great stress and discomfort. The family didn't recognize the reciprocal needs this role served: the mother took responsibility and control; the other family members gave up responsibility for their behavior.

Whether the problem is physical or psychological, the practitioner must take a holistic view of the family, rather than zeroing in on the identified problem.

For example, in a family with a diabetic member, the need to control the diabetes could have a powerful effect on the total structuring of the family. If the diabetic is a child, issues arise around who will give the child his medicine, who will be responsible for the diet, who will make the medical appointments, and who will become the most concerned and anxious about keeping the diabetes under control. If one parent in the family is responsible for maintaining the diabetic child, then one can imagine how a special relationship would develop between this parent and the child to the possible exclusion of other family members.

If the diabetes were suddenly no longer a problem, what would happen to that special relationship between parent and child and where would other family members fit into the overall relationship network? Whenever a family member has a problem there is a possibility that other members will set up a structure that causes two or more individuals to be over involved with each other to the exclusion of other family members. When this happens the immediate concern of the family may not be the major underlying problem. The important issue is how the problem has affected the relationship network within the family. A parallel issue concerns how the relationship would change if the problem no longer existed.

In summary, it is important for the practitioner to utilize a theoretical framework which gives meaning to behaviors which might otherwise appear as discrete or bizarre. A systems framework helps the practitioner formulate questions and strategies for intervening with families in a logical, consistent manner. These theoretical assumptions underlying a system approach to family focused intervention have a strong influence on how the therapist practises. They help the practitioner decide whom to see, when to see them and how to proceed in the therapeutic hour. They are guides which help the practitioner understand the family behavior he witnesses. Without these theoretical assumptions, the practitioner may rely only on his own feelings about the family interactions. These feelings are an unreliable guide since the practitioner's feelings about the family are likely to be quite different from the family's feelings about itself.

NOTES

[1]   This paper is a modified version of Chapter one in Freeman, D.S. Techniques in Family Therapy. New York: Jason Aronson, 1981.

REFERENCES

Gray, William and **Rizzo**, Nicholas. **1969**. 'History and Development of General Systems Theory'. In *General Systems Theory and Psychiatry*, ed. William Gray, Frederich Duhl, and Nicholas Rizzo. Boston: Little, Brown.
Speck, Ross V., and **Attneave**, Carolyn L. **1973**. *Family Networks*. New York: Pantheon.

Chapter 13 ·

Nurses, Families & Illness: A New Combination

Lorraine M. Wright and Janice M. Bell
Faculty of Nursing, University of Calgary

> We shall not cease from exploration
> And the end of all our exploring
> Will be to arrive where we started
> And know the place for the first time.
>   T.S. Eliot

THE NEW ROLE: FAMILY NURSING IN HOSPITALS

Nurses, more than any other health care professionals, have unique opportunities to work with families. This is primarily due to the number and variety of contexts in which nurses provide health care such as hospitals, homes, and work settings. Since the majority of nurses are employed in hospital settings (78.7% according to Canadian Nursing Statistics 1977), one might predict that most family work by nurses occurs in this context. Surprisingly, however, this is not the case. More emphasis to family work is given within community health settings rather than in hospitals; although in actual practice, family nursing in the community is not fully realized.

There are many factors which have prohibited or inhibited nurses from doing more family work. However, at present, there is an exciting turnabout in most clinical areas to encourage family work. In hospitals, nurses for many years spent much time and energy "shooing" relatives away - fathers out of labour and delivery areas, parents out of pediatrics, and family members away from the bedside of critically ill or dying members. Now, with the help of changes in hospital policy, the nursing profession is inviting family members back to participate in significant *family* events. Fathers, and sometimes other members of the family, are invited to labour and delivery rooms; arrangements are made for parents to stay overnight with small children; and hospices are being created for terminally ill patients where families are indeed welcome and in many cases provide the majority of care to their ill family members. Nursing is definitely moving toward more family-centered care but it is still the "squeaky" families who seem to obtain the most "grease", e.g., the upset families; the hostile families; the complaining families.

Nursing needs to be more cognizant that all families with a hospitalized family member need information and support. The family literature indicates that families have a capacity to care for their members in times of crisis. However, the arrival of the illness seems to fracture the unity of some families with the result that some lose this ability (Peck, 1974). The nurse may be able to provide support directly to families or indirectly by assisting them to support their own members.

It is encouraging to witness the movement towards more family work in hospitals by nurses and their demands for more knowledge and practice of family assessment and family interviewing skills. However, these changes in practice will continue to be slow until nursing changes its *thinking* with regard to *who* is the patient. This change in thinking will result in recognition of the impact of illness on the family, the influence of family interaction to the "cause" of illness, and the reciprocity between the two.

THE NEW "PATIENT": THE FAMILY

General systems theory postulates that a change in one part of the system affects change in other parts as well. When this premise is applied to the family system, the impact of illness affects *all* family members. Thus, our previous notion that the individual is the patient would now be revised to consider the family as the "patient".

The amount of disruption to a family unit when there is illness depends on: 1) the timing of the illness in the life cycle; 2) the nature of the illness; 3) the openness of the family system at the onset of the crisis; and 4) the family position of the ill family member (Herz, 1980). Recovery is based on social, cultural, education, economic, and medical resources of the family and the ability to communicate their emotions of anxiety, guilt, and grief (Hill, 1958). The family members in hospital settings are not only in the process of coping with the physical and emotional impact of a seriously ill family member, but are also trying to cope with new roles and demands. They have functioned in familiar routines and specific roles, and now these particular interrelationships are disrupted - if only for a short time.

To assess the impact that the illness has had on a family, it is well to explore the family's cognition with respect to their perception of the illness event (Aquilera & Messick, 1976). The perceptions of the family play a central role in determining what impact the illness has, what coping patterns are used, and ultimately, what physical and behavioral reactions will occur. People think about illness in different ways. It can be seen as a threat, challenge, enemy, punishment, weakness, relief, harm and/or loss (Weisman, 1978). If a family perceives the illness as a harm or loss, for example, they may need to grieve the loss of function or ability. If the family perceives the illness as a challenge, they may focus on the positive aspects and try to master the situation, rather than focus on the negative risks involved (Lipowski, 1970).

Several studies illustrate that illness may have a significant impact on family development, structure and/or functioning. Crain et al. (1966) studied the effect that diabetes has on the parents and siblings of diabetic children. They found that diabetes produces an intrafamilial crisis that leads to less agreement between the parents on how to handle the child, more marital conflict, and lowered level of marital integration. The family's responses to serious or chronic disease can be a significant determinant for recovery, i.e., a family can hasten the healing process. A study by Litman (1966) of 100 patients with a severe orthopedic disability found that 73% of those with a "good" response to rehabilitation had been receiving "positive" reinforcement whereas 77% of those with a "poor" response did not obtain this encouragement from their families. Benjamin (1978) studied families in which a child had recovered from an unexpected, acute, life-threatening illness. Subsequent family adjustment problems were observed such as a sense of helplessness, lack of control, and incomplete mourning experienced by parents. "Parental passivity, anxiety, and hypervigilance coupled with behavioral changes in the children set the stage for rapidly escalating over-activity and behavioral problems on the part of the children" (pp. 288).

When nurses begin to conceptualize the family as the "patient", the implications for clinical practice are numerous. Nurses in hospitals have a unique advantage in providing 24 hour care. This allows them to utilize the opportunities afforded by family visits. During the visiting period, the nurse can meet the patient's family or, better still, invite them to a family interview. This can be done by explaining that talking with families is a normal practice on the unit. Even a 15 minute interview could accomplish a great deal. By seeing the patient in his family context and observing family interaction, a greater understanding of the patient and the impact of illness on the family will be obtained (Northouse, 1980).

Opportunities are also available to emphasize the normalcy of their reactions to shock, confusion, and pressures which may be created by additional roles of parent, breadwinner, etc. (Atkinson et al., 1980). Many times families feel frightened, sad, and angry, but cannot connect these feelings to what has been happening to them. Validation by the nurse of a family member's affect can do much to alleviate a sense of aloneness by helping them make the connection between the experience of illness and their feelings of stress.

By making a special attempt in the family interview to answer questions and concerns, help them express their feelings, and include them in information or assist them to get information from the system, the nurse can provide the family with the tools for problem solving. Specifically, with regard to the family's perception of the illness, nurses can provide important information to help the family develop a realistic expectation about what the illness and treatment involves. Presented in a context of support, information about the illness, about procedures and their side effects, or information about what the family can do to prepare to adjust to the illness would be useful. In fact, the nature of the interaction itself might possibly be more important than the specific information provided (Cohen and Lazarus, 1980).

Additional resources may, at times, be necessary to provide assistance to families who seem unable to support their ill family member or who are having difficulties coping with the illness. The social worker, chaplain, volunteer, or family members of former patients with similar illness can all be utilized as additional support (Williams and Rice, 1977).

Therefore, while families can be a tremendous support system to the ill family member as he recuperates from illness, nurses can play an important role in maintaining and strengthening this vital support system. To conceptualize the family as the "patient" offers nurses in hospitals a wider view on one's lens for understanding the impact of illness on families and thus provides more intervention alternatives.

THE NEW CONNECTION: INFLUENCE OF FAMILY INTERACTION
TO THE "CAUSE" OF ILLNESS

The influence of linear thinking on the etiological models of disease has
created a classification of illness into those of purely psychological origins
(termed mental); those with a mix between psychological origin and physical
manifestations (termed psychosomatic); and those with physical origins and
symptoms (termed organic). However, systemic thinkers are quick to see
the fallacy of such a categorization. One cannot categorize disease or
creations of mind or body when both are intimately and exquisitely linked
together. However, the linear view of illness searches for factor A which
causes factor B which equals factor C.

Perhaps it is this kind of thinking which limited our conceptualization of
disease until the early 1950's. At that time, several researchers dared to
depart from the accepted psychological and biological theories of
schizophrenia to postulate that family communication, particularly the
dysfunctional double bind pattern of interaction, produced disordered
thought and behavior in family members (Bateson et al., 1956). Work in the
area of double bind communication provided a new model of mental illness
and had an enormous impact on the field of family therapy in particular,
providing it with the scientific stature necessary for increased acceptance
and practice. The result has been that while other psychological and
biological theories of mental illness still exist to explain susceptibility, the
family interactional theory has led to exciting developments in the
understanding and treatment of schizophrenia (Selvini Palazzoli et al., 1978)
and other dysfunctions. In a recent decade review of the family therapy
literature, Olsen et al. (1980, pp. 973) confirms that, "marital and family
therapy has gained credibility and emerged as a viable treatment approach
for most mental health problems."

This new epistemology led others to examine the influence or contribution
of family interaction to the "cause" of other types of illness. Anorexia nervosa
has been successfully treated by Selvini Palazzoli (1974) using this new
epistemology in a family approach. Salvador Minuchin and his colleagues
(1975) reported that certain types of family structure were related to the
development and maintenance of illness in children. These illnesses, which
included asthma, diabetes, anorexia and chronic pain, were thought to play a
major role in maintaining family homeostasis. These families were
characterized by enmeshment, overprotectiveness, rigidity and lack of
conflict resolution. Impressive treatment results were found when family
structure was altered to more adaptive functioning.

Grolnick's (1972) review of the literature with 129 references concluded
that, "family relationships do influence the onset and course of
psychosomatic illness and of many organic illnesses" (pp. 478). Weakland
(1976) coined the term "family somatics" and pointed to the need for
increased practical application of the family interactional viewpoint to illness,
even clearly organic pathology.

There, however, appears to be very little in the literature relating family
interaction to what is classed as "organic illness". Very few studies of this
nature have been published. One exception is a recent study by Steidl et al.

(1980) who reported family functioning was related to the patient's condition and adherence to treatment in a population of chronically ill patients on long-term dialysis. The specific areas of family functioning which were isolated included: strong parental coalition, respect for individuality in a context of closeness, and warm, affectionate and optimistic interactions. A positive relationship was found between the presence of these factors and the patient's condition and adherence to treatment.

The dearth of literature in this area is related to our lip service about "holistic", "integrated" health care which remains, in actuality, a dualistic model of treatment comprised of psychological vs. physical components, and individual vs. contextual components with no relationship between the parts. This model influences what we consider illness to be and "determines what we ask of, look for, and find in patients. In this way illness is *not* viewed, for the most part, as an inseparable part of the individual and his family." (Lewis et al., 1976, pp. 182, 183.) Unfortunately, nursing has not been immune from this fragmentation. However, it does appear that we are beginning to move away from the quest for single, specific causes of illness and are open to considering a complex of factors which influence each other in a circular fashion. Some of these factors are family-related.

Recently, a considerable body of evidence has accumulated which suggests that many serious illnesses, as well as being related to acknowledged physical causes, occur with some regularity following particular types of life experience. Holmes and Rahe (1967) developed a questionnaire to measure life events which required some degree of adaptation. The relationship of these life change events to illness was stated as follows: "It is postulated that life change events, by evoking adaptive efforts by the human organism that are faulty in kind or duration, lower body resistance and enhance the probability of disease occurrence" (Holmes and Masuda, 1973, pp. 172). It is interesting to note that approximately half of the 42 life change events may be related to family events or functions. In other words, it may not be change itself, but the context in which the change occurs that makes the event stressful, creating a ripple effect and affecting other important relationships.

A number of authors have suggested that family interaction can maintain illness (Anthony, 1970; Grolnick, 1972; Waring, 1977). Hoebel (1977) reported greater success in modifying high risk factors in coronary artery disease by changing family interaction which maintained the problem behavior rather than modifying the high risk factors themselves. Stern and Pascale (1979) have demonstrated that marital adjustment in patients with myocardial infarction may be a perpetuating factor in the course of their illness. Peck (1974) identified family dynamics which interfered with the rehabilitation of a disabled family member. However, Selvini Palazzoli et al. (1978) have begun to suggest that illness can serve a positive function or solution to impaired family interaction.

There is increasing evidence in the literature to support the connection of family interaction and illness. It is also evident that this idea is becoming more widely accepted but as yet has had limited impact in its application to nursing interventions.

SUMMARY

While nurses, families and illness may be a new combination in the health care system, it is hoped that once nurses internalize the belief that working with families is important, this combination will become less unique. As the uniqueness fades, more family nursing in hospitals will be provided which will reflect this new concept and be evidenced by knowledgeable family assessments and skillful family interviewing. It is exciting to not only observe, but be part of this evolution.

REFERENCES

Anthony, F.J. **1970**. 'The Impact of Mental and Physical Illness on Family Life'. 127(2). *American Journal of Psychiatry*, 138-146.
Aquilera, D.C. and **Messick**, J.M. **1976**. Crisis Intervention: Theory and Methodology. St. Louis: C.V. Mosby Co. 3rd ed.
Atkinson, J.H. et al. **1980**. 'The Family Meeting in Critical Care Settings'. 20(1). *The Journal of Trauma*, 43-46.
Bateson, G. et al. **1956**. 'Toward a Theory of Schizophrenia'. 1(4). *Behavioral Science*, 251-264
Benjamin, P.W. **1978**. 'Psychological Problems Following Recovery From Acute LIfe-Threatening Illness'. 48(2). *American Journal of Orthopsychiatry*, 284-290.
Cohen, F. and **Lazarus**, R.S. **1980**. 'Coping with the Stresses of Illness' in G.C. Stone et al. eds. Health Psychology - A Handbook. San Francisco: Jossey-Bass Publishers, 217-254.
Crain, A.J. et al. **1966**. 'Family Interaction, Diabetes, and Sibling Relationships'. 12 (Winter). *International Journal of Social Psychiatry*, 35-43.
Grolnick, L. **1972**. 'A Family Perspective of Psychosomatic Factors in Illness: A Review of the Literature'. 11(4). *Family Process*, 457-486.
Herz, F. **1980**. 'The Impact of Death and Serious Illness on the Family Life Cycle' in E.A. Carter and M. McGoldrick eds. The Family Life Cycle: A Framework for Family Therapy. New York: Gardner Press, Inc., 223-240.
Hill, R. **1958**. 'Generic Features of Families Under Stress'. 39(3). *Social Casework*, 139-150.
Hoebel, F.C. **1977**. 'Coronary Artery Disease and Family Interaction: A Study of Risk Factor Modification' in P. Watzlawick and J. Weakland eds. The Interactional View. New York: W.W. Norton, 363-374.
Holmes, T.H. and **Masuda**, M. **1973**. 'Life Change and Illness Susceptibility' in J.P. Scott and E.C. Senay eds. Separation and Depression. Washington, D.C.: American Association for the Advancement of Science, 161-186.
Holmes, T.H. and **Rahe**, R.H. **1967**. 'The Social Readjustment Rating Scale'. 11(8). *Journal of Psychosomatic Research*, 213-218.
Lewis, J.N. et al. **1976**. No Single Thread. Psychological Health in Family Systems. New York: Brunner/Mazel Publishers, 182-183.
Lipowski, Z.J. **1970**. 'Physical Illness, The Individual and The Coping Process'. 1(2). *International Journal of Psychiatry in Medicine*, 91-107.
Litman, T.J. **1966**. 'The Family and Physical Rehabilitation'. 19(2). *Journal of Chronic Disease*, 211-217.
Minuchin, S. et al. **1975**. 'A Conceptual Model of Psychosomatic Illness in Children'. 32(8). Archives of General Psychiatry, 1031-1038.
Northouse, L.L. **1980**. 'Who Supports the Support System?' 18(5). *Journal of Psychiatric Nursing and Mental Health Services*, 11-15.
Nursing in Canada: Canadian Nursing Statistics 1977. **1978**. Published by Minister of Industry, Trade and Commerce Health Division.
Olsen, D.H. et al. **1980**. 'Marital and Family Therapy: A Decade Review'. 42(4). *Journal of Marriage and the Family*, 973-993.
Peck, B. **1974**. 'Physical Medicine and Family Dynamics: The Dialectics of Rehabilitation'. 13(4). *Family Process*, 469-479.

Selvini Palazzoli, M. **1974**. Self-Starvation: From Individual to Family Therapy in the Treatment of Anorexia Nervosa. New York: Jason Aronson.

Selvini Palazzoli, M. **et al. 1978**. Paradox and Counterparadox. A New Model in the Therapy of Schizophrenic Transaction. New York: Jason Aronson.

Steidl, J.H. **et al. 1980**. 'Medical Condition, Adherence to Treatment Regimens, and Family Functioning'. 37(7). Archives of General Psychiatry, 1025-1027.

Stern, M.J. and **Pascale**, L. **1979**. 'Psychosocial Adaptation Post Myocardial Infarction: The Spouse's Dilemma'. 23(1). *Journal of Psychosomatic Research*, 83-87.

Waring, E.M. **1977**. 'The Role of the Family in Symptom Selection and Perpetuation in Psychosomatic Illness'. 28. *Psychotherapy and Psychosomatics*, 253-259.

Weakland, J.H. **1977**. '"Family Somatics" - A Neglected Edge'. 15 (Sept.) *Family Process*, 263-272.

Weisman, A.D. **1978**. 'Coping with Illness' in T.P. Hackett and H.H. Cassem eds. Handbook of General Hospital Psychiatry, Massachusetts General Hospital. St. Louis: C.V. Mosby Co. 264-275.

Chapter 14

The Impact of Critical Illness on the Family: Stresses and Responses

Karin Buchanan
University Hospital, Saskatoon

Illness and accident frequently produce loss, real or threatened, and this creates stress. One may consider a framework of stress as observed in hospital settings (see figure 1) and with this in mind identify some of the potential responses of families in crisis.

STRESSES OF CRITICAL ILLNESS ON THE FAMILY

(figure 1)

PRACTICAL PROBLEMS

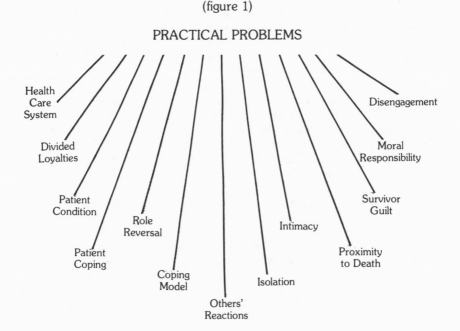

Practical Problems For many families, illness brings them to a strange city. Where do they stay? Who will look after the children, and where? For farmers, who will do the chores or finish the harvest? Illness means financial problems. It can mean loss of income if the sick person is a wage earner. Accommodation and travel to and from a hospital centre can be expensive.

When a middle aged bachelor goes home with severe perceptual problems after a stroke, who will come in and supervise him while his elderly mother goes out for groceries, goes to church, or just takes a break? When it comes to the practical problems of illness, this is only the tip of the iceberg.

Health Care System   All of us would like to think of ourselves as part of the solution, not part of the problem. The health care system can, however, create stress. There is the doctor who is too busy to give a thorough explanation in simple English; the nurse who is tired, overworked, and takes out her frustrations by snapping at a family member; the social worker who pushes too hard, too soon, for nursing home placement. There are hospital visiting regulations which may not easily accommodate a working man who has to go home and feed his children supper and then is only left with half an hour to visit his wife. There are long waits to get in to see a specialist, long waits for operating room time, long waits for hospital beds. We cannot deny it, the health care team as well as the health care system, may create problems.

Divided Loyalties   How does a woman decide whether to stay with her children at home in another community, or to visit her husband regularly in the hospital? I saw a woman whose husband remained deeply unconscious four months after his accident. At that time, she was still staying near the hospital, visiting daily and had left the care of the three small children, all under six, to their grandparents in a distant community. She saw the children only once a week when the grandparents brought them to the hospital. The way in which she dealt with her divided loyalties meant that her children ended up losing both a father and a mother.

When an accident occurs, several members of the same family may be involved. A small local hospital may keep the fully conscious child with a broken leg while mother is transferred to the city unconscious with a head injury. Grandma may have been killed. How does this family establish their priorities? Should they visit the child who knows that they are there, should they be with the woman who is critically ill and may die at any time, or should they be making preparations for Grandma's funeral?

Patient's Condition   The patient's condition may make visiting difficult for the family. The young woman whose husband and two children are severely burned in a house fire, may have to look at an unconscious child whose limbs are swollen to twice their size and whose hair has been burned off. For relief, she may leave the child's room to go to visit her husband who is conscious, but she sees him in extreme pain, and several days after the fire, his burns may begin to smell. Even we, the hospital staff, not knowing the patient, sometimes feel repulsion. Imagine what it would be like if it was someone that you loved.

Patient's Coping   How the patient is coping with the illness is many times an additional stress for family members, if the patient's style is incompatible with theirs. If the patient is withdrawn, bitter and resentful, or unrealistic about his capabilities, additional problems can be created.

When an eighty year old widowed man who has been able to live independently and travel to Florida, loses his leg because of a blood clot, he may be angry, bitter, and resentful about suddenly losing the independence of which he was so fiercely proud. Consequently, his son may be less willing to take him into his own home, because he does not know if his wife will be able to tolerate his father's angry outbursts.

Role Reversals   Illness frequently, at least temporarily, necessitates role reversals within the family structure, especially if the sick person is unable to make decisions on his own, or is in that grey area of being able to make them but not always reliably. It may be particularly difficult for the woman who has always let her husband make the decisions.

Most of us realize that by late middle age, we will have to participate in some decision making on behalf of our parents. However, accident or illness can completely upset the time table. Recently, a couple in their late forties were both injured in a car accident. The woman ended up unconscious, unresponsive, with little hope of functional recovery. Her husband had serious injuries, but his disability was only expected to be temporary. That accident forced the twenty year old son, the oldest of three children, to be the family head. He had to make decisions about the long term placement of his mother for chronic care, financial decisions concerning insurance and possible lawsuits, and decisions about his sixteen year old brother who was still attending school. This "head of the family" responsibility was thrust upon him, with the additional stress that he would eventually have to answer to his father for these decisions once his father had improved.

Coping Model   Illness forces the family members into being a coping model, good or bad. When there is a sick child, parents have an awesome responsibility. If they can successfully adapt to the emotional and practical demands of illness, while continuing to be loving and supportive to one another, they will facilitate, by their example, healthy adjustment in the sick child. Significantly, the siblings at home, also need the same modelling. By seeing their parents cry, they understand the depth of parental love, and as well, get permission to express their own grief. By seeing the parents laugh, enjoy their hobbies, and continue to show an interest in them, they develop a sense of security and a realization that life does go on despite the illness of the sibling.

Reactions of Others   Because families are networks, not just a set of isolated individuals, every family member must deal with the reactions of others.

When a twenty-five year old man who has never really been accepted by his in-laws because they feel he is an inadequate provider, finds himself facing those same in-laws after his wife has hemorrhaged during childbirth, he will be dealing with their accumulated hostility as well as blame, in addition to their hurt and sorrow. This obviously not only erodes a potential source of support, but causes an additional stress.

It is extremely common for people to be judgemental of the coping strategies of others. When young parents get an accurate assessment about their child's prognosis after a very severe head injury, they may actually decide that death would be preferable. However, they have to balance their decision against the frantic comments of family members, friends and clergy.

The grandparents may feel that to even discuss the fact that death may be preferable is in some ways forming a compliance with death and/or disability, and that the parents should be insisting that the child will have a full recovery.

This is an extremely important source of stress, partly because unresolved past developmental conflicts within the family network may resurface at this time. For example, when a young married male, especially one without children, becomes suddenly ill, it is common for the patient's mother to try to re-assume the role of mother, protector and nurturer. I have seen instances where a mother has tried to usurp the wife, to the point that the mother actually wanted to sign consent for surgery and make major decisions about her son's care. An overprotective mother, who has been struggling to let go of her son, will almost invariably at the time of his illness, end up in extreme conflict with her daughter-in-law.

On our ward, approximately 80% of the patients who are admitted for a serious illness or accident have a family member, who, because of these family conflicts, attempts to restrict which other family members may visit. These attempts at restricting visitors may then in turn create further conflicts.

Isolation   For many family members, emotional isolation is a significant problem. This may be especially true of single parents. It may also be especially true if the extended family network is particularly small, if there is geographic isolation, or if the nuclear family has purposely cut off communication with the extended family. Obviously, this sense of isolation is further increased if the nature of the patient's illness means that he or she is unable to communicate with a family member.

On our ward, there was a fifty five year old woman who was suffering from a brain tumor. She and her fifty seven year old husband had no children, had only one sibling each, and had moved from Ontario to Saskatchewan. They decided to concentrate on their primary relationship, consequently maintaining only minimal contact with their parents and siblings. For the previous 32 years, they had spent Christmas with just each other. Granted, they had a supportive and highly communicative relationship. However, they were so thoroughly enmeshed in each other that when this woman became unconscious because of her brain tumor, her husband's sense of isolation was profound. Although they had many superficial social contacts through his job, he boasted that they had not invited anyone into their home in the previous ten years, because they were "just happy with each other". This man suffered through the greatest stress of his life, his wife's illness, alone, because he had no one else to talk to, not even her. Four months after his wife's death, he died of a heart attack, although he had no previous history of a heart condition.

Intimacy   Although isolation is a problem for many, intimacy may be, at least temporarily, also a problem, either because people are unaccustomed to dealing with raw emotions, or because the patient's timing is not the same as the family's. For many years, a woman may have wished her husband could more easily show his feelings. He may have been a stalwart "tough guy" who she believed cared about her, because he stayed around and continued to provide for her and her family. But she may have wished for more obvious and frequent shows of emotions. However, when this man suffers a stroke in middle age and becomes weepy, sentimental, and very open about his feelings for the first time, she may feel both touched and relieved that her husband finally expressed himself, but also feel very threatened by the sudden show of unfamiliar intimacy.

Proximity to Death For most people, the mere proximity to death or possible death, is in itself an additional stress. When life is threatened, many people lose the sense of invulnerability which most of us normally possess. The usual conviction that accidents and illnesses only happen to other people and their families, gets painfully shattered. This scary realization can make people feel more vulnerable to all kinds of outside stresses. For example, most of us assume that chronologically, our parents are "doomed" to die long before we do. Therefore, as long as our parents are alive, we have a cushion or buffer zone against death. Consequently, when our parents are critically ill, no matter what age, even if they are in their nineties, we suddenly realize that we are about to lose our "buffer zone".

Survivor Guilt Survivor guilt is a term which became part of the psychiatric vocabulary during World War II. It was originally based on the guilt feelings in people over being the only, or nearly only survivor of a disaster in which others perished, particularly close friends or family members. We see the same syndrome when a number of people are involved in the same accident.

I met a twenty year old man following a two car collision. In that accident, the two occupants of the other vehicle were killed on impact. In the car in which this man was riding, the driver, his older brother, was killed on impact. His fiancée was killed and his fifteen year old brother lay in a coma for three weeks before he eventually died. This young man not only had to deal with his profound grief but cope with the fact that out of six people he was the only one to survive the accident. In this situation, the ever-present question, "why me?", takes on a new and twisted meaning.

Moral Responsibility There is an overwhelming moral responsibility when life and death treatment decisions have to be made. At some point, many people realize that there is a difference between prolonging living and what can really only be called prolonging dying. They realize that, although some kind of treatment or surgery is possible, it may not necessarily be required, right, or even kind to do it (Pearson, 1969).

If a man talks his eighty year old mother into risky major surgery, and then there are complications which leave her in a coma, he is left with the added responsibility of deciding how active treatment should be past that point. He may be in a tremendous moral dilemma. For those individuals who have a clear sense of what quality of life means to them as individuals, and more importantly, have heard the sick person say what quality of life means to him or her, the decision to withhold "heroic" treatment may be somewhat easier.

I now usually advise family members in this situation to talk it over with either a close friend or an immediate family member, but not with the extended family or beyond. This is because on follow up after the death of a loved one, I have rarely seen family members experiencing guilt for having requested that there be no heroic measures. However, I have seen some family members having extreme difficulty coping with the rumors, criticisms, judgements, and innuendos from the extended family and community, if others know about such a major decision.

Disengagement   Disengagement is the term which is used to describe the slight beginnings of emotional withdrawal that can take place during a terminal illness. When and if the patient begins to disengage himself from close family members, they may respond in kind by also withdrawing slightly. This is almost a form of emotional rehearsal for what is to come. However, if the patient's downhill course is a stormy one, interspersed with remissions and complications, then disengagement can become an additional stress, rather than a healthy process.

A sixty year old man was admitted to our ward having suffered a brain hemorrhage. His wife, a registered nurse, understood the potentially serious implications of his illness. The two of them talked before his surgery and the man expressed to his wife a great fear of becoming a "vegetable". He stated that he had had a good marriage, a full life, and he could face death with no major regrets. During surgery he bled, and then remained in a deep coma for several days. On the fourth day, his wife came to me and started to talk about the void that her husband's death would create in her life, and then started to discuss potential funeral arrangements. However, over the next week, her husband regained consciousness, and although he was paralyzed on one side he was able to communicate with her. Her hope was, of course, rekindled and she was once again very much enmeshed with him. At the end of the second week, her husband became suddenly unconscious from increased intracranial pressure. He was taken back to the operating room, a shunt was inserted, and he regained consciousness. Three weeks later, the shunt became infected and he was back in the operating room. Needless to say, that patient's course produced a confusing emotional imbalance for his wife as she tried to prepare for her future by disengaging herself.

What has been described is one framework which may be employed in looking at some of the potential stresses bearing down on family members, individually and collectively. Needless to say, these are stresses which individuals and groups can not easily "take in their stride".

Before we ever meet the family, a number of influences have already partially shaped what their group and individual responses to a life threatening situation will be. There are significant prior social circumstances and personal characteristics which are useful for us to know. These characteristics interact to make each particular individual family member unique. They are important in crisis intervention, so they will be reviewed briefly:

1. Who leans on whom?
2. How have they been getting along?
3. Has anything unusual happened lately? (Has the major wage earner just lost his job, has grandma just moved in, has the new baby just been brought home from hospital?)

4.   Who's around to help? What are the community and extended family's supports?
5.   How hard was it to get medical attention? (Particularly in a specialized referral centre, we are likely to see people who by the time they get medical attention have experienced a lot of frustration with the medical profession.)
6.   How did the accident or illness happen? (All too often accidents happen at a time of high family stress, especially immediately after arguments or conflicts.)
7.   What has he or she gone through in the past? (Crises that have been mastered individually, as well as those mastered by the family, build strength. On the other hand, crises that are only partly resolved are likely to have made the individuals more vulnerable.)
8.   Has he or she previously lost someone important through a death? Being in a life threatening situation makes many people relive previous grief, especially if they never apparently dealt with that grief. I have found that more than half of the people I see have needed to talk at length with me about previous significant grief before they are able to start sorting out their feelings about the present situation. In the Emergency Department, I saw a middle aged woman whose husband had fallen down a mine shaft and was dead on arrival. She cried, "it's so hard to lose a husband after only six weeks of marriage". I was surprised that this woman, in her fifties, had only been married such a short time. Then, as she talked, it became apparent that twenty two years *before*, she had lost her first husband in a farm accident, after only six weeks of marriage. She talked for half an hour about *that* loss ... commented that it helped to talk, and then started to tell me what kind of man her husband of twenty years had been. *This* was the husband she had just lost in a mine accident. By letting people talk about previous grief, we also get some idea of the strength and support they have utilized in the past, and what personal resources may be available to them in the present crisis.

Through interviewing, we may get some idea of the person's maturity level, intelligence, openness, coping skills, and not to be forgotten, motivation to cope. All of these things make the individual unique.

In order to understand some of the responses to the stress of illness, we should ask ourselves, how many people are well adjusted, not only to every aspect of their present life, but will remain well adjusted in the future, no matter how many problems they have? No one.

Adjustment is a dynamic process, not an end state. We are constantly going through attempts at various times to reach a level of reconciliation and adjustment to various crises and changes. We must remind ourselves of this in order to look at the responses of families to the stress of illness. I will review briefly the emotional responses that we may see immediately after an accident, or a sudden, serious illness. However, a few months later, if and when the patient dies, there can be a new crisis, and much of this feeling-response process will be repeated. If the patient survives, but does not recover to a level of functional independence then the family may go through some of these same reactions over the decision to place someone in a chronic care facility.

Margaret Epperson's (1977) work provides part of the framework for looking at common responses to critical illness. (see fig. 2)

RESPONSES*

(figure 2)

```
              Denial
Anxiety                        Remorse/        Sadness/
                               Guilt           Depression
              Anger


        Coping

                 Reconciliation  ───►  Adjustment
```

* 'Responses' is being used here as a loose 'blanket term' to encompass a defense mechanism, affective and behavioral responses, and unclearly defined processes.

High anxiety is the emotion most often felt first. It is characterized by great physical agitation ... the high pitched voice, tight muscles, and other body reactions like fainting and nausea.

There are two things that can be done. The first is to give brief accurate information about the condition of the patient and the next step in the treatment process. The second is to encourage family members to ventilate about the initial impact of the news of this sudden catastrophe, where they were, and what they were doing.

Denial of diagnosis is rare. However, intermittent denial of prognosis is extremely common (McCollum and Schwartz, 1972). Initially, it is a valid, healthy and useful defense, for it implies a kind of hope, a time limit to the present suffering, thus making the suffering more tolerable. However, we should not feed into it. If we do, this hope will become totally unrealistic against all physical evidence, will be prolonged and obsessive, and will interfere with treatment.

The single mother who intermittently denies that her child's leukemia will be terminal, especially initially, is basically just saying that she wants to have some small ray of hope. However, if this same single parent decides that it is too painful even to think about the possibility that her child has leukemia, then she is denying the diagnosis. This means that the child may not even be brought in for medical review, symptoms may be ignored, and effective treatment will be severely jeopardized.

The stronger and more insistent the denial, the greater the underlying fear and the more effort there has to be put into keeping up the defense, because the ego is so fragile (Wilson-Burnett, 1979). We must maintain balance by recognizing the need for denial as well as the need for the family to deal with the reality of what has happened, and what now is. Statements such as, "Mr. Smith, John was such a healthy boy, it must be difficult for you to believe that he is now paralyzed", are often helpful. Appropriately repeating such statements to the family conveys to them that we understand and accept their struggle with reality. However, these statements also act as a reminder of what is, without challenging the denial defense.

Anger may surface as the family's ability to deny the reality of the situation begins to break down. We have to help people find appropriate expression for their anger, so that it will not be internalized, thus lowering their self image, or displaced, which makes them start attacking other family members. It is our task to help the family focus on the real cause of their anger, which is frequently the patient. However, in our society it is unacceptable to express angry feelings towards one who is ill, and even more unacceptable to express angry feelings about a dead person. Therefore, this diffuse anger eats away at family members.

I have chosen to schematically show denial and anger in this fashion, (as is exemplified in figure 2) because although I feel that most individuals show some of both, people frequently move back and forth between the two. We are dealing with emotional responses, not necessarily with stages.

Guilt is a pervasive and debilitating and common response. When a child is sick or dies, the parents cannot explain it by saying, it is his own fault, or it is inevitable (as in old age) or it is his style of living (because he is a heavy drinker or smoker). Therefore, they frequently feel that the illness or death must have resulted from their own carelessness. Consequently, their feeling of guilt will be great. In their minds, it is a parent's job to notice the symptoms of an illness; it is a parent's job to prevent sudden accidental death (Kalish, 1969).

Guilt or at least a feeling of contributory responsibility is extremely prevalent following accidents. This sometimes has no relationship with reality. When it is someone we love, death even by natural causes is not seen as natural. When there is an accident, family members search for an answer to the question, "why", and, remembering all their safety lessons, remind themselves that accidents are preventable. As a family trying to answer that "why", they can always find a reason for feeling responsible and blaming themselves.

Guilt is felt for all the times they have ignored the patient, have hurt him, or have postponed occasions for enjoyment because of their own selfishness. Perhaps they thought they could make it up later ... but illness threatens to rob them of that "later". Therefore, they accuse themselves of short sightedness, impatience and neglect.

It is essential that we do not prevent people from expressing these feelings, even when they seem to us very inappropriate and irrational. Too often, we may be the block that prevents adequate ventilation of the many remorse feelings that are there. Cutting people off with a "there, there, it's not your fault", or a "just pull yourself together now" will not be helpful. After we have listened to these expressions of remorse, we can begin to inject some reality as to how much blame the family members can realistically accept; we can discuss what family members could have done to prevent this tragedy from happening. Usually, very little, if anything, could have been done to prevent it. What family members seem to need and want most during this phase, is a reassurance that they are "okay" people in spite of what has happened.

That special kind of sadness called grief is realistic and appropriate and almost always there. Some people just hide it better than others. The literature shows that a prolonged delay or complete avoidance of sadness as a response, because of the inability to bear the pain, indicates a less stable ego and more limited prognosis for eventual adjustment (Wilson-Burnett, 1979). It has generally been observed that the sooner and more acute the onset of depression, which is a type of stormy reaction sometimes most alarming to us as onlookers, the shorter it lasts and the more successful the eventual adjustment. This "reactive depression" does not in general respond to antidepressant medication. It runs its course when allowed time, "breathing space", expression, physical comforting and support.

Long standing, so called biological depressions can present quite different-ly. If we meet a family member who seems distant, depersonalized, mentally slow, with inappropriate anxiety and denial, it is worth getting some medical history on that person. Frequently, in such a situation, we will find that this person has had long standing problems with recurrent depressions, long before the present crisis. In several situations, I felt that a person's response was somewhat inappropriate in that he or she was immediately depressed following an accident, with almost no signs of anxiety. It turned out that these people had previously received shock treatments.

Sadness, as a reaction to profound loss, is a state which we as professionals must realize that we can not "cure". We can offer support, we can involve volunteers who can also offer support, companionship and some stimulation, but neither we nor any volunteer can replace the human being that has been lost. If we as human beings care about another, then this is the price that we pay for that caring.

Most people experience, to varying degrees, and in different sequence, all of these emotions. When they deal effectively with them, either on their own, or with outside help, we can say that they are coping.

I do not like the word "acceptance" because it connotes accepting the actual tragedy, almost as if it does not really matter that it happened. On the other hand, reconciliation connotes bringing all that has happened, and is felt, into harmony. It is a time of putting things in place, of being reconciled to the fact that something terrible has happened that deeply affects, and will continue to affect, the total family unit. Included in this period is a realistic sense of hope that, whatever hardships this tragedy may impose, the family can and will survive in its altered form. This is a time when mobilization of the family system's emotional and practical resources can effectively begin. When it works, we can say that people at that point in time are adjusting or making the best of a stressful situation.

What does it require of us to deal effectively with families responding to the stress of a serious illness? This kind of counselling demands that we be listeners who can bear to hear repetition; who will support the expression of feeling; will offer reassurance about the normalcy of feelings and behaviour when warranted; and will remain serene in the emergence of dependency, so that it is allowed to run its course toward growth from within. Most important, we must be able to tolerate other people's deep emotional pain with empathy, without prematurely cutting if off in order to relieve our own discomfort (Murray-Parkes, 1972).

In summary, serious illness can mean tremendous loss. It always produces some stresses on the family, individually, and as a dynamic network. There are significant prior social circumstances and personal characteristics which influence the emotional responses. There is a need to reduce the anxiety, reinforce the reality, focus the anger, lessen the guilt, and express the sadness. By doing this, either alone, or with help, the family will not only survive, but grow.

REFERENCES

Caine, Lynn. 1974. *Widow*. New York: Morrow.

Epperson, Margaret. 1977. 'Families in Sudden Crisis'. 2(3), Spring. *Social Work in Health Care*.

Kalish, R. 1969. 'The Effects of Death Upon the Family'. *Death and Dying*. Cleveland: Case Western Reserve Press.

McCollum, A.T. and Schwartz, H. 1972. 'Social Work and the Mourning Parent'. January. *Social Work*.

Murray-Parkes, Colin. 1972. *Bereavement: Studies of Grief in Adult Life*. New York: International Universities Press Inc.

Pearson, Leonard. 1969. *'Death and Dying'*. Cleveland: Case Western Reserve Press.

Wilson-Burnett, J. 1979. *Stress in Hospital: Psychological Reactions to Illness and Health Care*. New York: Longman.

Chapter 15

Chronic Pain & Family Dynamics

Ranjan Roy
University of Manitoba, Winnipeg

Many authors have clearly delineated a rationale for family involvement in assessment and treatment of psychiatric, medical and psychosomatic disorders including chronic pain (Engel 1980, Frank 1973, Livsey 1972, Meissner 1972, Mohamed et al. 1972). Family issues in relation to chronic pain remain somewhat poorly researched. Nevertheless, there has been a mounting interest in the function of the family in the etiology, prolongation and perpetuation of chronic pain (Engel 1959, Fordyce 1976, Violon 1980, Waring 1982). In addition, a common problem shared by chronic pain with other chronic disorders is the impact of the illness on the family system. The research interest that links family issues to chronic pain is of somewhat recent origin. Nevertheless, the implications of family factors in the etiology of a chronic pain problem (viz., migraine) is time honoured. Touraine and ˙Draper (1934), Olga Knopf (1935), Fromm-Reichmann (1934) and Wolff (1937), have observed the clinical significance of negative events in the family, negative emotional experiences during childhood, the patient's position numerically amongst his brothers and sisters and children who were accorded special privileges by adults in the etiology of migraine. It is noteworthy that most of the reports were of a clinical nature and did not furnish convincing research evidence to conclusively support their observations. These early works are simply mentioned to demonstrate that the significance of the family factors in the etiology of a condition as complex as migraine were and are thought to be highly relevant (Roy, under review).

The intricate complexities of the family dynamics in the etiology of chronic pain seem to have developed over the past 10 or 15 years and even then the interest is quite limited. The research conducted in this area generally speaking suffers from a lack of rigour (Roy, in press).

Research and clinical reports examining the contribution of family dynamics to the etiology and perpetuation of chronic pain broadly fall into three categories:

1. Role of family dynamics in the etiology of chronic pain
2. Role of family dynamics in the perpetuation of chronic pain
3. Various family oriented treatment strategies implemented to treat patients with chronic pain and their families.

FAMILY ETIOLOGY OF CHRONIC PAIN

Engel (1959) in a seminal paper developed the concept of pain-prone patient. He identified several characteristics associated with pain prone individuals which included a past history of a harsh and punitive childhood in which pain was regularly inflicted for discipline. For many of the individuals, adaptation to living requires that persistent experience of pain as a chronic symptom, whether accompanied by physical illness or not. Several authors have noted the importance of childhood family issues in the etiology of chronic pain.

Violon (1980) in a recent study of 13 cases of atypical headache and 15 cases of facial neuralgia found a uniform history of early affective deprivation which included battering and abandonment in over 80% of the subjects. Similarly, Swanson (1980) and his colleagues also found strong evidence of childhood trauma in a group of 13 female patients. The concept of pain prone patient has received further support from a study by Mersky and Boyd (1978) of 141 chronic pain patients. They discovered the patients without an organic cause for pain presented significantly more evidence of unhappy childhood than those with clear organic pathology for the pain. Patients who present a history of early childhood experience of affective deprivation and physical abuse and subsequent chronic pain are not uncommon in clinical practice as illustrated by the following cases.

Miss A.B., age 21.   This patient was referred to the pain clinic with complaints of abdominal pain for which no organic basis could be established. The referring doctor expressed grave concern about the psychological state of the patient and described her as depressed. The patient had a history of abdominal pain going back several years but the pain had significantly worsened at the time of referral to the pain clinic. In addition to abdominal pain, she also had a history of periodic headaches and menstrual cramps.

Her developmental history was very revealing. She was deserted by her father at age 2. This resulted in her mother having to go out to work and the patient was raised by different individuals from age 2 to age 8 years. She was informed by her mother that as an infant she had been subjected to physical abuse by the father; the matter was referred to the police but the man was never charged. When the patient was 8 or 9 years old her mother remarried. The patient became intensely jealous of her stepfather and took a serious dislike to him. To complicate matters further the stepfather turned out to be a strict disciplinarian and imposed a variety of rules and regulations on the children. The patient rebelled against it and was beaten on several occasions by him. He was also a heavy drinker and his violent behaviour became more generalized. In spite of physical abuse and emotional deprivation, this patient did relatively well in school completing Grade 12 education. This event coincided with her stepfather leaving home quite unexpectedly and the family found themselves faced with serious financial difficulties. About this time she was abandoned by her boyfriend just before they were about to get married. The patient presented a history of a great many problems in her interpersonal skills and had special difficulties in relating to men. On two separate occasions her boyfriends called off their engagement. The development of her latest abdominal pains coincided with her stepfather leaving home and the abandonment by her boyfriend. And after further exploration it was revealed that she had a consistent history of pain symptoms which coincided with stressful situations in her life.

Essentially, she presented several of the attributes associated with pain prone individuals such as the use of pain to expiate guilt, a history of suffering and defeat and a very harsh childhood which involved physical punishment which was regularly inflicted. In essence, experience of pain was incorporated defensively by the patient to bolster pre-existing patterns of behaviour. For her, adaptation to living required that persistent experience of pain as a chronic symptom.

Mrs. C.D., age 41. This lady was referred by an orthopedic surgeon for an investigation of chronic back pain associated with dizziness. Extensive investigation had failed to reveal any organic basis for this pain and the referring physician expressed concern about this patient's psychological state. This latest pain event was of 12 month duration although she had a history of back pain from her childhood. Her personal history was characterized by deprivation and neglect. The patient was 9 years of age when her father died and following that the family which included 3 other siblings and her mother lived almost permanently on welfare. She had very limited schooling and became pregnant at age 16. She immediately got married and had 6 children in quick succession. Her husband turned out to be a very heavy drinker, but on the whole was able to maintain his job and proved to be a good provider. Marriage was far from a stable one and they had several periods of separation, lasting from a few months to several years. At the time of her latest episode of backache she was having considerable problems with her 17 year old daughter who had left home earlier but continued to present very serious problems for the patient.

Formulation in this case was that the woman had experienced neglect in the family of origin which was also marked by loss of a significant figure, emotional and physical deprivation, resentment of a chronic nature and persistent feelings of hopelessness. She responded to any kind of environmental stress with an exaggeration of her pain symptom which further added to her sense of helplessness.

Mrs. E.F., age 30. This patient had a history of head pain dating back 17 or 18 years. Her family history was just as dismal as the other 2 cases. Her mother developed Multiple Sclerosis when she was 3 years of age and her father deserted the family one year later. Mother was hospitalized until she died and the patient was moved around from foster home to foster home. She was physically and sexually abused by a number of her foster parents and also her older sister who assumed the role of an authoritarian mother. The pain was very much a part of this patient's life from a very early age; she also presented several of the characteristics of the pain prone patient.

These three cases add some support to the notion of negative childhood experiences having an influence on subsequent development of chronic pain. It would be worth reiterating the six characteristics evident in pain prone patients.

1. the prominence of guilt and use of pain to expiate guilt.
2. the history of a harsh, punitive childhood in which pain was regularly inflicted for discipline.
3. the inability to express anger directly and the turning in of anger on one-self.
4. a history of suffering, defeat, and inability to tolerate success.
5. strong, usually unconscious, conflictual sexual impulses which appear symbolically as pain.
6. pain developed reflects loss or potential loss of another person.

Not all of these features may be present in all pain prone patients but a combination of these are frequently to be found. Pain proneness appears to be associated with the negative childhood experiences which inevitably include physical abuse; thus the initial experiences of pain. With this experience of pain is also associated accompanying feelings of total helpless-ness and unexpressed rage. The concept of pain proneness offers a theoretical framework which establishes a link between those early childhood experiences and subsequent development of chronic pain which is usually in response to unacceptable life situations. In that sense the pain for these individuals has extensive communicative significance. Pain for them could mean hurt, suffering or any other unpleasant emotions.

From a research point of view, however, a very important question remains unanswered. It is a fact that many individuals with negative childhood experiences, especially with a history of deprivation and abuse, subsequently develop depressive and personality disorders and other forms of psychosomatic illnesses. Why certain patients opt for the pain-prone route is a question which by and large remains unanswered and clearly merits further investigation.

FAMILY FACTORS IN PROLONGATION AND PERPETUATION OF CHRONIC PAIN

It is common knowledge that the techniques whereby a person may be induced into disability are numerous. A very simple illustration of that is if the parents have a strong desire to enhance the child's dependency on them, in the event of a child in late adolescence falling ill, they may very well engage in behaviour which will prolong the child's disability and keep him dependent on them. Along similar lines chronic pain in a spouse may relieve the partner of sexual and other marital responsibilities and the pain may be used to discourage the patient from making demands felt unacceptable to the partner. A third problem is associated with the concept of sick role which is assumed by an individual faced with an illness. This problem is very complex when the condition is a chronic one and the family members are in a dilemma in terms of determining their expectations of the patient (Gallagher, 1981). Family members in some ways reinforce the patient's illness behaviour or more specifically, pain behaviour and treat him as though he is a semi-invalid or they may take the opposite view that the patient, in the absence of any serious organic finding, does not in fact have a problem. Both perspectives are likely to create difficulties for the family as a whole.

In general terms, families do engage in what can be described as colluding behaviour with chronic pain patients. This has been evident in a number of studies. Swanson and Maruta (1980) found a very high level of agreement in patients with chronic pain and their families in the area of duration, location, severity, aggravating or relieving factors, influence of pain on other functions. For example, sleep, sexual life, work, etc., and medication factors predicted management problems and ultimately outcome. Their conclusion was that to maintain the patient's pain behaviour was essentially predictable of negative treatment outcome. The notion that the presence of a sick individual can provide homeostatis within the family system is a concept that has been around for some time (Waring et al. 1978). Communication emanating from undesirable mutuality and high level of collusion has been found to be a major reinforcer of patients' pain conditions. This matter has received some corroboration in recent research findings.

Block and colleagues (1980) found that patients with a solicitous spouse were inclined to report somewhat higher levels of pain than non solicitous spouses. Their conclusion was that patients systematically altered the report of pain level depending on their perception of spouses' response to pain behaviour and whether they believed the spouse to be observing the report. Along similar lines Khatami and Rush (1978) observed that perpetuation of chronic pain is often a consequence of interpersonal factors and is used for attention seeking purposes and avoidance of responsibilities. On the reverse side are the family members who often view the patient as 'sick' or incapacitated and lower their expectations of the patient. This then sets the scene firmly for perpetuation of the pain problem.

Significant contribution to the understanding of the problem of perpetuation has come from intensive work done by Fordyce (1976a, 1976b). He adopts a learning model for pain behaviour, explains that when a patient's pain problem is persistent, "not for seconds or minutes, but for months and years, the person becomes vulnerable to the facts of learning or conditioning". It stands to reason that for a patient suffering from chronic pain there has to be some form of pain behaviour or manifestation of the fact that the individual has chronic pain. It is also a matter of common sense that family and friends who surround this patient will be required to respond to the pain behaviour of the patient. Those responses according to Fordyce (1976b) act as positive or negative reinforcers for the pain. Understandably the spouse in that situation plays a highly significant role as will be evident in some of the case illustrations which follows.

Mr. G.H. age 53. Mr. G.H. came to Canada from England and set up a business. Just prior to being involved in an automobile accident his business ran into serious financial difficulties. The patient from all accounts received minor whiplash injury, failed to respond to conservative treatment and his pain continued to worsen. Subsequently, two years following the accident he was referred to the pain clinic. During the initial interview, the patient gave very little evidence of suffering and denied any emotional difficulties. He attributed all his problems to the accident and the injury as is so common with pain patients. He expressed a great deal of anger and hostility towards the health care professionals who had singularly failed to remove his pain. His contention was that if only his pain were removed, he would return to normal living. He refused to admit that his major business setback had proven to be an enormously disappointing and emotionally upsetting experience. Soon after his inception into the pain clinic he and his wife were interviewed together and following is a summary of those sessions.

Mrs. H. was puzzled and vexed by her husband's condition and shared a great deal of his anger towards the health care profession. Once she got beyond the stage of being angry she managed to focus her attention on their marital relationship and the strain that Mr. H.'s condition had placed on that relationship. Virtually all the family related responsibilities had shifted from the patient to his wife. She had to manage the finances, listen to the problems of the children and in addition had to go out to work for the first time in their married life. Her husband did not have any organic problem; she wondered if he was imagining his pain. She was at a total loss as to how she should treat him and what could she realistically expect from him. She gave an example of how in one instance he attempted to bring in a bag of groceries from the car to the house and in the process exhibited a great deal of pain behaviour by loudly moaning and groaning. She quickly rushed to his rescue and grabbed the bag. She had felt very frustrated sexually and at least considered discussing with Mr. H. the possibility of trying out positions that might be comfortable for him, but was actively discouraged by the patient. On a few occasions when he tried to have sexual intercourse, he experienced serious pain in the low back region. What troubled Mrs. H. more than anything else was the loss of a partner with whom she could share her thoughts and feelings, who now was irritable most of the time and depressed all the time.

The question obviously is the manner in which Mrs. H. contributed to the perpetuation of pain behaviour in the patient. The way it was done was remarkably simple. She fully accepted the idea of her husband being ill and incapacitated. Although she had periodic doubts about it, she kept those doubts to herself and in addition she felt she had lost all her rights to be angry with a man who was in pain and suffering. This set up a vicious circle of manifestation of pain behaviour by the patient and equally reinforcing behaviour on the part of the wife and the rest of the family.

Miss I.J. age 22. The patient was referred to the pain clinic with complaints of persistent abdominal pain which had been thoroughly investigated and found to be without an organic cause. She was a health professional and worked in a local hospital. She lived at home with her parents. The history of the pain dated back to her menses, which commenced at age 11, and over the years her pain had worsened. For the past 2 years she had had severe pain.

The history revealed that she had made several attempts to leave home but always returned to the fold of her family. Her family continued to express a great deal of concern about her condition and she was at the receiving end of a great deal of attention. The parents were very reluctant for her to leave home and actively encouraged the patient to stay with them so that she could be "properly looked after". Other than her work, she participated very minimally in social activities and spent most of her leisure hours lying on the couch in the living room and watching television. She was engaged to be married and her inception into the pain clinic coincided with the forthcoming marriage which was 3 months away at the time. Her parents by and large were in favour of the marriage but were also concerned about her future husband's ability to take care of their "sick" daughter. Another complicating factor was that the patient's fiancé had obtained out of town employment. This was particularly disturbing for Miss J. but she continued to deny any anxiety associated with that factor. She went through with her marriage and moved to a town several hundred miles away with her husband. It lasted three months and she persuaded her husband to return to her hometown where she could be closer to her parents.

This case is an example of undesirable mutuality and an unconscious need on the part of the patient and her parents to maintain a state of permanent bond. Unquestionably, Miss J. was immature, dependent and somewhat lacking in interpersonal skills. On the other hand, disabled status presumably contributed significantly to the homeostatis of the family. It was evident that the parents encouraged her dependency status which was attained by maintaining their focus on their sick child. This, in turn, enabled them to retain their relationship which otherwise might have been in jeopardy. There was some evidence of marital discord which unfortunately was never totally unravelled.

Mrs. K.L. age 39. The patient was referred to the pain clinic with complaints of persistent abdominal pain. She had had multiple surgeries but the pain remained unabated; in addition there was some evidence of addiction to narcotic analgesics. She presented a rather intriguing history of a marriage which was characterized by serious disharmony and physical abuse directed toward her by her husband. There was a child age 9 in this marriage who was presenting behavioural problems at the time. Investigation of the marital relationship revealed a rather complex picture. Mr. L. was a very heavy drinker and spent most of his free time at bars with friends. Frequently he came home drunk and engaged in serious physical violence towards his wife. These physical attacks had on one occasion resulted in the patient's admission to hospital. No charges were ever laid against this man.

He took very little responsibility for family affairs; he continued to have high expectations of his wife and when she complained of pain he quickly rushed her off to the nearest emergency where she obtained a quick relief with an injection of morphine. This pattern had persisted for several years.

What this tragic case helps to illustrate is the ease with which pain behaviour is encouraged and how it serves a purpose for the "well partner". Mr. L. had virtually no commitment to his marriage, he drank excessively and would not involve his wife in any part of his life. She was afraid of him and periodically she used her pain complaint to get out of his "excessive" sexual demands. On most occasions she got some attention from him through her pain complaint. He not only encouraged this pain behaviour but actively played a significant part in her dependency on drugs. As long as she remained ill and disabled, he could justify his life style and non-involvement in family affairs and it was clear that he had a high level of investment in maintaining the unhealthy family system. He even justified his drinking and un-involvement with the family on the grounds of his wife's illness. What good is a sick wife? The tragedy of this case was that his own action contributed so significantly to the perpetuation of his wife's problem.

FAMILY TREATMENT FOR CHRONIC PAIN

Interest in family approach to treating chronic pain is of relatively recent origin. Despite that there has been a considerable proliferation of literature describing multitude of modalities of family treatment in the context of chronic pain. These approaches include operant conditioning, cognitive family therapy, social system intervention and other types of behavioural intervention with the families (Cameron 1972, Hudgens 1979, Khatami and Rush 1978, Lieberman 1970, Minuchin 1975, Wolff 1973). Most of the reports are clinical in nature but there are a few controlled studies attempting to evaluate specific treatment methods (Roy in press).

Research in this entire area remains somewhat neglected. A recent review of the literature failed to reveal a single study which had attempted to compare relative merits of two different family treatment modalities or family treatment vis-à-vis the other forms of treatment (Roy, in press).

Waring (1982) in recent years has examined in great detail cognitive family therapy for treating patients with chronic pain and their families. Cognitive family therapy is a technique that facilitates marital intimacy through cognitive self disclosure. Liebman and his colleagues (1976) have extensive experience in structural family therapy approach in treating families with children who presented problems of abdominal pain. Fordyce (1976a, 1976b) and Hudgens (1979) have extensively used operant conditioning methods with emphasis on training spouses to counteract the pain reinforcing behaviour in the patients.

Engaging the families of chronic pain patients presents certain problems. The family members tend to take an organic view of the pain and cannot readily appreciate the need for family therapy (Roy, 1981). Secondly, any suggestion of family involvement raises the possibility in the minds of family members that they might have been in some ways responsible for the patients' problem and once again they manifest defensive behaviour. In spite of these problems several authors have reported various examples of family treatment, some of which are recorded below.

Lieberman (1970) for instance, described a woman who suffered from migraine headaches for 15 years. Her husband ignored her at all times except when she had these headaches. They were treated by correcting the husband's attention (adapted strivings) and the maternal and wifely behaviour of his wife. They had to restructure their marriage as a consequence of which the husband became more appropriately attentive to his wife and learned to ignore or pay only minimal attention to her headaches. When she did have a headache she was expected to take care of it herself. Their sex life improved, generally there was an improvement in the quality of the family life. The patient managed to obtain a job for which she received a lot of encouragement from her family members. She continued to have minor headaches but they ceased to be problematic.

Waring (1982) described in detail cognitive approach to family therapy which is described through case illustration.

This case is that of a 42 year old married woman who presented with a complaint for arthritis. The woman expressed a great deal of anger and frustration regarding her husband's prolonged period of absence from home and surmised that he might be involved with another woman. Initially the husband failed to show for two appointments for joint sessions. Following her discharge he brought her to the clinic for a follow up visit and on this occasion he was willing to participate in his wife's follow up interview. Waring began by exploring their thoughts and feelings about each other and particularly the way they viewed the patient's improvement. Having determined respective thoughts about the matter he obtained a detailed family history. It emerged that she had experienced many losses including being abandoned by her first husband. He left her for another woman. It was quite apparent that she and her present husband had a good relationship but Waring observed that they rarely talked about sexual problems. Her husband came from a large family, he was very young when his father died and the family was raised by the mother. Sexuality was not discussed in the family and his first marriage ended when his wife deserted him. This couple got married at a time when they were both experiencing a great deal of loneliness. Soon after she became physically ill and the communications between them related to her illness and the sexuality virtually came to an end. Waring learned in the process of therapy that the couple really never discussed their relationship which could account for lack of argument in the marriage and also for her inability to share her concerns and lack of knowledge about sexuality with her new husband. He disclosed that his masculine image suffered a set back in his relationship with women which called for tenderness and expression of finer feelings. She acknowledged that her pain did bring her some extra attention. She also expressed her fear that her lack of interest regarding sex could eventually lead to another marital breakdown. Waring concluded that at the end of treatment, the couple had "better understanding of each other and were able to maintain an improvement in marital adjustment".

The case of Mr. G.H. was discussed earlier in the chapter. Mr. G.H. agreed to enter into conjoint family therapy. The approach used was the McMaster

Model which was developed by Epstein (1978) and his colleagues. This particular approach calls for critical assessment of the communication patterns and role functioning within a family system. In adherence to this approach, the couple was encouraged to negotiate with each other in developing a clear set of expectations and to reach an agreement that they would feel free to express their feelings and emotions towards each other. This was particularly valuable for Mrs. H. who felt severely constrained in communicating her feelings of anger towards the patient, especially when he adopted a posture of helplessness and withdrawal. On his part, Mr. G.H. acknowledged that he had by and large abrogated all his family responsibilities and needed to take some steps to reassume his role as a father and a husband with the family. This couple made good progress after six sessions and they continued to maintain their improvement at subsequent follow up visits which lasted a year.

Treating Mr. and Mrs. K.L. whom we met earlier was much more problematic. Mr. L. had a serious personality disorder plus, as mentioned earlier, was a very heavy drinker and the success of the therapy depended on his commitment to 1) his discontinuance of drinking 2) refraining from physically abusing the patient. For her part she could no longer run to the emergency room at the hospital at the first sign of pain and discomfort. They remained in treatment for about 6 months but made only nominal gains. He stopped physically abusing his wife but continued to drink. While the frequency of her visits to emergency did decrease she was not able to stop them altogether.

These cases are not meant to demonstrate the efficacy of family treatment but rather that in some selective cases family treatment proved to be successful. It is worth reiterating that not all individuals coming into the pain clinic either need or agree to family treatment. Incorporation of family dimensions in the investigation with all patients coming into the pain clinic however, is essential (Minuchin 1975, Waring 1978).

CONCLUSION

The problem of chronic pain has been described as an epidemic. The consequences of pain on the patient and family is frequently devastating (Violon 1982). It often results in the loss of occupational role and quickly renders the sufferer into the state of a semi invalid (Tunks and Roy 1982). The problem of chronic pain is extremely complex and therefore the approach to treatment has to be equally complex and has to include every facet of the patient's life. Medical treatment alone has proved to be singularly incapable of dealing with this difficult problem. On the other hand combined psychological, social and medical therapies and in more recent years family therapies have come to play an important part in the treatment of chronic pain.

This chapter has attempted to raise some critical issues related to the family factors as they influence etiology, perpetuation and treatment of chronic pain. Research in this whole field is singularly inadequate, yet from a clinical perspective it should be equally clear that family dimension is an extremely important one and cannot be ignored. The intention is to have a comprehensive understanding of the pain problem and its impact upon the family system as a whole. Family dynamics, as an etiological factor with chronic pain is not altogether convincing, on the other hand it is clear that families can and do contribute to the perpetuation of pain behaviour and family intervention at least in some cases is clearly beneficial.

It is imperative to adopt a family approach to the understanding of chronic pain which necessitates a comprehensive assessment of family related issues. Those issues of necessity must include family history of pain, a comprehensive marital history and detailed understanding of the patients' and the spouses' backgrounds. Finally, convincing rationale is required to explain to the patient and the family the need for engaging the whole family in therapy.

REFERENCES

Block, A.R., Kremer, E.F. and Gaylor, M. 1980. Behavioural Treatment of Chronic Pain: The Spouse as a Discriminative Cue for Pain Behaviour. 9. *Pain*, 243-252.

Cameron, Roy. 1982. Behavior and Cognitive Therapies, in eds. R. Roy and E. Tunks, Chronic Pain: Psychosocial Perspective in Rehabilitation Factors. Baltimore: Williams & Wilkins.

Engel, G.L. 1959. "Psychogenic" Pain and the Pain Prone Patient. 26. *American Journal of Medicine*, 899-918.

Engel, G.L. 1980. The Clinical Application of the Biopsychosocial Model. 137. *American Journal of Psychiatry*, 535-544.

Epstein, N.B., Bishop, D.S. and Levin, S. 1978. The McMaster Model of Family Functioning. 4(4). *Journal of Marriage and Family Counselling*, 19-31.

Fordyce, Wilbert. 1976a. Behavioral Methods for Chronic Pain and Illness. St. Louis: C.V. Mosby.

Fordyce, W. 1976b. Behavioral Concepts in Chronic Pain and Illness, in Davidson (ed.). The Behavioral Management of Anxiety, Depression and Pain. New York: Brunner/Mazel, 147-188.

Frank, J.D. 1973. Persuasion and Healing. Baltimore: John Hopkins University Press.

Fromm-Reichmann, Frieda. 1934. Contribution to the Psychogenesis of Migraine. 4. Psychoanalysis Review, 773-788.

Gallagher, E.B. and Wrobel, Sylvia. 1981. The Sick-Role and Chronic Pain, in eds. R. Roy and E. Tunks. *Chronic Pain: Psychosocial Factors in Rehabilitation*. Baltimore: Williams & Wilkins.

Hudgens, A.J. 1979. Family Oriented Treatment of Chronic Pain. 5 (Oct.). *Journal of Marital and Family Therapy*, 67-78.

Khatami, M. and Rush, J. 1978. A Pilot Study of the Treatment of Out-Patients with Chronic Pain: Symptom Control, Stimulus Control, and Social System Intervention. 5. *Pain*, 163-172.

Knopf, O. 1935. "Preliminary Report on Personality Studies in Thirty Migraine Patients". 82. *Journal of Nervous and Mental Disease*, 270-285.

Liebman, R., Honig, P. and Berger, H. 1976. Integrated Treatment Program for Psychogenic Pain. 15. *Family Process*, 397-405.

Lieberman, R. 1970. Behavioral Approaches to Family and Couple Therapy. 40. *American Journal of Orthopsychiatry*, 106-118.

Livsey, C.G. 1972. Physical Illness and Family Dynamics. 8. *Advance Psychosomatic Medicine*, 237-251.

Meissner, W.W. 1966. Family Dynamics and Psychosomatic Processes. 5. *Family Process*, 142-161.

Merskey, H. and Boyd, D. 1978. 5. Emotional Adjustment and Chronic Pain, 173-178.

Minuchin, S. 1975. 'The Use of an Ecological Framework in the Treatment of a Child', in E. Anthony and C. Koupernik (eds.). The Child in His Family. New York: Wiley.

Mohamed, S.N., Weisz, G.M. and Waring, E.M. 1978. 'The Relationship of Chronic Pain to Depression, Marital Adjustment, and Family Dynamics'. 5. *Pain*, 285-292.

Roy, Ranjan. 1981. 'Chronic Pain and Social Work'. 6. Health and Social Work, 54-62.

Roy, Ranjan (under review). Personality and Psychiatric Aspects of Headache. *Psychotherapy & Psychosomatics.*

Roy, Ranjan (in press). Marital and Family Issues in Patients with Chronic Pain, Psychotherapy and Psychosomatics.

Swanson, D.W., Swenson, W.M., Maruta, T. and Floreen, A.C. 1978. The Dissatisfied Patient with Chronic Pain. 4. *Pain*, 367-378.

Swanson, D.W. and Maruta, T. 1980. The Family's Viewpoint of Chronic Pain. 8. *Pain*, 163-166.

Touraine, G.A. and Draper, G. 1934. "The Migrainous Patient". 80. *Journal of Nervous and Mental Disease*, 1-23.

Tunks, E. and Roy, R. 1982. 'Chronic Pain and the Occupational Role' in eds. R. Roy and E. Tunks, Chronic Pain: Psychosocial Factors in Rehabilitation. Baltimore: Williams and Wilkins.

Violon, A. 1980. "The Onset of Facial Pain: A Psychological Study". 34. *Psychotherapy and Psychosomatics*, 11-16.

Violon, Anita. 1982. The Process Involved in Becoming a Chronic Pain Patient, in eds. R. Roy and E. Tunks, Chronic Pain: Psychosocial Factors in Rehabilitation. Baltimore: Williams and Wilkins.

Waring, E.M. 1977. The Role of the Family in Symptom Selection and Perpetuation in Psychosomatic Illness. 8. *Psychotherapy and Psychosomatics*, 253-259.

Waring, E.M., Mohamed, S.N., Boyd, D.B. and Weisz, G. 1978. Chronic Pain and The Family: A Review. Presented at the Second World Congress of the International Association for the Study of Pain, Montreal, Canada.

Waring, E.M. 1982. Conjoint and Marital Therapy, in eds. R. Roy and E. Tunks, Chronic Pain: Psychosocial Factors in Rehabilitation. Baltimore: Williams and Wilkins.

Wolff, H.G. 1937. "Personality Features and Reactions of Subjects with Migraine". 37. *Archives of Neurology and Psychiatry*, 895-921.

SEXUALITY AND PHYSICAL DISABILITY

The general public tends to view the physically disabled as beings without sexuality. This stereotype has pervaded the human services in that many practitioners disregard the sexual needs of the disabled either through a lack of adequate awareness or perhaps because of the sense of discomfort they may feel in dealing with the sexual concerns of disabled people.

The heightened awareness of the importance of the theme of sexuality, in services to the physically disabled, is evidenced by the expanding literature on this subject. At the 1981 Banff Conference, which focused on the disabled from the perspective of family practice, much interest was generated in regard to this aspect of service delivery. The quality and relevance of the material presented on this topic justified its inclusion as a separate section in this book.

James Gripton and Mary Valentich ("Sex Counselling of Clients with Physical Illnesses and Disabilities") consider sexual concerns that may be tied to physical disability and which may be appropriately met by sexual counselling. A classification is offered of sexual dysfunctions related to impairment, disability or medical treatment. An overview is offered of the most salient themes in the assessment of sexual concerns and several therapeutic approaches are considered.

Derek Jehu ("Implications of Physical Disability for Sexual Function and Rehabilitation") offers a thoughtful consideration of the implications of specific physical disabilities on sexual function. Spinal cord lesions, diabetes mellitus, arthritic disorders, cancer and myocardial infarction are each studied as frequently treated physical conditions which individually present a unique context for sexual dysfunction. A detailed presentation of interventive alternatives is offered in dealing with sexual disabilities consequent to these organic conditions.

Attitudes held by occupational therapists and physiotherapists toward sexual rehabilitation of the chronically ill and the disabled are considered in the last chapter within this section. Leah Quastel ("Sexual Rehabilitation of the Physically Disabled and Chronically Ill") surveyed these two professional groups in British Columbia to explore the range of functions that were being performed by occupational therapists and physiotherapists in dealing with the sexual rehabilitation of the chronically ill. Attitudes were assessed in regard to which of six tasks related to sexual functioning were considered to be important as unique occupational therapy and physiotherapy responsibilities in sexual rehabilitation services. The perceived status of other health care professionals in offering these services to the physically disabled was reviewed. The survey sought to clarify whether occupational therapists and physiotherapists were adequately prepared to perform these roles in sexual rehabilitation and further, whether their attitudes and beliefs served to guide the extent of their involvement. This attitudinal survey does serve to highlight those factors that may facilitate or hinder the provision of services that deal with this important aspect of the rehabilitation of the physically disabled.

Chapter 16

Sex Counselling of Clients With Physical Illnesses and Disabilities

James Gripton and Mary Valentich
Faculty of Social Welfare, University of Calgary

Sex counselling is a rapidly growing area of practice in social work, psychology, nursing, medicine, occupational therapy, physiotherapy and pastoral counselling. It is a problem solving process designed to alleviate a client's stress about sex-related problems. Clients may be individuals, couples, families, or small groups. The duration of intervention may extend from a single interview to weekly interviews over three or four months. Sex counselling has a strong educative component, and the theoretical perspectives upon which most sex counselling is based are cognitive, behavioral and interpersonal communication theories. Sex counselling as used here is more encompassing that sex therapy (Jehu, 1979; Kaplan, 1974; Masters and Johnson, 1970) which is concerned with sex problems of individuals and couples that include orgasmic and erectile difficulties, level of sexual interest and painful intercourse.

The range of sex problems addressed in sex counselling may be categorized as follows:

Developmental Problems - Problems arising from ignorance, confusion, conflict or inability to perform in relation to sexual norms for a specific age and gender role.

Compatibility Problems - Frustration arising from inability to realize important sexual goals with one's sexual partner(s).

Performance Problems - Specific performance incapacity that prevents realization of sexual goals.

Preference Problems - Problems arising from social oppression or from preference differences with one's sexual partner(s) that interfere with opportunities for preferred modes of sexual expression.

Sexual Oppression Problems - Impediments to sexual expression that are effected by oppressive attitudes or sanctions applied to persons by virtue of their social status.

Health Related Problems - Impediments to preferred modes of sexual expression or realization of sexual goals; or threats to sexual self-image arising from physical impairment or medical treatment.

Gender Role Related Problems - Sexual problems arising from gender role conditioning and differential gender roles.

Life Style Related Problems - Sexual problems arising from sexual role expectations of an adopted life style.

Reproduction Related Problems - Sexual problems related to control of reproduction and the child bearing experience.

Sexual Trauma Related Problems - Problems arising from a traumatic sexual experience such as sexual harassment and sexual assault.

Gender Identity Problems - Problems of confusion or conflict related to gender identity.

Sexual Orientation Problems - Problems involving confusion about one's orientation or distress related to identification of orientation.

Sexual Obsessions - Sexual behavior such as fetishism which is repetitive in nature and problematic for the individual or partner.

Forensic Problems - Problems related to sexual expression that is against the law.

This classification of clients' sexual problems aims to be exhaustive but not mutually exclusive. Clients may experience problems in several categories and intervention may be directed to several concerns. Thus a man who has suffered a heart attack may believe it is now necessary for him to restrict his sexual activity, thereby creating frustration for his partner and lessening their mutual sexual pleasure. If there is an extended period of recovery in hospital, the lack of privacy for any kind of sexual expression may be frustrating for the patient and his partner. After recovery he may find that he is no longer able to maintain a fast-paced life style. This may result in a lowered self-esteem which in turn leads to diminished confidence in sexual abilities. The result may be performance problems. Thus, the sex problems experienced by a man disabled by cardiac illness may relate to health, sexual oppression, incompatibility, life style and performance.

INTERACTION OF SEX, IMPAIRMENT, DISABILITY AND HANDICAP

Impairment refers to the organic component of the injury or process of disease. Disability is the functional component, or the limitation of function imposed by the impairment, and the individual's psychological reaction to it. Handicap refers to the social component, the manner and degree in which the primary impairment and functional disability limit the performance of social roles and relations. The distinction among impairment, disability and handicap has been made by Susser and Watson (1971). This article is primarily concerned with functional and social components of illness and injury.

A growing literature attests to the greater awareness of counsellors in health care of the sexual concerns of patients with chronic illnesses or physical injuries. The sexual interests and capacity of the brain damaged (Verduyn), the blind (Scholl, 1974), the deaf (Fitz-gerald and Fitz-gerald, 1979), individuals and renal disease (Levy, 1979), neuromuscular disease (Anderson et al., 1979) and cardiac illness (Friedman, 1978), and persons with spinal cord injury (Cole, 1975) have been recognized and documented. It would be premature to claim that sexual oppression in the form of negative attitudes of care givers and denial of opportunities for sexual expression has been substantially eliminated. The sexual rights of individuals with health problems are, however, being widely acknowledged. The trend is toward encouraging the sexual expression of the disabled and expanding their opportunities to do so, either with partners or through fantasy and self-stimulation.

A number of dimensions are important in understanding the interaction of sex and illness, disability and handicap. The first relates to the sexual developmental tasks accomplished by the individual prior to onset. Early onset means that the individual will encounter difficulty in accomplishing the sequence of sexual developmental tasks that lie ahead (Robinault, 1978). Those whose disability occurs at a later stage will experience the trauma of sexual loss differently. The person with a relatively stable disabling condition is in a different situation than the person who has a deteriorating physical condition with concomitant loss in sexual functioning. While a progressive condition provides the person with time to make adjustments to the disability, there may be an ongoing sense of grief which interferes with maintaining satisfying sexual functioning.

Another dimension is the severity of the sexual loss which results from the health problem. The loss may be minimal, requiring no more than a change in position during love making or it may be major, as when the capacity for erection or genital sensation is lost.

A third dimension which influences the interaction of sex and impairment is the availability of a partner and the partner's response. While individuals with an illness or disability often feel demoralized and unworthy of another's sexual attention and love, the person with a supportive partner will more readily develop a satisfying sexual relationship. There will be emotional hurdles to overcome but time and energy will not be taken up with searching for a partner. Some of these individuals may never have experienced a sexual relationship and the nature of their disability may effectively preclude that possibility. For others, institutional health care may enforce social isolation and severely limit opportunities for sexual expression.

The following is a comprehensive description of the diverse ways in which impairment, disability or medical treatment may affect a person's sexual experience and/or sexual performance:

1. Adverse effects on physical sexual performance.
   1.1 Effects on structure and/or function of the genital system.
   1.2 Effects on level or stability of sexual interest.
   1.3 Impediments to sexual communication, verbal or non-verbal.
   1.4 Restrictions on sexual repertoire because of amputation, lack of ambulation or coordination.
   1.5 Loss of sensory response to sexual stimuli.
   1.6 Effects on reproductive capacity.
   1.7 Effects on contraception.

2. Adverse effects on psychosexual development, experience and satisfaction.
   2.1 Inaccurate and/or inadequate understanding of the implications of impairment for current and prospective sexual performance and experience.
      2.1.1. Client may have unfounded fears that continuation of sexual activity will aggravate impairment or will be fatal.
   2.2 Negative effects of impairment or disability on sexual self-image.

2.2.1   Client may consider self inadequate as a sexual person because he/she cannot meet performance norms or suffers loss of sexual sensation.

2.2.2   Client views self as an inadequate sexual person or abnormal because of the belief that persons with his/her particular impairment or disability should not be interested in sex. This may lead to denial of sexual interests.

2.2.3   Client may consider self an inadequate sexual person because disability is considered to have reduced sexual attractiveness. The impairment or disability may have led the client to adopt a negative or distorted body image.

2.2.4   Client may attempt to maintain an adequate sexual self-image by denying limitations imposed by disability on sexual performance.

2.2.5   Inadequate sexual self-image may contribute to lowered self-esteem.

2.2.6   Impairment or disability may create problems of personal hygiene that may undermine a client's positive sexual self-image.

3.   Negative effects on gender identity.

3.1   Gender identity is threatened because of inability to perform certain aspects of normative gender role, and this in turn affects sense of self as an adequate sexual person.

3.2   Gender identity is threatened because normative sexual performance or appearance is viewed as a necessary condition of masculinity or femininity.

4.   Adverse social effects.

4.1   Sexual oppression through social attitudes that negate the sexuality and/or restrict the sexual expression of persons suffering from the client's impairment or disability.

4.2   Negative attitudes or responses of partners to sexuality of the client.

4.3   Negative attitudes or responses of other significant persons in the life of the client, including health care givers, to the client's sexuality.

4.4   Obstacles to communication about sex imposed by anxieties, fears, distaste or disapproval evoked in others by the client's impairment or disability. These inhibiting feelings or attitudes may be toward the impairment or the disability itself, or toward the continuing sexual interests on the part of the sufferer.

ASSESSMENT OF SEXUAL CONCERNS

Assessment of sexual concerns includes a psychosexual development history. Policies of the organization that employs the counsellor, the counsellor's theoretical persuasion and the presenting concerns will determine how lengthy and detailed a history is obtained. Important issues to be examined in depth are: what loss in sexual functioning has occurred because of the impairment, disability or medical treatment; what psychosexual stage of development had the individual attained at the time of the impairment or disability; what changes in sexual functioning have occurred since that time; and what is the outlook for the future.

The assessment is also concerned with the individual's attempts to deal with the sexual implications of impairment, disability or medical treatment. How informed is the individual and the sexual partner? What kind of help has been sought? How has the person attempted to minimize negative sexual consequences, and to affirm his/her sexuality through seeking or maintaining relationships, or substituting and compensating for sexual activities that are no longer possible? How well has the individual succeeded in maintaining gender identity through symbolic activities or redefinition of gender role?

Assessment of sexual functioning does not focus solely on the individual experiencing loss, but also considers social relationships and living situation. Impairment and disability are often perceived negatively by friends, family and even health care givers. The disabled are assigned inferior status and sexual rights are often denied:

> All disabled persons share with us a heritage traditionally rooted in avoidance, censorship, and suppression of open discussions of sexual growth and development. This is carried even further for the disabled, since they are usually pre-judged by society either as "not interested in sex" or as "oversexed" (Fitzgerald and Fitz-gerald, 1979, p. 22).

Disabled children and adolescents may be denied participation in sex education programs. Sex segregation or restricted opportunities for heterosexual contact, lack of privacy and punitive rules forbidding sexual activity are not uncommon experiences of disabled persons who live in institutions. It is important, therefore, to ascertain what sexual oppression clients have suffered, and how this has affected their perceptions of themselves as sexual beings.

A wide range of measurements of sexual knowledge, attitudes, values, experiences, fears, interests and satisfaction are available. These can facilitate assessment, measurement of client change and evaluation of counselling effectiveness. They should be used selectively with the disabled, however, since they have been developed and standardized with able bodied subjects, and many are intercourse focussed.

Sexual assessment presumes that both client and counsellor are ready to discuss sexual concerns. Because of the strong cultural taboo about talking about sex, however, both client and counsellor may be reluctant to broach the subject. The counsellor may rationalize unwillingness to initiate discussion about sex as respect for the client's privacy and the client's right to determine what problems will be presented to the counsellor. With disabled persons, however, the overriding considerations are the importance of affirming their sexuality, giving permission to them to express sexual concerns and letting them know that help is available. If the client fails to raise the subject, the counsellor should ask about sexual concerns despite the risk of causing embarrassment.

INTERVENTION

Sexual concerns are likely to be only one of a number of adaptation issues involved in counselling the disabled. Consequently a counselling plan should be formulated with the client to determine how sexual concerns will be treated in conjunction with other problems. Goal attainment scaling is one useful procedure for specifying and assigning priority to counselling goals and developing a counselling contract (Garwick, 1976).

The PLISSIT model (Annon, 1974) of sex counselling is useful for delineating levels of intervention. PLISSIT is the acronym for Permission, Limited Information, Specific Suggestions and Intensive Treatment. In many instances, sexual concerns can be relieved by giving the client permission to continue sexual activity in which they are currently engaged or to decide about future sexual behavior. Permission is not to be construed as unrestricted endorsement of whatever sexual activity the client is involved in or contemplating. Value conflicts are often the central issue in sexual concerns, and value clarification techniques are an important part of giving permission. It must also be understood that permission includes supporting clients in refraining from sexual activities of which they disapprove, and in resisting the pressure of partners or others to participate in these activities. Other concerns may be resolved by providing limited information. Ignorance, misinformation, myths and irrational ideas about sex abound, and these frequently are the basis of sexual concerns that can be alleviated by accurate information. Counsellors should be well informed, not only about the implications for sexuality of the impairments that their clients suffer, but also about the sexual misinformation that prevails about these conditions.

Many clients can be helped in relation to adverse effects of impairment on physical sexual performance through a combination of permission and specific suggestions. The latter relate primarily to behavioral exercises prescribed for clients. They include the sensate focus exercises developed by Masters and Johnson (1970) to overcome performance problems. Disabled clients and their partners can be given permission to try ways of love making that differ from traditional preoccupations with male dominance, intercourse and orgasm. Specific suggestions in the form of behavioural homework can provide for graduated, non-anxiety provoking exploration of new sexual activities. With information provided by the counsellor, by others with similar impairments, and through audio-visual materials, clients can discover ways of compensating for sexual losses. Counsellors should also be knowledgeable about sexual prostheses (Diokno, 1978; Maddock, 1980) and mechanical aids such as vibrators. There may also be specific physical exercises and drug or hormonal treatments that may restore some loss of sensation or sexual interest (Mooney et al., 1975).

Cognitive restructuring is an important approach in sex counselling for the disabled. The negative effects of impairment on sexual development and satisfaction can be extremely demoralizing, and a client may be overcome by feelings of failure and worthlessness, not only as a sexual being, but also as a man or woman. Cognitive restructuring can help disabled persons to redefine their sexual selves in ways that are congruent with rational ideas. Irrational ideas about perfection in sexual performance and negative global self-definitions require strong challenges before clients can begin to reorganize their sexual lives in ways that are satisfying for themselves and their partners. Ellis' (1974) Rational Emotive Therapy helps the individual to identify and dispute irrational ideas that give rise to unpleasant or immobilizing feelings and unproductive responses to situations, and to develop more constructive and satisfying responses. Other useful techniques are counsellor self-disclosure, thought stopping and guided imagery.

Behavior modification techniques can assist disabled persons and their partners to overcome anxiety about changes in sexual performance, explore new modes of sexual expression, and re-establish sexual relationships with partners. These include relaxation training, systematic desensitization, sensate focus exercises, role playing and behavior rehearsal (Cormier and Cormier, 1979; Kanfer and Goldstein, 1980; Rimm and Masters, 1979).

Improving sexual communication is a particularly important aspect of sex counselling. Able-bodied couples can develop satisfying sexual relationships with a minimum of discussion about sex simply by conforming to cultural norms of sexual interaction and behavior. This is unlikely to happen with disabled persons who must develop idiosyncratic modes of sexual expression that fit their conditions. It can only be achieved if the disabled person is able to communicate sexual needs comfortably and clearly to a partner, and perhaps to family members, friends or care givers. It will often rest with disabled persons themselves to teach others by initiative and example to overcome difficulties in sexual communication. Sexual communication skills can be taught by the counsellor through such techniques as assertiveness training, counsellor modelling, role playing and behavior rehearsal.

It is not unusual for the disabled person's partner to be the principal focus of sex counselling. The major obstacle to helping the disabled client to make the best of his/her sexual capacity may be the partner's negative feelings about the disability, his/her reluctance to adopt new modes of sexual activity, anger or discouragement about the loss of an able-bodied partner, fear of being sexually unresponsive to a disabled partner, or anxiety about aggravating the partner's impairment through sexual activity.

CONCLUSIONS

Providing sex counselling to the disabled often has ramifications for the counsellor beyond interaction with disabled clients and their partners. If one is the first professional in an organization to counsel clients about sexual concerns, colleagues may question one's professional competence and integrity, and administrators may oppose this innovation. Counsellors will also discover that disabled persons' rights are often denied by prejudicial attitudes of individuals and discriminatory policies of organizations. In these situations the appropriate role for the counsellor is to act as advocate for the disabled. For many of those who work with the disabled, this will merely be an extension of the advocacy role they have already adopted in relation to the other discrimination against the disabled. The counsellor may undertake case advocacy to advance the rights of a particular client, or social advocacy to change policies and practices that infringe on the sexual rights of groups of

240 Treating Families With Special Needs

the disabled (Fischer, 1978; Terrel, 1967). Advocacy is especially challenging when the target is the counsellor's employing organization or immediate colleagues.

Effective sex counselling of the disabled involves application of counselling strategies and techniques that have been found successful in dealing with other personal concerns. Application must be based upon the counsellor's understanding of the client's impairment, disability and handicap and how this affects sexual expression, sexual relationships and view of self as a sexual person (Anderson and Cole, 1973; Griffith et al., 1975; Heslinga et al., 1974; Labby, 1975; Maddock, 1975). In addition to knowledge of disability and sexuality, it is important that the counsellor recognize the rights of the disabled to rewarding sexual expression, be comfortable with his or her own sexuality, and have come to terms with the personal meaning of impairment, disability and handicap.

REFERENCES

Anderson, F., **Bardach**, J. and **Goodgold**, J. **1979**. Sexuality and neuromuscular disease. *Rehabilitation Monograph No. 56*. New York: Institute of Rehabilitation Medicine and The Muscular Dystrophy Association.

Anderson, T.P. and **Cole**, T.M. **1973**. Sexual counseling of the physically disabled. 58. *Postgraduate Medicine*, 116-123.

Annon, J.S. **1974**. *The behavioral treatment of sexual problems: Vols. 1 and 2*. Honolulu: Enabling Systems.

Cole, T.M. **1975**. Sexuality and the spinal cord injured. In R. Green (Ed.), *Human sexuality: a health practitioner's text*. Baltimore: Williams & Wilkins.

Cormier, W.H. and **Cormier**, L.S. **1979**. *Interviewing strategies for helpers*. Monterey, Calif.: Brooks/Cole.

Diokno, A. **1978**. Penile prosthesis. In *Expanding Thought*. USA: Squibb.

Ellis, A. **1974**. *Humanistic psychotherapy*. New York: McGraw-Hill.

Fischer, J. **1978**. *Effective casework practice*. New York: McGraw-Hill.

Fitz-gerald, D. and **Fitz-gerald**, M. **1979**. Deaf people are sexual too. In *Sexuality and deafness*. Kendall Green, Wash.: Pre-College Programs, Gallaudet College, 7-17.

Friedmann, J.M. **1978**. Sexual adjustment of the post-coronary male. In J. LoPiccolo & L. LoPiccolo (Eds.), *Handbook of sex therapy*. New York: Plenum Press.

Garwick, G. **1976**. The rudiments of goal attainment scaling. In J. Brintnall & G. Garwick (Eds.), *Applications in goal attainment scaling*. Minneapolis: Program Evaluation Resource Center.

Griffith, E.R., **Trieschmann**, R.B., **Hohmann**, G.W., **Cole**, T.M., **Tobis**, J.S. and **Cummings**, V. **1975**. Sexual dysfunctions associated with physical disabilities. 56. *Archives of Physical Medicine and Rehabilitation*, 8-13.

Heslinga, K., **Schellen**, A.M.C.M., and **Verkuyl**, A. **1974**. *Not made of stone: the sexual problems of handicapped people*. Springfield, Illinois: Charles C. Thomas.

Jehu, D. **1979**. *Sexual dysfunction: a behavioral approach to causation, assessment and treatment*. New York: Wiley

Kanfer, F.H. and **Goldstein**, A.P. (Eds.). **1980**. *Helping people change*. New York: Pergamon Press.

Kaplan, H. **1974**. *The new sex therapy*. New York: Brunner/Mazel.

Kaplan, H. **1975**. *The illustrated manual of sex therapy*. New York: Quadrangle.

Labby, D.H. **1975**. Sexual concomitants of disease and illness. 58. *Postgraduate Medicine*, 103-111.

Levy, N.B. **1979**. The sexual rehabilitation of the hemodialysis patient. 3(1). *Sexuality and Disability*, 60-65.

Maddock, J.W. **1975**. Sexual health and health care. 58. *Postgraduate Medicine*, 52-58.

Maddock, J.W. **1980**. Assessment and evaluation protocol for the surgical treatment of impotence. 3(1). *Sexuality and Disability*, 56-66.
Masters, W. and **Johnson,** V. **1970**. *Human sexual inadequacy*. Boston: Little, Brown.
Mooney, T.O., **Cole,** T.M. and **Chilgren,** R.A. **1975**. *Sexual options for paraplegics and quad-raplegics*. Boston: Little, Brown.
Rimm, D.C. and **Masters,** J.C. **1979**. *Behavior therapy: techniques and empirical findings*. New York: Academic Press.
Robinault, I.P. **1978**. *Sex, society and the disabled*. New York: Harper and Row.
Scholl, T. **1974**. The psychosocial effects of blindness: implications for program planning in sex education. 68(5). *New Outlook for the Blind*, 201-209.
Susser, N.W. and **Watson,** W. **1971**. *Sociology in medicine* (2nd ed.). London: Oxford University Press.
Terrell, P. **1967**. The social worker as a radical: roles of advocacy. 1. *New Perspectives*, 83-88.
Verduyn, W.H. **(unpublished paper)**. Sexuality issues in brain injury adjustment: a summary. Available from author, Rural Family Practice Clinic. Reinbeck, Iowa, 50669.

Chapter 17

Implications of Physical Disability for Sexual Function and Rehabilitation

Derek Jehu
School of Social Work, University of Manitoba

This chapter is predicated on three assumptions. First, that disabled people are not asexual, they are sexual human beings like able-bodied people. Sexuality is often equated with physical attractiveness and good health, while the disabled are considered to lack interest and ability in sexual expression; this is the cultural stereotype of the "sexless invalid". In fact, only very rarely does a disability have such a totally destructive effect on sexual functioning; it is much more usual for any impairment to be of a temporary or partial nature.

The second assumption is that sexual expression and sexual satisfaction should be facilitated with disabled persons, though not imposed on them. For instance, this may involve facilitating mobility so that disabled persons have opportunities to meet partners; ensuring their privacy, particularly in institutions; and the controversial issue of direct assistance from caregivers in preparing for or engaging in sexual activities. It is, of course, for the individual or couple concerned to decide to what extent and in what form they wish to express themselves sexually.

The final assumption is that adequate attention to sexual functioning ought to be an integral part of health-care and rehabilitative services. The need for such provision is readily apparent in the light of the substantial proportion of disabled people who do experience sexual difficulties that are associated with their disabilities. For example, Stewart (1975) surveyed a group of 212 physically disabled people between 20 and 64 years. He found that obstacles to sexual satisfaction were being experienced currently by 54% of this group, while an additional 18% had experienced such obstacles at some time since their disablement, making a total of 72% who had experienced sexual difficulties.

Such difficulties are sometimes a direct result of the physiological impairments involved in the disability or in its treatment by surgery or medication. Sexual difficulties may also arise from the client's psychological reactions to these experiences. Even when there is a physiological impairment, its effects may be influenced by psychological factors; for instance, a temporary or moderate physiological impairment of sexual capacity may persist or worsen if the client becomes unduly anxious or depressed about this. Some common psychological reactions to disability, surgery and medication are listed in Table 1 and illustrated later in this chapter (for fuller discussion see Jehu, 1979).

Table 1. Psychological reactions to disability, surgery and medication

Anxiety and Avoidance Reactions	Impaired Self Concept
• Fear of harm	• Body image
• Fear of failure	• Gender identity
Depressive Reactions	• Self esteem
• Chronic pain	Relationship Difficulties
• Life threatening illness	• Fear of rejection
• Changes in form and functioning of body	• Partner discord
• Dependence on others	
• Restriction of social/occupational activities	
• Lowering of social status and self esteem	

Some methods of rehabilitation that may be employed to prevent or alleviate sexual difficulties associated with disability are listed in Table 2 under sub-headings indicating the major, though not the exclusive, purpose of each method (for fuller discussion see Jehu, 1979). The application of specific methods with particular disabilities is illustrated throughout the remainder of this paper.

Table 2. Some methods of sexual rehabilitation

General Therapeutic Conditions	Reduction of stress
• Therapeutic relationship	• Relaxation training
• Causal explanation	• Desensitization
• Prognostic expectancy	• Flooding
Sexual Assignments	• Guided imagery
• General pleasuring	• Thought stopping
• Genital stimulation	• Modeling
• Sexual intercourse	• Vaginal dilatation
Specific Procedures	Sexual enhancement
Provision of information	• Classical conditioning
• Verbal	• Biofeedback
• Bibliographical	• Hypnosis
• Audio-visual	• Exposure to erotic material
Modification of attitudes and beliefs	• Pelvic muscle exercises
• Sanctioning	• Drugs/hormones
• Self disclosure	• Prosthetic/mechanical aids
• Role playing	Relationship enhancement
• Cognitive restructuring	• Increasing positive exchanges
	• Communication training
	• Problem solving training
	• Assertiveness training
	• Heterosocial skills training.

SPINAL CORD LESIONS

A wide range of sexual difficulties in both men and women are associated with spinal cord lesions arising from injuries (Higgins, 1979), tumours, inflammation, multiple sclerosis (Lundberg, 1978) or spina bifida (Dorner, 1977; Wabrek, Wabrek and Burchell, 1978).

To some extent at least, the difficulties are likely to be due to the physiological impairment of the central nervous system mechanisms that subserve sexual responses, although psychological reactions may also be involved in some cases (Higgins, 1979, Teal and Athelston, 1975).

The retention of sexual responses by spinal cord injured men is summarized in Table 3, although it should be noted that there are many methodological deficiencies in the studies from which these proportions are derived (Higgins, 1979). The major reason for the wide range in residual capacity is variation between clients in the level and completeness of the lesion. Generally speaking, lower level lesions are more destructive of sexual response than those at higher levels, and the same is true of complete compared to incomplete lesions.

Table 3. Retention of sexual responses by spinal cord injured men

Response	Proportion of men retaining (%)
Erection	48.2 - 91.7
Ejaculation	0.0 - 50.0
Orgasm	2.0 - 16.0

About 85% of spinal cord injured people are male, while only 15% are female. This may be one reason why the sexual responses of spinal cord injured women have been even less well investigated than those of their male counterparts. In the best study to date (Bregman, 1975, 1978) the results are not altogether clear but they seem to indicate that about 90% of the 31 spinal cord injured women experienced vaginal lubrication and about 73% could reach orgasm.

Apart from the impairment of specific sexual responses, there are other common physical sequelae of spinal injuries that may have an adverse effect on sexual functioning. For instance, involuntary defecation or urination may occur during intercourse. This may also be precluded or disrupted by an abnormality of the trunk and lower limbs, such as an occurrence of muscular spasms that are strong and unpredictable, or by weakening of the bones through atrophic changes so that they are easily fractured in some coital positions.

Turning now to the sexual rehabilitation of clients with spinal cord lesions, one basic point is to help them and their partners to understand that the sexual difficulty is due to client's medical condition rather than to more personal faults such as lack of virility or loss of love, and it is especially important to convey this when the disability is of a less visible kind like multiple sclerosis.

Such clients and their partners commonly share the cultural stereotype of the disabled as asexual, and they may be confused by the occurrence of sexual desire and responses, or fear that sexual performance is beyond their capacity. Therefore, they need to be informed that a spinal cord lesion does not inevitably entail loss of sexual capacity, but that when this does occur it is often temporary rather than permanent, and usually partial rather than complete. Thus, many people with spinal cord injuries may take up to six months to recover from spinal shock, and improvement in sexual response may occur for up to two years after the injury. Depending on the level and completeness of the lesion, a person may be able to become aroused either as a reflex response to tactile stimulation of the genitals, or in response to other forms of sexual stimulation which are mediated by the brain, if not to both kinds of stimulation. While spinal cord lesions are often accompanied by losses of sensation in certain areas of the body, it is also true that heightened sensitivity to erotic stimulation may occur in other areas. For instance, sensation may become more acute at the body level just above the sensory loss, and this area may become a new or enhanced erogenous zone.

It follows from this variation in the sexual effects of spinal cord lesions that clients and their partners are likely to benefit from help and encouragement to explore the many options for sexual expression that probably remain open to them. Basic to this exploration is the idea that sexual satisfaction can be gained in many different ways; worthwhile and pleasurable sexual activity is not limited to strenuously performed genital intercourse culminating in climax.

One example of this exploration of sexual options is the discovery and exploitation of the residual capacity for arousal either by genital touching, or by other forms of stimulation, when both are no longer effective for the client. In particular, the recall or imagining of sexual activities and sensations in fantasy can serve as a potent source of arousal, which sometimes culminates in an experience of orgasm.

Similarly, exploration can usefully be directed towards the discovery of any new or enhanced erogenous zones, following sensory losses elsewhere on the body.

Spinal cord lesions may entail severe motor limitations which restrict the positions for intercourse that are feasible for the client, so that the exploration of alternatives such as the side-by-side or rear entry positions may be highly desirable. When a male client has erectile difficulties the couple may like to experiment with the so-called "stuffing technique", in which he or his partner stuffs his flaccid penis into her vagina and she holds it there by voluntary contraction of her pubococcygeal muscles. The sensation of penetration can be very satisfying to both partners (Mooney, Cole and Chilgren, 1975).

For those couples who find genital intercourse difficult or impossible it is especially important that they explore and enjoy other forms of sexual expression, including kissing, hugging, caressing, massage, mutual masturbation, oral sex, and the use of prosthetic aids such as vibrators. One form of prosthesis that is of growing importance in the treatment of erectile difficulties due to irreversible medical conditions is the penile implant.

A relatively simple device consists of one or two semirigid, foam filled, silicone rods which are surgically implanted in the penis. The result is a permanent state of partial erection sufficient to permit intromission and without impairment of penile sensation, orgasm or ejaculation. The erection can usually be concealed against the stomach in normal clothing, and a later version of the prosthesis includes a hinge that permits it be raised or lowered as appropriate. Sotile's (1979) review includes outcome data on 623 patients with silicone rod implants in 22 studies. He deems the outcome to be satisfactory in 89.1% of cases, in that there was sufficient penile rigidity to allow sexual intercourse to take place. Surgical complications, mainly infection, occurred in 16.7% of cases.

A more sophisticated inflatable hydraulic type of implant consists of two silicone rubber cylinders which are inserted into the penis and then connected by tubing to a reservoir in the provesical space. The radiopaque fluid in this reservoir can be pumped into the cylinders by means of a bulb actuator situated in the scrotum so that the penis becomes erect. It can subsequently be returned to the flaccid state by means of a release valve in the pump. Once the apparatus is implanted surgically, the client then operates the bulb himself in order to inflate or deflate his penis. This prosthesis yields a full erection and does not impair penile sensation, orgasm or ejaculation. It also has the appearance of a normal penis and a partner need not be aware of the prosthesis. Sotile (1979) reviews the outcome of inflatable implants in 117 patients reported in six studies. According to the criterion stated above he judges 95.7% of them to be satisfactory, although the rate of complications at 31.2% is higher than for the silicone rod prosthesis. This is understandable in view of the more complex nature of the inflatable prosthesis and most of the complications arising from it are due to mechanical problems. Since Sotile's review was completed, very similar results from the inflatable prosthesis are reported for two further series of 63 (Furlow 1978) and 245 (Scott, Byrd, Karacan, Olsson, Beutler and Attia, 1979) patients.

In order to explore and utilize certain means of sexual expression, including genital intercourse, an individual or couple may need the assistance of a caregiver in preparing or positioning for lovemaking. This is obviously a sensitive topic involving an invasion of customary privacy and possible embarrassment for the clients, as well as non-traditional professional demands upon the caregiver, but it is a matter that has to be confronted if sexual expression is to be facilitated effectively for some disabled people and their partners.

One aspect of preparing for sexual activity is the management of bowel and bladder functions. These organs should be emptied before lovemaking so that involuntary voiding is less likely to occur during intercourse, and there are various ways of dealing with catheters and ostomy appliances that some clients will need to learn (Mooney et al, 1975).

Women with spinal cord lesions and their partners need to understand that this disability does not diminish fertility and that it is not a contraindication to pregnancy. It follows that appropriate contraceptive advice is required if an unwanted pregnancy is to be avoided (Mooney et al, 1975, Task Force on Concerns of Physically Disabled Women, 1978a, 1978b; Thornton, 1979).

The last point I want to make on the sexual rehabilitation of clients with spinal cord lesions is the vital importance of good communication between them and their partners. Thus, for some it may be advantageous to provide specific training in the communication skills (Dunn, Lloyd and Phelps, 1979) required to accomplish tasks such as meeting and relating to potential partners in a confident manner so that they are more likely to respond positively to the client; dealing with the myths about the disabled, such as that they are asexual, and being able to communicate sexual feelings and preferences; engaging in the mutual exploration of the many options for sexual expression discussed above; and the mutual resolution of potential problems like bowel and bladder control, muscular spasms, and methods of contraception.

This last point on the importance of good communication, as well as several other matters discussed in the context of spinal cord lesions, are equally relevant to other disabilities and will not be reiterated in the following briefer discussions of some of these other conditions.

DIABETES MELLITUS

One of the commonest organic causes of erectile dysfunction is diabetes mellitus. In a typical study (Barnett, 1973) of sexual difficulties among 175 diabetic men it was found that 49% suffered from erectile dysfunction, 2% from premature ejaculation, and 1% from retrograde ejaculation. The incidence of erectile dysfunction was not related to the control, duration or severity of the disease. In another study (Rubin & Babbott, 1958) erectile dysfunction was found to be related to age; among diabetic men aged between 30 and 34, the incidence was 25%, while in those between 60 and 64 it rose to 74%.

There has been considerable controversy over the nature of the physiological impairment contributing to erectile dysfunction in diabetic men; neurogenic, endocrine, and vascular factors have all been implicated but there now seems little doubt that damage to the autonomic nervous system is at least partly responsible in many cases (*British Medical Journal,* 1974). To the extent that neural damage is responsible, the erectile dysfunction is irreversible. This does not necessarily imply a similar poor prognosis for the erectile problem when this arises either from physical causes, such as transient period of hypoglycaemia or general ill health, or from the client's psychological reactions to diabetes. For instance, he may become anxious about his sexual performance after learning that it can be adversely affected by diabetes or following a temporary loss of erectile capacity due to the kind of transient physical causes mentioned above.

In order to plan a suitable programme of sexual rehabilitation it is of course desirable to decide whether a client's erectile dysfunction is due to an irreversible organic condition or to some other physical or psychological cause. In recent years, this differential diagnosis has been facilitated by the technique of nocturnal penile tumescence (NPT). During an average night's sleep people have four or five periods of dreaming during which they exhibit rapid eye movement (REM). In physiologically unimpaired males these periods of REM sleep are invariably accompanied by full or partial erections.

A recent example of the application of these findings is a study by Marshall, Surridge and Delva (1981). Taking a 3 mm increase in penile circumference as their criterion for the occurrence of NPT, they found that they could correctly allocate 95% of their subjects to organic or psychogenic categories by applying the decision rule of designating as organic those subjects who exhibited two or less episodes of NPT, and as psychogenic those exhibiting three or more episodes of NPT. There was no significant difference in the total amount of REM sleep between the two groups, but more of it was accompanied by erections in the psychogenic cases compared to those with an independently established organic basis.

The equipment and facilities needed to measure NPT are not always available, and it is costly and sometimes inconvenient to bring the client into a sleep laboratory for two or three nights. Consequently, it is encouraging that Kockott, Feil, Revenstorf, Aldenhoff and Besinger (1980) have reported almost 100% success in allocating to organic and psychogenic categories on the basis of patients' replies to six questions in a semi-standardized clinical interview. Analysis of the replies to these six questions indicated that compared to the psychogenic patients, the organic patients had significantly less strong erections during foreplay, during masturbation, and spontaneously, including waking erections. The erectile capacity of organic patients was as bad or worse during masturbation as it was during sexual contact. Compared to the psychogenic patients, the organic patients reported less anxiety during sexual activity, and they avoided it less.

As far as the sexual rehabilitation of diabetic men is concerned, suitable medical treatment is essential in all cases; those whose erectile dysfunction is due to an irreversible organic cause may wish to consider a penile implant, and any psychological factors may be alleviated by appropriate procedures from among those listed in Table 2, bearing in mind many of the more general points made in the discussion of spinal cord lesions.

The effect of diabetes on the sexual functioning of women is at present undetermined. There is a direct conflict of evidence over whether diabetic women have more difficulty in reaching orgasm compared to non-diabetic women (Ellenberg, 1977; Kolodny, 1971). Furthermore, in one major study (Ellenberg, 1977) it was found that diabetic women who showed clear evidence of neurological abnormality were not more sexually dysfunctional than other diabetic women who did not show signs of neural damage. The results of this study concerning the incidence of sexual dysfunction in diabetic women and the role of neuropathy as a cause of these difficulties are markedly discrepant from the equivalent findings in respect of male diabetics, and at present there are no adequate explanations for these discrepancies.

ARTHRITIC DISORDERS

Some degree of sexual difficulty is reported by a high proportion of arthritic patients (see review by Richards, 1980), and this is readily understandable in the light of the impediments to sexual activity presented by the inflammation, pain, stiffness, immobility and deformity of the affected joints and connective tissues. For instance, the involvement of a woman's hip joints may prevent her from abducting and externally rotating them so that it is impossible for her to have intercourse in the male superior position with her partner lying between her open legs. Similarly, a man whose lower spine is painful or rigid will be unable to engage in thrusting movements during intercourse. In a recent survey (Ferguson & Figley, 1979) of 70 women and 30 men suffering from arthritic disorders it was found that 54% of the women and 56% of the men reported sexual difficulties, with pain being the major problem in both sexes.

Without underestimating the contribution of pain and the other impediments mentioned above to the sexual difficulties of arthritic people, it is likely that other physical and psychological factors may also play a part. Relevant physical factors include fatigue, and the side effects on sexual functioning of the medication used to treat arthritis, such as corticosteroids and narcotics.

The stresses and limitations entailed by the disability may also evoke psychological reactions such as lowered self-esteem and depression, which may in turn have adverse effects on an arthritic person's confidence in heterosocial relationships, interest in sex, and sexual performance. His or her partner may also be inhibited by fear of inflicting pain on the arthritic person during sexual activity. Some support for the importance of such psychological reactions arises from the fact that relief from pain, for example, by hip replacement, is not regularly followed by an alleviation of sexual difficulties (Richards, 1980). Patients may wholly attribute these difficulties to their pain when other causal factors are also operating.

Turning to the sexual rehabilitation of arthritic persons, again many of the general points discussed in the context of spinal cord lesions are applicable, especially the exploration of various positions for intercourse and of other forms of sexual expression. More particularly, surgical procedures to replace or improve mobility of joints may he helpful in some, though not all, cases. Clients may be advised to use for sexual activity those periods during the day when their mobility, energy and comfort are at their highest; most arthritic people do have such times. Analgesics or muscle relaxants may be taken before sexual activity in order to reduce pain during intercourse.

CANCER

The sexuality of clients suffering from various forms of malignancy is an especially neglected area in rehabilitation and research (see review in Kolodny, Masters and Johnson, 1979).

Many of these clients will experience sexual difficulties as a result of physiological impairments arising either from certain side effects of malignancy, such as anaemia, anorexia, muscle atrophy, and neurological deficits; or from the methods used to treat the malignancy, such as chemotherapy, surgery, and radiation. The psychological reactions of clients and their partners to the malignancy are also likely sources of sexual difficulty. For instance, this may result from feelings of anxiety, anger and depression evoked by the life-threatening nature of cancer, as well as the pain and mutilation often associated with its treatment. These physiological and psychological causal factors are illustrated in the following discussion of the sexual implications of two common forms of cancer.

Breast Cancer

The commonest form of cancer among women is cancer of the breast, and it is most usually treated by a radical or simple mastectomy.

At present, only very limited evidence is available on the sexual implications of this disability and its surgical treatment, although there are some preliminary indications of difficulties being experienced. For instance, Maguire (1978) found that mastectomy patients reported many more sexual problems than did a control group of benign breast tumour biopsy patients. At a 4-month postoperative follow-up, 40% of mastectomy patients reported difficulties, compared to 11% of control group patients. At 1 year follow-up, the equivalent figures were 33% of the mastectomy patients, and 8% of the controls. Similarly, in a retrospective pilot study of women who had undergone mastectomies an average of eight years previously, it was found that a third of them had not resumed intercourse within six months of their surgery, and that there were pre-postoperative decreases in the frequencies of the woman initiating sex, of breast stimulation, of intercourse, and of female orgasm (Frank, Dornbush, Webster, & Kolodny, 1978).

There are some physical side effects of breast cancer and its treatment that may adversely affect sexual functioning (Kolodny et al, 1979), but the psychological reactions of the woman and her partner are likely to be especially important sources of sexual difficulty. While these reactions are varied in their nature, intensity, and duration, some of them do appear to be very prevalent (Meyerowitz, 1980). For example, depression, anxiety, and anger are commonly reported responses to concerns about relapse and death, mutilation by surgery, and rejection by a partner. The woman's body image and self-concept are often damaged, a reaction which is readily understandable in the light of the importance of the breast as a symbol of femininity and attractiveness in our society (Polivy, 1977). There is evidence also that while most men adjust well to their partner's mastectomy, there are others who have marked difficulty in this regard (Wellisch, Jamison, and Pasnau, 1978).

Among the particular points to be noted on the sexual rehabilitation of mastectomy patients and their partners (Witkin, 1975, 1978, 1979) is the need for them to confront the loss of the breast. The woman is likely to fear that her partner will find the incision site repulsive and cease to desire her sexually, while he may be concerned that he will react to the wound in ways which indicate distaste for her. To overcome these concerns it is often suggested that the partner should be present and assist when dressings are changed in the "safe" and supportive environment of the hospital, as well as after discharge. The couple also need to be reassured that the resumption of sexual activities, including intercourse, is feasible and safe, and advice may be given on the use of an appropriate male superior position while the woman is still weak after the operation and the site needs to be protected. Finally, many mastectomy patients will wish to obtain a properly fitted breast prosthesis, and some may want to consider the possibility of reconstructive breast surgery.

Cancer of the colon or rectum

Malignancies of the colon or rectum are among the commonest forms of cancer in men. These disabilities are often treated by the surgical excision of some part of the colon, together with the rectum. Additionally, a colostomy is constructed by bringing a remaining portion of the colon to a stoma, or opening, in the abdominal wall through which faeces are discharged, usually into a bag.

Substantial proportions of men who have undergone this surgical intervention appear to suffer both erectile and ejaculatory difficulties, although more systematic evidence is lacking (Kolodny et al, 1979). In particular, retrograde ejaculation occurs in perhaps half such cases. This problem can be defined as the involuntary discharge of semen into the bladder rather than through the urethra, so that the client may still be able to have erections and orgasms, but there is no visible ejaculate. This is collected from the internal sex organs and deposited at the base of the urethra in the usual way, but the normal reflex closure of the internal sphincter at the neck of the bladder does not occur. Consequently, the semen flows backwards into the bladder instead of being propelled forward by the muscular contractions of orgasm (Jehu, 1979).

This problem of retrograde ejaculation is due to neural damage incurred as a side effect of the surgical excision of the rectum. Such damage may also contribute to some of the other sexual difficulties exhibited by colostomy patients. In addition to this physiological impairment, however, there are many psychological factors that may contribute to such difficulties. These factors include the common concerns and reactions arising from the diagnosis of cancer that are discussed above, but some issues are of particular relevance to colostomy patients. They often fear that the stoma will be damaged during sexual activity. Another potential source of distress is the possibility of any leakage, noise or odour from the stoma or appliance during lovemaking. Such patients may believe that the disease or surgery has completely destroyed their sexual capacity. In many cases they suffer damage to their body image and self concept as a result of changes in excretory function and the stoma itself. Finally, they may regard themselves as much less attractive, if not repulsive, to a partner, who it is feared may therefore reject or desert them.

It follows that these issues are among those that need addressing in the sexual rehabilitation of colostomy patients and their partners. Reassurance needs to be given that the stoma does not prevent sexual activity, including intercourse, and that this will not damage the stoma in any way. Couples also need help in understanding that the disease and surgery have almost certainly not completely destroyed the patient's sexual capacity. In particular, if he suffers from retrograde ejaculation, they need to know that this in itself does not inevitably entail any impairment of erection or orgasm, although these other difficulties are associated in some cases. Advice may be given about the management of the colostomy when preparing for or engaging in sexual activity. For instance, the patient should irrigate his bowel and apply a clean covering to the stoma with a deodorant in the case of a regulated colostomy for which a bag is not required. In other cases, a secure, opaque, and odour-free appliance should be used, which can be attractively covered if desired. Suggestions can also be made about positions for intercourse that the couple may find helpful in adapting to the colostomy. Finally, some colostomy patients who suffer from erectile dysfunction arising from irreversible neural damage may wish to consider the possibility of a penile implant.

MYOCARDIAL INFARCTION

Sexual difficulties are common among men who have experienced myocardial infarction. These difficulties include lack of sexual desire, erectile dysfunction, ejaculatory problems, lowered frequency of intercourse, and failure to resume intercourse after the heart attack (Friedman, 1978, Kolodny et al, 1979; Mehta & Krop, 1979; Papadopoulus, 1978; Wabrek and Burchell, 1980). At present, no satisfactory data is available on the sexual functioning of women who have experienced myocardial infarction, therefore this discussion is focussed upon male clients.

An occasional coronary patient may experience sexual difficulties as a side effect of organic factors such as antihypertensive medication or chest pain, but in the vast majority of such patients these difficulties are psychogenic in origin. Thus, a man may react with anxiety, depression, avoidance, and an impaired self-concept, to the threats to his survival, life style, and sexual and marital relationships which he perceives as necessary consequences of his heart attack (Krop, Hall and Mehta, 1979). In particular, coronary patients and their partners are very prone to fear a repeat infarct or sudden death during intercourse, therefore they often avoid it. Apart from the deprivation this entails, there is some evidence to suggest that rather than decreasing the risk of another infarct, such avoidance might actually increase this risk because of the stress associated with abstinence (Wabrek & Burchell, 1980).

It follows that a major task in the sexual rehabilitation of coronary patients and their partners (Freidman, 1978; Kolodny et al, 1979; Masur, 1979; Sanders and Sprenkle, 1980; Stein, 1980) is very specifically to inform and reassure them that it is safe to resume sexual activities, including intercourse in the vast majority of cases. There is good evidence that the typical middle aged male patient can fulfill the physiological demands of resuming intercourse within an established marital relationship, without incurring significant risk of a repeat infarct (Hellerstein & Friedman, 1970; Masur, 1979; Stein, 1977). Similarly, the risk of death during intercourse in such relationships is extremely low, although it appears to become appreciably higher if the man is with an extramarital partner in an unfamiliar setting, especially if he has recently eaten a heavy meal and/or consumed alcohol (Massie, Rose, Rupp and Whelton, 1969; Ueno, 1963). Naturally, these general statements must be tailored to particular patients in the light of individual characteristics such as general health, exercise tolerance, severity of damage to the heart, frequency of pain or arrythmias, age, and preinfarct sexual activity.

Additionally, more specific advice is given concerning the resumption of sexual activity. This should be built up gradually through holding, touching, caressing, and masturbation, to intercourse performed in a non-strenuous manner. The patient should not engage in intercourse within 2 or 3 hours of consuming large amounts of food or alcohol, or when he is fatigued or emotionally upset. If chest pain or tightness occur during sex, the patient should slow down or terminate the activity, and his physician should be informed. These symptoms can be reduced by a supervised exercise programme, by taking nitroglycerine or a long-acting nitrate shortly before sexual activity, or by the use of a beta-adrenergic blocking agent, such as propranolol, on a regular basis.

CONCLUSION

This chapter is focused upon the sexual difficulties experienced by disabled people as a result of their physiological impairments or psychological reactions, operating either singly or in combination.

In conclusion, I want to emphasize that such difficulties can arise also from the conditions in the disabled person's environment, especially when this is an institutional setting. For instance, there is often a serious lack of privacy; accommodation may be in inadequately partitioned dormitories, doors cannot be locked, staff members do not knock before entering, residents are forbidden to spend time in each other's rooms, and this ban may even extend to spouses. These restrictions are not simply matters of architecture or regime, they reflect the negative attitudes towards sexual expression by disabled people that are held by some institutional administrators and staff members.

Sexual rehabilitation programmes for disabled people and their partners may well require attempts to improve such environmental conditions as well as to alleviate the effects of physiological impairments and psychological reactions. Finally, it is important to note that as far as the latter tasks are concerned, only some topics which are relatively specific to particular disabilities are discussed above, and in practice these are likely to be encompassed in a more comprehensive and individualized rehabilitative programme comprising a number of methods from among those listed in Table 2.

REFERENCES

Barnett, D.M. 1973. Diabetic impotence unrelated to treatment. October 8. *Hospital Tribune.*

Bregman, S. 1975. *Sexuality and the Spinal Cord Injured Woman.* Minneapolis: Sister Kenney Institute.

Bregman, S. 1978. Sexual adjustment of spinal cord injured women. 1. *Sexuality and Disability*, 85-92.

British Medical Journal 1974. Editorial. 2. Diabetic autonomic neuropathy, 2-3.

Dorner, S. 1977. Sexual interest and activity in adolescents with spina bifida. 18. *Journal of Child Psychology and Psychiatry*, 229-237.

Dunn, M., Lloyd, E.E., and Phelps, G.H. 1979. Sexual assertiveness in spinal cord injury. 2. *Sexuality and Disability*, 293-300.

Ellenburg, M. 1977. Sexual aspects of the female diabetic. 44. *The Mount Sinai Journal of Medicine*, 495-500.

Ferguson, K. and **Figley**, B. **1979**. Sexuality and rheumatic disease: a prospective study. 2. *Sexuality and Disability*, 130-138.

Frank, D., **Dornbush**, R.L., **Webster**, S.K., and **Kolodny**, R.C. **1978**. Mastectomy and sexual behavior: a pilot study. 1. *Sexuality and Disability*, 16-26.

Friedman, J.M. **1978**. Sexual adjustment of the postcoronary male. In J. LoPiccolo and L. LoPiccolo (Eds.), Handbook of Sex Therapy. New York: Plenum.

Furlow, W.L. **1978**. The current status of the inflatable penile prosthesis in the management of impotence: Mayo Clinic experience update. 119. *Journal of Urology*, 363-364.

Hellerstein, H. and *Friedman*, E.J. **1970**. Sexual activity and the post-coronary patient. 125. *Archives of Internal Medicine*, 987-999.

Higgins, G.E. **1979**. Sexual response of spinal cord injured adults: a review of the literature. 8. *Archives of Sexual Behaviour*, 173-193.

Jehu, D. **1979**. *Sexual Dysfunction: A Behavioural Approach to Causation, Assessment and Treatment*. Chichester: Wiley

Kockott, G., **Feil**, W., **Revenstorf**, D., **Aldenhoff**, J. and **Besinger**, V. **1980**. Symptomatology and psychological aspects of male sexual inadequacy: results of an experimental study. 9. *Archives of Sexual Behaviour*, 457-475.

Kolodny, R.C. **1971**. Sexual dysfunction in diabetic females. 20. *Diabetes*, 557-559.

Kolodny, R.C., **Masters**, W.H. and **Johnson**, V.E. **1979**. *Textbook of Sexual Medicine*. Boston: Little, Brown.

Krop, H., **Hall**, D., and **Mehta**, J. **1979**. Sexual concerns after myocardial infarction. 2. *Sexuality and Disability*, 91-97.

Lundberg, P.O. **1978**. Sexual dysfunction in patients with multiple sclerosis. 1. *Sexuality and Disability*, 218-222.

Maguire, P. **1978**. Psychiatric problems after mastectomy. In P.C. Brand and P.A. van Keep (Eds.), *Breast Cancer: Psychosocial Aspects of Early Detection and Treatment*. Baltimore, Md.: University Park Press.

Marshall, P., **Surridge**, D., and **Delva**, N. **1981**. The role of nocturnal penile tumescence in differentiating between organic and psychogenic impotence: the first stage of validation. 10. *Archives of Sexual Behaviour*, 1-10.

Massie, E., **Rose**, E., **Rupp**, J. and **Whelton**, R. **1969**. Sudden death during coitus - fact or fiction? 3(3). *Medical Aspects of Human Sexuality*, 22-26.

Masur, F.T. **1979**. Resumption of sexual activity following myocardial infarction. 2. *Sexuality and Disability*, 98-114.

Mehta, J. and **Krop**, H. **1979**. The effect of myocardial infarction on sexual functioning. 2. *Sexuality and Disability*, 115-121.

Meyerowitz, B.E. **1980**. Psychosocial correlates of breast cancer and its treatments. 87. *Psychological Bulletin*, 108-131.

Mooney, T.O., **Cole**, T.M. and **Chilgren**, R.A. **1975**. *Sexual Options for Paraplegics and Quadriplegics*. Boston: Little, Brown.

Papadopoulos, C. **1978**. A survey of sexual activity after myocardial infarction. 3. *Cardiovascular Medicine*, 821-826.

Polivy, J. **1977**. Psychological effects of mastectomy on a woman's feminine self-concept. 164. *Journal of Nervous and Mental Disease*, 77-87.

Richards, J.S. **1980**. Sex and arthritis. 3. *Sexuality and Disability*, 97-104.

Rubin, A. and **Babbott**, D. **1958**. Impotence and diabetes mellitus. 168. *Journal of the American Medical Association*, 498-500.

Sanders, J.D. and **Sprenkle**, D.H. **1980**. Sexual therapy for the post-coronary patient. 6. *Journal of Sex and Marital Therapy*, 174-186.

Scott, F.B., **Byrd**, G.J., **Karacan**, I., **Olsson**, P., **Beutler**, L.E., and **Attia**, S.L. **1979**. Erectile impotence treated with an implantable, inflatable prosthesis. 241. *Journal of the American Medical Association*, 2609-2612.

Sotile, W.M. **1979**. The penile prosthesis: a review. 5. *Journal of Sex and Marital Therapy*, 90-102.

Stein, R.A. **1977**. The effect of exercise training on heart rate during coitus in the post-myocardial patient. 55. *Circulation*, 738-740.

Stein, R.A. **1980**. Sexual counseling and coronary heart disease. In S.R. Leiblum & L.A. Pervin (Eds.), *Principles and Practice of Sex Therapy*. New York: Guilford Press.

Stewart, W.F.R. **1975**. *Sex and the Physically Handicapped*. Horsham: National Fund for Research in Crippling Diseases.

Task Force on Concerns of Physically Disabled Women. 1978. *Within Reach: Providing Family Planning Services to Physically Disabled Women* (2nd ed.). New York: Human Sciences Press. (a).

Task Force on Concerns of Physically Handicapped Women. 1978. *Toward Intimacy: Family Planning and Sexuality Concerns of Physically Disabled Women* (2nd ed.). New York: Human Sciences Press. (b).

Teal, J.C. and **Athelston, G.T. 1975.** Sexuality and spinal cord injury: some psychosocial considerations. 56. *Archives of Physical Medicine and Rehabilitation*, 264-268.

Thornton, C.E. 1979. Sexuality counseling of women with spinal cord injuries. 2. *Sexuality and Disability*, 267-277.

Ueno, M. 1963. The so-called coition death. 17. *Japanese Journal of Legal Medicine*, 535.

Wabrek, A.J. and **Burchell, R.C. 1980.** Male sexual dysfunction associated with coronary heart disease. 9. *Archives of Sexual Behaviour*, 69-75.

Wabrek, A.J., Wabrek, C.J. and **Burchell, R.C. 1978.** The human tragedy of spina bifida: spinal myelomeningocele. 1. *Sexuality and Disability*, 210-217.

Wellisch, D.K., Jamison, K.R. and **Pasnau, R.O. 1978.** Psychosocial aspects of mastectomy: II. the man's perspective. 135. *American Journal of Psychiatry*, 543-546.

Witkin, M.H. 1975. Sex therapy and mastectomy. 1. *Journal of Sex and Marital Therapy*, 290-304.

Witkin, M.H. 1978. Psychosexual counselling of the mastectomy patient. 4. *Journal of Sex and Marital Therapy*, 20-28.

Witkin, M.H. 1979. Psychological concerns in sexual rehabilitation and mastectomy. 2. *Sexuality and Disability*, 54-59.

Chapter 18

Sexual Rehabilitation of the Physically Disabled and Chronically Ill

Leah Quastel
Rehabilitation Medicine, University of British Columbia

A considerable amount of literature has been published in the past decade and a half emphasizing the need for health professionals to pay attention to the sexual aspects of rehabilitation of physically disabled and chronically ill clients.

Occupational therapists and physiotherapists are key members of the rehabilitation team; their daily contact with clients for self care and activities of daily living (ADL) training provides an intimate climate for the raising of sexual related concerns. However, a gap appears to exist between rhetoric and practice. It is claimed that, in practice, the subject of sexuality and sexual functioning is treated in a sterile and misinformed manner by therapists and other health professionals. The reason for this is attributed to inadequate knowledge, negative attitudes and lack of clear delineation of roles.

Such accusations raise questions about what specific tasks related to sexual rehabilitation are the domain of occupational and physiotherapist and what roles and attitudes currently guide their behaviour in practice.

This chapter will describe a study that focused on the roles and attitudes toward sexual rehabilitation of chronically ill and disabled clients of therapists in British Columbia. Specific answers to the following questions were sought: (1) What tasks related to the physical aspects of sexual rehabilitation of the chronically ill and disabled are performed by occupational and physiotherapists? (2) Which tasks are considered to be important in the unique constellation of services offered by occupational therapists and physiotherapists? (3) Are occupational therapists and physiotherapists adequately prepared to perform the tasks they believe to be important? (4) Which team member should primarily be responsible for the performance of sex-related physical rehabilitation tasks? (5) What attitudes and beliefs guide the behaviours of occupational therapists and physiotherapists in regard to sexuality and sexual rehabilitation of the disabled and chronically ill?

The impact of answers to these questions will be reverberating through undergraduate, graduate and continuing education programs for therapists; they will present a challenge to reformulate our goals in rehabilitation work with disabled and chronically ill clients and their families and to rethink our own values and beliefs concerning the nature of the total rehabilitation process.

BACKGROUND TO THE PROBLEM

Since 1975 the School of Rehabilitation Medicine, University of British Columbia, has offered a "sexuality curriculum" as a part of the regular undergraduate program. It starts in second year with a consideration of the relationship between reproductive and other uses of sexual activities. Physiology of male and female sexual responses is outlined; motor activities required for different sexual practices are analyzed. The concept of sex norms is discussed and sexual behaviour practices of the current decade are portrayed.

In third year sexual problems of able bodied and disabled are contrasted under categories of sex response difficulties, sexual disinterest and sex activity problems. In the fourth year sex growth and development patterns are related to physical, mental and social functioning. Problems caused by developmental handicaps, chronic illness and physical disability are illustrated by case presentations.

Exam results have indicated that students do their homework diligently, however, when students arrive at clinics for fieldwork placements they cannot transfer that knowledge into practice without further instruction. Further instruction is rare. Obviously the "sexuality curriculum" is weak in many respects. The emphasis on knowing and understanding leaves the student puzzled as to what to do and what therapeutic service they can offer clients, particularly in the apparent absence of role models in the community to demonstrate therapeutic tasks. Indeed, what are the tasks of physiotherapists and occupational therapists related to sexual aspects of rehabilitation? Prior to expansion and revision of the sexual curriculum it appeared essential to investigate the perceptions of practising therapists, the 'role models', regarding sexual aspects of rehabilitation.

REVIEW OF THE LITERATURE

A number of issues have been raised by concerned authors in medical, nursing. occupational therapy, physiotherapy and rehabilitation related literature.

A recurring theme, appearing first in 1969 and continuing to the present day is the failure of therapists to offer any services in sexual rehabilitation (Bucy, 1969; National Paraplegic Association, 1973; Griffith and Trieschumann, 1975; Evans, et al., 1976; Sidman, 1977; Conine, et al., 1979). Bucy (1969) called this failure neglect of professional responsibilities. Sidman (1977) claimed therapists turn away when patients ask questions about sexual functioning and sex activities. The National Paraplegic Foundation compared sexual rehabilitation to an unwanted stepchild.

The second important issue raised is the lack of knowledge and skills of rehabilitation personnel, including doctors, concerning sexual rehabilitation needs of clients (Krelenbaum and Love, 1979; Conine, et al., 1979; Isaacson and Delgate, 1974). Masters and Johnson (1966) found doctors know no more and no less than the average college graduate about sexual functioning. Conine, et al. (1979) administered a 45 item test of facts, myths and mythology regarding sexuality and the spinal cord injured patient to 30 physiotherapists directly involved in rehabilitating adults with spinal cord injuries. Subjects' scores ranged from 25 to 39 correct responses. Only 4 items were recognized correctly by all subjects.

Not only do health personnel appear to be ill informed, but are unable to respond to patients' inquiries due to their personal negative attitudes toward sexual issues (Sha'ked and Flynn, 1978). Fontaine (1976) found educators in schools of nursing equally ill informed and negative in attitude and wondered who would teach the teachers.

There is general agreement in the literature that sexual rehabilitation must be a part of the total rehabilitation program; this aspect of rehabilitation should not be closeted but rather included within the context of activities of daily living training (Sidman, 1977; Doughty, 1977; Keal, 1979). However, there is uncertainty concerning which members of the team are or should be qualified to perform tasks related to sexual rehabilitation. Individual team members' responsibilities are not precisely defined (Szasz, 1978; Conine, 1980).

Despite the repeated exhortations to therapists to provide service in this "neglected", "stepchild" aspect of rehabilitation, few authors were specific about what that service should be. Only Conine, et al. (1980) directly addressed tasks related to sexual rehabilitation. Part of that study focused on an intensive search of the literature to identify activities of daily living services aimed at the physical aspects of sexual adjustment. Six tasks were culled from a variety of resources and posed in the form of a questionnaire concerning importance, performance and adequacy of preparation for each task. One hundred and fifteen professionals (26 O.T.'s, 45 P.T.'s, 44 R.N.'s) in a large midwest American metropolis responded to the questionnaire. The findings of that study indicated that less than 33% of the 115 subjects participated in *any* of the six delineated tasks, and the majority felt inadequately prepared to do so although they considered the tasks important.

Regional and cultural differences exist regarding professional attitudes and practices in North America, particularly in subjects as sensitive as sexuality and sexual functioning. Thus it seemed unreasonable to generalize from results of a midwestern American city professional population study to attitudes and practice in British Columbia. The review of the literature confirmed the legitimacy of the questions which initiated the present study: "What are the roles of the O.T.'s and P.T.'s in sexual rehabilitation", and "What attitudes and beliefs guide their behaviour in response to sexual rehabilitation needs of disabled and chronically ill clients?"

METHOD

The questionnaire devised by Conine, et al. (1980) was adapted for use in the present study. A preliminary respondent profile sought information concerning professional affiliation, type of employing agency, student clinical teaching responsibilities, where and when basic professional training was acquired and whether or not the respondent had been exposed to sexual rehabilitation education. Only those respondents with responsibilities for activities of daily living training of chronically ill or disabled adults were requested to fill out the questionnaires.

The first questionnaire listed the six identified professional tasks (see Table 1). For each task answers were sought to the following questions: 1) Do you perform this task? 2) Is the task important in the repertoire of

Table 1. Distribution of Responses of Therapists to Their Participation in Tasks Related to Sexual Aspects of Rehabilitation (N = 197)

Task Category	Participate in Task		Is Participation Important		Is Preparation Adequate		Who SHOULD Perform this Task				
	Yes	No	Yes	No	Yes	No	MD	RN	OT	PT	Other
1. Take a sexual history as part of ADL or other routine evaluation and provide information.	11 6%	185 94%	143 77%	42 23%	28 15%	165 85%	84 44%	16 8%	44 23%	7 4%	39 21%
2. Train the patient and his/her partner in personal care and hygiene related to sexual activity.	8 4%	186 96%	130 70%	56 30%	29 15%	162 85%	22 11%	97 51%	50 26%	5 3%	18 9%
3. Instruct patient in management of ileal conduit, indwelling catheter, diaphragm, or other devices for sexual activity.	2 1%	192 99%	117 64%	67 36%	14 7%	176 93%	38 19%	114 58%	26 13%	3 2%	16 8%
4. Provide information and intervention for the control of excessive spasticity, painful joints, and phantom sensations that may interfere with sexual activity.	42 22%	152 78%	174 92%	15 8%	50 26%	141 74%	23 12%	2 1%	36 19%	111 59%	17 9%
5. Advise patient on proper positioning for coitus when difficulties of balance, loss of limb, or cardiovascular dysfunction exist.	25 13%	171 87%	165 88%	22 12%	44 23%	145 77%	32 17%	5 3%	39 21%	91 49%	20 10%
6. Adapt the environment of pre-partum and post-partum disabled women to their ADL needs and associated medical risks.	18 9%	174 91%	160 85%	28 15%	52 27%	137 73%	13 7%	7 4%	124 65%	35 18%	13 6%

services offered by your profession? 3) Is your preparation adequate for performing the task? 4) Who, in your opinion, *should* primarily be responsible for performing the task?

Space was provided for suggestions concerning tasks, other than the six listed, related to sexual rehabilitation which the therapist performed or believed to be important. Additional comments concerning the tasks were invited. The questionnaire subsequently asked respondents not participating in any of the tasks to state reason(s): 1) My employing institution does not approve. 2) There is no demand. 3) I consider these services more injurious than beneficial. 4) I feel totally unprepared. 5) Other reasons.

The second questionnaire consisted of fifteen attitude and belief statements regarding sexual rehabilitation and education (Table 2). The respondent was asked to indicate agreement or disagreement with each item and invited to comment freely.

The sample was drawn from the British Columbia Society of Occupational Therapists' current membership list and the Association of Chartered Physiotherapists and Massage Practitioners of British Columbia list of licensed physiotherapists. The questionnaire with a covering letter of explanation was sent to all active physiotherapists and occupational therapists in British Columbia. Cooperation was solicited and anonymity of response guaranteed.

The data was analyzed at the University of British Columbia Computer Center by means of SPSS frequency distribution and cross tabulations.

RESULTS

Responses were received from 664 therapists (46% return). One hundred and ninety-seven (30%) claimed responsibility for activities of daily living training of chronically ill and disabled adults. Therefore, results were computed for 197 professionals composed of 118 physiotherapists (60%), 56 occupational therapists (33%) and 13 combined OT/PT therapists (13%). It should be noted here that until the past decade many university programs in Canada offered a combined physio and occupational therapy degree. Such is still the case at the University of British Columbia; consequently some health facilities in B.C. hire a therapist to perform both physiotherapy and occupational therapy services.

Respondents work in Rehabilitation Centres (57, 30%), General Hospitals (80, 40%), Public Health Units (20, 10%), Extended Care Facilities (21, 11%), Personal and Intermediate Care Facilities (7, 3%) and Private Practice (12, 6%). Two-thirds of the respondents supervise students in the clinical training portion of their education program.

Fifty-two (26%) of the 197 respondents received their basic professional education at the University of British Columbia, 58 (30%) were educated at other Canadian universities and 87 (44%) were foreign trained graduates. Eighty-two (42%) respondents had graduated eleven or more years ago, 71 (40%) had completed basic education four to ten years prior to the study and 36 (18%) were recent (within three years) graduates. More than half the respondents (107, 54%) were never offered information about sexual rehabilitation; the remaining 46% had received information at school (23%), at work (17%) and at workshops (6%).

The first four questions posed in the study were presented in the form of the six tasks shown in Table 1.

Although all six tasks were identified by two or more subjects as being performed, seventy-five percent of respondents (87 P.T.'s, 51 O.T.'s, 9 O.T./ P.T.'s) did not participate in any of the six tasks shown in Table 1. Only Tasks 1, 4, 5 and 6 were being carried out by 5% or more of the respondents. Task 4 is the one most frequently addressed by P.T.'s and O.T.'s in this study (22%). This task focused on therapeutic intervention for the control of spasticity, painful joints and phantom sensations that may interfere with sexual activity.

The majority of subjects rated all six tasks as important in the repertoire of services offered by physio and occupational therapists. While there was close agreement on the importance of tasks 4, 5 and 6, opinion was divided as to the importance of tasks 1, 2 and 3. At least 25 respondents commented that these tasks should be emphasized as part of the total rehabilitation program but were skeptical that delivery of these services was occurring by physiotherapists, occupational therapists or any other team members.

As the data in Table 1 show, over 70% of therapists feel inadequately prepared to perform each of the six tasks. Many respondents commented on inadequate preparation to deal with social/emotional problems as well as the physical. A typical comment read: "I believe this is a vital area especially to an individual's rehabilitation. However, no one seems to be willing, nor is anyone educationally prepared to tackle this. Consequently people are discharged from hospital and sexual rehabilitation has been totally ignored. Someone needs to be trained!" Although the majority of respondents (over 60%) believed that all six tasks were important in the repertoire of services offered, 26% or less thought therapists should primarily assume responsibility for three of the six tasks. As can be seen in Table 1 therapists perceive Task 6 as the domain of occupational therapists and Tasks 4 and 5 as the domain of physiotherapists. Many respondents commented on the desirability of a team approach to all aspects of rehabilitation in preference to task allocation; others expressed the need for a specialized sex therapist on the team. Some therapists commented: "Let the patient approach the person with whom he/she is most comfortable. Occupational Therapists and Physiotherapists should be prepared but shouldn't take the initiative."

In response to the question concerning reasons for lack of participation 'lack of preparation' was cited on 78 responses and 'no demand for the performance of these tasks' on 57. A typical comment read: "There is no demand but this could be because no one feels adequately prepared to assume the responsibility. If there was someone, many patients' problems would come to light."

Only one therapist cited the notion that 'such services would be more injurious than beneficial' as a reason for non-participation. Seven respondents claimed the employing institution would not approve. One therapist wrote: "Sex is a taboo subject with one of the doctors here...under these circumstances I prefer not to participate." Twelve therapists were self-employed and pointed to the circumstances of their private practice as a reason for lack of participation in sexual rehabilitation tasks. Several therapists commented that physicians and social workers perform the tasks in their centres; (approximately 14) stated presence of a specially trained sex counsellor as the reason for non-participation in sexual rehabilitation.

Table 2. Distribution of Responses of Therapists to Statements of Attitudes or Beliefs Regarding Sexual Rehabilitation (N = 197)

Statement	Agree	Disagree
1. Sexuality is an important dimension of health care and the rehabilitation process.	195 99%	4 1%
2. Sexuality and sex drive remain intact, although physical disability or chronic illness may impose alterations in sex acts.	190 96%	7 4%
3. In assessing a patient for activities of daily living, all aspects should be considered: physical, occupational, recreational as well as sexual.	190 96%	7 4%
4. In evaluating a chronically ill or disabled adult for activities of daily living, therapists should ask routine questions concerning the patient's sexual history.	114 58%	78 42%
5. Probing into the sex life of the disabled would be a source of irritation or embarrassment.	100 51%	80 49%
6. History taking and discussion of sexuality should be done within the context of the patient's total problem.	189 96%	8 4%
7. Sexual rehabilitation should not be encouraged in the hospital.	24 12%	173 88%
8. Information on sexuality should be made available to patients.	197 100%	0 0%
9. Occupational Therapy/Physiotherapy patients have questions related to sexuality and their disability or illness.	187 95%	9 5%
10. Medical aspects of sexuality should be integrated into the basic curricula of professional programs.	197 100%	0 0%
11. Rehabilitation team members should try discussing sexuality and sexual functioning with disabled or chronically ill patients and with colleagues.	179 91%	16 9%
12. Occupational Therapists/Physiotherapists should not become involved in the sexual aspects of rehabilitation of the disabled.	23 12%	173 88%
13. Occupational Therapists/Physiotherapists should leave the discussion of sex to other rehabilitation team members.	24 15%	168 85%
14. Most Occupational Therapists/Physiotherapists do not know enough about the medical aspects of sexuality and sexual functioning.	182 92%	15 8%
15. Practice in tasks related to sexual rehabilitation of chronically ill or disabled should be incorporated into the basic curricula of professional programs.	189 96%	8 4%

Table 2 shows the distribution of responses to statements of attitudes and beliefs regarding sexual rehabilitation. Therapists were unanimous in their agreement that: a) medical aspects of sexuality should be integrated into the basic curricula of professional programs; b) information on sexuality should be made available to patients. Respondents were in close agreement that: a) sexuality is an important dimension of health care and the rehabilitation process; b) sexuality and sex drive remain intact, although physical disability or chronic illness may impose alterations in sex acts; and c) practice in tasks related to sexual rehabilitation should be incorporated into basic curricula of professional programs.

On all but two items therapists were in close agreement. They were divided in opinion with regard to routine questioning concerning the patient's sexual history and whether probing into the sex life of the disabled would be a source of irritation or embarrassment. In response to the latter item one therapist commented: "I am the one who is embarrassed. I feel ambivalent and inadequate." In response to the statement that patients have questions related to sexuality one respondent wrote: "Patients have many questions but often they feel inhibited about or unsure of whom to approach with their questions or anxieties."

Responses to the statements of attitudes or beliefs indicated that physiotherapists and occupational therapists have a positive attitude toward sexual rehabilitation. The data were congruent with self ratings of adequacy of preparation for performance of the sex tasks listed in Table 1. Responses were also consistent with written statements requesting educational programs to help bridge the competency gaps.

Respondents were asked to comment on the tasks and list others they performed or believed to be important. Written comments indicated general approval of the tasks presented. Occupational therapists protested the inadequacy of a study addressing only the physical and not the psychosocial aspects of sexual rehabilitation. Relationship formation, sexuality and sex appeal, sexual self image, emotional support and reassurance, and anxiety management were perceived by many respondents as client rehabilitation needs requiring the helping skills of occupational therapists. Respondents writing the above comments were divided in opinion as to the adequacy of their preparation.

Further suggestions concerned needs of people with particular disability or medical conditions and patient education needs. These suggestions included: a) advice for back pain, sprains, and/or disc sufferers and post-surgical orthopaedic conditions; b) birth control and venereal disease education; c) alternate methods of sexual activity and satisfaction; and d) information about child-bearing potential. Therapists commenting about the above sexual rehabilitation needs generally felt inadequately prepared to offer any services.

Data analysis of the cross-tabulations yielded few significant differences in task participation and attitudes between occupational and physiotherapists, type of employing agency, place of basic professional education or length of time since graduation. Therapists who were exposed to sexual rehabilitation education at work and at workshops tended to participate in more tasks than those who had no educational experience or were offered information at school.

DISCUSSION

Is there really a need for sexual rehabilitation? Sex related social and cultural changes of the 70's demand an affirmative answer to this question. Authors have documented how young handicapped people who suffer effects of cerebral palsy, diabetes and spinal cord injury, (to name but a few conditions) are begging for help (e.g. Szasz, 1978; Conine, et al., 1979). The not-so-young sufferers of pulmonary disease, arthritis and stroke are speaking out as well (Sidman, 1977). The subjects of the present study seemed to know this very well.

Many authors claim that occupational therapists and physiotherapists do not as yet have the skills and knowledges to address the issues of sexual rehabilitation of physically handicapped persons. The results of the present study appear to confirm these observations. Although all the tasks are being performed by some therapists, three-quarters of the subjects indicated a general lack of participation and rated their adequacy of preparation as low. As to the tasks listed, the majority of respondents felt they were important in the repertoire of professional skills. No respondent commented negatively about the tasks and new tasks suggested tended to indicate needs of patients with particular conditions rather than specific helping skills.

Conine, et al., (1979) stated: "Psychological problems may be more commonly treated by specialists in psychiatry, counselling and social work." Occupational therapist respondents disagreed and indicated, one or two rather forcefully, that some aspects of psychosexual adjustment were of considerable concern to Occupational Therapists and fell within the domain of services offered by that professional group.

Despite the importance of the tasks, as indicated by the majority, when asked who optimally should perform the tasks therapists prefer to "turn away", as Sidman (1977) puts it, or delegate the responsibility to another team member. Only Task 6 is embraced overwhelmingly by Occupational therapists and Tasks 4 and 5 by physiotherapists. This reluctance, as well as lack of participation cannot be attributed to negative attitudes. In fact therapists' attitudes are generally positive. A far more plausible interpretation lies in the expressed feelings of inadequacy. It is part of human nature to avoid doing activities for which we feel ill prepared. In our attempts to rationalize actions we tend to ascribe the responsibilities to others.

A close examination of responses to question 4; who *should* perform this task, indicates as suggested in the literature review, uncertainty as to which team members are or should be responsible for sexual rehabilitation tasks. Sexual rehabilitation of the chronically ill and physically disabled has been persistently neglected for so long that attempts to redress past neglect raises issues of role overlap, role ambiguity and fear of overstepping professional territorial boundaries. Thus, sexual rehabilitation needs of clients continue to fall between the cracks of who does what.

Therapists do not appear to have faith in physicians' willingness to assume the responsibilities as outlined in the delineated tasks. Respondents were more likely to ascribe the task of sexual history taking and provision of information to doctors. Less than 20% of the study subjects perceived the other five tasks as physician 'domain'. Over half the respondents viewed nurses as primarily responsible for personal care and hygiene training related to sexual activity, as well as instruction in the management of ileal conduit, indwelling catheter, diaghragm and other devices. Yet, in surveying 44 R.N.'s, Conine, et al. (1980) found 20% or less nurses actually perform these tasks.

The issue of a specialized sex counsellor was raised by therapists whose units do in fact employ such health personnel as well as those who do not. The specialized sex counsellor/therapist is a vital and much needed team member. However, the presence of a highly trained person in sexual rehabilitation should stimulate participation of other team members rather than isolate sexual aspects of rehabilitation as a special issue. The literature exhorts therapists to assume these tasks as part of activities of daily living training and the total rehabilitation process and not to closet it as a separate entity. Perhaps for some respondents a special sex counsellor is wishful thinking. The practicality of yet another health professional in every facility is questionable. Economic factors indicate that this will occur only in a few highly specialized metropolitan centres.

The tasks appear to loom somewhat larger than common sense dictates. "High level of skills required and years of training", as cited by some respondents, is indicative of apprehension rather than reality. Who on the team other than Physiotherapists and Occupational therapists have the skills and knowledges to evaluate and intervene therapeutically for positioning, muscle strength, joint range of motion, adapted devices, and environmental adaptations?

Most therapists who indicated 'other' as the person who *should* perform the task wrote either doctor, social worker or sex therapist. The literature is clear concerning physicians' failure to address sexual aspects of rehabilitation. In this author's experience social workers do indeed counsel patients on sex related issues, take histories and provide information; however, they rarely participate in activities of daily living training of the physically disabled and chronically ill. Adoption of these tasks by occupational therapists and physiotherapists would be viewed as a welcome collaborative effort by social workers concerned with rehabilitation and family related issues.

In embracing wholeheartedly the team approach to rehabilitation, health professionals may sometimes overlook the intent of the concept. Common goals do not necessarily mean common skills. Therapists who advocated a team approach to all aspects of rehabilitation rather than task allocation appear to miss the essential issue. Indeed all members of a rehabilitation team must pay attention to the sexual aspects of rehabilitation, but each member does so by applying his special professional skills. Task allocation is what teamwork is all about.

The reluctance of health personnel to address sex related rehabilitation needs of clients, their personal anxieties, rebuffs of patient' sexually oriented questions and negative attitudes have been well documented in the literature (Nigro, 1975; Stubbins, 1977; Diamond, 1974). The present study revealed a reluctance of British Columbia physiotherapists and occupational therapists to participate in the sexual aspects of rehabilitation; however, the study indicates that personal anxieties and lack of involvement are associated with inadequate preparation rather then negative attitudes. These findings are similar to the results of the study conducted by Conine, et al. (1980). They differ only in relative participation rates: more therapists in British Columbia participate in environmental adaptations for pre-partum and post-partum disabled women than do therapists in a midwestern U.S.A. center.

Curricular concerns initiated the present project. The inadequacy of professional preparation of therapists to participate in sexual aspects of rehabilitation as revealed in the study have policy implications for health service providers and educators. Since the majority of respondents viewed all six tasks as important in the repertoire of professional skills, the basic undergraduate curriculum should be revised to include competency acquisition in all six tasks. If the potential role models, the workers in the field, perceive themselves as inadequately prepared then remedial planning must certainly include extensive educational programs for them as well. Indeed numerous respondents requested continuing professional education courses, resource material and reading lists.

The importance of sexual self image and self worth of the disabled and chronically ill should be of particular concern to policy makers and rehabilitation workers alike. Diamond (1974), Anderson, et al. (1975), and many others have found that patients who were able to make satisfactory sexual adjustments were more apt to be educable, livable and self content; those who could not were more likely to express their disability symbolically through feelings of insecurity and helplessness. Thus the sexual rehabilitation needs of clients reverberate throughout the total rehabilitation process. The more adequately prepared health workers become to address sexual related issues the more likely will rehabilitation efforts be successful in helping clients and their families make satisfactory life adjustments.

The interpretation of the findings of this study and generalizations are limited by the nature of the instrument used for data collection. The precise wording of questions asked, and the questions themselves may have biased respondent perceptions. The sample was limited to one province of Canada; view of therapists elsewhere in the country may differ. As is always the case in mailed questionnaires, the perceptions of respondents do not necessarily reflect opinion of non-respondents.

ACKNOWLEDGEMENTS

This study was supported in part by a grant from the Faculty of Medicine, Research Co-ordinator Committee, University of British Columbia.

I am indebted to Dr. Tali Conine, Director, School of Rehabilitation Medicine, U.B.C. for her generous support, assistance and guidance.

REFERENCES

Anderson, P. and **Cole**, M. **1975**. Sexual Counseling of the Physically Disabled. 58. *Postgraduate Medicine*, 117-23.
Bucy, P.C. **1969**. Paraplegic: The Neglected Problem. 49. *Physical Therapy*, 269-272.

Conine, T.A., **Christie**, G.M., **Hammond**, G.K. and **Smith**, M.F. **1979**. An Assessment of Occupational Therapists' Roles and Attitudes Toward Sexual Rehabilitation of the Disabled. 33. *American Journal of Occupational Therapy*, 515-519.

Conine, R.A., **Christie**, G.M., **Hammond**, G.K. and **Smith**, M.F. **1980**. Sexual Rehabilitation of the Handicapped: The Roles and Attitudes of Health Professionals. 9. *Journal of Allied Health*, 260-267.

Conine, T.A., **Disher**, C.S., **Gilmore**, S.L. and **Fischer**, B.A.P. **1979**. Physical Therapists' Knowledge of Sexuality of Adults with Spinal Cord Injury. 59. *Physical Therapy*, 395-398.

Diamond, M. **1974**. Sexuality and the Handicapped. 35. *Rehabilitation Literature*, 34-40.

Doughty, S. **1977**. Arthritis and Sexuality. 24. *Australian Association of Occupational Therapy*, 31-34.

Evans, R.L., **Haler**, E.M., **Defreece**, A.M. **1976**. Multidisciplinary Approach to Sex Education of Spinal Cord Injured Patients. 56. *Physical Therapy*, 541-545.

Fontaine, K.L. **1976**. Human Sexuality: Faculty Knowledge and Attitudes. 24. *Nursing Outlook*, 174-176.

Griffith, E.R., **Trieschumann**, R.B. **1975**. Sexual Functioning in Women with Spinal Cord Injury. 56. *Archives of Physical Medicine Rehabilitation*, 18-21.

Isaacson, J. and **Delgato**, H.E. **1974**. Sex Counseling for those with Spinal Cord Injury. 55. *Social Casework*, 622-627.

Keall, B. **1979**. Sexual Problems of Physically Handicapped People - A Pilot Survey. (Nov.). *New Zealand Journal of Physiotherapy*, 21-23.

Krelenbaum, F. and **Love**, K. **1979**. Sexual Counselling for Spinal Cord Injured Males. 46. *Canadian Journal of Occupational Therapy*, 47-53.

Masters, H. and **Johnson**, E. **1966**. *Human Sexual Response*. Boston: Little, Brown and Co.

National Paraplegic Foundation. **1974**. Sex: Rehabilitation's Stepchild. *National Paraplegic Foundation*. Chicago, Ill.

Sha'ked, A. and **Flynn**, R.J. **1978**. Normative Sex Behavior and the Person with a Disability: Training of Rehabililation Personnel. 44. *Journal of Rehabilitation*, 30-32.

Sidman, J.M. **1977**. Sexual Functioning and the Physically Disabled Adults. 31. *American Journal of Occupational Therapy*, 81-85.

Szasz, G. **1978**. "Sexuality Curriculum for the Physiotherapist and Occupational Therapist." In Rosenzweig, N. and Pearsall, B.P. (Eds.). *Sex Education for the Health Professional: A Curriculum Guide*. New York: Grune and Stratton, 175-185.

INDEX

Sanders, J.D., 253
Saulnier, K., 152
Scholl, T., 234
Schulman, G.L., 121, 123-125
Schumer, F., 116
Schwartz, H., 214
Schwartz, W., 160
Scott, F.B., 247
Seabury, B.A., 65
Seitz, S., 23
Seltzer, M., 69
Selvini Palazzoli, M., 2, 77,
  81, 84, 91, 92, 95-101, 104,
  105, 107, 202, 203
sensate focus exercises, 238
sex
  counselling, 233-240
  interaction with impairment,
  disability and handicap,
  234-240
  related problems, 233, 234
  therapy, 233
sexual
  concerns, assessment of, 236,
  237
  expression, 233
  function and the chronically
  ill, 257
  function and the disabled, 11,
  243-254, 257, 258
  oppression, 236
  protheses, 238, 246, 247
  rehabilitation for the disabled, 243-254, 257-267
  rights of the disabled, 239, 240
sexuality curriculum, 257, 258
Sha'ked, A., 259
Shanahan, T., 63
Shands, H.C., 94
Shontz, F.C., 3
Sidman, J.M., 258, 259, 265
Simon, A.W., 126
single parent family, 113, 114,
  116-120, 127
Skinner, H.A., 69, 70
Sluzki, C.E., 62
Sobell, L.C., 69
Sobell, M.B., 69, 70
social network, 151-161, 196

social networks
  quantifiable factors
  density, 151, 152
  direction, 151, 153
  frequency of contact, 151, 153
  multiplexity, 151, 153
  size, 151, 152
Soper, P.H., 77
Sotile, W.M., 247
Spanier, G., 68
Spanier Dyadic Adjustment
  Scale, 68
Spark, G.M., 120
Speck, R.V., 154-156, 196
Speigal, T., 4
Spouse Hardship Scale, 69
Sprenkle, D.H., 253
Statistics Canada, 117, 118, 121
Steidl, J.H., 202
Stein, M.J., 203
Stein, R.A., 253
Steinglass, P., 60, 62, 65
Stern, P.N., 125
Stewart, W.F.R., 243
Stuart, R., 30
Stubbins, 266
Susser, N.W., 234
Swanson, D.W., 5, 220, 222
systems approach
  six levels of, 4
Szasz, G., 259, 265

Task Force on Concerns of Physically Disabled Women, 247
Tavormina, J., 21
Teal, J.C., 245
Terrel, P., 240
Tharp, R., 20
theory
  circular cybernetic, 93
  communication, 45, 59, 97, 166
  community organization, 191
  cybernetics, 59, 93
  family, 60
  family systems, 134, 192
  information, 93
  interactional, 113
  learning, 166
  personality, 192
  role, 59, 166
  social structure, 192

977 - SOLD 3
27653